DEADPAN

MINORITARIAN AESTHETICS

General Editors: Uri McMillan, Sandra Ruiz, Shane Vogel

Minoritarian Aesthetics promotes scholarship that develops a minor position toward aesthetics and an aesthetic stance toward minoritarian experience. The aesthetic—the domain of sensation, beauty, value, taste, (dis)pleasure, and the sublime—instructs not only representations and judgments of the social, but the relational bonds that form between objects, subjects, and entities across spatial-temporal domains.

DEADPAN: THE AESTHETICS OF BLACK INEXPRESSION

TINA POST

DEADPAN

THE AESTHETICS OF BLACK INEXPRESSION

TINA POST

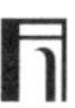

NEW YORK UNIVERSITY PRESS New York

NEW YORK UNIVERSITY PRESS
New York
www.nyupress.org

References to Internet websites (URLs) were accurate at the time of writing. Neither the author nor New York University Press is responsible for URLs that may have expired or changed since the manuscript was prepared.

Please contact the Library of Congress for Cataloging-in-Publication data.
ISBN: 9781479811205 (hardback)
ISBN: 9781479811212 (paperback)
ISBN: 9781479811229 (library ebook)
ISBN: 9781479811243 (consumer ebook)

New York University Press books are printed on acid-free paper, and their binding materials are chosen for strength and durability. We strive to use environmentally responsible suppliers and materials to the greatest extent possible in publishing our books.

The manufacturer's authorized representative in the EU for product safety is Mare Nostrum Group B.V., Mauritskade 21D, 1091 GC Amsterdam, The Netherlands. Email: gpsr@mare-nostrum.co.uk.

Manufactured in the United States of America

10 9 8 7 6 5 4 3 2

Also available as an ebook

CONTENTS

Color plates appear as an insert following page 130.

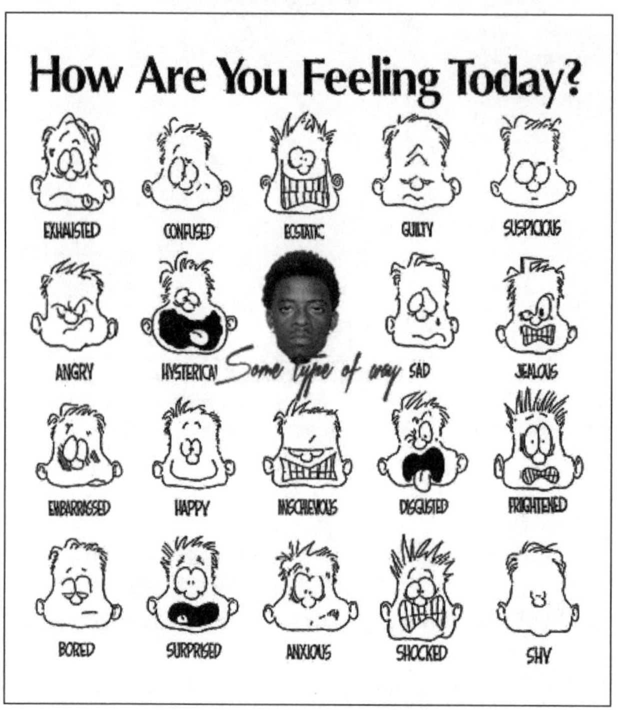

Figure I.1. Rich Homie Quan T-shirt design, “Some Type of Way.”

INTRODUCTION

Some Type of Way

If you can't be free, be a mystery.
—Rita Dove

In October of 2014, an online purveyor of hip-hop paraphernalia promoting rapper Rich Homie Quan's single "Some Type of Way" offered the image shown in figure I.1 as an option for on-demand T-shirt ordering. The picture has since been scrubbed from the internet, presumably due to copyright infringement. Most of the image is lifted directly from Jim Borgman's blandly ubiquitous "How Are You Feeling Today?" cartoon, which surely hangs, in poster form, in a middle-school guidance counselor's office near you. Borgman's cartoon features a 5 × 6 grid of emotions as expressed by the face of a boy who is white in race and hue. The emotions include the obvious—happy, angry, sad—as well as some more thoughtful selections—ashamed, smug, lovestruck. The boy's face repeats serially: in each pear-shaped iteration his mouth, eyes, eyebrows, and hair perform each named emotion in turn.

The majority of Quan's image is identical to Borgman's. Two rows of emotions have been removed to make the image closer to square.[1] Beyond this, there are only two differences. First, an image of Rich Homie Quan's head appears in place of one of the centermost Borgman illustrations. Unlike the cartoons that surround it, Quan's image is photographic, and in color. Also unlike the cartoons, Quan's image does not embody a readily identifiable emotion: Quan neither smiles nor frowns; his eyes reveal no scowl nor twinkle of joy. He is, for all intents and purposes, expressionless. Second, the caption has also been changed. In lieu of "frustrated" Quan's caption reads "Some type of way." And rather than the tight, black, all-caps lettering that accompanies and names all other emotions, "Some type of way" is in a sprawling, bright red script. This lettering is larger and more dramatic than the contained, if still cartoonish, letters that surround it.

The uncredited image offers a subtle and savvy commentary on emotion and expression. The realism of Quan's picture carries a wealth of affective information in its photographic detail and its rich color, even if no obvious emotion can be ascribed to it.[2] His realistic black face also interrupts the assumption of ubiquitous, universal, deraced whiteness. The caption, too, communicates information in its form and its deviation from the tight lettering that surrounds it; it is looser, faster, larger, and, in its color, suggestive of brashness, speed, or lusciousness. There is a tension between form and content here: the words themselves name Quan's single, of course, but they also evoke a nebulous affective stance.

At the time of this writing, the top definition of "some type of way" on the popular, crowdsourced *Urban Dictionary* is "A phrase meaning I'm unable to express the complexity of the emotion at the moment. Can be used seriously or in jest."[3] The contributor adds the following usage examples: "*That ain't even how you spose to talk to nobody. I'm feelin some type of way about ya dumb ass*" and "*I'm feelin some type of way about this nigga callin me in the hoe hours of the morning.*" Both of these black dialect examples tip toward the negative—someone has interpellated the speaker in a way she finds displeasing. At the same time, however, her words suggest fondness or intimacy—in the first example, "ya dumb ass" reads as a chiding term of endearment (as opposed to, say, "you stupid motherfucker"); in the second, the speaker is frustrated with her suitor but not obviously done with him. An *Urban Dictionary* entry from August 17, 2012, concludes with the labels "#loss for words, #complicated emotions, #words fail me, #mixed feelings, #emotional"—a list that highlights how the irruption of "some type of way" as non-naming is a pointed intervention into Borgman's chart of feelings. Ultimately, Quan gives us a lack of expression and an abundance of aesthetic affect.

I begin with this image because it distills so much of the play between expression and inexpression, whiteness and blackness, serious engagement and mocking commentary, that lies at the heart of this project. In short, *Deadpan* is an investigation of the aesthetic affects at work at the intersection of blackness and embodied inexpression. In this book I chart deadpan gestures, and their contexts, to see what is activated through their use. Though this book is not, and could never be, a comprehensive account of the registers of black inexpression, I ultimately claim deadpan as a black performative mode analogous to the inscrutability that runs through accounts of Western encounters with Asian and Asian American subjects. If "inscrutability" marks the nexus where the "unreadable" Asian meets narratives of Asian unreadability, the place where the inexpressive black person meets narratives of black inexpression is what I am calling the realm of deadpan aesthetics. Like Asian inscrutability, deadpan might be projected by an observer or performed by the observed; the deadpan's aesthetic functions operate with or without the intention of the subject who performed it. Not every instance of black inexpression is necessarily deadpan, but the lively exchange between black embodiment and cultural narratives of black subjectivity makes deadpan a formidable cultural trope.

DEFINING DEADPAN

"Deadpan" appears to be a twentieth-century coinage, most likely of vaudeville extraction, that combines "dead" (inanimate) with "pan," a slang term for face.[4] Dictionary definitions of the term emphasize expressionlessness, but also intention or affectation—that is, the deadpan's nature as performance.[5] Common usage often implies a generally flattened affect and/or a degree of contextual discord—being impassive in circumstances that might call for expressiveness, or stating an absurdity with seeming seriousness—and this quality is what we recognize in deadpan comedy. Yet comedy is not the gesture's only home. We can find the deadpan as well in the boxing ring, on the dance floor, in the art gallery—all places where the valences of comedy may or may not hold.

The first usage of "deadpan" listed in the *Oxford English Dictionary* (OED) is from the *New York Times* in 1928, where it referred to the playing of a role with expressionless face.[6] However, the term "dead pan" appeared in the sports pages of American newspapers some five years earlier, when a *Los Angeles Times* article referred to Argentine boxer Luis Firpo as "Dead Pan Louie."[7] While the newspaper offers no indication of how Firpo acquired this moniker, black vaudevillian Tom

Fletcher recalls in his memoirs that black performer Dan Washington, who had been a cast member of *In Dahomey* (featuring George Walker and Bert Williams), helped train Firpo in 1923.[8] If "deadpan" did originate in vaudeville, it was perhaps through the stages of the Theatre Owners Booking Association (TOBA), the vaudeville circuit for African American performers—which suggests that deadpan may have been, from its inception, a black performance mode. That the earliest mentions of deadpan occur in the contexts of the boxing ring and the vaudeville stage suggests how deadpan can imbricate the body as well as the face, and in this book, too, I locate deadpan as a constellation of facial and corporeal expression. Indeed, I assume that deadpan can involve the body or leave the face behind entirely.[9]

Whether live or in photography, film, or painting, the face is generally the first place one looks for the emotional information that informs the affective charge of an encounter. Nevertheless, as I have previously suggested in agreement with V. I. Pudovkin, if this first affective source is insufficiently revealing, the result is not *no* affective information but rather that the viewer will assemble affective information through whatever surrounds and supports the inexpressive subject.[10] Affective meaning can be gleaned from optic, haptic, or kinesthetic sensoria instead of the face—or, more accurately, *alongside* the face. Cultural actors can play into this dynamic knowingly or unknowingly. This makes the deadpan a remarkably malleable performative—a surface quiet that affects its audience through genre, material surroundings, and sensoria.

Because inexpression does not necessarily interrupt relation's informational circuit, I follow Édouard Glissant in his belief that opacity is not, in itself, a refusal of relation.[11] Consequently, I endeavor to respect the historical subject's opacity—their right not to be known—*and* to endorse a poetics of relation that does not demand legibility. Perhaps an analogy is helpful here. To my mind, the relations available through the deadpan's lack recall Duke Ellington's 1944 description of an airshaft—that narrow and nondescript space between buildings. Although definitions of the airshaft emphasize it as a kind of non-space, empty save for air,[12] in Ellington's description it is instead a space full of information and vibrancy:

> You get the full essence of Harlem in an air shaft. You hear fights, you smell dinner, you hear people making love. You hear intimate gossip

floating down. You hear the radio. An air shaft is one great big loudspeaker. You see your neighbors' laundry. You hear the janitor's dogs. The man upstairs' aerial falls down and breaks your window. You smell coffee. A wonderful thing, that smell. An air shaft has got every contrast. One guy is cooking dried fish and rice and another guy's got a great big turkey. Guy-with-fish's wife is a terrific cooker but the guy's wife with the turkey is doing a sad job. You hear people praying, fighting, snoring. Jitterbugs are jumping up and down always over you, never below you. That's a funny thing about jitterbugs. They're always above you. I tried to put all that in "Harlem Air Shaft."[13]

In Ellington's notice, the airshaft is not empty, but rather is a vehicle for sights and smells and sounds, an arena for contradiction and action. Though it is no one's home in itself, the airshaft amplifies all that is homey in Harlem, both the good and the bad. The deadpan is like this. In the pages that follow, photography, painting, theater, and sculpture all meet and mingle in the deadpan's space.

The deadpan performance may give the impression that its emptiness offers nothing, just as the airshaft might. This may be the end of intention for some performers, and it may be the end of reception for some witnesses. Yet, like the airshaft, the deadpan's blank surface also allows it to act as a vehicle for all manner of other information. Even as the airshaft withholds a sense of itself as a location, the airshaft of Ellington's description is a kind of sensory echo chamber where intimate details not *of* the airshaft but *adjacent* to it accrue and come to life. Just so, even as the deadpan refuses some part of an encounter, it amplifies other details for those witnesses, like Ellington, who are primed to notice. This happens regardless of whether the deadpanned actor intends it to. Many canny actors use the malleability of the deadpan to their advantage, and in some of the following chapters I take up for discussion cultural actors who knowingly play with the deadpan's affects. In this work as a whole, however, proving artistic intent is less important to me than exploring what deadpan aesthetics can enact or enable regardless of the conscious intention of the performer.

To understand why, consider Arthur Rothstein's Farm Security Administration (FSA) photograph of a girl, Artelia Bendolph, in a window in Gee's Bend (fig. I.2). The affective economy of this image relies on the interaction between the girl and the cabin in which she appears.

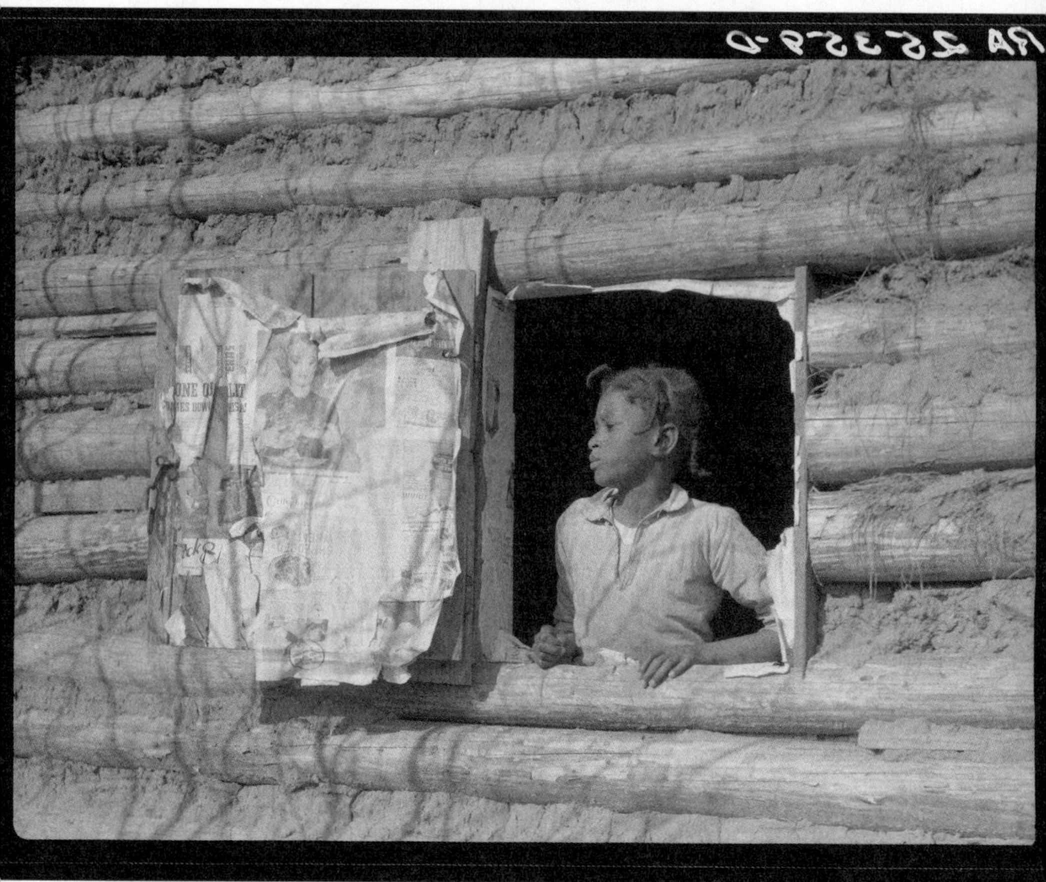

Figure I.2. Arthur Rothstein, girl at Gee's Bend, Wilcox County, AL, April 1937. Library of Congress.

This is largely a matter of compositional line: the lines of her braids find subtle echoes in the grass that helps to seal the cabin's chinks, and in the photograph's grayscale, the brown of her sunlit arms finds its closest companion in the clay or mud sealant of the image's upper-left corner. Furthermore, the image of a white woman on the newspaper covering the shutter opposite Bendolph casts the girl more deeply into the cabin, both through their contrasting grayscale tones and through their disjunctive narrative suggestions.[14] While Bendolph is surrounded by the cabin it is really the black square of the window that primarily frames and situates her. Between the natural cabin and the distinguishing void, the girl is at once earthy and transcendent, embodied and present.

I do not feel I can name, exactly, an expression here. Although Bendolph's eyebrows are slightly knitted, she might be worried or pensive, or she might be squinting against the light. She does not seem happy, nor does she necessarily seem sad. To this viewer, she seems, more than anything else, contained. She is contained within herself, and within the house. Indeed, what is remarkable about this image is how much the girl seems *of* the cabin as well as *in* it—whether she lives in the cabin or not, in the space of the photograph this cabin is hers. To be clear, I do not mean to suggest that she reveled in poverty, nor that she was in some way suited to this social environment, nor that she is herself mimetic of it. Rather, Bendolph becomes an object under the camera's gaze. Her (in)expression helps facilitate this impression, even if it is not the direct cause of it.

Was Bendolph performing her containment? At a minimum, one might concede the likelihood that she understood that in sticking her head out of a cabin window, she became a public figure, whatever the public (though "the public" generally carries a hegemonic hue), and therefore wore an appropriate front for someone (regardless of whether that "someone" is the photographer). Furthermore, if we acknowledge that the photographer might have been among those for whom Bendolph donned her performative front, we might further conclude that she implicitly or explicitly understood the conventions of portraiture well enough to know that inexpression is a traditional choice. We are called to consider the possibility that she understood the possibility of conveying her selfhood through the conjunction of her (in)expression and her surroundings. Perhaps Bendolph volunteered herself for the surveillance of her existence among the objects that surround her—which is another way of saying that she might "work" with the material that is the cabin as much as the photographer does. As Uri McMillan has argued, "objecthood provides a means for black subjects to become *art* objects" (emphasis added),[15] and if we give full credit to Bendolph as a subject, Rothstein's photo offers a striking example of such performativity.

What, if anything, changes if Bendolph did not purposefully perform inexpression? Not much, I would argue. If she is lost in thought, captured by the photographer in a moment of "awayness," her interiority, rather than her performative agency, comes to the fore.[16] Sadly, the acknowledgment that black people have interior lives, and that moments of black quietude happen in whiteness's view, remain poignant critical interventions even in the twenty-first century. However, highlighting the fact of the girl's interior life does not provide access to the nuance of it.[17] Furthermore, while I believe in the importance of black interiority, claiming it through representational visuality is no straightforward affair.[18] In the end, the girl remains part of the image's overall affective ecology. Bendolph herself—who she is, what she intends, and why—remains opaque.

As a way to respect such opacity, I follow in the tradition of Sylvia Wynter and José Esteban Muñoz in bringing a practice of decipherment to the objects, images, and performances of *Deadpan*. "Rather than seeking to 'rhetorically demystify,'" Wynter explains, "a deciphering turn seeks to decipher *what* the process of rhetorical mystification *does*. It seeks to identify not what texts and their signifying practices can be interpreted to *mean* but what they can be deciphered to *do*, and it also seeks to evaluate the 'illocutionary force' and procedures with which they do what they *do*."[19] Wynter's deciphering practice highlights action and process over meaning—or, perhaps more accurately, locates meaning *in* process and its results. For this reason, Wynter's method is a natural fit for theorists who are interested in discussing what a performance enacts while leaving intact some of the variable mysteries of its meaning. This approach is well suited to queer and minoritarian performance and performance reception, as Muñoz makes clear.[20] For Muñoz and those scholars who follow in his line, minoritarian positions also come by their meanings in and through the processual—through lived practices that render these identities in forceful yet contingent ways. To decipher minoritarian performance, then, is first to recognize it as unfolding, lively, and incomplete. In order to attend to what the deadpan does as one such performance, I ascribe to expressionlessness only those meanings that I find in its aesthetic processes.[21] Perhaps fittingly, this has led some readers to feel that this entire work is a bit deadpanned. A reader looking for the hidden depths of expressionless black subjectivities will not find them here.

I limit my interpretative work to the aesthetic sphere and its affects for several reasons. First among these is the subjective nature of reading inexpression, and my concomitant skepticism of the viewer's ability (including my own) to resist projecting emotion and/or narrative onto an expressionless or nearly expressionless face. In truth, there probably is no such thing as an expressionless face. Emotion and cognition flit across our faces in spite of ourselves. Furthermore, given time and inclination, people can and will find meaning in even the stillest visage. We will read stress or cheer in the subtle depths of a wrinkle; we will find significance in the turnings of the corner of a mouth. Relatedly, in absence of clear emotion people too often attempt to read physiognomy on the one hand, or abstraction and metaphysics on the other. And as a wealth of scholarship shows, this split isn't race neutral.[22]

On the side of abstraction, there are examples like Noa Steimatsky's *The Face on Film*, a dense and lyrical treatise on faciality explicitly drawn to "films in which facial legibility is always courted and deferred, where expressivity is irreducible to a name or a code, or is otherwise resistant, where it is withdrawn or else crystalized in such way that the face becomes its own barrier."[23] Although her primary concern is the enigmatic face in film, Steimatsky refuses a distinction between cinematic faces and the faces we encounter every day,[24] and her argument—that treating the face as a dispositif helps illuminate its synecdochic, contradictory, and transformative capacities—is sustained with examples of faciality drawn from photographic portraiture, ritual masks, painted religious iconography, and so forth. She also draws from discussions based on the still image (such as Roland Barthes's in *Camera Lucida*), furthering the sense that her observations about the ambiguous or inexpressive face are meant to find broader applications.

In its conclusions, Steimatsky's text lands again and again on the ineffable—skin's texture becomes authentic presentness, the unbeautiful hermetic face contains the essence of trauma, the mysteries of subjectivity permeate the screen test. Yet only one black visage appears in this account of the "archaic power" of the face: that of the servant in the painting *Olympia* by Édouard Manet.[25] And even when she does appear (and in a chapter with a section titled "The Epidermal and the Written," no less), the black woman isn't given mention within the text itself. In short, when the face is a marker of subjectivity, temporality, interiority—anything less tangible, less *markable* than flesh—blackness falls away. Steimatsky's text is in no way especially egregious in this regard; I name her book only because of its clear adjacency to my own concerns. Such constant omission would seem to confirm Calvin Warren's assertion that (white) metaphysics requires blackness's non-being.[26]

Phillip Brian Harper wrestles with this problem in his book *Abstractionist Aesthetics*.[27] He argues that, while all representational depiction is by necessity abstraction of a sort, abstraction works differently for whiteness (which is able to achieve neutral universality) and blackness (which remains indexical). Through close readings of artworks by Vanessa Beecroft and Kara Walker, as well as through close readings of viewers' critical responses, Harper shows how difficult it is for abstracted visual representations of blackness to shake the legacies of earlier abstractions, be they the social-political construction of fungible chattel property or the social-historical imaginaries of racial caricatures. On the other hand, if racial content is so abstracted as to disappear, the import of abstraction as *black* representation disappears as well. "This is not to say that contemporary visual imagery can *never* achieve critical abstractionist effect," Harper explains. "Rather, the point is that [. . .] it cannot *reliably* do so."[28]

If blackness is consistently written out of abstraction, it is consistently written into base embodiment. From history to art history, history of medicine to cultural studies, scholars have documented how whiteness built its sense of its own exceptionalism by insisting on race as a matter of biological difference confirmable through physiometric regimes.[29] I will say more about blackness and the evidentiary body, but for now I would simply register the aesthetic interaction between black expressionlessness and evidentiary physiognomy. An example of such a link is John Reekie's image of post–Civil War bone pickers (fig. I.3). In Reekie's photograph, one central black figure crouches so that his head is in line with a row of skulls on a stretcher. The parallelism of the bone picker's cranium and the skulls runs through his body, with his clothes in line with the clothes of the deceased, his boots in line with their boots. In addition to the main living subject's alignment, the image constructs a parallel between the five skulls on the gurney and the five bone pickers, who together form an oval at the photograph's center.

This image is not simply memento mori—given the freshness of the Civil War's massive death toll, no such reminder was needed. Moreover, this image contains none of the opulent forgetfulness that classically couches the deathly reminder. On the contrary, this image nominates the plainly clothed black body as interchangeable with death and its evidence of gruesome, fragmented harm. Is this meant to secure the black American as the cause of the war, for better or worse? Does this image wish to suggest the uselessness of these deaths, its leveled soldiers now no different from the non-being of blackness?

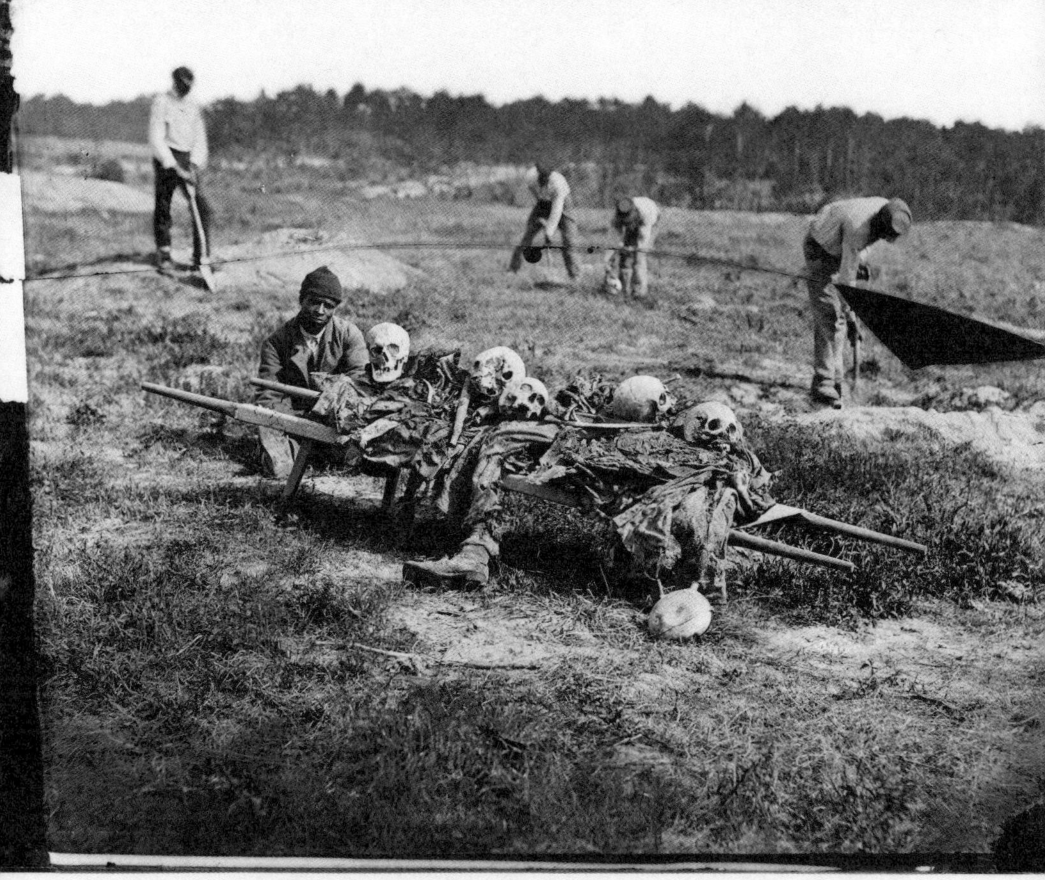

Figure I.3. John Reekie, African Americans collecting bones of soldiers killed in the battle, Cold Harbor, VA, April 1865. Library of Congress.

Indeed, does the black sitter wish to level an accusation of the same? I cannot say. But while I cannot name the intention or emotions of the subjects, I can name the affects of the image overall (somber, grave, cynical) and even those of the inexpressive subjects within the image's affective ecology (ironic, absent, perhaps numbed). And I am certain that the rhetorics of this image would be irrevocably changed if these workers exhibited a nameable emotion, be it sadness, or disgust, or deference. Ultimately, then, I can say that the image's rhetorics are buttressed by the workers' lack of clear expression (and, indeed, that of the skulls—no smilers, these). This buttressing effect is why I treat deadpan as a gesture, rather than as an expression, even when I locate that gesture in the face.

While the literature on gesture is extensive and variable by discipline, I draw from its use in dance and movement studies and, in particular, Carrie Noland's influential theorization of the gestural in her work *Agency and Embodiment*.[30] Building on the work of Marcel Mauss and his students, Noland frames gesture as a technique of the body that is simultaneously a site of cultural conscription and one of individual resistance. If expression generally implies an emotional underpinning and the promise of emotional "truth," the gestural might convey emotion or might instead repeat a convention of a cultural field (or both). The gestural acknowledges the power of cultural transmission while leaving room for individual agency and complication. In other words, as a culturally specific, culturally encoded phenomenon, the gestural—including those gestures of the face that we call facial expression—might be consciously or unconsciously performed, performed according to tradition or improvised.[31] They might reveal the interior state of the subject, or they might reveal the nature of a social situation. How might one characterize this gesture, exactly? Lauren Berlant, in their work on black performance artist Pope.L, uses the phrase "showing up to withhold" to characterize a deadpanned performance event.[32] Building upon Berlant's insight, in this book I collect embodied and artistic gestures that trade in a combination of visibility and withholding, especially, but not exclusively, the withholding of facial expression.

RACE AND INEXPRESSION

A reader may very reasonably wonder what is inherently black in the combination of visibility and withholding. To a certain extent, the answer is: nothing whatsoever. People of every race can and do perform inexpression, whether strategically or unconsciously. But, as Kim F. Hall succinctly states, race is "fundamentally more about power and culture than about biological difference"; race plays (and has long played) a role in "organizing relations of power."[33] Kobena Mercer writes that "blackness-as-otherness is symbolically central to Western culture's self-understanding precisely because it marks the interior limit that surrounds what is unseen and unknown within the dominant epistemological regime of power and knowledge, which does indeed fuse violence and visuality into the spectacularization of black bodies."[34] In the simplest terms, this book posits the aesthetic field as a place where power's organizing relations play out—that is, I take race in general, and blackness in particular, as aesthetic and aestheticizing constructions.

Given the organizational power of race, the stakes of legibility run high for minoritarian subjects, who often encounter overdetermined expectations of when and how their subjectivities should be (il)legible via their embodiment. Concretely applied, this means if there's nothing inherently black about the inexpressive face, there *is* something distinct about the affects and narratives that congeal around black inexpression. This is true not only for blackness. Freighted interpretations of expressionlessness run through Native American and Asian cultural archives, and each carries narrative and aesthetic valences of its own. I am particularly indebted to colleagues in Asian and Asian American studies who have shown the trope of Asian inscrutability to be remarkably consistent in its invocation, and remarkably protean in its deployment.[35] For example, in his exploration of the cultural aesthetics of pain, Eric Hayot traverses centuries, beginning with an encounter from 1606, to illustrate the West's inability to recognize Chinese pain. Through both hypothetical and historical examples, Hayot documents Europeans' consistent failure to imagine that the relationship between pain's physical evidence (a grievous wound) and its subjective expression (a yell or cry) is culturally constructed. To the European, the "inscrutable" Chinese subject refused to present honest and open information about its body, even as that same subject discursively represented, to its European observers, a precultural corporality.[36] Yet Hayot also proposes that the charge of inscrutability is not necessarily just a Western projection, insofar as some pained Chinese subjects may indeed have performed the "wholesale rejection of an aesthetic model predicated on the opposition between inside and outside, experience and expression [. . .], not a refusal but simply an absence of the aesthesis that represents representation as the movement from presence to mimesis."[37] In other words, inscrutability lives at the nexus of performance and interpretation.

Observing twenty-first-century constructions of Asianness and Asian Americanness, Summer Kim Lee names a mode of Asian American asociality that is "against relatability, but for relation."[38] Without taking up inscrutability per se, she describes a phenomenon in which Asian Americans' desire to "stay in" renders them illegible.[39] Given the historical position of Asian Americans as "subjects neither wholly resistant nor complicit with the social schemas, movements, or discourses around them," Lee helpfully frames Asian Americans' purported failure to be well-rounded as "mapp[ing] onto language around the loner, the awkward nerd, the one who does not work well in groups or with others, the one who cannot socialize properly, who does not take part in enough extracurricular group activities. In other words, to not be well-rounded means to not be that social: to be alone, to not be personable, to not be a good team player or cooperative collective member. On the other side of this, to be well-rounded is to be white."[40] When (interracial) group dynamics around the Asian American fail, Lee argues, this failure is located not in the group, nor in the space between the group and the Asian American, but rather in Asian Americans themselves—in their mysterious resistance to being "personable." Lee does not stop with this diagnosis, however, but argues that Asian American asociality is a minoritarian practice that "points toward the desire to want to relate, to show up for one another, but when one is ready, and in ways that alter the horizon of what constitutes the social, and the political projects, collectivities, affiliations, and models of care born out of it."[41]

In each of the above examples, inscrutability is not only a projection of the Western mind but *also* an aesthetic wielded by the Asian or Asian American subject themselves. On the one hand, racial constructions are built through the performances of racialized people—individuals whose skin color, phenotype, and/or genetic heritage causes minoritarian identification (by themselves and by others).[42] Sometimes these performances explicitly engage the history or experience of being racialized, sometimes not. On the other hand, racial constructions are fed by an *imaginary* of race built in the minds of white (and sometimes other) Americans. This imaginary is sometimes indebted to the actual performances of racialized people and sometimes not. Race—at least in the twentieth-century American iteration that informs most of this project—is an amorphous and ever-shifting conglomeration, built in the space between what a diverse set of people perform themselves as and what other Americans imagine them to be. Race is *also* overdetermined, but as Stuart Hall notes, as unrelenting as these constructions can seem, they are never total, and never unchallenged.[43] I also agree with Ju Yon Kim that "most racial stereotypes implicate the mundane, which enlivens their flattened portraits with the small details of how people walk, speak, eat, or hold their bodies."[44] Therefore, at times I will move quickly between embodied blackness (or blackness as performed by black people) and symbolic blackness (or blackness in the cultural imaginary). Indeed, this slippage is part of my point. Sometimes black people, who are busy inhabiting their subject positions with little or no attempt to perform a trope, nevertheless feed the cultural imaginary of blackness. And sometimes black people quite consciously inhabit the broader cultural imaginary of blackness and do so to their own ends. Sometimes white people observe and copy the former, sometimes the latter. Blackness, in the end, is what we collectively make of it. To acknowledge it as so nebulous and so shifting is not to discount its coercive or conscriptive nature but rather to say that the threads of its web are constantly pulled at, broken, and rewoven.

Like blackness, deadpan exists in the contested territory between performance and interpretation. And, just as for the Asian or Asian American, narratives of black inexpression interact with lived blackness through cultural constructions that both preexist and are influenced by those instances in which black people perform something like it. These constructions include the insistent corporeality mentioned above; the messy subject-object imbrication that, as Saidiya Hartman has explained, is a legacy of the constructions of America's chattel slave laws; and the simultaneous hypervisibility and invisibility that Nicole Fleetwood has explored in depth, and that, I would argue, accounts for the ways that black studies has shuttled the promise of black "freedom" (inasmuch as it is believed in) between the fugitive and the opaque.[45] They also include the assumption that performances of blackness that are colorful, loud, happy, funny, witty, or joyous represent natural or true black expression and sociality.[46] As a consequence of this assumption, a performance that is quiet, brooding, resistant, or circumspect becomes a cue to look for the social circumstance that is *disrupting* the black American's naturally expressive state. This in turn fosters a siloing of African American expressivity, whereby viewers interpret a performance of black subjectivity through an aesthetic or a sociological lens based on its affect.

As a case in point, we might take Margaret Bourke-White's ironic images of black people waiting in a food queue, taken in Louisville, Kentucky, in 1937.[47] One photograph (fig. I.4) shows a dense line of expressionless black figures. Dressed in coats and hats, carrying bags and pails, they seem crowded and immobile. A few of the black subjects look toward the camera; most look away. They seem insular as they stand in single file, inviting viewers to interpret serial black solitude, rather than community, in their number. Forming their backdrop is

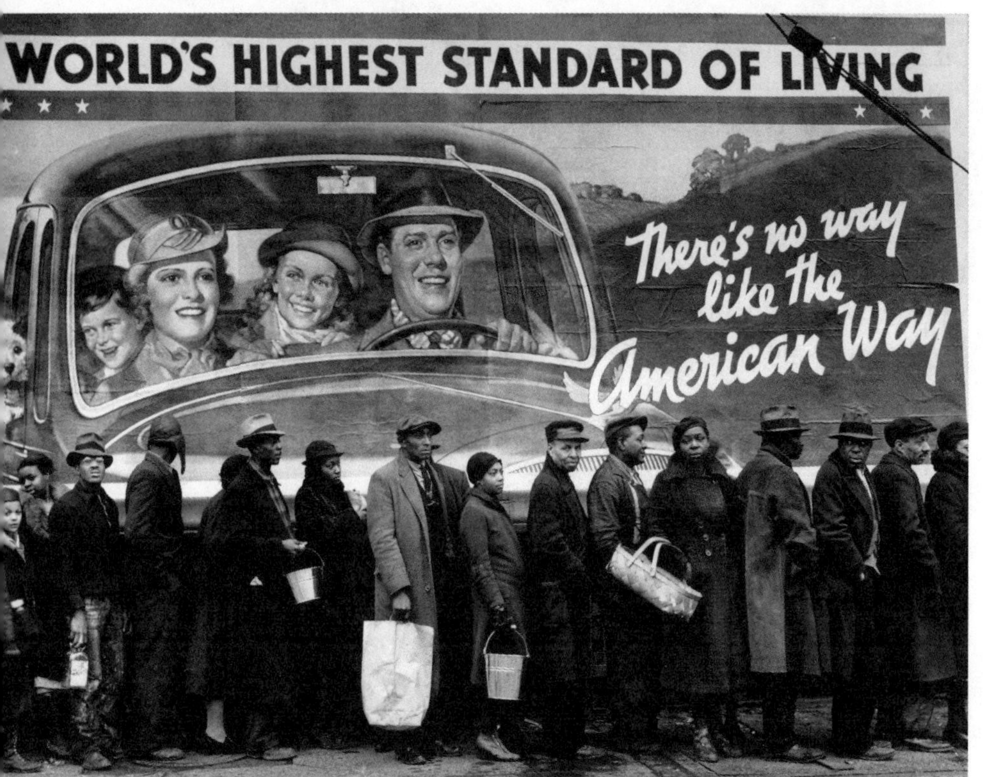

Figure I.4. Margaret Bourke-White, African American flood victims lined up to get food and clothing from Red Cross relief station, February 1, 1937.
The LIFE Picture Collection. Shutterstock.

a massive billboard that features a white nuclear family driving in a car—mother, father, daughter, son, dog—rendered in a healthful and vaguely Rockwellian pop realism. Large block letters, accompanied by stars, proclaim "WORLD'S HIGHEST STANDARD OF LIVING." A second set of script letters announces, "There's no way like the American Way," a phrase that acquires a biting, unintended meaning in the interplay between the imaginary scenario on the billboard and the factual black subjects who wait for food below it. Moreover, the image's framing makes the car seem as though it would run over the subjects were it real; the image suggests not only that the American way is unequally available but that it is made real for a few on the backs of the many.

However, this is only the more famous of *two* pictures Bourke-White took of the scene; a second image, seen in figure I.5, features the same billboard and a food line of hungry black Americans. This image's

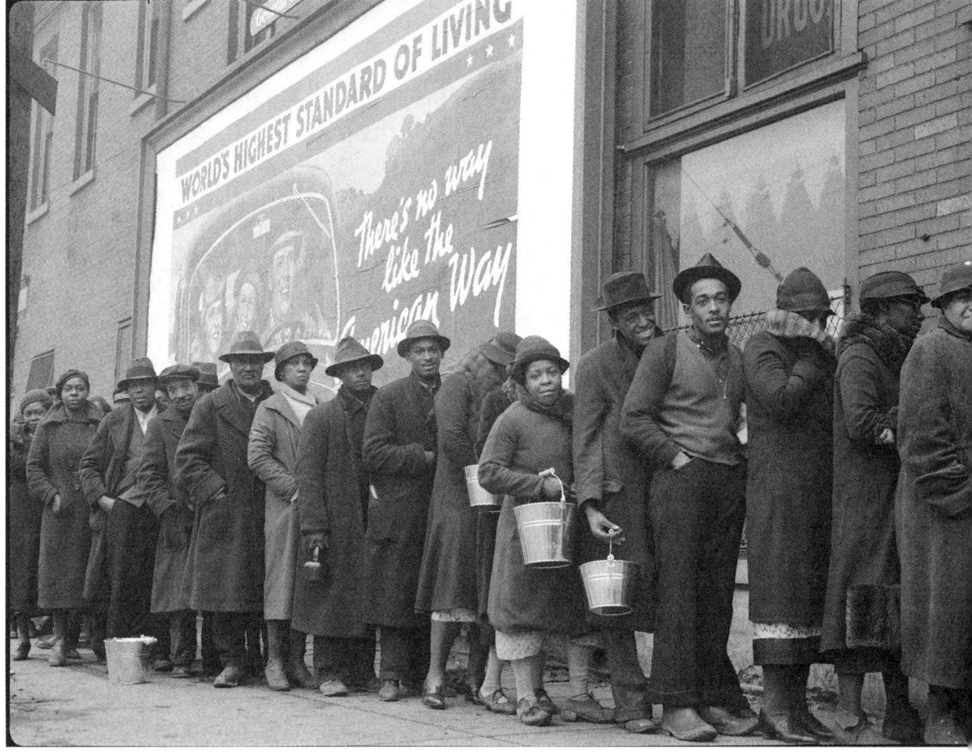

Figure I.5. Margaret Bourke-White, African American flood victims lined up to get food and clothing from Red Cross relief station, February 2, 1937.
The LIFE Picture Collection. Shutterstock.

affects are very different from those of the first image, a result of the changed camera angle and the expressions of the pictured subjects, who are not so uniformly expressionless as those in the first. Many more of these subjects look into the camera, some smiling. Others turn their faces away or hide in their collars. Moreover, some seem to engage with their neighbors in line—in particular the gentleman fifth from the right, who appears to be laughing at, or with, the woman who has hidden her face in her coat lapel. The billboard appears but is no longer featured; instead, what comes alive are the black subjects themselves and the shiny pails with which they wait. The image feels far more communal, at least to this reader, than the image previous. If the dates on the images are correct, Bourke-White returned to the food line a day later to take the second image. One might surmise that Bourke-White suspected some quality was missing from her first day's work. And yet it is the first image that has become the iconic one. Surely this is, at least in part, because the rhetorics of the first image are clear and forceful. Yet mightn't it also be due to the ways that the black subjects of the first image *bolster* the desired rhetorics, insofar as the inexpressive black subjecthood they perform indicts the color line?

Expressionlessness has obvious utility in social encounters, especially encounters of unequal power distribution—and these are the terms that have governed the day-to-day experiences of many black Americans for most of US history. Further, expressionlessness can convey a sense of restraint, a virtue woven into America's puritanical heritage and consequently threaded through black Americans' uplift endeavors as well. Yet a focus on sociological utility has tended to emphasize the black deadpan directed toward white audiences to the neglect of the black audiences who might simultaneously witness its performance. Moreover, the interruptive assumption has overlooked the affective capacities of deadpan performance and elided ways that a sociologically driven response can still send an aesthetic signal. Sociological forces might inspire deadpan performances, certainly, and the deadpan has lubricative potential. My work is indebted to sociologists such as Erving Goffman and Michel de Certeau, to say nothing of W. E. B. Du Bois.[48] But when invoking Du Bois's racial veil, one does well to remember that a veil is itself an aesthetic object. I agree with Richard Iton that "political intention adheres to every cultural production."[49] My focus on aesthetics is, therefore, not meant to obscure the relationship between aesthetics and politics but rather to attend more closely to its "minor-key sensibilities."[50] Like Robin D. G. Kelley, I look to everyday performances that might seem perfectly reasonable, if not necessarily "relevant"—and to those artworks that elucidate how, in one more Iton turn of phrase, "what appears to be merely compliance or complacency is usually more complicated, and that resistance and contestation can take many different forms."[51]

That said, I do not wish to overstate the resistance that occurs in these pages. In general, I share Jeffrey Ferguson's concern that scholars can, for very understandable reasons, overinvest in racial narratives of resistance. As he notes, "The broad and diverse discourse on African Americans has yielded many books, but only two basic stories: those of suffering and resistance. Whether through exaggeration, understatement, denial, or intricate combination, all others derive from these two. [. . .] As a leading concept of modernity, as a multiform social and political reality, and as lived experience, race has stood out for the extreme way that it manifests both the persistence of suffering and the great hope that by fighting against it human beings might deliver itself from its grasp."[52] Since Ferguson's 2008 caution, queer-of-color critique has, to my mind, positively altered performance studies and race and ethnic studies through its insistence that people do not always resist oppression (and that one man's oppression might be another man's pleasure), nor do they consistently desire those values that are generally considered "good." Nevertheless, I have found it remarkable how often, in the course of presenting this work, I have been asked whether deadpan is a strategy of resistance. My answer is generally "Maybe." Deadpan might enact deference or denial, quietude or aggression, resistance or acquiescence. Like any performance, it depends on the settings, the costumes, the dramaturgy, and the audience. Bleak political and sociological realities form the backdrop of much black inexpression, and I take the quest for resistance to represent, as often as not, a desire for techniques of survival. But present realities should not circumscribe the potentialities of deadpan gesture.

Among those potentialities is a surprising measure of mobility. As scholars at the nexus of race and performance studies have argued, enactments of racial ways and knowledges are born of particular lived experience, and yet *also* can be abstracted and then mobilized. Racialized subjects can externalize and then play against their inherited cultural and aesthetic habitus.[53] People *outside* of a particular racial embodiment can also adopt the embodied ways and knowledges they have witnessed, or invented, in an other. Importantly, this adoption doesn't have a singular look to it. I find most discourses of appropriation unsatisfyingly vague for this reason. It is, of course, troubling when one group adopts the cultural ways of another for exploitation, or for cynical—or even thoughtless—financial gain. And white cultural producers do receive disproportionate adulation and financial reward for copying the innovations of American subcultures, often with an entire corporate apparatus of support. But it also happens that cross-racial and cross-cultural encounters change tastes, that techniques of the body permeate cultures consciously and unconsciously, that culture moves like water.

One author who has named modes of cross-racial borrowing very carefully is dance scholar Susan Manning. Manning names as "metaphorical minstrelsy" the method by which modern dancers borrowed from blackness. Metaphorical minstrelsy's referential embodiment does not rely on an explicit impersonation (as in blackface, for example); rather, as in the example of Helen Tamiris's *Negro Spirituals*, performed from 1928 to 1944, a performer embodies "Nobody Knows de Trouble I See" or "Git on Board, Lil Chillen," using movement techniques to evoke bondage and freedom—a metaphorical impersonation.[54] As Manning points out, this metaphorical impersonation bears a readily identifiable mark of racial origin or reference, and this mark indicated, in the 1930s, the skill of the white modern dancer who, through their artistry, could enact what a black dancer could only do "naturally." From the 1940s on, however, "metaphorical minstrelsy became a residual convention in modern dance, as choreographers embraced the representational conventions of mythic abstraction"—the "universal" (deraced, and therefore white) subject.

Another important theorist of cross-racial adaptation is art historian Darby English, who, in *1971*, reverses the directional arrow of aesthetic mixing. "Racial discomposure" is his name for when race begins to come apart at its seams through aesthetic means, revealing itself to be constructed and contested.[55] However, he only reads the discomposure of blackness through abstract aesthetic means, leaving whiteness intact and abstraction a deracinated (mythic) endeavor. English has his reasons for his focus on blackness in particular. Viewers recognize blackness only in its clearest representational forms, he says, and art criticism implicitly or explicitly demands that black artists portray or signal blackness in their work. Barring this, viewers will go so far as to insert narratives and symbols of blackness, even in the case of black abstractionist painters. This, he writes,

> violates the moral right of the artist, contravenes her practical claim to inconsistency, opacity, and voluntary disclosure in her work—and to have some say in the construction of its consequence. [. . . "Black abstraction"] holds out for an aesthetic experience that seems to me insufficiently distinct from the kind of absolute self-knowledge—and correspondingly, absolute knowledge of strangers—we are over-encouraged to have in our everyday world. What we miss in an experience so saturated with meaning is the concentrated, open-ended intimacy that comes from not knowing, from being left unsure—discomposed, as the case may be—by the things and beings of the world.[56]

I share English's sense that blackness is often overwritten with assumed knowledge, and that the assumptions of blackness can, in turn, function oppressively. Yet if English is suggesting that to overtly link blackness and abstraction would inevitably contravene abstraction's opacity—which is to say that opacity has no register *as* a register of blackness—I must respectfully disagree.[57] In reading English's work I find myself wondering: Why must we forgo blackness in order to also be opaque? Why give the right to opacity over to whiteness (or to neutrality as personified by whiteness)? Why cede blackness as inevitably known and knowable?

In the pages that follow, I hope not only to highlight instances of black illegibility (or opacity or disappearance) but also to show illegibility's efficacy for the black subject. In doing so, I build upon scholarly foundations concerning modes of black reserve, especially the accounts of opacity, fugitivity, impersona, and stillness produced by Daphne Brooks, Huey Copeland, Shane Vogel, and Harvey Young, respectively.[58] Though it is related to all of these modes, deadpan is not synonymous with any of them. Deadpan may be opaque, but it need not be spectacular, as are the afro-alienation acts Brooks narrates. Like the fugitive artworks Copeland describes, deadpan may help the subject disappear, but it doesn't necessarily absent the black body. Like the performances Young points to in *Embodying Black Experience*, deadpan comprises a repertoire of black subjectivity across time, but it isn't necessarily still. And like Lena Horne's impersona, as described by Vogel, it withholds something critical and often desired, though it does not necessarily forward hostility in its place. Deadpan may be aloof, yet its performed reservation may also extend from humility.

Two other modes of black inexpression are worth explicit mention here, particularly for the ways they might double-encode. The first of these is signifying, alternately spelled signifyin' or signifyin(g) in black letters. Henry Louis Gates, Jr.'s seminal essay "The Signifying Monkey" surveys a number of its kaleidoscopic meanings, among them "a rhetorical practice that is not engaged in the game of information-giving"; "a '*technique* of indirect argument or persuasion'; 'a language of implication,' 'to imply, goad, beg, boast, by *indirect* verbal or gestural means'" (after Roger D. Abrahams, emphasis in original); and "trope-a-dope" (after Kimberly W. Benston). In black usage, Gates explains, "one does not signify something; rather, one signifies *in some way*."[59] Signifying bears a likeness to the deadpan not so much in its strains of one-upmanship but rather in the ways it can subtly encode one meaning to a listener in the know while leaving the uninitiated with a different sense of meaning. A second mode of double-coded inexpression is dissemblance. Most famously theorized in an African American women's context by Darlene Clark Hine, "the dynamics of dissemblance involved creating the appearance of disclosure, or openness about themselves and their feelings, while actually remaining an enigma."[60] While shielding the performer's inner life from the white observer, dissemblance surely also helped signal to black observers the degree to which the white person before them was felt (or not felt) to be "safe." Deadpanning isn't a form of dissemblance, just as it isn't a form of signifying—the deadpan does not pretend at openness, after all—but the deadpan is another in the matrix of ways that black people have marshaled inscrutability as a technique for surviving oppression—especially when it might also provide information to fellow black people familiar with the technique. But again, the fact that it *can* be used as resistance doesn't mean it *must* be. Rather, the deadpan walks an affective tightrope of (in)sincerity, (in)vulnerability, and (dis)honesty in its (non)revelation—a flexibility that can be turned to various ends.

CHAPTER OVERVIEWS

In addition to contributing to the literature on black modes of reserve, another of my goals for this book is to contribute to our understanding of the ways black subjects exist and invent under the visual strictures of racialization. I want to know what recourse we have in the visual field, and what poetics we might create under, with, and against the unavoidable regimes of sight. The chapters that follow are organized to move from the most visually apparent instances of black inexpression to the most abstracted; accordingly, this book begins with black deadpan in the guise of expressionlessness black faces, and it ends with black deadpan as it is performed by a *white* actor. Each chapter is concerned with the deadpan's aesthetic action, or the combination of visibility and withholding as it is embodied within a specific context (whether or not the actor is fully aware).

In the first chapter, "Subjectivity and Self-Specimenization," I consider the expressionlessness performed in portrait photography from the mid-nineteenth through the mid-twentieth century. Using insights gleaned from Janice Neri, Shawn Michelle Smith, and Mark Seltzer, I argue that deadpan allows the black subject who desires respectability to simultaneously perform the positions of specimen and empiricist, bolstering the black subject's claim to a place in modernity. I show how photographers both white and black, progressive and regressive, have contributed to the variable—if nevertheless formidable—formation of evidentiary blackness, as have the black subjects who have embraced or distanced themselves from that construction.

In the next two chapters I take up how gendered racialization contributes to deadpan's gestural workings. While I do not believe in a gender binary, I believe that the historical tendency to interpret bodies binaristically and through the lens of sex means that on the whole, inexpressive black men have been more prone to being interpreted as threatening, and inexpressive black women have been more likely to experience modes of invisibility (which does not preclude the visibility of being being sexually desired). This is the case despite the ungendering of the black female named by Hortense Spillers, and the simultaneous invisibility and hypervisibility that runs throughout all black life and letters.

In the second chapter, "Minimalism and the Aesthetics of Black Threat," I examine the longstanding association of black inscrutability with a sense of looming or impending threat. "Threat," in my usage, is indebted to Brian Massumi, who describes it as an affective effect born of unactualized danger—an unresolved and unresolvable surplus of foreboding. Citing writers from Thomas Jefferson to Tom Wolfe, I show that white Americans persistently interpret black inscrutability as threatening, and that black Americans strategically perform blackness as foreboding. Taking up this persistent interpellation of blackness within American culture, and enlisting Michael Fried's "Art and Objecthood" to think about the aesthetics of looming, in this chapter I examine engagements with the paradigm of black threat through minimalist sculpture and performance by Adrian Piper, Martin Puryear, David Hammons, and Robert Morris.

In the third chapter, "The Opacity Gradient," I attempt to parse aesthetics of calibrated visibility and withholding by thinking through discrete points of visual saturation. At one end of opacity's density gradient are the "dark points of possibility," to quote Daphne Brooks, that constitute the most opaque aesthetic acts.[61] In these performances, the subject can simply be overlooked, or their presence so taken for granted as to no longer register. At the other end of the gradient are performances of material transparency—instances where the subject is seen through, rather than seen and not noticed. Such performances are transparent rather than invisible because, like a scratch or a glare on glass, the aesthetics of transparency can draw attention to subjects who would otherwise merely facilitate another sight. The difference between being looked over and looked through might seem slight, but it resides in the affective density of presence, which is to say that the presence of the opaque figure is meant to be felt if not seen, while the transparent subject is meant to escape even affective notice. Put another way, the difference between opacity and transparency is the difference between the window and the wall. While both escape notice most of the time, if a pane of glass disappeared, it might take you a moment to notice; if a similar-sized piece of wall disappeared, you would note its absence immediately. Between these poles of transparency and opacity, I name three other aesthetic strategies of gradated saturation: sheerness, obscurity, and awayness.

In chapter 4, "Excess and Absence (or, The Negro Believes ______)," I examine Young Jean Lee's *The Shipment* and Branden Jacobs-Jenkins's *Neighbors*, plays that stage excessive blackness through both stereotyped characters and stereotyped forms. Revisiting Angeline Morrison's article "Autobiography of an (Ex)Coloured Surface," I argue that the mode of racial deadpan executed in these works is analogous to that at work in the monochrome, the deadly serious joke of resolute unknowability. While Morrison likens unknowability to the passing mixed-race subject, I argue that darker instances of blackness can also perform indeterminacy, and that *Neighbors* and *The Shipment* show how, as in the monochrome, excessive blackness can become an act of evacuation.

I conclude with a chapter titled "Buster Keaton's Black Deadpan." In this chapter I argue that Keaton, the paradigmatic example of (white) deadpanning, activated well-rehearsed cues that invoked blackness in the white imagination. In his combination of insentience and indestructibility, his subtle recycling of minstrel tropes, and his rare but tellingly timed excursions into blackface, Keaton marshaled blackness in a way that his performances of expressionlessness further underscored. In focusing on the history of Keaton's performative evolution, I also work to recover the figure of Willie Riddle/Carruthers, Keaton's forgotten personal assistant, to emphasize that everyday performances of blackness, as well as their minstrel stage counterparts, surrounded and bolstered Keaton's creative life.

This book does not present a comprehensive view of black inexpression. Instead, I begin to sketch a picture of how black individuals might use gestures of withholding and inexpression within visuality's racial regimes. To this end, I lean heavily on an African American context, as it is one I know well. I have aimed, in other words, for a cohesive account of deadpan in one cultural context, rather than attempting a comprehensive or comparative one. It is my hope that a deep consideration of deadpan's gestural significance in one context provides a springboard to others, so that we might understand the ways that deadpan might move through the black diaspora.

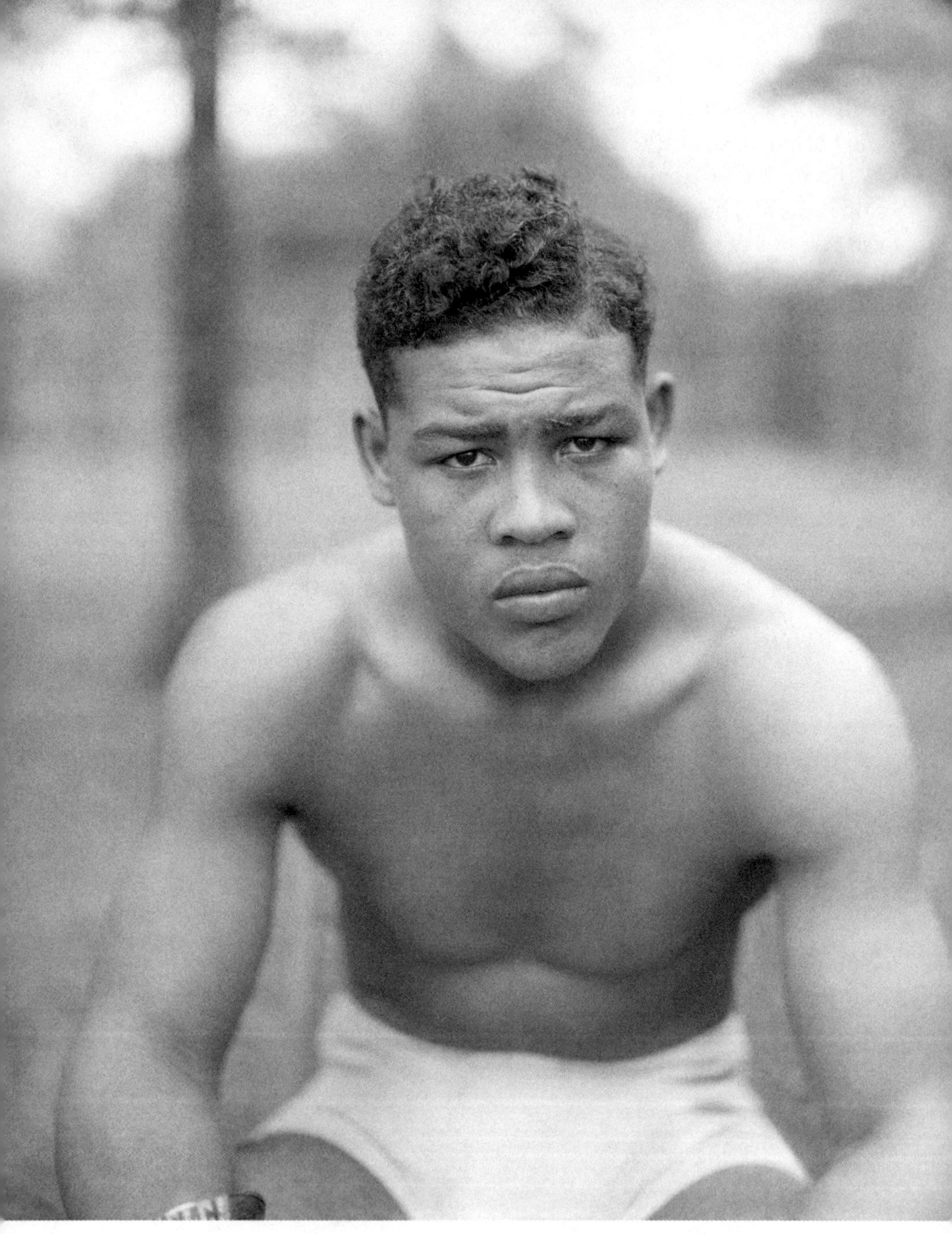

Figure 1.1. Joe Louis, “A front view closeup of the Brown Bomber cold stare and ‘dead pan,’” August 1936. Photo: Bettmann/Getty Images.

1

SUBJECTIVITY AND SELF-SPECIMENIZATION

> Pronouncing one's specificity is not enough if one is to escape the lethal, indistinct confusion of assimilations; this specificity still has to be put into action before consenting to any outcome.
>
> —Édouard Glissant, *Poetics of Relation*

> In order for self-determinations to count as self-determinations, they have to be observed as such.
>
> —Mark Seltzer, *The Official World*

This book began, for me, with Joe Louis, world heavyweight champion 1937–1949 (fig. 1.1). While he has largely fallen away from—or, perhaps more accurately, been sublimated into—the study that follows, I nevertheless invoke him here as a touchstone and point of departure. Louis was famously deadpanned. He rarely smiled or frowned in his public life. He could stroll through throngs of fans with the humility of a man going out for a quart of milk, and he entered and exited the boxing ring in much the same way. Each of his wins as champion was taken in stride with the same placidity as his single, spectacular loss.

Louis's inexpression earned important mention in the press from the get-go.[1] While he was still an amateur fighter, a news article called him "'Poker Face' Joe Louis."[2] One year later, the *Baltimore Afro American* quoted a reporter as saying, "His dead pan will make him famous."[3] As Louis rose in the boxing ranks, public interest and society page stories took up the preoccupation with his expressionlessness, and reported somewhat obsessively the social circumstances in which his deadpan held (baseball, funerals, and nightclubbing, no; dancing, yes). Biographers consistently draw a portrait of someone naturally inarticulate, a consequence of his modest education, natural shyness, and a speech impediment suffered in his youth.[4] But they also stress the stage direction of Louis's uplift-minded managers, John Roxborough and Julian Black. The two were determined to craft a fighter allowed to fight for the heavyweight crown—which had been barred to black fighters for some years—and they set rules for Louis in order to construct an unthreatening public persona. Though Louis claimed in his autobiography that his managers did not set down a list,[5] the general rules outlined in early biographies had, by 1973, solidified into a recurrent seven-point list:

1 He was never to have his picture taken alongside a white woman.
2 He was never to go into a nightclub alone.
3 There would be no soft fights.
4 There would be no fixed fights.
5 He was never to gloat over a fallen opponent.
6 He was to keep a "dead pan" in front of the camera.
7 He was to live and fight clean.[6]

As codified in this apocryphal but ubiquitous list, Louis's deadpan was central to the project of respectability as his managers conceived it—as central as humility, honesty, and a diminished threat of miscegenation.

Yet expressionlessness isn't *inherently* respectable. Nothing in an inexpressive face signifies dignity, manners, or any of the other associations that are bound up in respectability—at least not in any simple, direct way.[7] Moreover, not so many years after Louis's heyday, the inexpression of boxers Sonny Liston and George Foreman was interpreted as menace rather than respectability.[8] I began this book as an attempt to discern how a single performative gesture could signal so variously. In this first chapter, I want to consider the original provocation: why would someone believe that inexpression communicated respectability? In answer, I propose that deadpan can communicate respectability to the extent that it relays a successful occasion of self-specimenization.

By successfully performing respectability, I posit, the black subject demonstrates engagement in the empirical acts of cataloguing and visualizing, and, in turn, externalizes those acts for others to witness. Certainly, displays of contemporary standards of beauty or propriety, displays of wealth or professionalism, and displays of adherence to the values of property ownership or familial obligation contribute to performances of respectability in their own right. But these sociological fronts ultimately, and perhaps most critically, display the self-referentiality that indexes a black subject's ability to act as the scientist as well as the specimen. Although we usually focus on the end product of respectable comportment, the importance of such a performance, I argue, lies not in respectable comportment per se but rather in the black subject's demonstration of their modernity through their ability to specimenize—*and*, ironically, in the implicit concession that they are themselves an appropriate or an inevitable specimen.[9] Consequently, portraiture's play for respectability reveals that a Du Boisian double-consciousness—"this sense of always looking at one's self through the eyes of others"—is a product not only of the color line, but more particularly of the racialized subject's attempt to prove their qualifications for modernity by turning the evidentiary eye inward.[10]

THE SPECIMEN

In March of 1860 seven enslaved people were brought to the portrait studio of South Carolina daguerreotypist Joseph T. Zealy. Harvard naturalist and comparative anatomist Louis Agassiz had arranged for their appearance at the studio and, most likely, their appearance within the photographs. A polygenesist, Agassiz believed in the separate origins of man's various races, and the fifteen surviving daguerreotypes seem to have been produced in support of Agassiz's preoccupation with human taxonomy. While the most frequently reproduced of these images show the seven individuals nude from the waist up (see fig. 1.2), three of the men also appear nude in full-body shots: frontal, side angle, and rear views.

Agassiz's daguerreotypes recur in African American cultural criticism for obvious reasons, including the ways they harken to the long and often devastating relationship of racialized people to science and medicine, the complicated role of photography in African American representational histories, and the history of the display of racialized people. These daguerreotypes are also deeply affecting, although for seemingly contradictory reasons. For some viewers, these images are unshakable because of the clear objectification of the individuals pictured. For others, the poignancy of the images resides in the clear and present subjecthood of the people who were, according to records, named Alfred, Delia, Drana, Fassena, Jack, Jem, and Renty. Do these photographs tell the story of their situation, or of their subjectivity? Are the two synonymous? Can one acknowledge that as a fact and also deny it as a truth?

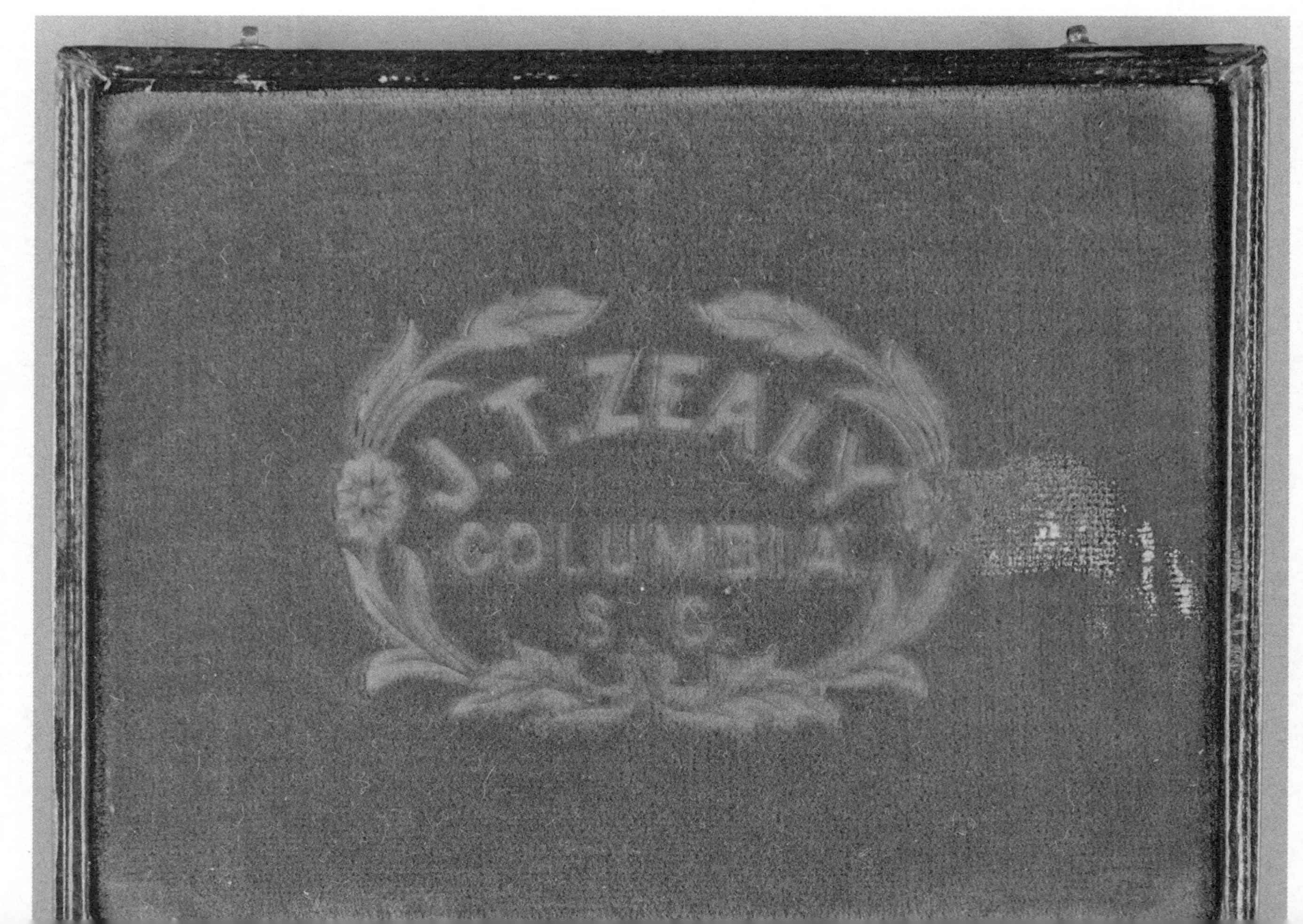
J. T. ZEALY
COLUMBIA
S. C.

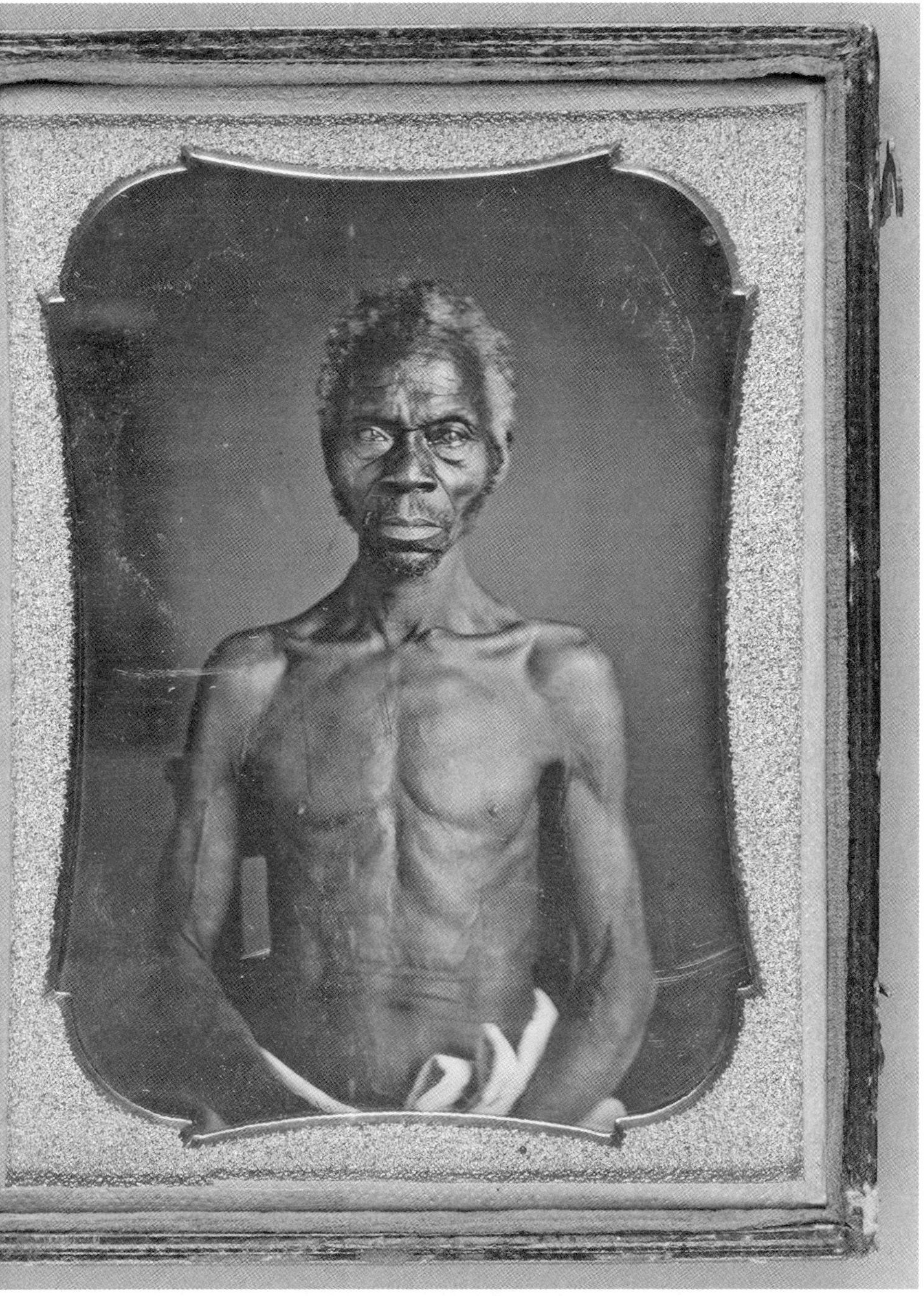

Figure 1.2. J. T. Zealy, Renty, Congo, on plantation of B. F. Taylor, Columbia, SC, March 1850. Commissioned by Louis Agassiz for his study on Polygenism. Mounted quarter plate daguerreotype in case, black male, nude to waist, front view. Courtesy of the Peabody Museum of Archaeology and Ethnology, Harvard University, 35-5-10/53037.

Concomitantly, critics struggle with the question of the agency of these little-known figures. Performance scholar Harvey Young offers a brief survey of critical attempts to attend to this problem, highlighting the language of performance that runs through them. Art historian Cherise Smith, he notes, says that Delia "gazes into the camera, *appearing* calm, yet painfully aware of her inability to change the situation" (emphasis added).[11] Although Smith's point was that Delia has very little agency, Young sees in the choice of the word "appearing" the potential to control the appearance of the self through comportment and facial expression. Young also notes that Alan Trachtenberg, who attempted to locate the slaves' possible agency, suggested they were "performing the role of specimen." For Trachtenberg, to enact of the role of specimen is to portray an alienated and objectified self. He writes,

> By obeying his commission to present them as bodies rather than persons, as biological speciments, Zealy allows them to be as they are: black slaves constrained to perform the role of specimen before the camera. The absoluteness of their confinement to this *role* [emphasis added] has the unintended effect of freeing their eyes from any other necessity but to look back at the glass eye staring at them. Their gaze defies the scrutinizing gaze aimed at their nakedness, and challenges the viewer of these daguerreotypes to reckon with his or her own responses to such images.[12]

For Trachtenberg, the role of specimen affords the enslaved the power, if not to control, then to affect. For Trachtenberg, this power is located in the gaze's "acute awareness of the spectator." Building on the work of a Roman portraiture scholar, he argues for a lineage from Roman busts to the Agassiz daguerreotypes, in that both picture the seen *being* seen. This innovation of late antiquity marks a significant evolution in portraiture, for "the subject's awareness of being in the presence of a spectator who shares his space and 'narrative time' opens a wedge between mask and self, persona and person—between self-presentation and self-awareness."[13] Trachtenberg also notes a discrepancy between Agassiz's daguerreotypes and the subjects of Roman portraiture, however, only insofar as Roman busts portrayed figures of "dual identity: a social persona and actual individual."[14] The enslaved have no such duality to enact. "Without a public mask to mediate their encounter with the lens," Trachtenberg says, "the eyes of the enslaved Africans can only reveal the depths of their being—for, as naked slaves, they are permitted no social persona."[15] For Trachtenberg, the layers of the photographic in the Agassiz daguerreotypes exist in the layers of observation but not in the social personas of the portrayed, who are denied such masks. Implicitly, Trachtenberg argues that "specimen" is not itself a social persona.[16]

For his own part, Young sees the enslaved person as enacting something, though for Young, this enactment is not so much *beyond* what Agassiz had determined for them as *through* it. Young theorizes that enslaved people's understandings of their selves—or at least the present conditions of their selfhoods—were likely informed by iterative instances of the stilled black body as much as by the enslaved body at work and in motion. Following Maurice Merleau-Ponty's theory that self-awareness arises by looking at another, or through the look of another, Young theorizes that slaves would have recognized, and constituted, their own experiences of stillness and captivity by observing fellow slaves' immobilizations—confined in ship holds, on auction blocks, in holding cells.[17] Stillness is resonant in this instance because, as Young reminds his readers, the daguerreotype initially required its subjects to be still for upwards of three minutes, though by 1860 the technology had advanced so that subjects may have needed to be still for closer to one full minute.[18] For Renty and the other slaves photographed for Agassiz, the stillness of the photographic process might have been not (only) a new objectification, but another of the myriad moments of motionlessness required in slavery. In stilling their bodies for the camera and, perhaps, in witnessing one another's performed stillness, the enslaved person enacted an immobility that belonged to their internalized repertoire of selfhood.

As Young describes this experience of subjectivity, the fact that stillness is ordered by white captors *coexists* with motionlessness as a mode of survival being modeled by, modeled for, and shared among black subjects. Such iterative stillness means that the affective registers of these daguerreotypes reside, in part, in the way that their subjects are "futured."[19] The viewer interacts with this futured stillness both within and beyond the daguerreotype's frame. He writes, "To look at Alfred [. . .] is to see a person who consciously is enacting motionlessness. His performance becomes atemporal. [. . .] Alfred stands still and still stands."[20] Young's theory suggests that affective resonance threads through a temporal foreshortening or folding between then (stands still) and now (still stands).[21]

Young's discussion of temporality provides a helpful pivot from the Agassiz daguerreotypes to photographic capture more generally, for other theorists of visuality have discussed photography's temporal folds. In *Camera Lucida*, for example, Roland Barthes includes a picture of a young man to illustrate his concept of *punctum*—the "sting, speck, cut, little hole" or "prick" through which an image wounds its viewer, an "element which rises from the scene, shoots out of it like an arrow, and pierces."[22] The young man, who might be considered handsome, leans against a wall and stares directly into the camera. His gaze is intense, though his posture is disaffected and his expression is inscrutable. His hands are shackled. The man's name was Lewis Powell (also Paine or Payne), and his picture was taken a little more than two months before he was hanged for his role as a co-conspirator in the Lincoln assassination (fig. 1.3). Barthes captions the photograph, "He is dead and he is going to die . . ."; in this knowledge—in this temporal fold—lies the punctum of the image for Barthes.[23]

Technology and ethics scholar Michael Sacasas considers this and other images of Powell in an essay titled "Dead and Going to Die." For Sacasas, as for Barthes, the image is affecting; Sacasas describes its effect on him as "haunting." Yet for Sacasas, the punctum of the image lies in the "modernity of Powell's subjectivity."[24] To better illustrate this modern subjectivity, Sacasas includes, as a counterexample, the picture of a stiff nineteenth-century couple. He posits that, uncomfortable with the camera's objectification and unsure how to regain subjectivity, most subjects of nineteenth-century photographs stared blankly into the camera—that is, they remained objects—or they performed their subjectivity by adopting the roles of stock characters (statesmen or lovers, for example). Although Sacasas doesn't cite Trachtenberg, the earlier scholar said more or less the same thing when he wrote that early photography's "sitters were encouraged and cajoled to *will* themselves, as it were, into a desired expression—in short, a role and a mask which accord with one's self-image."[25] In contrast to such subjects, Sacasas argues, Powell plays himself:

> To ward off the objectifying power of the camera, [Powell] had to play himself before the camera. Simply *being* himself was out of the question; the observer effect created by the camera's presence so heightened

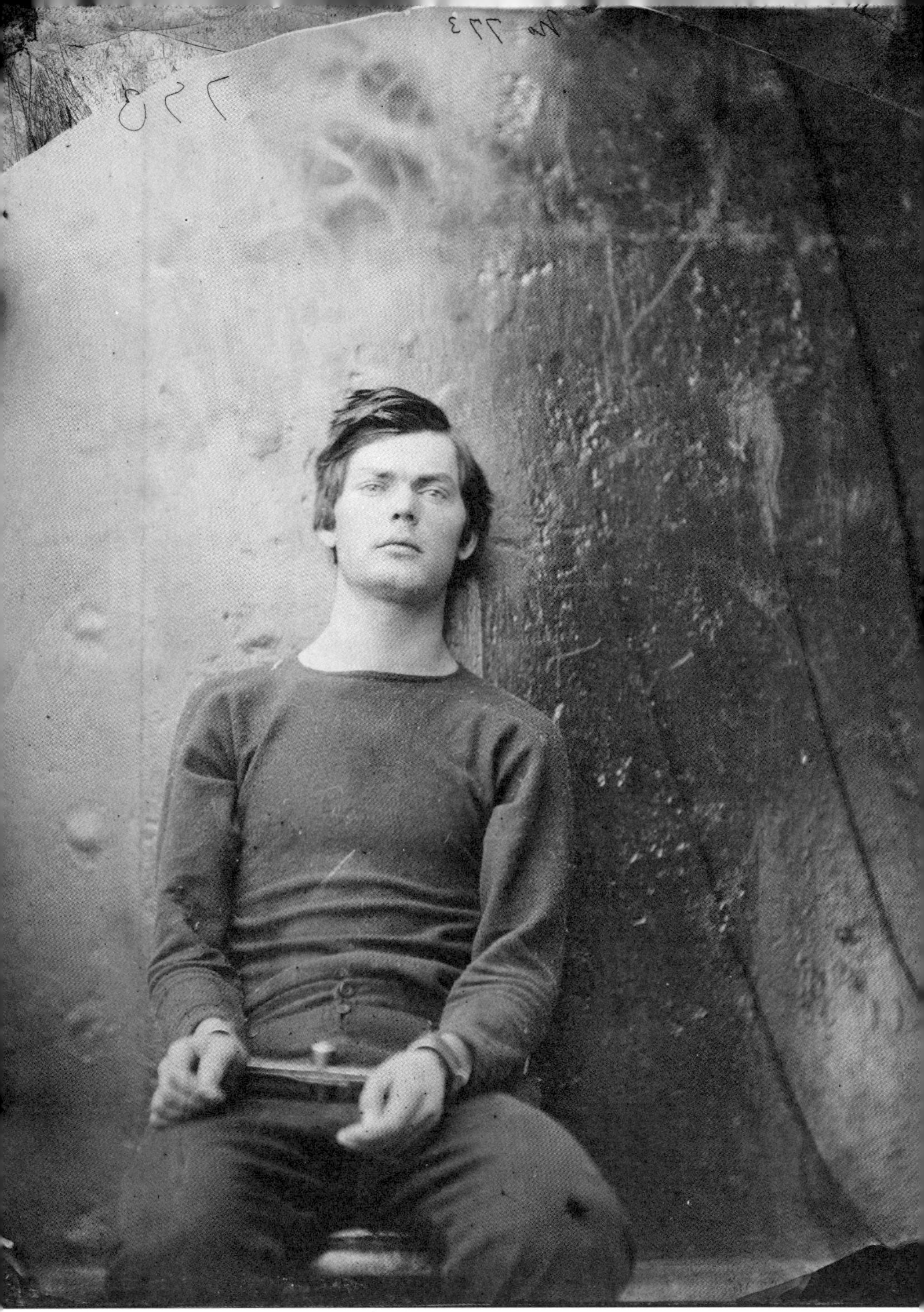

Figure 1.3. Alexander Gardner, Lewis Payne, in sweater, seated and manacled, Washington Navy Yard, DC, April 1865. Library of Congress.

> one's self-consciousness that it was no longer possible to simply be. [. . .] The camera does not allow us to forget ourselves. In fact, as with all technologies of self-documentation, it heightens self-consciousness. In order to appear indifferent to the camera, Powell had to perform the part of Lewis Powell as Lewis Powell would appear were there no camera present.[26]

It was impossible for Powell to *be* himself for, as Sacasas explains, "simply being" implies a self-forgetfulness that was interrupted by the camera's gaze. Notably, Sacasas doesn't suggest that Powell performs his appearance as if *no one* were present; rather, he performs as if the *camera* were not present.

If self-forgetting under the camera's gaze was impossible for all subjects of nineteenth-century photographs, how did Powell, in particular, arrive at his different mode of performative subjectivity? Sacasas posits that it was born out of Powell's resistance to being photographed, for Powell's image was taken against his will. As photographer Alexander Gardner attempted to capture his picture, Powell shook his head to blur his image in exposures. After being struck for this attempt, Powell resigned himself to the camera's objectification, and Sacasas locates Powell's performative innovation in this outward resignation and inward resistance. Sacasas also posits that Powell's relationship to violence may have "prepared him for this work against his psyche."

Two points of Sacasas's brief essay are of particular interest. The first is the suggestion that the ability to *perform* modern subjectivity (which is not to say modern subjectivity itself) might be the result of an individual's resistance to compulsory objectification in image-making, for, compelling as Powell's portrait is, he was hardly the first subject (or the last) to be photographed against his will or to inhabit a particularly alienated subjectivity. If Sacasas's affective theory is correct, Agassiz's daguerreotypes might be so moving to the modern viewer because they display a particularly *modern* subjectivity, that of the alienated subject who is playing, rather than simply being, himself.[27] Furthermore, Sacasas's theorization suggests that the enslaved individual might have been uniquely endowed to perform this modern subjectivity, since, in Sacasas's formation, such a performance is born out of an individual's resistance to compulsory objectification. This is why the camera's presence was different for Powell than the presence of Gardner alone. Yet for racialized subjects of the nineteenth century, compulsory objectification was such a matter of course that these individuals might be said to have existed under what Lauren Berlant has named "conditions of crisis within the ordinary."[28] No camera would have been necessary for black people in America to meet the conditions of Powell's performative innovation.

A second point of interest—shifting from the subject to the viewer—is the suggestion that the recognition of modern subjectivity begets an affective punctum in the modern viewer. Yet Sacasas doesn't explain why the recognition of modern subjectivity *in and of itself* would be affecting. If one attempts to account for this through the specific terms of the performance Sacasas observes, rather than speculate about what might be affecting about modern subjectivity in general, one finds oneself repeating, with a difference, a sentence from above: the ability to perform *modern* subjectivity might have been born out of an individual's resistance to compulsory objectification in image-making.

To summarize Sacasas's hypothesis, then: the performance of modern subjectivity is born of compelled objectification, which results in alienated subjectivity, which structures (or at least primes) an affective result in a viewer. In this, Sacasas's theorization goes one step further than Trachtenberg's. For Trachtenberg, the reciprocity performed in simultaneous acts of looking and being looked at is paramount. He acknowledges that "in spite of the coerciveness they represent—*or perhaps, in an ironic reversal of intention, because of it*—[the daguerreotypes] possess a power of communication that reveals more than most conventional portraits" (emphasis added).[29] And like Sacasas, he feels hailed even into his contemporary moment. "The illustrations are trapped within a system of representation as firmly as the sitters are trapped within a system of chattel slavery," Trachtenberg writes. "And they powerfully inform us of our own entrapment."[30] Though visual entrapment speaks to Trachtenberg across time, he stops short of calling this structure of feeling a feature of modernity. For Sacasas, on the other hand, it is precisely the modernity of alienated subjectivity that provokes the viewer's affective response.

Of course, identifying the ability to perform modern subjectivity (or to be alienated from it) depends on a delineation of what constitutes modern subjectivity in the first place, and here Denise Ferreira da Silva's work is helpful. Ferreira da Silva writes a genealogy of Western subjectivity that charts Western philosophy's successive attempts to locate an autonomous and reasoning "I" against the incursions of exterior forces—a project that became more difficult amid the rise of science and its increasing evidence of everything's affectability, including the autonomous reasoning of man. The creation of racial hierarchies is, in her account, the consequence of white Western minds attempting to preserve their imperviousness by scripting the global others they encountered as more primitive and more affectable, less autonomous and less reasonable. Put differently, the advent and growth of empiricism in the West meant that the "others of Europe," as Ferreira da Silva names them, were converted to specimens of affectability.[31]

The history of racism in science's evidentiary looking is extremely well established in black studies, and indeed is so powerful that Paul Gilroy opens his most influential text, *The Black Atlantic*, with a reminder that "scientists did not monopolize either the image of the black or the emergent concept of biologically based racial difference" and that "both were centrally employed in those European attempts to think through beauty, taste, and aesthetic judgment that are the precursors of contemporary cultural criticism."[32] While Gilroy's plea to attend to aesthetics as well as science is close to my heart, it would be a mistake to overlook the countless times aesthetics has *abetted* science. One can call to mind illustrations of the comparative beauty, anachronism, or freakishness of skulls and genitalia detailed by scholars such as Sander Gilman and Brian Wallis; the overlapping scopophilia and pornotroping underwriting ethnographic photography illuminated by Suzanne Schneider; or the carte de visite images of the "white" slave children of New Orleans, which were ostensibly produced to raise funds for the National Freedmen's Relief Association, but did so by offering the lay scientist–cum–legal expert the opportunity to examine and draw conclusions about the formerly enslaved based upon the bodies of evidence quite literally in hand.[33] In each of these instances, compelled objectification results from the *union* of science and hegemonic visual aesthetics.

SPECIMEN LOGICS

The specimen—from the Latin root *specĕre*, to look, or look at—is a distinctly modern invention, springing, as it does, from the empiricism that characterizes the Enlightenment.[34] The earliest instance of the word, a now-obsolete usage for "a means of discovering or finding out;

an experiment," dates to 1610; its more contemporary usages appear by middle of the seventeenth century. The science-specific specimen appears by the middle of the eighteenth century ("an animal, plant, or mineral, a part or portion of some substance or organism, etc., serving as an example of the thing in question for purposes of investigation or scientific study; in extended use: of a person").[35] To the extent that modernity entails the meeting of nature and technology—which is one way to think of empiricism's method—the specimen poignantly encapsulates modernity's impulses.

With this provenance in mind, works such as Janice Neri's *The Insect and the Image* show how the visual logics of the Agassiz daguerreotypes long preceded the advent of photography. If, as Alan Sekula has argued, photography consolidated and carried science's evidentiary impulses and methods into the twentieth century, the visual conventions of what Neri calls "specimen logic" are recognizably in place from the beginning of the sixteenth century.[36] Beginning with Albrecht Dürer's 1505 illustration of a stag beetle, Neri shows how image-making was a crucial vehicle for understanding the natural world through the production of specimen images that "entice," "inviting us to imagine them as inhabitants of a timeless space of display, and to imagine ourselves as their possessors."[37] Specimen logic's visual techniques, she explains, involve presenting an isolated object before a blank background, depicting it in high detail, and providing multiple views of the same object. These practices "[turn] nature into object [. . .] by removing them from their habitats, environments, and settings."[38] Only those items that can be discretely separated from their contexts are suitable for specimenization. Indeed, building on the words of art historian Lee Hendrix, Neri suggests that the visual strategy of "isolat[ing] the specimens from one another as pure visual data" is what distinguishes the act of "specimenizing" from that of "simply depicting specimens."[39]

The significance of specimen logic lives not only in the visual conventions it would establish but also in the ways that it helped (white, mostly male) individuals create artistic and scientific personas. Specimen logic allowed collector-artists "to construct themselves as the gatekeepers to a strange and fascinating new world"; moreover, this classificatory gatekeeping unfolded within the early modern period's "taste for the esoteric and the bizarre that is usually associated with [courtly] mannerism."[40] In other words, even as citizen-subjects created specimens, specimens consolidated artistic-scientific personas and practices—that is, individual and societal roles for citizen-subjects to inhabit with (and against) observed curiosities and othernesses. Furthermore, the observer's relation to the specimen elevated the practices of both collecting *and* isolating the specimen from the collection for extended observation and image-creation. As Neri explains, "drawings provided a space in which individual objects could be taken out of the context of the collection for prolonged and concentrated examination. The results of these investigations were visual images that stress the physical presence of the specimens and present them as highly individualized objects. The drawings are suffused with a mood of serious contemplation."[41]

Note the tight knot between collection, observation, and thought. The act of observational image-making helps establish which objects constitute a specimen—what should be collected in order to be closely observed. As Neri writes, "Early still life painters contributed to the construction of insects as collectable objects *by making them visible as appropriate items for a collection*" (emphasis added).[42] In other words, specimen logic is a conceptual framework that can (and did) change observational objects without changing the frame. Finally, if the specimen yokes the acts of collecting, isolating, and producing visual images to the advent of thought and knowledge, another critical element of its logic was that visual images could, in turn, be collected, isolated, exchanged, and possessed. "Specimen logic was also part of the commodification of nature that was central to global trade and commerce during the early modern period," Neri writes, and her work carefully delineates networks of circulation and exchange.[43]

Scientific empiricism created and proliferated the specimen during the rise of transatlantic encounter, empire, and industrial capitalism—all of which are foundational to the common account of modernity. In *The Black Atlantic*, Gilroy highlights the violence and illogic of the modern era's systems (slavery, empire, global capitalism) in order to urge a reconsideration of the Enlightenment's underlying principles and, by extension, of modernity itself. For Gilroy, any account of Western modernity should feature the brutality and terror of slavery and colonialism as inherent to, rather than an aberration of, Enlightenment logics. "Successive generations of black intellectuals," he reminds his readers, have articulated "critiques of modernity [. . .] nurtured by a deep sense of the complicity of racial terror with reason."[44] As an evidentiary body held up to empirical examination, the specimen is made subject to modernity's violent demands precisely through the Enlightenment's putative rationality, and this was in place (as implied by Ferreira da Silva text) long before the nineteenth-century scientists upon whom Ferreira da Silva focuses most closely. Indeed, it is hard to overstate the specimen's relationship to the racialized body, and the extent to which it ran in tandem with Europe's conquest of the so-called new world and its enslavement of Africans and others.

As but one example, take the first pathological examination recorded in the Western Hemisphere, which was conducted in the Dominican Republic in 1533. The Roman Catholic Church authorized the examination in order to determine whether a set of conjoined twin girls, who were born in Santo Domingo and lived for nine days, had one soul or two.[45] Their autopsy, which was recorded by El Capitan Don Gonçalo Fernández de Oviedo y Valdés, found its way into the *Annals of Medical History* in 1924. In the excerpts that appear in that journal, Oviedo gives no clear indication of the racial parentage of the girls. Their father, Juan Lopez Ballestero, was formerly of Sevilla. Nothing is mentioned of the mother beyond her name, Melchiora, which carries at least some association with the biblical magi's dusky otherness (especially in the context of the relatively early date of encounter). Regardless of the race of the children, however, the *Annals*' account makes clear that the evidentiary body was central to the Europeans' cross-racial encounter (and, I would add, remained so in 1924).

The *Annals*' article on the autopsy is six pages long; the first two and a half offer an account of Oviedo's life and parentage. The authors, A. Peña Chavarría and P. G. Shipley, praise Oviedo's empirical eye:

> He was omniscient in the knowledge of his day, and [the "Historia," from which the autopsy account is drawn] is abundant evidence of this fact. He wrote ably of the customs and habits of the savage people he found about him and, though neither a botanist nor an entomologist, his descriptions of the fauna and flora of the New World were above reproach. He was no physician but he has left good records of some of the diseases of the tropics. He recorded the case history quoted below, clearly and thoroughly in excellent language and style, missing no important detail.[46]

Oviedo's linked observations of plant and animal life, foreign human bodies, illnesses, and "monstrosities" were noted in detail worthy of praise many centuries later, by others no less enamored of specimens.

When Oviedo first returned to Spain in October of 1515, the authors tell us, he "carried with him a most amusing cargo of presents for his sovereign, six cannibal caribs, the first sugar from the western world to reach Europe, cassia fistula, six Indian girls and thirty parrots."[47] Again, both Oviedo and the journalists of 1924 show a preoccupation with exhibit and examination, and, for both, the racialized specimen seems far down what Mel Chen calls the animacy hierarchy.[48]

Oviedo visited the day after the twins' birth, Peña Chavarría and Shipley relate, "in the company of the important officials, priests, scientists and residents of the city and the neighboring country." He observed that "each of them would have been a beautiful woman, had they lived and not been joined" ("Cada una dellas fuera mujer hormosa viviendo si no estuvieran assi juntas").[49] He noted the details of their bodies—which I will not here reproduce except to say they included those Oviedo deemed flawless and fine as well as those of their conjoinment—as well as details of the babies' behavior (which reveal rather more about the people around them than the twins themselves). As Peña Chavarría and Shipley summarize, "Oviedo observed that when they were stripped and put on exhibition, both began to cry, but when they were dressed again one became quiet, although the other continued to scream for a short time."[50]

Oviedo also attended the children's postmortem examination, which, as noted above, was conducted to determine how many souls they contained. "We are inclined to believe," the *Annals*' authors state, "that this uncertainty was instrumental in securing the ready consent of the parents to a postmortem section, an uncommon procedure in that time and place, when medical investigation of the dead was even less approved by the laity than it is today."[51] It seems pertinent that the church not only determined that anatomical investigation was warranted—which speaks volumes about the church's relationship to empiricism at this historical juncture—but also arrived at this conclusion in the midst of the cross-racial intermingling of Indigenous, African, and European peoples on the shores of the Spanish colonies. Put differently, it seems likely that, regardless of whether the twins themselves were racialized, the racialized encounter of the Americas suggested their bodies as evidentiary.

MODERNITY'S PERFORMANCE REVIEW

As Mark Seltzer sees it, the "official world"—his name for the modernity most familiar to the contemporary Western bourgeois subject—is characterized by three main criteria. First, the modern world notices itself. Second, it notices its processes. Third, modernity questions its own nature "with an unremitting and unsparing intensity."[52] Seltzer offers concrete examples to help us get our heads around all this, "isotopias" that operate in the same way. One is the suspense novel and the "microworlds" that populate it: the office, the train car, the game space of the tennis court.[53] Another is the abstract modern artwork. For Seltzer, the modern world "interrogates itself with an unremitting and unsparing intensity as to its own nature and singularity."[54] In this, the modern world follows Clement Greenberg's ideals of modernist abstraction, in which a maker "turns in upon the medium of his own craft," "not in order to subvert, it but to entrench it more firmly in its area of competence."[55] For Greenberg, the task of the artwork in any given medium is to discover and exploit those traits unique to it; similarly, Seltzer's official world observes itself in order to produce itself.

While Seltzer's illustrative novels and artworks are helpful, I cannot help but note that performance haunts his depictions. The official world, he says, "comes to itself by *staging* its own conditions."[56] "The artwork *stages* what it does, and, in doing so, *enacts* what it shows."[57] Modernity's isotopias are "*staging areas of reenactment*," and—much like a play stage—spaces of simultaneous motion and "suspended animation."[58] Modernity's internal systems "[allow] for, or [require], externalization for validation," which, at the level of the human, seems simply a requirement for an audience. Seltzer calls this a paradox between interior life and "reenactive institutions," a term reminiscent of Richard Schechner's "twice-behaved behavior."[59] Furthermore, the subject must "systematically manage himself: to state intentions as reenactments."[60] Strikingly, Seltzer's language of performance at times collapses into a language of science and its specimens, as when Seltzer likens the official world's stage (an "overlit [zone] of action and reenactment") to "a glass cell."[61]

In *The Player's Passion*, Joseph Roach offers an extended consideration of the link between acting and science, showing that what it is to convincingly body forth a role depends upon a given episteme's sense of how a body rightly registers and conveys an emotion. "What is true of the history of scientific thinking is true also of the history of theatrical theories," he teaches us. "If each age prides itself on having attained the right answers about how the world works, it prides itself equally on being able to view theatrical expressions of human feeling that are more realistic and natural than those of the previous age." Leaps in acting technique correspond to seismic shifts in the scientific understanding of bodies and emotions because "the central issues of psychology and physiology, by whatever names they are known, are not remote abstractions to the performer, but literally matters of flesh and blood."[62] If Roach shows that the epistemologies of science and acting are inevitably linked, Seltzer's work suggests the that this connection is present not only for the professional actor, but also for the pedestrian actor tasked with presenting a self inside of the official world.

In his earlier work *Bodies and Machines*, Seltzer discusses modernity's regulation of performative subjectivity through scientific management. As he narrates, the machine-age birth of Taylorism brought new levels of regulation and *self*-regulation.[63] Feeling themselves always watched, workers performed accordingly.[64] This theme is reprised in *The Official World*, now with the language of stages, performance, productions, and puppets: "Intentions are extroverted [. . .] and perspicuous only to a super-observer or over-seer, who may be there or not. [. . .] The distinction then seems to be between mindfully mindless devotees and *marionettes* of administrative reason, iterative ascetics and irrational work ethics. The scene *stages* the conversion to the Taylorized work ethic, one that systematically divides cognition and motion and acts into parts, so *performance* and *production*, doing and being done, can be separated and administratively recombined" (emphasis added).[65] I would like to highlight here that such self-administration, such mindful devotion to overseers who may or may not be present except for internally (where they certainly are), and such concern with passivity and upward mobility, are essentially the crux of black subjectivity for those African Americans who have invested in respectability as the performance of modern selfhood. Put differently, if respectability is the art of self-management, uplift is a process of machine culture. Most fundamentally, respectability and Taylorism share the self-reflexive acts of self-assessment and self-regulation, which depend upon a degree of alienated selfhood. This allows us to consider respectability's performance of proxy selfhood as a *technological* procedure, morphing "ascetic training into aesthetic conditioning to a continuous, self-stressed, virtuoso performativity."[66] In all, the subject of modernity must self-alienate enough to self-monitor and self-stage, just as does the actor of Bertolt Brecht's "alienation effect."[67] And indeed, Seltzer further describes "reincarnation exercises" that might as well be a school of acting: "training [. . .] in repetitive self-annihilation in the service of serial self-projection."[68] The twist is that, just as in Sacasas's modernity, the actor is training to self-annihilate in order to play herself.

Ultimately, what has been too overlooked in discussions of respectability is not the phenomenon of evidentiary looking, nor the insidiousness of respectability's demand to anticipate such a look, nor even the extent to which this insidiousness can come to define a portion of classed, gendered, and hued black experience. Rather, what seems too thinly acknowledged is the extent to which such (self-)specimenization is a minoritarian attempt to meet the preconditions of racialized admission to modernity itself. What matters most, in other words, is not the outcome but the *process*.

Finally, we return to the mystery of how Louis's deadpan communicated respectability. We can see respectability—which is to say performed modernity—not in the fulfillment of his scripted role but in his public performance of the "self-distancing and avertedness" of modern subjectivity.[69] While Seltzer doesn't name the boxing ring as a game space of the official world, take Joyce Carol Oates's assertion that although she is unable to consider boxing a metaphor for anything else, she is able to consider *life* a metaphor for boxing, "for one of those bouts that go on and on, round following round, jabs, missed punches, clinches, nothing determined, again the bell and again and you and your opponent so evenly matched it's impossible not to see that your opponent *is* you: and why this struggle on an elevated platform enclosed by ropes as in a pen beneath hot crude pitiless lights in the presence of an impatient crowd?—that sort of hellish-writerly metaphor."[70] What could be more unremittingly indoor, self-observed, autotropic, than timed round after timed round on a roped, elevated, brightly lit platform, where it is "impossible not to see that your opponent *is* you"? It seems clear that the microworld of the boxing ring bolstered Louis's performance of self-regulation. But if the boxing ring perfectly distills modernity's official world, offering up a space for enacting one's modernity, so, too, does the photography studio.

THE EVIDENTIARY SUBJECT

If photography proffers the black body as evidence, here I want to highlight the ways that black subjects attempt to turn their specimenization to their advantage by yoking evidentiary subjectivity to their evidentiary bodies. This is of course not a new observation, though perhaps it is a new restatement of what we've long known about the project of respectability and the layered surveillances it requires.[71] Those who attempt to visually render evidentiary black subjecthood have already conceded that blackness will be scrutinized.[72] Moreover, this conjoined concession and compensatory technique is a longstanding one. One can see the force of evidentiary subjecthood in Sojourner Truth's election to bare her breast to prove her womanhood, and to shame (and emasculate) her persecutors, for example.[73] In this act, one can see as well that respectability's visuality does not run *counter* to the project of specimenization; it is rather the other side of the same coin, an attempt to beat specimenization at its own game by presenting an evidentiary subject over and above and alongside an evidentiary body.

Believing (perhaps rightly) that the black body *will be* evidentiary, respectability attempts to present visual evidence of its own choosing. An example of this is detailed in Shawn Michelle Smith's outstanding *Photography on the Color Line*, which examines the 363 photographs W. E. B. Du Bois provided as part of the American Negro Exhibit of the Paris Exhibition of 1900. These were organized into two subsections: *Types of American Negroes, Georgia, U.S.A.*, and *Negro Life in Georgia, U.S.A.* Smith reads the photographic images from Du Bois's exhibition individually and together. She also notes instances where images from the Paris Exhibition recur in Du Bois's other rhetorical projects in order to argue that the images "collectively function as a counterarchive that challenges a long legacy of racist taxonomy, intervening in turn-of-the-century 'race science' by offering competing visual evidence."[74]

Smith emphasizes that Du Bois's visual albums entered a much broader and more fraught field of ethnographic display within the grounds of the Paris Exposition, which included, for example, a Dahomeyan village. Such ethnographic displays contrasted "primitive savagery" with European order. In the context of such display, Smith argues, Du Bois "signified" on the conventions of scientific image-making by pairing frontal and profile images in *Types of American Negroes,* hauntingly following the photographic conventions of race science. Smith hypothesizes that Du Bois courted this association purposefully, in order to "'signify on' the formal visual codes of scientific photography, repeating those visual tropes 'with a difference' in order to invert the dominant significations of those particular photographic signs."[75] While Smith doesn't focus on the title of this part of the exhibition, Du Bois's use of "types" in relation to the visual archive title both underscores and complicates Brian Wallis's argument that Agassiz's photographs should not be considered portraits at all. Smith's savvy reading of Du Bois suggests the extent to which portraiture and type may overlap.[76]

Furthermore, Smith points out that forty-eight of the images of *Types of American Negroes* recur in Du Bois's *The Health and Physique of the American Negro* (1906), in which he cropped the images to focus on heads and shoulders. For Smith, this visual choice more closely echoes the work of eugenicist Francis Galton, an association furthered by Du Bois's decision to delineate details of subjectivity alongside visual evidence. In lieu of names, Du Bois presents "numbered notations of physical features, moral character and intellectual aptitude—the very categories of racial classification outlined by Francis Galton: '#10. Brown, mass of curled hair; short and plump; usual mental ability, cheerful and good character'; '#39. Light yellow, long, nearly straight hair; large and plump; slow, but willing.'"[77] For Smith, this is another repetition with a difference, for even though the photographs' form mimics that of scientific evidence, the individuality and personality of those pictures nevertheless shine through. "In the overlapping 1900 and 1906 photographs," she notes, "students clearly have come before the camera with forethought: their neat, crisp clothes are embellished with pins, and here and there a lilac adorns a lapel." For my own purposes—and in inversion of Smith's syntax and focus—it is equally relevant that "most of these young men and women have managed to assume a serious countenance for the photographer."[78]

Smith also observes that the portraits within *Types of American Negroes* that do not mimic scientific conventions follow instead those of middle-class portraiture. In these images, "The camera has been placed at a greater distance, to show more of the body and surrounding accoutrements. Large feather hats, formal Victorian dresses, ornate chairs, lace curtains, plants, books, and statuettes come to fill the photographic frame. African American 'types' turn out to be middle-class gentlemen and ladies."[79] Again the expression adopted by the subjects is a critical part of Du Bois's endeavor and Smith's reading of it. In those exhibition photographs known to have been taken by photographer Thomas Askew, for example, the men are typically "positioned at a slight angle to the camera [. . .] but more often just off to the side of center, assuming the lofty gazes of contemplation that signal interiority." Of one in particular, Smith writes, "His expression appears serene and quiet, thoughtful but not overly dreamy."[80] If not inexpressive or inscrutable, this expression is at least minimal.

Du Bois also uses physical space in the companion album, *Negro Life in Georgia*, as a means of "transposing [the black body] from the realm of (racist) science to that of class and culture."[81] Unlike those Farm Security Administration (FSA) photographs discussed below, Du Bois absents the black body from scenes of rural poverty, instead showing black men, women, and children in bourgeois settings—the lawyer's home, the horse-drawn carriage, the piano bench of the drawing room—that emphasize "polish, control, and stillness [and] the relationship of master to servant to animal that structures class hierarchy."[82] Family members standing before their large and well-kept home adopt "far-off looks of nobility and striving, gazing out in different directions."[83]

Smith's excellent analysis of Du Bois's visual efforts helps to illuminate a persistent problem for black modern subjectivity. As Smith sees it, the visual archives Du Bois assembled for the Paris Exhibition "[highlight] the transmutation whereby people are transformed into evidence and, vice versa, whereby such 'evidence' is also always a marker of subjectivity in another register, for another viewer."[84] I would like to both say that this is true and insist that the display of subjectivity is not an antidote to modernity's evidentiary demands but rather another instance of them. Smith herself comes close to acknowledging this in her discussion of *The Health and Physique of the American Negro* when she writes that "Du Bois uses Galton's scientific terms and visual forms of documentation—he replicates Galton's methodology—to reach very different conclusions." While Smith highlights the difference in conclusion, I want to highlight instead the similarity in method. If Du Bois's albums trade in the hope that they can control what evidence the viewer will see in the racialized body or subject—control, in other words, the *outcome* of looking—the *process* of evidentiary looking remains the same.

Perhaps it is unsurprising that one should see this operation clearly in the work of the theorist of double-consciousness, "this sense of always looking at one's self through the eyes of others, of measuring one's soul by the tape of a world that looks on in amused contempt and pity."[85] But this evidentiary impulse drives the visuality of the black subject in remarkably different contexts. One can see it at work, for example, in *12 Million Black Voices* (1941), which pairs Richard Wright's sociological narration of black struggle with Edwin Rosskam's curation of images from FSA archives.[86] Wright's social realism envisioned subjects as products of their circumstance, and, in contrast to Du Bois's attempt to divorce the black body from physical environments of degradation or poverty, offers a visual indictment of conditions that shape black life. Though Rosskam's selections include black people smiling, dancing, and singing, the preponderance of his images show subjects of minimal expression laboring or ensconced in settings of privation and disrepair. The expressionlessness displayed by some of the pictured subjects played an important role in the polemics of this visual archive.

Consider two examples from FSA archives. The first, by Arthur Rothstein, shows a smiling black man and child with a wagonload of cotton (fig. 1.4). The caption explains that the man is a rehabilitation client, but even without this context we can see that this is an image of well-being. The image foregrounds—both literally and affectively—the warm relation between the boy and the man, whom one assumes to be the child's father. Paired in button-down shirts and denim overalls, the two smile at one another as the father holds the child's ankle in reassurance or protection. The boy sits on bolls of a seemingly copious harvest, one hand buried in its white, the other upturned at ease in his lap. His laces are tied and his socks are white. The light is bright. The building in the background appears square and intact. The wood of the wagon is relatively new, exhibiting no weather staining or warping. The people exhibit warm individuality, and the background hints at orderliness. Many such images exist, yet these are not the photographs that have become iconic of midcentury American blackness. Too much individuality comes through the subjects' facial expression and the expression of their relation.

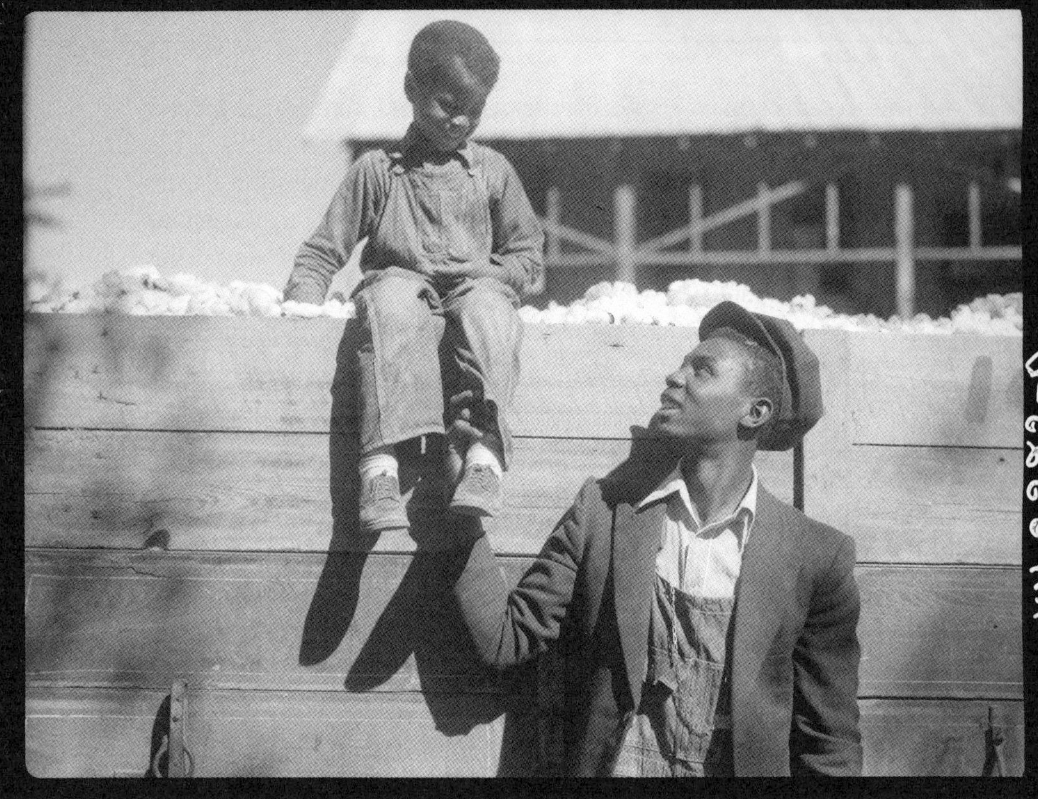

Figure 1.4. Arthur Rothstein, rehabilitation client, Smithfield, Johnston County, NC, October 1936. Library of Congress.

Instead, the culturally iconic FSA image is more like Marion Post Wolcott's image of dusty, exhausted vegetable workers waiting to be paid (fig. 1.5). These vegetable farmers hover at the verge of being lost as subjects in the throng of the wagon and its surrounding crowd: the crush of bodies, the iterative jackets and slacks and boots and hats, the hands folded one over the other again and again in waiting. But if they are almost lost as subjects, they are well situated as specimens. The vertical frame of the wagon sets them apart visually. The hat of the man whose head is turned down toward his shoe further divides the men into two visually consumable pairs. The hats of these other four are almost, but not quite, in line with the rows of hats on either side, the slight elevation emphasizing their faces (and their neutral cast) against the backs of others' heads. The men in the wagon are not any of the other men, but, the image says, they could be, and perhaps they might as well be. One can find evidence of individualism, a punctum, some dear detail to render each man a rounded and full example of humanity.

Yet the visual rhetorics of the photograph ask us to consume the four workers as representative examples culled from the larger assembly of anonymous black workers, like the central bone picker of figure 1.3. And while each of the men might *deserve* the empathetic acknowledgment of the viewer, such acknowledgment may not be the treatment they *desire* as they perform being solitary together. If the details of their framing were in Wolcott's hands, the performance of expression was in their own.

Without losing sight of the ways that the aesthetics of black rural impoverishment made certain images highly digestible for American publics (and haunt perceptions of an unpolished or backward black urbanity even into the present day), I want to suggest that we lose much in the assumption that blackness was somehow always captured off guard in these images—that it was caught in its "natural" state, or in some way amplified by the photographer rather than her subjects. I see no reason to suppose that the dusty, exhausted vegetable workers were

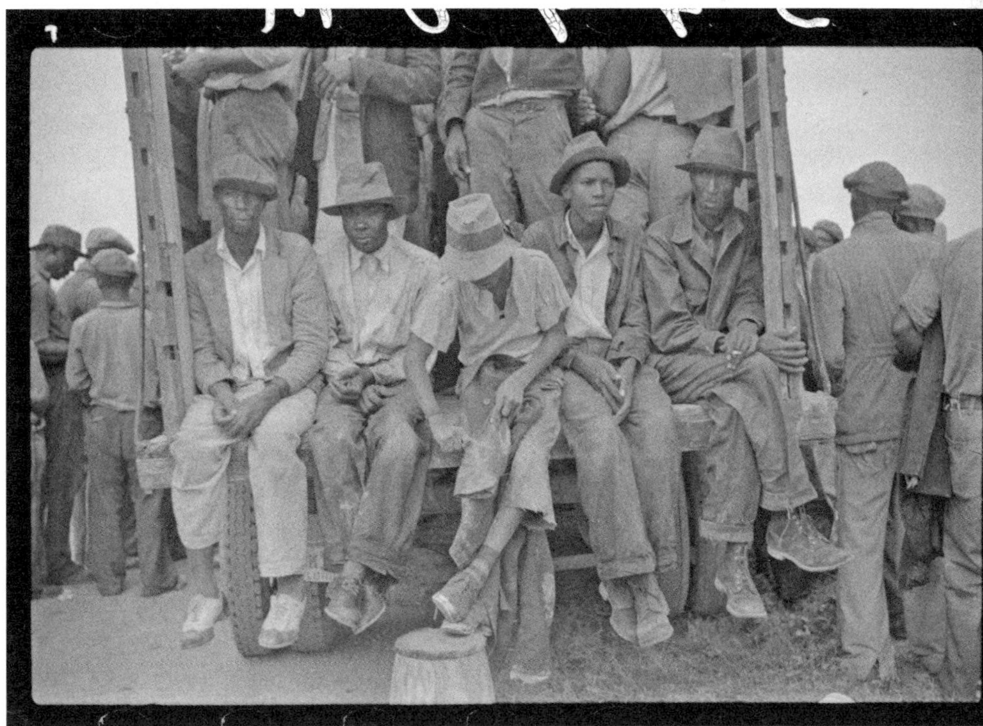

Figure 1.5. Marion Post Wolcott, vegetable workers, migrants, waiting after work to be paid, near Homestead, FL, [February?] 1939. Library of Congress.

less in control of their performance of selfhood than the smiling father and son. I can imagine any number of reasons for the pictured men to minimize their individualism or expressiveness, including frank exhaustion. Whatever the motivation, however, one effect is support of the photograph's visual rhetorics, which portray a bleak picture of black agricultural life that runs counter to the racist trope of happy black ruralism, proffering instead a serial and minimal black subjectivity. In other words, the deadpan is a fruitful aesthetic partner in the sociopolitical realm of documentary portrait photography both because it cues up the sense that a "problem" is interrupting African American performativity *and* because it enlivens the background to make assertions about the nature of that problem. I assert this because while the canonicity of certain images suggests that Americans desire, or at least validate, particular visual and affective rhetorics around blackness, it is important to leave open the possibility that black subjects *are among those Americans*. Expression carries one set of risks, inexpression another.

Finally, if the self-alienating, Jekyll-and-Hyde performance of scientist-and-specimen offers the black subject a speedy means of demonstrating modernity's self-regulation, respectability isn't the only available vehicle. Moreover, *aesthetic* modernity is complicated terrain—as enamored of the primitive as the future—and the black subject's position within modernity is, too, contested. Consider this passage by Zora Neale Hurston, which details her experience listening to a jazz orchestra at the New World Cabaret together with a white acquaintance:

> This orchestra grows rambunctious, rears on its hind legs, and attacks the tonal veil with primitive fury, rending it, clawing it until it breaks through to the jungle beyond. I follow those heathen—follow them exultingly. I dance wildly inside myself; I yell within, I whoop; I shake my assegai above my head, I hurl it true to the mark *yeeeeooww*! I am in the jungle and living in the jungle way. My face is painted red and yellow, and my body is painted blue. My pulse is throbbing like a war drum. I want to slaughter something—give pain, give death to what, I do not know. But the piece ends. The men of the orchestra wipe their lips and rest their fingers. I creep back slowly to the veneer we call civilization with the last tone and find the white friend sitting motionless in his seat, smoking calmly.
>
> 'Good music they have here,' he remarks, drumming the table with his fingertips.[87]

Hurston feels dismayed that the white gentleman failed to be moved by the music. The underlying suggestion—since the music is depicted through her bodily experience—is that he fails to notice the physical change in her. We see none of her exterior appearance, but her internal assegai waving does not break the surface enough for her acquaintance to still even his fingers in response. Perhaps her companion is unusually unobservant. Or perhaps *Hurston is unusually still*. Perhaps what is most readily visible is not the intensity of her feeling or the obliviousness of her companion, but the composition of her withholding.

Critics have pointed to a tension, in the works of predominantly white male modernist designers, between spare exteriors and more lush, exotic interiors. In her work *Second Skin*, literary theorist Anne Anlin Cheng takes up this perceived division, and shows it to be instead a case of entanglement. Cheng does so with a focus on skin. Skin, she writes, is "a medium of transition and doubleness: it is at once surface and yet integrally attached to what it covers [. . .], a vibrant interface between the hidden and the visually available."[88] Through her reading of skin, Cheng questions the austere modernist exterior as a field untouched by the primitive interior, and she does so in order to reassert the many ways in which Josephine Baker's visual archives, and modernism's archives at large, reveal a deep play with racialized surface. In so doing, Cheng writes the black subject into aesthetic modernism—and not only as the other upon whom the white male modernist has always secretly relied. Rather, if interiors and exteriors are entwined and enfolded, Cheng's revision grants access to the aesthetic of an austere surface to those whose dark skin had been considered the mark of a primitive interior. In other words, if high modernist aesthetics actually depend upon the entanglement of the sleekly modern and its primitive counterpart, the placid surface that seems to have accompanied Hurston's jungle trip is no simple accident but rather her fulfillment of a modernist entanglement that presupposes her "native" side. This re-figuration of austere exteriors allows us to reconsider inexpression performed in the context of rural poverty, and its associations with past, primitive, or unmodern black lives.

MASK IS/MASK AIN'T

If it is true that deadpan can bolster performances of respectability as self-observation in and alongside compulsory visibility, it is also true that some specimens are more specimen-y. In order to account for this, I return to Neri's assertion that it is the *isolation* of individuals as visual data that distinguishes the mere depiction of specimens from the act of specimenizing. Moreover, and ironically, it seems that the isolation of the figure in specimen photos—from other people, and from time-bound props—makes the subjects more deeply compelling. Trachtenberg and Sacasas felt themselves powerfully interpellated in their modern present by the figures of Agassiz's daguerreotypes, after all. In order to understand the specimen's ideal affective location outside of time, consider two photographs by Richard Avedon.

In an outtake of Avedon's 1963 portrait session with an elderly black man named William Casby, Casby sits on a porch in Algiers, Louisiana, surrounded by family members in what might be called Sunday dress (fig. 1.6).[89] The patriarch might wear a slight smile, though it is hard to say. We cannot see his neck, which suggests that he is bent slightly, protectively, over the baby nestled in his arms. He seems proud of the baby, or the family as a whole, and this sense of pride is supported by the upturned camera angle. One girl smiles openly. Other family members wear expressions much harder to name without risking an act of conjecture. To my eye, the family's pose and demeanor instantiates the formulaic aesthetic of respectability. But while we can see evidentiary self-discipline in the predictable poses and muted subjectivity of the family, we also see a large piece of white paper or canvas, presumably meant to provide a bright, neutral background. A fold in the sheet's lower left suggests thickness or stiffness, while a small tear in the upper right communicates some measure of impermanence or disposability, and it is readily apparent that this sheet is affixed with quantities of tape. Ostensibly hung as the backdrop, the sheet instead acts as a set piece in this photograph, which frames the family such that clapboard shows at the photograph's edges and a chain-link fence, complete with AMCO sign, runs before the family. Visually, this provides the family with a frame. But what kind of frame? Rather than the iconic Avedon white, the family is framed by earthy and inelegant domesticity in the guise of traditionally inexpensive siding and fence.

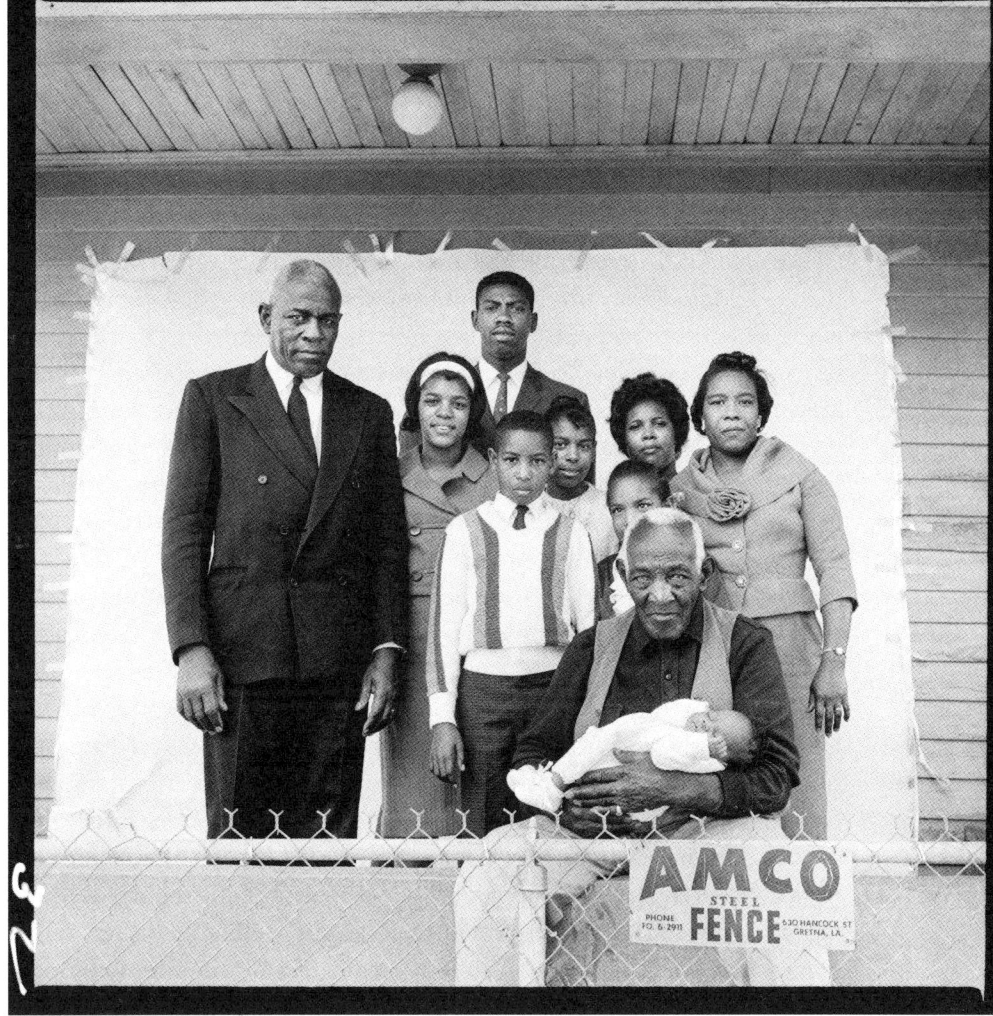

Figure 1.6. Richard Avedon, William Casby and family, 1963. © The Richard Avedon Foundation.

According to the Richard Avedon Foundation, this photograph is one of many outtakes that the Foundation pulled from Avedon's contact sheets, and they selected it for publication posthumously. Had Avedon selected this or any of the other outtakes, they contend, "the final print would have most certainly cropped into the white concealing any other visual markers outside it."[90] While the camera angle renders such cropping of this particular image incredibly difficult (insofar as the standing men's heads overlap with the affixing tape), this might well be precisely the reason the image was not selected for publication by Avedon himself. Instead, the image was selected as supporting archival material for publication in the Avedon Foundation's re-release of the iconic and visually stunning *Nothing Personal* (1964/2017),[91] a James Baldwin text with Avedon illustrations. And one can easily understand why they chose to include this image. It is a beautiful photograph.

Nevertheless, in drawing attention to this photograph's framing of the Casby family, my intention is not to spotlight the choices Avedon made as a photographer, nor the choices his Foundation made as a curator of his images, so much as it is to consider the source of this image's cultural currency. Indeed, the uptake of this particular photograph by sources like the *New Yorker* confirm that it is a deeply compelling one.[92] My concern here is to question what makes this image so culturally resonant at our present historical juncture when we previously elevated a different one.

Avedon took a much more famous photograph of the family patriarch, which, like the image of Powell, appears in Barthes's *Camera Lucida*. In this close-up of Casby, we see a long, oval face bearing the marks of time (fig. 1.7). Casby's dark skin is furrowed along his brow, his nose bridge, and around his mouth, these last dark lines further emphasized by the small bit of his vest that makes it into the image frame. Not enough clothing is visible to register much information; rather, it echoes the tonal light and shadow of Casby's face itself. We are closer to this face than we would be in life to any but the most beloved, rendering the portrait all the more intimate. Casby is roughly shaven and a few white hairs peek out of his nose; the effect is to render him not disconcertingly rough but rather evidentiarily honest. Here is a *true* specimen of the formerly enslaved, these poignant details of humanity announce, supported by even more visual rhetoric. Avedon has set the image focus so tight that the tip of Casby's nose, to the front, and his ears, to the back, are slightly blurred. What *are* in focus are Casby's eyes, looking directly back at the viewer. They are slightly filmy, and their emphasis renders Casby even older. Given the mythical association of blindness with second sight, Casby takes on a timelessness, like the old man in the basement of Jean Toomer's "Kabnis."[93]

What's more, in comparing Avedon's two images, we see in the family portrait that Casby has a fairly full head of white hair, which has here in the individual portrait disappeared into the white of Avedon's background. This makes Casby's face seem longer and older and more mask-like, which is indeed the quality that compels Barthes: "Since every photograph is contingent (and thereby outside of meaning),

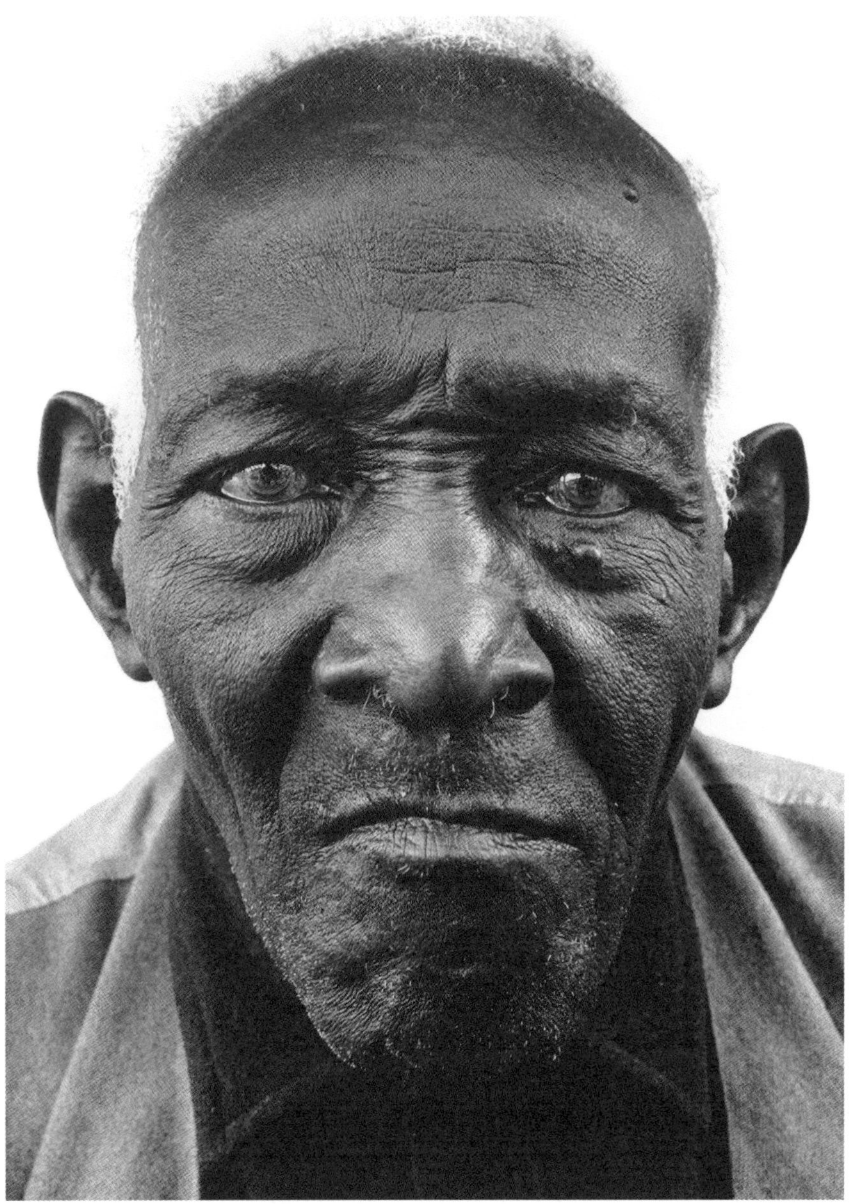

Figure 1.7. Richard Avedon, *William Casby, Born in Slavery*, 1963.

Photography cannot signify (aim at a generality) except by assuming a mask. It is this word which Calvino correctly uses to designate what makes a face into the product of a society and of its history. As in the portrait of William Casby, photographed by Avedon: the essence of slavery is here laid bare: the mask is the meaning, insofar as it is absolutely pure (as it was in the ancient theater)."[94]

By this point in his text, Barthes has already asserted that a photograph is contingent in the philosophical sense: it is phenomenologically true. A photograph is by necessity *of* something, he says, as opposed to a text's movement from description to reflection.[95] For Barthes, in order for a photograph to enact signification (of history, of society), meaning must come through a mask; therefore, Casby's face becomes the mask of slavery. While this objectification of Casby the subject is troubling, it is also familiar: in this face, we are expected to see the temporal fold to Jack or Renty, doubly enacted through Barthes's caption: "William Casby, Born a Slave. 1963."[96] One can note, too, the way that this mask becomes animate through its objecthood. Casby's face signifies not only *as* an object (a mask), but *because* it is an object. No other prop or object comes to signify in tandem with, or in lieu of, William Casby. Yet lacking those affective objects, Barthes does not instead offer a speculative reading of Casby's subjecthood.[97] Rather, the lack of any *other* signifying object demands that Casby himself must fill the role. He is the avatar of slavery and therefore—even as a free black man of the middle-late twentieth century—modernity's specimen.

I suspect that our recent cultural election of Casby's family portrait is exactly attributable to the way that it frames the white background against which Avedon's subjects usually stand, so that—in a manner consonant with FSA photographs—expressionless blackness is situated within its social environment. The inexpression of the black family members sets the viewer on a quest for details of subjectivity, yet our informational circuit is not limited to their clothes, hair, and proximity to one another, but also includes the wood and wire that defines their abode beyond the white set piece. Once again, the expressionless black subject becomes evidentiary of society as much as selfhood. Or, perhaps more accurately, this image highlights the black subject whose selfhood is conceived and projected in tandem with society. Its taped layers of artifice and hope highlight the nexus of performative subject and framing photographer much more clearly than the FSA photographs that haunt its clapboard margins. This picture lays bare the conditions of its making, the multidirectional arrows of the evidentiary bodies and subjectivities. While a difficult assertion to prove, my supposition is that the family offers a more palatable image of blackness at our particular juncture in the pendulum swing of social history. It depicts respectability, striving, love—things that we rightly want for blackness. The singular portrait of Casby—also beautiful—seems to capture an essence of something—but what? As Barthes suggests, Casby doesn't function culturally as a singular man—he's a mask and an essence of history or enslavement or race.

When discussing the Agassiz daguerreotypes, Trachtenberg, like Barthes, uses the language of the mask, but Trachtenberg's interpretation is Barthes's inverse: "Without a public mask to mediate their encounter with the lens, the eyes of the enslaved Africans can only reveal the depths of their being—for, as naked slaves, they are permitted no social persona."[98] Note the ways the two align in their all-or-nothingness: for Trachtenberg, the isolated, inexpressive black subject has no societal mask to impart his meaning; for Barthes, the isolated, inexpressive black subject has no meaning but his societal mask. Either way, Trachtenberg and Barthes remove the black subject from a traditional sense of history or temporality, abstract him to an archetypal non-time or all-time. William Casby, a lasting specimen for contemplation.

Ultimately, black subjects who perform expressionlessness without the aid of material surroundings rarely achieve the individual subjectivity that might be granted to white subjects pictured in the same way. For the black subject, one possible avenue of interrupting specimenization is the tool of expression itself (which is, of course, not the subject of this book). Another option is to ensure that the body remains in a context, to use the inevitability of objects' signifying force to forward the sense of subjecthood one wishes to convey. A third is to introduce what Lauren Berlant calls "processual awareness." Their article "Thinking about Feeling Historical" describes the circumstances of the AIDS crisis and the Iraq war, and the ways in which their representative subjects, Essex Hemphill and George W. Bush—living "on the verge of *something*"—find themselves "*stopping to think*."[99] Hemphill and Bush's stoppage is not without consequence. Rather, it "jams the machinery that makes the ordinary appear as a flow."[100] Importantly, Berlant says that such stoppage creates a processual awareness that can give shape in the midst of crisis, although "giving shape is not the same as solving the problem of crisis, or having the right emotions about it."[101] The aesthetic question of shaping, they suggest, is "how to find form without distracting from the gravity of the real." While Berlant discusses poetry and speech, I want to ask: what would such a stoppage *look* like? What would it look like to cause—to enact—"processual awareness" within a moment of visual crisis? What would be its embodied form? Is there a way to perform the self-observation required of modernity without acquiescing to (self-)specimenization of the black body? Alternately, is there way to enact a processual awareness of specimenization within the official world's scopophilic regimes?

I propose that this is precisely the accomplishment of a number of Rashid Johnson's early photographic images. Johnson's photographic print *Jonathan with Hands* (fig. 1.8), for example, has striking resemblances to Avedon's image. The photograph is a close, frontal portrait, spanning roughly from the subject's shoulders to the top of his head. As in Avedon's image, the subject's hair disappears into the background, which is here black rather than white, and now the subject's shoulders disappear as well. And—once again, as in the portrait of Casby—the camera's focus is such that, even in this tight image, the closest and farthest parts of the subject begin to blur. While the contents of the picture are most salient here, two other contextual details are relevant. First, the image belongs to the Homeless Series, and while it is not my intention to conflate homelessness with former enslavement (especially as Casby was photographed before a home), one can imagine a scenario in which an image of an inexpressive black homeless subject would serve an analogous function to the image of the formerly enslaved, presenting the evidentiary specimen of social and historical meaning, face transfiguring into modernity's archetypal mask. Second, the photograph was produced through a nineteenth-century photographic process known as Van Dyke brown printing, a technique similar to cyanotyping. The evocation of the nineteenth century in the sepia-toned paper print allows past black conditions to ghost the image.

If there are similarities to the Avedon photograph, however, the differences are noteworthy. In Johnson's print, we do not see the subject's face. Instead, we see the slightly out-of-focus rectangular expanse of a forehead and, in arresting detail, the backs of Jonathan's hands, which

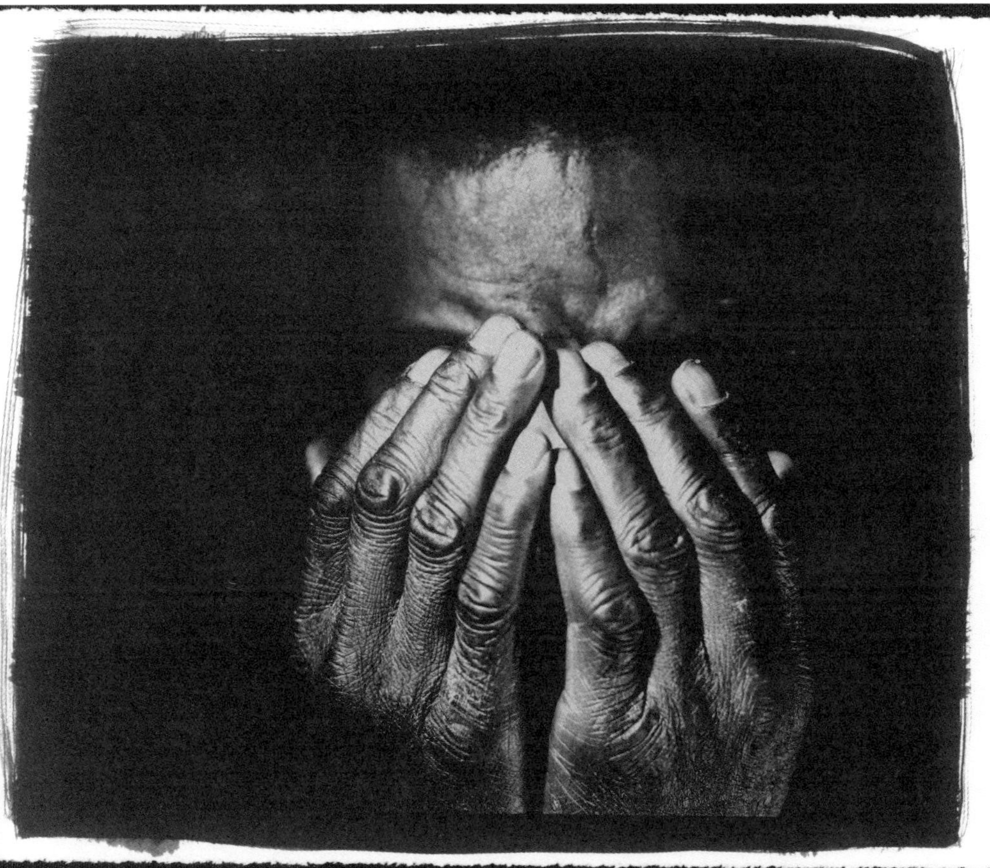

Figure 1.8. Rashid Johnson, *Jonathan with Hands*, 1997. Van Dyke brown print, 56.7 × 60.3 cm (image); 57.5 × 77.2 cm (paper). © Rashid Johnson. Courtesy of The Art Institute of Chicago / Art Resource, NY.

are held before his face so that his fingertips align with his brows. In its simultaneous visibility and withholding, the image deadpans. A black subject appears in order to be observed, yet he interrupts that observation, displaying his modern self-awareness without presenting his evidentiary face. Furthermore, one notes that the title is not *Jonathan's Hands*, but rather *Jonathan with Hands*, insisting both that Jonathan remains present in the photograph and that the hands we see are not a substitute specimen, but rather their own prop of subjectivity. In short, Johnson's image proffers the black subject for observation while also interrupting the viewer's ability to see all or part of the isolated face. Instead, hands and/or part of a black face confirm the black subject's self-reflexivity in their performed awareness of the camera's gaze, even while they interrupt the evidentiary strength of the photograph. Jonathan is a black modern who subverts his specimen status by making himself into a bad specimen.

If Johnson's image presents one method for reclaiming black subjectivity under surveillance, it is not the only one. The examples of the next chapter, I argue, do not attempt to escape the gaze so much as they attempt to demonstrate a nuanced black subjectivity in the face of one interpellation of black inexpression: that of the black subject as an a priori threat.

2

MINIMALISM AND THE AESTHETICS OF BLACK THREAT

A man of clear ideas errs grievously if he imagines that whatever is seen confusedly does not exist; it belongs to him, when he meets with such a thing, to dispel the mist, and fix the outlines of the vague form which is looming through it.

—John Stuart Mill, from "Bentham," *Early Essays*

In the August 1966 issue of *New York*, a New Journalism–style article by Tom Wolfe describes a meeting in support of the Black Panther Party's legal defense, held at the home of Leonard and Felicia Bernstein. Wolfe begins his essay, "Radical Chic: That Party at Lenny's," with a dream Leonard Bernstein had on his forty-eighth birthday. In the dream, Bernstein delivered to the starched crowd of Carnegie Hall an antiwar message, which took the form of declarations of love. Or rather, he attempted to deliver it, for his efforts to convey this simple message were interrupted, again and again, by a spectral "superego Negro," who rose up from the curve of the grand piano to narrate the audience's embarrassment. This black man isn't described except through his words, which are noticeably detached and condemning: "The audience is curiously embarrassed," he says. "The audience thinks [Bernstein] ought to get up and walk out. The audience thinks, 'I am ashamed even to nudge my neighbor.'"[1]

Wolfe intends "the Negro by the piano" to be the overriding metaphor of Leonard and Felicia's Bernstein foray into social justice via the Black Panther Party—hence the dream figure's place at the opening of the essay.[2] Just as the black figure in Bernstein's dream reveals the absurdity of his antiwar pronouncements, so does the Black Panther Party reveal the superficiality of liberal New York. As in the dream, humiliation follows the Bernsteins as their social justice narrative spirals away from them: Felicia intended to have a meeting and yet the press makes it into a party; Leonard intended the meeting to be informational and yet Jewish organizations make him out to be a Panther-loving traitor to Israel. They *meant* well. Still, Wolfe's essay suggests, those who attend and host such parties are more interested in posing alongside a cause célèbre than in truly righting social wrongs.

Twelve or thirteen Black Panther Party members were present at the Bernsteins' meeting, but Wolfe's narration centers on one: Don Cox, field marshal of the Black Panther Party and the meeting's primary speaking guest. And although Cox's words are represented in the essay, Wolfe's greater preoccupation is with Cox's performative presence. Wolfe writes of Cox's cadences, his clothing, and his movement through the space of the Bernsteins' apartment. Throughout Wolfe's essay, Cox is at once visible and yet unknowable. It's certainly possible that this was exactly the subjectivity that Cox wished to project. It's also possible that it was a product of Wolfe's literary construction. Certainly, Wolfe builds his metaphors to highlight this nexus of visible and unknowable, even going so far as to turn Cox into the literal embodiment of the dream figure that opened his essay: "And a tall back man rises from behind one of Lenny's grand pianos . . . *The Negro by the piano* . . . The Field Marshal of the Black Panther Party has been sitting in a chair between the piano and the wall. He rises up; he has the hardrock look, all right; he is a big tall man with brown skin and an Afro and a goatee and a black turtleneck much like Lenny's, and he stands up beside the piano, next to Lenny's million-dollar *chatchka* flotilla of family photographs."[3] Like the black man in Bernstein's dream, Cox looms, indelibly out of place. He is described as "hardrock" in a thoughtfully elegant home. Moreover, Cox's rise from the chair transforms the chatchkas atop the piano into a flotilla, metaphorically setting these pieces abob in the wake of his obtrusive physical presence. To this reader, the most striking thing about the description of this figure is how very *unspectral* he is in spite of his uncanniness.

A photograph of this moment accompanied Wolfe's text (fig. 2.1). Stephen Salmieri's image captures Felicia Bernstein at the photograph's center. She is, however, at a good distance; her face is sized to fit into one of the frames on the piano, which are perhaps somewhat less insubstantial than Wolfe's text would lead one to believe. In the middle distance are some of Cox's listeners: a black woman turned away from the camera and, as the caption tells us, the lawyer Leon

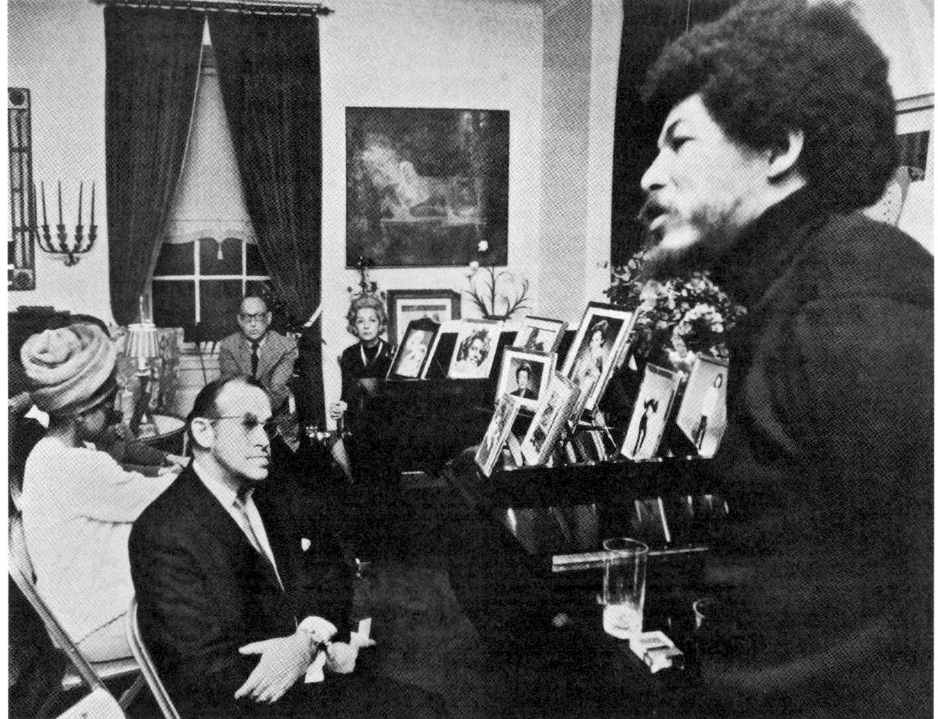

Figure 2.1. "Hard by the million-dollar chatchkas, Don Cox. Leon Quat, a lawyer for the 'Panther 21,' listens," 1970. Photo by Stephen Salmieri. *New York* magazine.

Quat. On the far right-hand side of the image, so close as to be slightly out of focus, is Cox himself. Cox's head and torso run from the very top of the image to the very bottom. His black turtleneck runs three-quarters of that length, rendering the better part of Cox as a long, black shape. His blurred face appears in profile, perhaps mid-word but not obviously so. In fact, compared to the clearer faces of the smiling photographs or the audience members who lean in postures of attention and concern, it's hard to say anything at all about Cox's expression or bearing *except* that the image confirms his presence as distinctly unspectral: he is undeniably present, even as his blurriness disturbs the haptic certainty of his image. The situation of Cox at the far right of the image, large and out of focus, reinforces the sense of his looming.

In the opening photograph of the article, Cox also looms. The image (fig. 2.2) is of the Bernsteins along with Cox. Leonard sits in an armchair; on his right, Felicia perches on its arm and leans into him. Cox stands on Leonard's other side. Felicia wears a smile that

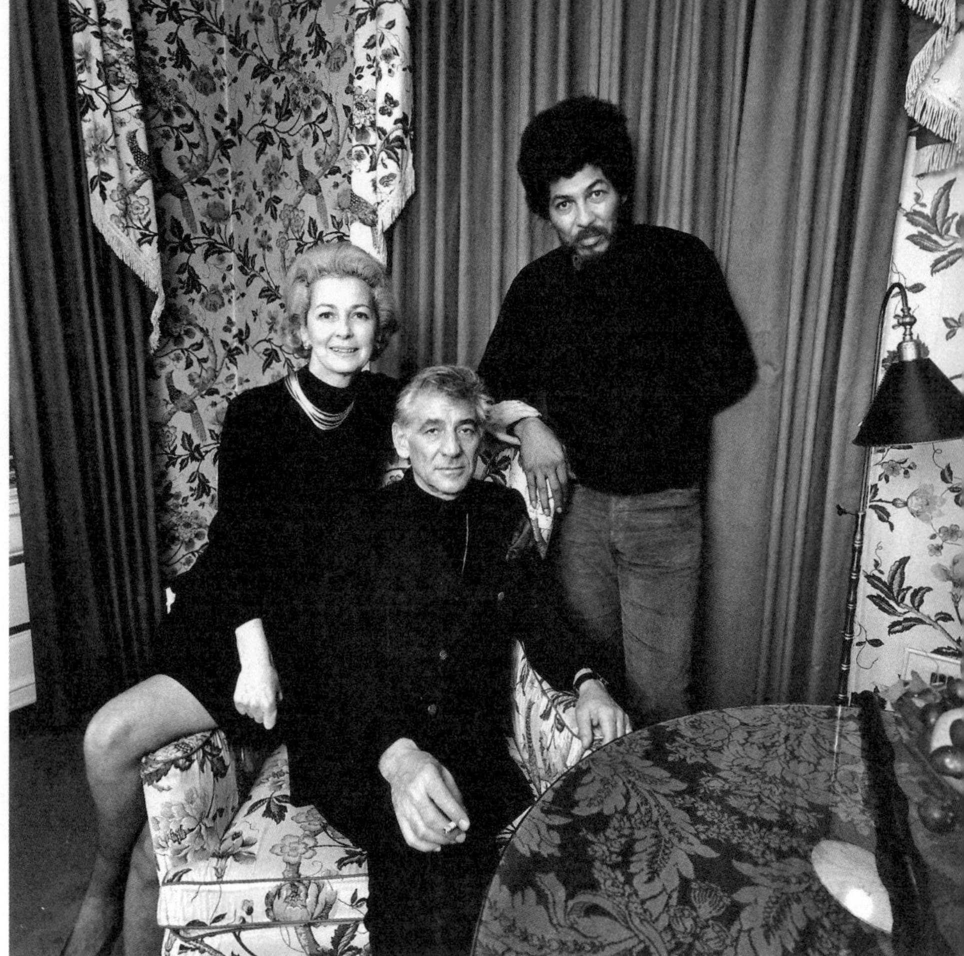

Figure 2.2. "Felicia and Leonard Bernstein and guest Don Cox," 1970. Photo by Stephen Salmieri. *New York* magazine.

is set off by the bright arch of her necklace. Leonard's face is fairly inscrutable. The corners of his mouth might be the slightest bit upturned, but it is hard to say. In lieu of clear expression, the viewer is given Leonard's centered position, the embodied lean of his wife, and an explosion of floral décor, all positioning Leonard as the head of a domestic space.

Beside them, Don Cox looms. This is partly a matter of height and distance. As Leonard and Felicia both sit, their faces are inches away from one other. Cox leans into them only slightly. He might have moved behind the chair for closer proximity; instead he stands slightly apart, a head taller and a foot away. Felicia's hand on his wrist does nothing to draw him into the couple's circuit. Instead it highlights

Cox's hand hanging next to Bernstein's face, an object apart. Cox does not appear to smile or frown. Instead, the notable aspects of his face are his large eyes and thick eyebrows, and their complement in the thick downturn of Cox's mustache. Cox's sense of looming is exacerbated by the camera angle, which looks down on its subjects and therefore subtly emphasizes Cox's standing presence through the lines of the background curtains, which are wider at the top than at the bottom. While the photograph ostensibly centers the three, the magazine's layout team expanded the image onto the recto page, with Cox's left shoulder falling into the gutter. As a result, he once again appears as a large, dark figure on the margin.

Here is the second definition of "loom" in the *New Oxford American Dictionary* (the first concerns the object used for weaving):

> Loom[2]
> *verb*
> [no *object*] appear as a shadowy form, especially one that is large or threatening: *vehicles loomed out of the darkness.*
> - (of an event regarded as ominous or threatening) seem about to happen: *there is a crisis looming | higher mortgage rates loomed large last night.*
>
> *noun*
> [in *singular*] a vague and often exaggerated first appearance of an object seen in darkness or fog, especially at sea: *the loom of the land ahead.*
> - the dim reflection by cloud or haze of a light that is not directly visible, e.g., from a lighthouse over the horizon.[4]

Loom's definition is tied to a sense of threat, which might be rooted especially in large size or other forms of exaggeration. Additionally, looming is an affect of future imagining—to loom is to *seem* about to happen. Finally, looming's sense of threat is linked to opacity or indiscernibility: darkness, haze, and fog obscure clear viewing.

This chapter takes up the aesthetics of looming to show how specific performances can evoke or intervene in the free-floating association of blackness and threat. In the lexicon of affect theorist Brian Massumi, threat is an abstract yet immanent quality made tangible in the world through the tangibility of emotion, an ambient "felt quality."[5]

Because threat is atmospheric, it is freed from the need to instantiate. It is "independent of any particular instance of itself, in much the way the color red is a quality independent of any particular tint of red, as well as of any actually occurring patch of any particular tint of red." Just as "red" needn't attach to a particular shade or patch of red, "threat" needn't relate to any actualized danger—on the contrary, threat is made real precisely through its *non*-actualization. This is because threat is a foreshadowing, "the anticipatory reality in the present of a threatening future" or "the felt reality of the nonexistent, loomingly present."[6]

Massumi's use of the word "nonexistent" is an important detail in my willingness to attach "threat" to "blackness," for I do not mean to suggest, in so doing, that blackness is itself a vehicle of danger, but rather that others feel danger there and that this makes our shared reality. Massumi argues that threat is a manifesting affect—that is to say, as a feeling that self-fulfills as reality, an affect that becomes a fact because *the affect is itself the overriding fact*. Because threat has yet to arrive (and never *can* arrive and still be threat), "its nature is open-ended. It is not just that it is not: it is not in a way that is never over. [. . .] There is always a remainder of uncertainty, an unconsummated surplus of danger."[7] This unending quality renders threat unmoored, self-renewing, and nebulous. In other words, it makes no difference if this "might be" is, by evidential standards, unreal. Threat is rendered real through the affective workings of a conditional future.

To summarize three qualities of threat, then: (1) threat does not need to be factually real to be affectively factual; (2) threat is rooted in the unmet future, which makes it interminable and inconsummate; and (3) threat involves the affective as atmosphere, as loomingness. These qualities of threat accrue particular resonance in tandem with blackness—or, more accurately, in tandem with the persistent cultural tendency, in America, to sense blackness generally, and black masculinity in particular, as potential menace. This tendency is especially acute (and historically weighty) in instances where white individuals project black threat onto black bodies and then respond to that projection with terror and rage. This viewing paradigm accounts for Darren Wilson's characterization of eighteen-year-old Michael Brown as a "demon" capable of "bulking up to run through the shots" that Wilson fired at him, fatally.[8] This viewing also enfolds the longstanding (and ironic) white cultural terror of black male rapists—a self-renewing and largely inconsummate future-imaging that nevertheless spawned (and spawns) real fear and real violence.[9]

These examples of violent response are far too frequent, and are important to reckon with. Furthermore, they rightly raise the question of why I do not frame the aesthetics that inflect such encounters as aesthetics of "dread" rather than "threat."[10] Implicit in this question, I think, is the acknowledgment that as astute as Massumi's diagnosis is, it is unlikely to correct the prevailing sense that threat is located within the looming object rather in the perceiving subject, (or, at a minimum, somewhere between the object and its perceiver). Said differently, even after acknowledging that threat, of necessity, poses no real violence, isn't there a still a danger in the rhetorical attachment of blackness and threat? To this I would answer absolutely, yes. Nevertheless, black performing subjects sometimes embrace this danger themselves, whether to perform threat on its own terms or slightly askance. My goal is not to extract actors' intentions (nor to deny that they might have some), but instead to read the e/affects of deadpan's mobilization. And if one is concerned with what the performer (or performing object) bodies forth through deadpan, the instantiation of threat, rather than the perception of dread, will be the primary focus, even if recognizing that instantiation depends, at times, on reading the negative space that surrounds (white) dread.

Moreover, dread isn't the only affective response to black threat. As scholars such as Jennifer Doyle point out, people react to aesthetic stimuli with an unpredictable range of emotions.[11] Threat is not exempt from this range. Reactions to threat might include studied obliviousness, fascination, attraction, idealization, or pity. And while culture might overdetermine reactions to threat as perceived in or alongside blackness (and culture certainly has scripted the conjunction of blackness with threat in the first place), instances abound in which white *and* black people view black threat with something other than terror and rage. Consider Norman Mailer's description of George Foreman in *The Fight*, which oozes a kind of begrudging awe rooted in the fetishized overlap of Foreman's blackness and his menace.[12] Alternately, consider how James Baldwin consistently casts black threat as the promising young understudy ready to step into the American dilemma should love or forbearance ever fail to show.[13]

One might argue that these reactions are troubling in their own right. I welcome that work, but it isn't mine. I am troubled by the implications of Massumi's analysis of threat for blackness, even while (or especially because) I can't see that it yields wrong results. The fact that threat, as an affective reality, is born from the unactualized—indeed that it *must* be born from the unactualized—helps explain its persistent, sticky surplus. If indeed threat has no true referent but self-renews atmospherically, that bodes badly for black futures. And yet isn't that exactly what we see happening in the ambient and self-perpetuating associations that cause black school children to seem older and garner more severe punishment, or that cause black people to be killed more often by police?[14]

If the overwriting of threat onto blackness will not be quick to disappear, it is at a minimum worth better understanding those responses that are not rage and violence. Beyond that minimum, though, I hope that clues for exhausting the surplus of threat, or for subtly editing the cultural script around blackness and menace, might lie in aesthetic response. Therefore, in this chapter I explore rejoinders to the paradigm of black threat through the works of four minimalist artists: Adrian Piper, Martin Puryear, David Hammons, and Robert Morris. Their sculptural and performative works enfold the visual and the embodied, for black threat lives in just this concatenation of the visual (black) and the embodied (threat). But I also choose them because their mode *is* minimalist, and is therefore, I think, specially poised to register black threat's aesthetic.

Of these artists, Morris is the only one who is consistently framed as minimalist, and while I believe all four work within minimalism's purview, they do not all themselves embrace the label. Puryear, for example, has said that that he "tasted [minimalism] and spit it out"—specifically citing the prefabricated as the rejected tenet.[15] Given the narrow confines of minimalism as the art establishment has curated it, it is not surprising that some artists have eschewed the label. As Maurice Berger has argued, critics attempting to name and define minimalism linked a cadre of white male artists whose philosophical and stylistics concerns were not necessarily as coherent as the critical narrative would lead one to believe.[16] Many of the presumably defining characteristics of minimalism—such as prefabrication—do not squarely apply to Morris, for example. The result of this narrow and self-perpetuating definition of minimalism is that a small band of artists qualifies. Some artists (such as Eva Hesse or Martin Puryear) are written out of an originating impulse and into a "postminimalism" while others (Morris) are written in, arguably based more upon the art establishment's reading of the maker than the reading of the work.

John P. Bowles has argued that Adrian Piper is among those artists who have been written out of minimalism's lineages through the tautology that first produced the canon of minimalism out of white male artists, and then denied the works of non-white and non-male artists as minimalist. Bowles set out to reinstate Piper as a minimalist practitioner through her early object-based works, suggesting that as Piper claimed a racialized body in her art, she moved away from minimalist and conceptualist works that elevated an unexamined universalism.[17] Other critics claim Piper for minimalism due to her own embrace of the label—and here I am thinking particularly of Maurice Berger in *Minimal Politics*, in which he discusses Piper's *Black Box/White Box* (1992).[18] Beyond honoring Piper's self-identification, Berger argues that minimalism, like its close cousin conceptualism, is always already political. As a consequence, Berger is able to situate Piper within minimalism's boundaries well after Bowles would have her abandon them. If minimalism's objects are performative, he reasons, then the demand for relation is itself a political act. This is all the more true when that object is a performing body.

I agree with Berger, but want to push a bit more on minimalism's deraced onto-epistemological politics. For though Berger takes up *Black Box/White Box*—a piece about the Rodney King beating—as a signature example of minimalist politics, he says relatively little about the racial specificity of this artwork (or indeed of any of Piper's works) beyond noting that racial specificity is important to it. Yet over and over in Piper's works—in *Black Box/White Box*, *Vote/Emote*, *Cornered*, and a host of other works—the political relation in question is charged with a sense of threat.

Unsurprisingly, most of the artists I see as responding to black threat belong to historical moments of especially fraught racial relations; moreover, these moments carried a heightened sense of crisis around black visuality in particular. Artists working in the late 1960s and early 1970s brought the racial activism of the broader culture into New York's art world in hotly contested ways.[19] Artists working in the late 1980s and early 1990s did so against the backdrop of race as a photographic and televised spectacle that included the 1992 beating of Rodney King and the ensuing LA riots, the televised confirmation hearings of Clarence Thomas, the invocation of Willie Horton in the

1988 election, and the darkening of O. J. Simpson on the cover of *Time* magazine.[20] While the distinct political reality of these moments is less my focus than the trans-historical interpellation of blackness into paradigms of threat, I here remind readers of the historical realities that surround my case studies so that their particularities can help color the argument that follows.

ART AND OBJECTHOOD

In performance studies, scholars discussing minimalism still largely labor under the critical terms of engagement set by Michael Fried in "Art and Objecthood." Fried is, famously, no fan of minimalism (or, as he prefers to call it, literalism). For Fried, minimalist artworks are too stubbornly persistent in their objecthood. He explains, "There is [. . .] a sharp contrast between the literalist espousal of objecthood—almost, it seems, as an art in its own right—and modernist painting's self-imposed imperative that it defeat or suspend its own objecthood."[21] Modernist painting, in other words, *transcends* its objecthood in a way that minimalist art cannot or will not. Fried asserts that literalist art is essentially theatrical because it relies on the creation of a situation, namely the viewer being made stubbornly aware of herself in relation to the object in space. For Fried, this awareness necessarily "*distances* the beholder—not just physically but psychically" (emphasis in original). This distancing becomes, for Fried, a core element of minimalist aesthetics. As he says, "the beholder knows himself to stand in an indeterminate, open-ended—and unexacting—relation *as subject* to the impassive object on the wall or floor. In fact, being distanced by such objects is not, I suggest, entirely unlike being distanced, or crowded, by the silent presence of another *person*" (emphasis in original).[22]

Fried goes on at some length about the disquietingly anthropomorphic qualities of minimalist art, in spite of his simultaneous concern with minimalism's stubborn persistence in objecthood. He is helped along in this by the fact that minimalist sculpture is often roughly the size of a person—quite an intentional choice, as Robert Morris explains in his "Notes on Sculpture." Unsettled by the minimalist object's anthropomorphic size, Fried ascribes it a character: the "work in question has an inner, even secret, life," he says; "obtrusiveness and, often, even aggressiveness" are its traits.[23]

The charges Fried levels against minimalism bear a great resemblance to discourses that surround the black subject. For example, Fried begins his essay by introducing minimalist art as "the expression of a general and pervasive condition" belonging to "the history—almost the natural history—of sensibility."[24] The language of "condition" has ample parallels in discourse that equates blackness with social problems, including the roughly contemporary Moynihan report (1965)—officially titled "The Negro Family: The Case for National Action"—with its characterization of female-headed black households as a "tangle of pathology."[25] Yet more poignant than the general "condition" is the turn to natural history in tandem with it, a rhetorical move rampant in the literatures of racial hierarchy. In particular, Fried's invocation of a natural history *of sensibility* evokes nineteenth-century racial discourses. As Kyla Schuller details extensively in *The Biopolitics of Feeling*, a profoundly influential school of American biologists, following in the tradition of evolutionary theorist Jean-Baptiste Lamarck, located racial difference primarily in divergent levels of impressibility.[26] For the neo-Lamarckians, impressibility was a refinement of the nervous system that determined how responsive a population was to its environment. The more refined a race, the greater its sensibility—and the greater the danger that undesirable forces might induce a slide back down the evolutionary ladder. According to this philosophy, the black race was a vestigial holdover; black individuals felt less, both physically and emotionally. Accordingly, Fried's sense that a literalist artwork is dumbly inexhaustible—which explains his own preference for the literalist label—resonates with the myth of black durability. Minimalist art is "inexhaustible," he writes, "not because of any fullness—*that* is the inexhaustibility of art—but because there is nothing there to exhaust."[27]

Finally, the consignment of minimalist artwork to an object status resonates with critical black studies because of the ways Fried *also* grants these minimalist objects a set of intentions and limitations—a liveliness, as it were. In other words, the minimalist object is, for Fried, *simultaneously subject and object*—or, to borrow a phrase from Saidiya Hartman, a "curious hybrid of person and property."[28] Hartman uses these words to describe the American chattel condition, in which "the acknowledgment of the slave as subject was a *complement* to the arrangements of chattel property rather than its remedy" (emphasis added).[29]

The slave's doubled existence was a creation of the law and those who made it. Yet, Hartman points out, it came to characterize the resistances of those who lived under such conditions, too. In the practice of "stealing away," for example, Hartman spies an exploitation of "the bifurcated condition of the black captive as subject and object by the flagrant assertion of unlicensed and felonious behavior and by pleading innocence, precisely because as an object the slave was the very negation of an intending consciousness or will."[30] This double-edged resistance resonates with the oppositional stance Fried sees, and disdains, in the minimalist object—its willful assertion of presence and its refusal to transcend human relation (which is, for Fried, treasonous) and, *concurrently*, its stubborn reliance on its own objecthood. As Fried lingers on the anthropomorphic dimensions of the willful object—its uncanny near-person size—the embodied black subject haunts his margins even more. To be clear, I am not suggesting that Michael Fried was secretly writing about race all along.[31] Rather, the aesthetics of minimalist art as Fried sees them are consistent with ways that black subjects have been, and continue to be, described—obstinate, aggressive, secretive, untranscendent, inexpressive, and above all, stubbornly, uncomfortably, theatrically *present*.

The imputation of these traits to black Americans has been present since the birth of the nation, and is, importantly, tied to a sense of affective impenetrability. Even at the beginnings of the American republic, black countenances perturbed Thomas Jefferson for reason of their inscrutability—and, already, this perturbation was juxtaposed with looming violence. In his *Notes on the State of Virginia*, in answer to the rhetorically posed "Why not incorporate blacks into the state?" Jefferson replies,

> Deep rooted prejudices entertained by the whites; ten thousand recollections, by the blacks, of the injuries they have sustained; new provocations; the real distinctions which nature has made; and many other circumstances, will divide us into parties, and produce convulsions which will probably never end but in the extermination of the one or the other race.—To these objections, which are political, may be added others, which are physical and moral. The first difference which strikes us is that of colour.—Whether the black of the negro resides in the reticular membrane between the skin and scarf-skin, or in the scarf-skin

itself; whether it proceeds from the colour of the blood, the colour of the bile, or from that of some other secretion, the difference is fixed in nature, and is as real as if its seat and cause were better known to us. And is this difference of no importance? Is it not the foundation of a greater or less share of beauty in the two races? Are not the fine mixtures of red and white, the expressions of every passion by greater or less suffusions of colour in the one, preferable to that eternal monotony, which reigns in the countenances, that immoveable veil of black which covers all the emotions of the other race?[32]

In the space of a few sentences, Jefferson moves from black people's recollections of injuries sustained and the possible eventuality of race war to the "immovable veil of black" that obscures the emotions of black people through their inability to blush. In 1781–2, when Jefferson composed *Notes*, a quick associative leap connected black inscrutability with black threat.

What's remarkable is how much the impression of unreadability in blackness has been maintained over time—even though (or perhaps partly because) blackness *also* came to be associated with excess emotion. This, too, was in place in Jefferson's writings: he argued that black people's lack of self-regulation could be seen in their loving (not tenderness but eager desire) and their sleep (too easily sloughed when amusements were to be had).[33] White observers are not the only ones to write excess emotion into blackness, however. In the 1920s and 1930s, such excess was embraced by a section of black culture makers; it runs through Zora Neale Hurston's "Characteristics of Negro Expression," to name but one example.[34] Yet as rendered in Hurston's folk tales (as well as in "Negro" folk tales relayed by white authors such as Joel Chandler Harris), excessive black expressiveness is in no small part duplicitous. And if black expression cannot be trusted, what can be known of black expression?

Much has been written about verbal tricksterism in the form of signifyin'. Deadpanning is different from signifyin' (as well as dissemblance) in important ways: for one thing, deadpanning presents an inscrutable face rather than a false one; for another, deadpan does not necessarily invite intimacy or trust as signifyin' and dissemblance do (even if only to abuse or refuse them).[35] Yet if black deadpanning is not a form of signifyin', it certainly bears a relation in its determination to withhold and its ability to back-foot a white counterpart. Discomfited white observers might frame black duplicitousness as more or less transparent, or more or less sinister. But whatever that nuance, the suspicion of duplicity is stubbornly present. Take, for example, a quotation from *Esquire*—a magazine on the forefront of presenting the nation's race problem in the middle decades of the twentieth century. In an article that questioned the wisdom of pressing the South to change its ways with speed, the author wrote (with an excruciatingly misguided sincerity): "And there were other questions for the heart: What would happen to the virtues of that paternalism which had bound black and white together in a relationship that, however unprogressive, was often warmly human in its sharing? If the Southerner *knew* he did not understand the lesser figure in this bond, was it not frightening to be forced to comprehend that this friendly, agreeable and sympathetic soul that jollied him and nursed his children was in reality a total stranger who changed vocabularies at quitting time?"[36]

In this representative quotation the white man knows, deep down, that the black folks who surround him are strangers—persons unknown. While far less explicitly tied to countenance than in Jefferson, there is nevertheless the sense that the black caretaker before the white protagonist is an unknown *and unknowable* entity. Once again an immovable veil of black obscures the true emotions of the black person at hand; once again this is a source of affective threat. If Jefferson felt that skin itself precluded him from knowing black people, the source of their obscurity is somewhat less clear in the 1962 *Esquire* article. There is a greater sense of agency on the part of the black figure, whose "change in vocabularies" seems voluntary if also socially inevitable. As black demands for justice became more strident, the implicit belief in the determined *performance* of inscrutability seems to have grown—with no lessening of the commensurate sense of its threat. It makes sense, then, that an artist would turn to performance to explore the arranged American marriage between blackness and threat. And in her Mythic Being performances of the 1970s, this is exactly what Adrian Piper did.

ADRIAN PIPER

Although my original intention was to dive directly into these performances, I must begin with a more recent occasion of withholding. Adrian Piper declined permission for images of her artworks to be included in this text. Though I wrote to explain the orientation of the Minoritarian Aesthetics series and my own commitment to the constructed nature of race, as well as this book's inclusion of artists such as Robert Morris and Buster Keaton in its discussions of black performance, I received the explanation that my "request does not comply with Adrian Piper's policy of not participating in racially segregated events or publications."[37]

It's hard to know where to begin with this wrinkle. One supposes this stance is an expansion of Piper's disappointing withdrawal from the 2013 exhibition *Radical Presence: Black Performance in Contemporary Art*—though not, as Uri McMillan points out in his excellent coda on this decision, from the catalogue of the exhibition.[38] I do not believe this book is a racially segregated work. Furthermore, given that images of the artworks I discuss are widely available, their omission from these pages is more a matter of lost convenience for my reader than it is a blow to my argument.[39] But never mind this book. Piper's position, at least as it was articulated when she withdrew from *Radical Presence*, is that an artwork measured within the world of black art cannot be measured truly—that the yardstick is not of the same length within the world of black art as across a wider swath of art production. On the face of it this might seem a reasonable position. But when artworks produced by white artists are surrounded by and judged against other such works, they are not subject to the accusation that the ruler is missing some inches. Ironically, Piper's refusal of "segregated" black company implies that black art production must lack variety at best, or quality at worst. For this assumption to hold—that is, for a black artist–produced artwork to need artwork born of a different racial origin in order to find something to rub up against, or to truly know its worth—blackness must be monolithic. Moreover, for black art to *necessarily* form an ineffective corpus for productive judgment, blackness must inescapably inhere in the artworks themselves, having transferred, somehow, from the makers to the artworks. Certainly, this *can* happen—there is art of racially explicit content or racially allusive form—but I don't believe it *must*. Similarly, while I believe the curation of all black-produced artworks can be (and indeed, has often been) guilty of unsophisticated groupings or essentialist assumptions, I don't think this is the only way that all black artists can be brought together.

In any event, as McMillan has already suggested, Piper's withholding has had the effect—strategic or not—of heightening her visibility in and as black art. Rather than showing up to withhold, Piper's latest position withholds to show up. As a look at her earlier works will demonstrate, this is no new trick. Whether or not Piper's recent decision not to participate in projects organized around race is a "performance" in an intentional way, the decision itself performs a consonance with earlier performance works.

The most famous example of this is the Mythic Being persona, which, in John P. Bowles's words, Piper did not so much create as "[appropriate] from the popular imagination" when, around September of 1973, Piper donned a mustache, Afro wig, sunglasses, and cigar, to stride about New York City as a man.[40] In addition to making appearances on the streets of New York, the Mythic Being also made his way into the pages of the *Village Voice*, accompanied with thought or speech bubbles containing quotations from Piper's own journals. Eventually this two-dimensional iteration of the Mythic Being took over, spawning photographic artworks in which Piper used the signifiers of black masculinity to her channel feelings of anger, resentment, or horniness.

Piper's false mustache, Afro wig, shades, and dark clothing are generally framed, rather simply, as the costuming of a stereotypical black male persona. This much is true, but these objects not only portray stereotypical blackness but also render the "stereotypical black male" as a kind of minimalist object. Further, through this minimalist objecthood, Piper grafts the aesthetic affects of looming into her performance. For example, in the triptych *It Doesn't Matter* (1975), the Mythic Being says in block letters, "It doesn't matter who you are / if what you want to do to me / is what I want you to do for me." In the first panel—the darkest of the three—the Mythic Being stands level to the viewer, one arm bent upward and holding a cigarillo while the other extends, palm forward, as though signaling the viewer to stop. In the next two panels, his previously extended arm is held across his chest and underneath the upturned arm in a posture at once closed and powerful. Meanwhile, the viewer's perspective comes closer and lower. By the third panel, the viewer is essentially positioned at crotch level, looking up at the mythic being as though poised for fellatio.[41] Through this depiction of looming, Piper wields the threat implicit in deadpanned black masculinity, here explicitly tied to sexuality.[42]

My reading of the Mythic Being builds on the work of Uri McMillan, who importantly focuses on the art object as an avatar of Piper and *for* Piper in her intellectual journey as an artist and philosopher. I will follow instead the affects and aesthetics of the Mythic Being himself—that is, what his objecthood allowed and allowed for, whether or not the artist herself intended or noticed. Said differently, while I concur with McMillan's concern that the Mythic Being has become "a think-piece on race and racism" at the expense of its beginnings as "a bodily and psychological experiment in transcending the boundaries between subjecthood and objecthood to become an art object," my own purpose is to think the first part of this equation through the second.[43]

To do so, I return briefly to Wolfe's "Radical Chic" to excavate one more detail about the minimalist aesthetics of the Black Panthers. Oddly, at least three times in the course of his essay, Wolfe emphasizes the "reality" of Cox and the other Panthers, and seats this reality in stereotypical objects:

> Anyway, the white guests and a few academic-looking blacks were packed, sitting and standing, into the living room. Then a contingent of 12 or 13 Black Panthers arrived. The Panthers had no choice but to assemble in the dining room and stand up—in their leather pieces, Afros and shades—facing the whites in the living room. As a result, whenever anyone got up in the living room to speak, the audience was looking not only at the speaker but into the faces of a hard front line of Black Panthers in the dining room. Quite a tableau it was. It was at this point that a Park Avenue matron first articulated the great recurrent emotion of Radical Chic: "These are no civil rights *Negroes* wearing grey suits three sizes too big—these are *real men*!"[44]

The woman's observation links black "realness" with strident masculinity. But this "realness" is also wedded to the materiality of the Panthers' sartorial effects. The reality of their physical presence is transferred into their "leather pieces, Afros, and shades." Ironically, though this lends them the impression of being "*real* men," the Panthers are hardly bodies at all, but rather a conglomeration of accoutrements. The objects that constitute the Black Panthers' dress come to contain their very presence; they become fetish objects and *as such* contain black manhood.

Moreover, Wolfe makes this move over and over in his essay. At another point he writes, "Christ, if the Panthers don't know how to get it all together, as they say, the tight pants, the tight black turtlenecks the leather coats, Cuban shades, Afros. But real Afros, not the ones that have been shaped and trimmed like a topiary hedge and sprayed until they have a sheen like acrylic wall-to-wall—but like funky, natural, scraggly . . . wild [. . .] —*these are* real men!"[45] Here the definitive presence of black manhood is fetishized into Afros, shades, and leather jackets, alongside tight pants and black turtlenecks. Oddly, no sense of bone or muscle fills out these pants and turtlenecks—no bulge of calf or pectoral, no sinewy line of neck. Instead, the closest the Panthers come to live embodiment is when their Afros form scraggly brambles in lieu of topiary hedges. Wolfe continues: "Shootouts, revolutions, pictures in *Life* magazine of policemen grabbing Black Panthers like they were Viet Cong—somehow it all runs together in the head with the whole thing of how *beautiful* they are. *Sharp as a blade*" (emphasis in original).[46] And with this introduction of a blade, Wolfe revisits the leap that Jefferson made centuries before: blackness can't quite be read, and surely there is danger there.

Besides this whiff of danger, Cox and the other Panthers are characterized through their size, movement, and wardrobe. Upon their introduction, Wolfe writes, "That huge Black Panther there in the hallway, the one shaking hands with Felicia Bernstein herself, the one with the black leather coat and the dark glasses and the absolutely unbelievable Afro, Fuzzy-Wuzzy scale in fact—is he, a Black Panther, going on to pick up a Roquefort cheese morsel rolled in crushed nuts from off the tray, from a maid in uniform, and just pop it down the gullet without so much as missing a beat of Felicia's perfect Mary Astor voice . . ." Wolfe once again draws our attention not so much to the personage of the Black Panther but to the objects that signal that personage—the Afro, the dark glasses. The quotation, too, reveals that these particular object symbols of this particular blackness have an affective result (and it is an incommensurate affect to that of Roquefort cheese, whatever affect that might be).

Wolfe notes a certain titillating incredulity flowing through the party's white attendees as a result of the Panther's "reality," writing, "Harassment & Hassles, Guns & Pigs, Jail & Bail—they're *real*, these

Black Panthers. The very idea of them, these real revolutionaries, who actually put their lives on the line, runs through Lenny's duplex like a rogue hormone."[47] In addition to being a rogue hormone, the particular blackness of the Panthers is described as "delicious," "funky," and an "electrifying spectacle."[48] It brings romance and excitement; it generates emotional momentum.[49] As Wolfe repeatedly reveals through the figure of Cox, these affects are generated not through anything the Black Panther says or even does, but rather through the fact of his incredible yet undeniable presence. They are generated, in other words, through the phenomenon Fried names as "the literalist espousal of objecthood"—the aesthetics of black threat.

Returning to Piper by way of these observations, one can see how, in donning the stereotypical markers of a certain mode of black masculinity, Piper "operated as a confrontational art object," in McMillan's words.[50] Furthermore, one can see how the Mythic Being embodied something more than stereotype. Stereotype *abstracts* particularity, substituting an imagined idea—and certainly the Mythic Being does this. But the Mythic Being also *effaces* particularity through the objects that represent inscrutable black looming. Put differently, the accoutrements Piper adopted do not just call up stereotype, they use that stereotype to force the (presumably white) viewer into an awareness of him- or herself in relation to the anthropomorphized object before them, and to beg an affective response.

The Mythic Being therefore bears more than a passing resemblance to Piper's *Untitled Performance at Max's Kansas City*, in which Piper "made an object of herself with the intention of defending her autonomy from the imposing presence of those around her. Sealed off from sensory perceptions, she would present herself as insular and individualistic."[51] Piper wore street clothes, a blindfold, gloves, and nose- and earplugs. These objects are a far cry from the symbolic clothing of a Black Panther, but they similarly assert themselves over the presence of the person who wears them, eclipsing her singularity and forcing relation in objecthood. Piper ultimately felt that the piece—which was executed as part of an exhibition—was less successful than she had hoped. The attendees, for the duration of the performance, used the space of Max's as a performance venue rather than a bar. Piper didn't bump into enough people, and she wasn't obtrusive enough to cause in her viewers the excitement of being hailed as subjects in relation. In short, her objecthood didn't loom.[52]

Piper's invocation of black threat through the Mythic Being is not *simply* a matter of embrace, as it may at first glance seem. Take, for example, the images and text of *I Am the Locus* (1975). Visually, *I Am the Locus* trades in the aesthetics of looming. As the panels proceed, the Mythic Being comes closer to the photographic frame, increasing in size and forcing the viewer into ever more direct relation, while also obscuring individuality with the stereotypical objects of inscrutability and threat (Afro, shades). As many others have noted, Piper's idiosyncratic textual additions, which represent the Mythic Being's interiority, run counter to his anonymity. More significant to my mind is the way the text also runs counter to the visual register's subject/object arrangement. The panels of *I Am the Locus* declare in uppercase lettering: "I am the locus of consciousness / surrounded and constrained / by animate physical objects / with moist, fleshy, pulsating surfaces . . . / Get out of my way, asshole." Piper's text locates consciousness in black objecthood and unknowability in the white subjects that surround the Mythic Being. In so doing, *I Am the Locus* explicitly invokes objecthood and looming but complicates its terms, seeding consciousness in the looming figure against the historical interpretations that surround inexpressive blackness.

MARTIN PURYEAR

Martin Puryear, an African American visual artist whose primary medium is sculpture, also nuances the relation of black objecthood and consciousness. Puryear openly acknowledges blackness as an occasional subject. His explicit engagement with figures of black history, including James Beckwourth and Booker T. Washington, suggests that he's not an artist who wishes to foreclose race as a valid site of inquiry. Yet critics seem tentative to engage Puryear's African American identity as an aspect of his work.[53] Curator Margo Crutchfield illustrates this point when she writes, of Puryear's engagement with African American subjectivity, "While a number of his sculptures specifically reference his African American heritage, Puryear's work for the most part transcends the specific for the most universal concerns."[54] Crutchfield's syntax pits African American heritage *against* universal concerns; his artwork attends to one thing *or* the other. Implicitly, Crutchfield suggests that any given piece *does not* reference his African American identity *unless* that reference is made explicit.

Yet surely it is possible for the works of a black artist to deal with universal concerns as they manifest in the particulars of African American subjectivity.

Too often, an artist's engagement with the "universal" is announced as the proper abandonment of a bodily (and raced) particularity, as if one might effortlessly leap from embodied specificity to universal humanity, somehow leapfrogging their nexus in selfhood. Yet selfhood is that liminal space in which the particular and universal meet and are negotiated, and it should therefore be possible for the subject to engage universal themes within that space without abandoning the racialized bodily. Curator John Elderfield seems to allow for the possibility when he says that Puryear's sculptures "halt us in contested areas where the artist's freedom of thought met the resistance of the external world, and deep spaces of imagination opened in the attainable."[55] Though his engagement with race in Puryear's work is also, on the whole, quite limited, Elderfield suggests that Puryear's sculptures unfold in the negotiated space between the individual and the world, between imagination and pragmatism—a space we might call selfhood. To my mind, this also suggests that universals ("deep spaces of imagination") can *also* reflect particular histories ("the attainable") in the mediated space of subjectivity.

Elderfield warns against interpreting Puryear's sculpture as "some unmediated outflowing of his private self"—a valuable caution.[56] Far from asking Puryear's engagement with subjectivity to stand in as "unmediated outflowing," my intention is to highlight the ways the (raced) self might *never* be an unmediated outflowing. A number of Puryear's works, I argue, can be read as embodying or performing a mode of black selfhood through the conjunction of their presence and their materiality. They insist on the prerogative of the black subject to loom as an object. Yet even as they insist on the prerogative of an object to loom, Puryear's works also defuse the sense of danger that characterizes black threat through the beauty of their handcraftsmanship.

Martin Puryear's *Self* (1978) is a dark, heavy-looking form, one suggestive of a smooth, massive stone rising out of the earth (fig. 2.3). Puryear described *Self* as looking "as though it might have been created by erosion, like a rock worn by sand and weather until the angles are all gone."[57] It is large—indeed, at 69 × 48 × 25 inches, the sculpture is many inches taller than most viewers. *Self*'s large size and its appearance of weight and solidity make the sculpture formidable, as it

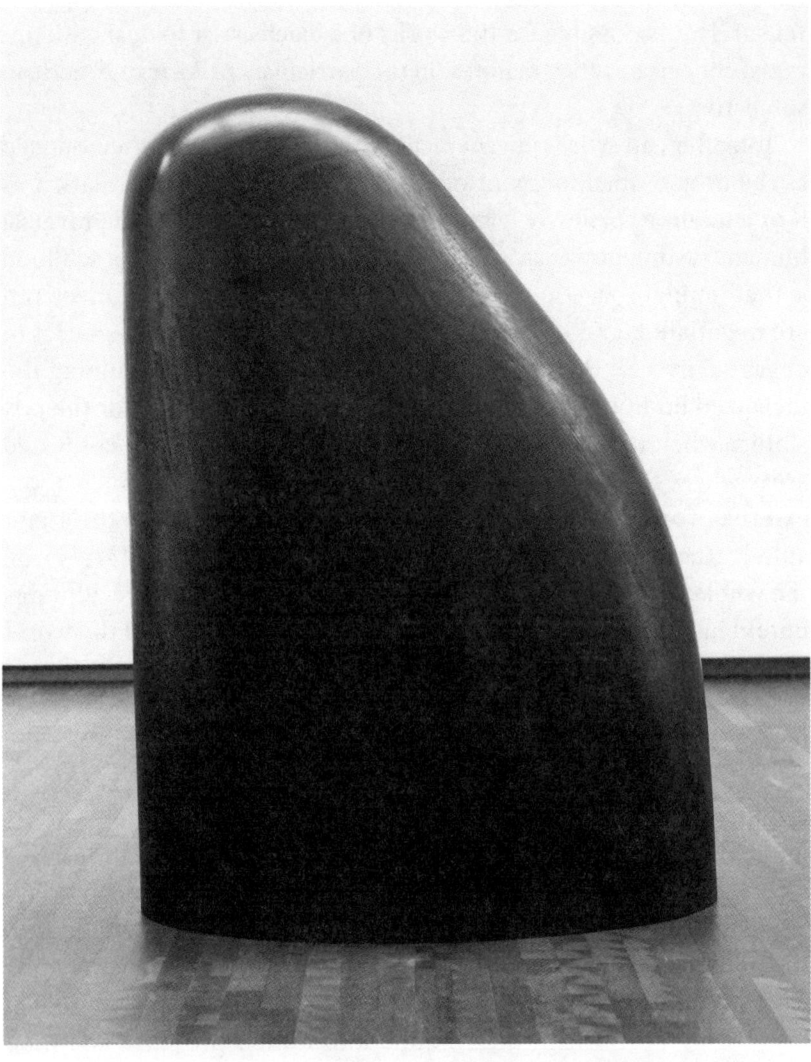

Figure 2.3. Martin Puryear, *Self*, 1978. Painted and stained cedar mahogany, 69 x 48 x 25 in. © Martin Puryear. Courtesy of Matthew Marks Gallery.

places its viewers in the phenomenological relation so characteristic of minimalist works. Its heaviness is illusory, though: *Self* is a work of laminated cedar and mahogany, thin layers enclosing a hollow core. The sculpture is surprisingly lightweight.

Untitled (1997) is somewhat similar (fig. 2.4). Another hollow, dark monolith, *Untitled* (1997) is more reminiscent of a head, evoking the concept of selfhood not through its title but through its shape. As with *Self*, *Untitled* is a figure of outsized proportions—it is only one inch shorter than *Self*—and it presents a similarly smooth, rounded, and polished surface. As Crutchfield points out, this surface both absorbs and reflects light, thereby adding to its sense of unbroken enclosure.[58] Like *Self, Untitled* seems impenetrable, but not unalterable. For one thing, the sculpture's surface reveals more of the seams of its assemblage. If it invites associations with stone forms, it is because the shape—by teetering at the edge of figuration—harkens to stone

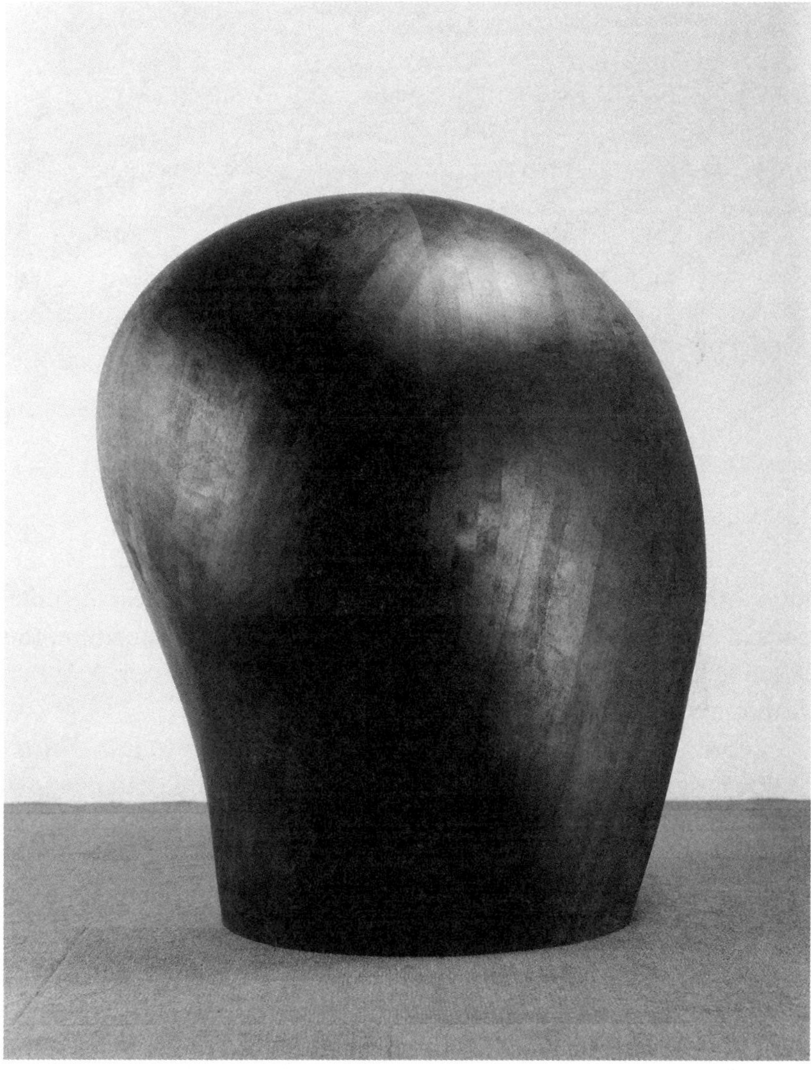

Figure 2.4. Martin Puryear, *Untitled*, 1997. Painted cedar and pine, 68 × 57 × 51 in. © Martin Puryear. Courtesy of Matthew Marks Gallery.

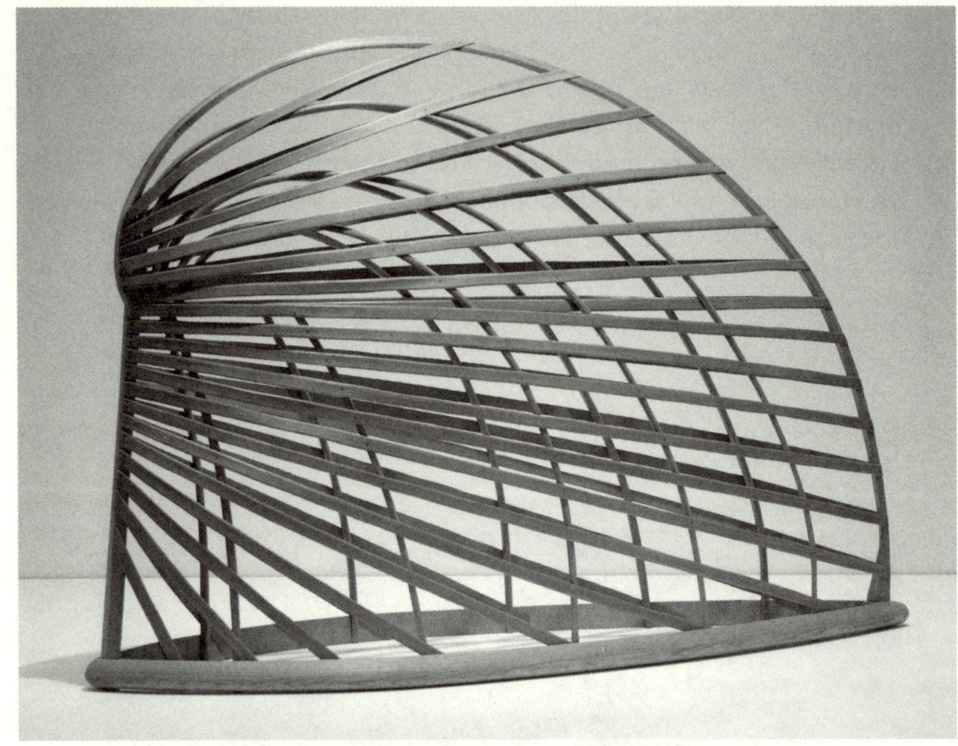

Figure 2.5. Martin Puryear, *Bower*, 1980. Sitka spruce, pine, and copper tacks, 64 ¼ × 94 ⅝ × 26 in. © Martin Puryear. Courtesy of Matthew Marks Gallery.

monoliths carved by human hands. Both sculptures suggest the influence of external elements (whether environmental or human) on the shape of the object and, in turn, on the space of the interior. And Puryear thinks a great deal about the interior.

According to the artist, in *Self* (and, it would follow, in *Untitled*), hollowness "remain[s] locked away inside, inaccessible and unknowable to others."[59] Yet Puryear plays with the inaccessibility of the interior in other works (fig. 2.5). In *Bower* (1980)—a bit reminiscent of *Self* in shape, but constructed as an airy frame of Sitka spruce and pine—the artist offers "a contrasted imagining of a secret place hidden in full view."[60] This self is not worn down, but built. This work is penetrable; its airiness matches its lightness. Yet it is also a body that maintains clear boundaries. It has a delineated volume, and while its interior is permeable, it nevertheless remains distinct from its surroundings.

Several recurrent themes of Puryear's work are present in these works: the tension between exterior appearance and internal space; the relationship between the visible and invisible surface (as in *Bower*, where the exterior of the sculptural form is delineated by gap as well as substance); and, I think, in the concept of selfhood as formed in the spaces between self-directed technologies of making (such as in the techniques of assembly that shape these wooden sculptures) and the effects of external forces on an originary body (as in the reductive sculptural techniques or erosive elements that shape the rock forms they harken to). Puryear's sculptures, in other words, propose a mediated black American subjectivity in which the self is formed not simply through the wearing effects of social or elemental forces, nor through a pure self-making, but rather through a negotiated crafting and shaping of self in dialogue with other forces. Moreover, the presentation of interiority that is delimited and yet available, hidden and yet discoverable, protected and yet vulnerable, interacts with the representational legacies of black subjectivity in particular and generative ways.

Puryear builds objects that can evoke those affects of looming that so define minimalism: they are large enough to force viewers into a phenomenological relation, large enough to tip into the anthropomorphic and, yes, the theatrical. Art critics have described Puryear's sculptures as "unfamiliar objects that encourage but frustrate a wish to identify them,"[61] and as "elemental forms remarkable for their unusual beauty and metaphoric resonance." Surely these impressions are compounded in objects (like *Self* and *Untitled*) that are dark and impenetrable. The ambiguous forms of Puryear's anthropomorphic objects result in a desire for relation *and* an unsurety about the nature of that relation—just the impossibly delicious combination that Tom Wolfe ascribed to the Panthers.

Yet if Puryear's objects loom through their size and their unreadable form, they also refuse to threaten through the substance and surface of their material subjectivities. Their carefully (one wishes to say "lovingly") handcrafted surfaces; their material composition of wood, a warm medium; and their quietly waiting and sometimes visible interiors all invite a deeper relation than does shape alone. Indeed, Puryear has said of *Self* that its hollowness "gave rise to the title and to the notion of the work as a place as much as an object."[62] Puryear suggests that the object's hollowness does not mean emptiness so much as an awaiting presence. Nothing about this presence invites the affective relation that is threat. For one thing, its phenomenological constitution (as a place as much as an object) suggests a receptive rather than aggressive stance. For another, its material qualities—the evidence of its careful making, its warm material—might be interpreted as placid or inviting.

"Puryear's protagonist is a quiet one," critic Robert Storr has said, "and, although it may yearn for peace and perhaps transcendence, never, in the manner of the expressionist self, does it proclaim aloud its erstwhile struggles."[63] Storr's statement does a great deal of work in a short space, and is therefore worth parsing a bit. To begin with, Storr references "Puryear's protagonist" as though it is possible to identify a singular character in Puryear's works. Although Puryear's works present a coherent vision, I am resistant to naming a singular protagonist in them, as that would veer close to insisting that the artist has (re-)produced autobiography, rather than social vision, through his works. Still, regardless of whether a singular protagonist may be found in Puryear's works, subjectivity is a recurrent motif—and if Puryear's works do not proclaim expression*ist* selfhood, neither do they decline to express selfhood. Rather, in their material, form, and processes, Puryear's works speak to a black subjectivity that does not shy away from objecthood but rather insists on its nuanced ability to speak to, and for, blackness.

DAVID HAMMONS

If Piper largely (though not exclusively) embraces the aesthetics of black threat and Puryear largely (though not exclusively) rejects them, David Hammons takes the most ambivalent stance of the artists I discuss here. His 1993 sculpture *In the Hood* (fig. 2.6) is a ready example of this ambivalence in the way it combines the high visibility and charged symbolic structure of a hoodie with the absence of the young black male who presumably occupies it. Like the other works in this chapter, Hammons's sculpture insists that there is something or someone to witness while simultaneously refusing some aspect of that act's fulfillment. The piece trades in the anthropomorphic objecthood of the minimalist object, not only in referencing human form but in that the work is mounted well above the ground: it looms. For viewers who have been conditioned to fear men in hoodies, the piece may well feel threatening due to its height, its suggestion of human form, its dark and shadowy hue, and its association with black crime. Yet while

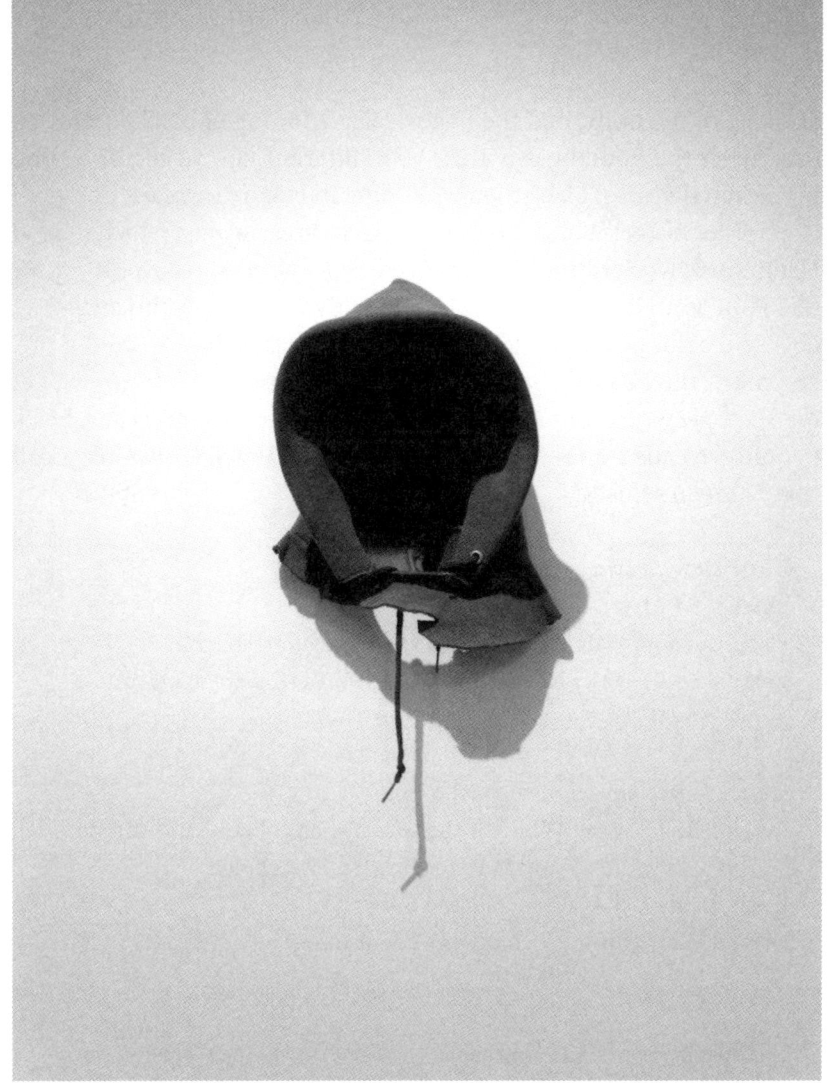

Figure 2.6. David Hammons, *In the Hood*, 1993. Athletic sweatshirt hood with wire, 23 × 10 × 5 in. Tilton Family Collection.

Hammons presents his viewers with a symbol of blackness, there is no physiognomic blackness here. *If the object will stand entirely for blackness,* he seems to suggest, *then let it. I'm out.*

But if the black body is fugitive in *In the Hood*, neither is it quite free. The symbolic structure that would entrap blackness feels too ready to claim its own—at least in *this* political moment, when Trayvon Martin's death looms as a not-so-distant and dreadfully recurrent future-past. The hood lacks a head, but also its own body, and the cut at the neck is jagged. For the black spectator, the violence of that cut, the absence of the body, and the historical sectioning of black bodies on display let the hood bear witness to a different violent history—one perpetrated *against* black men—standing in lieu of the black body.

Another historical instantiation of black threat against which to read Hammons's work is the July 1968 issue of *Esquire*. The cover story for this issue is an interview with James Baldwin. Though the magazine cover bills this article as "James Baldwin tells us all how to cool it this summer," the heading on the article instead asks, "How can we get *the black people* to cool it?" (emphasis added). In this interview, black people are called on to cool the nation's rising racial tensions, a call that Baldwin refuses:

> ESQ: How can we get the black people to cool it?
> JAMES BALDWIN: It is not for us to cool it.
> ESQ: But aren't you the ones who are getting hurt the most?
> JAMES BALDWIN: No, we are only the ones who are dying fastest.
>
> [. . .]
>
> ESQ: Is there any white man who can . . .
> JAMES BALDWIN: White by the way is not a color, it's an attitude. You're as white as you think you are. It's your choice.
> ESQ: Then black is a state of mind too?
> JAMES BALDWIN: No, black is a condition.
>
> [. . .]
>
> You talk about us as though we were not there. The real pain, the real danger is that white people have always treated Negroes this way. You've always treated Sambo this way. We always were Sambo for you, you know we had no feelings, we had no ears, no eyes. We've lied to you for more than a hundred years and you don't even know it yet. We've lied to you to survive. And we've begun to despise you. We don't hate you. We've begun to despise you.
>
> And it is because we can't afford to care what happens to us, and you don't care what happens to us.[64]

Baldwin reiterates that blackness is a condition, in counter-distinction to whiteness, which is a choice. Fried's language of condition echoes once again. He then describes the ways blackness is called into this condition through the equation of blackness with a lack of feeling, a

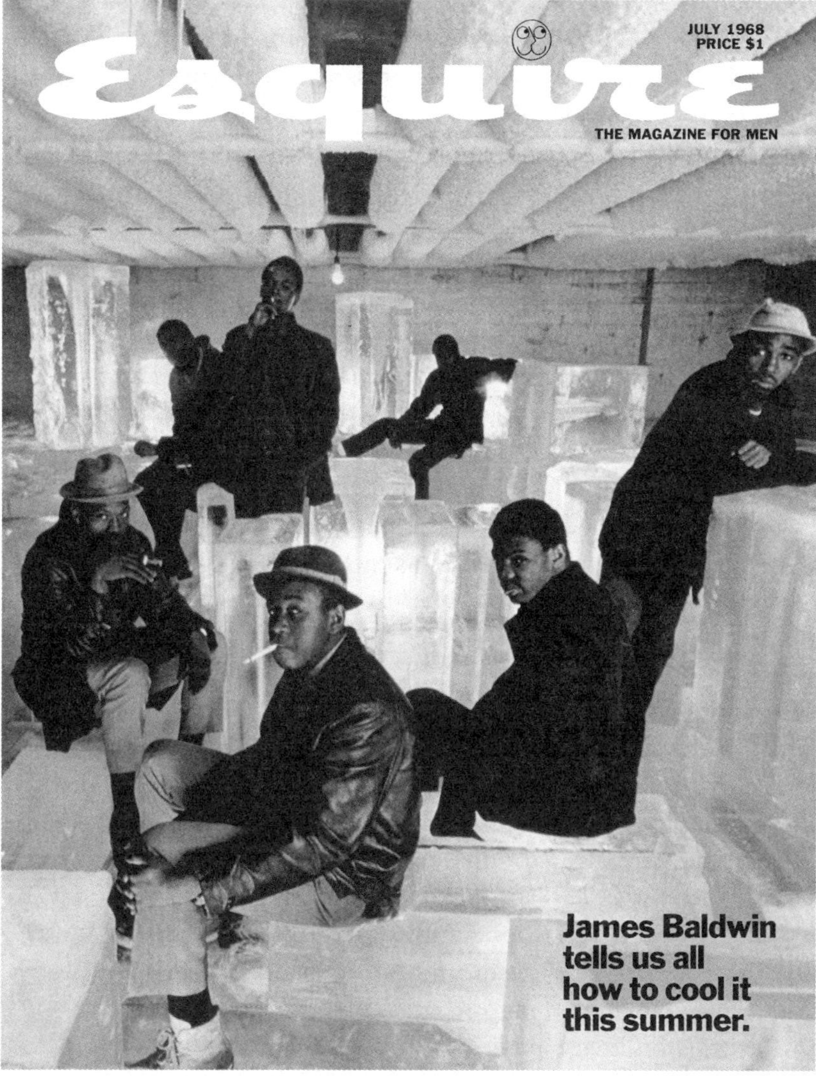

Figure 2.7. George Lois, *Cool It*, 1968. *Esquire*.

lack of sense—no ears, no eyes—like Piper at Max's Kansas City—and situates disingenuousness and threat as the natural consequence.

The incendiary and now legendary art director George Lois designed the magazine cover that accompanied Baldwin's interview (fig. 2.7). The image features seven young black men arrayed in an ice warehouse. They sit on ice, lean against it, and stand among blocks of it (and each other); they smoke and leer at the camera (or at the photographer) with a certain aloof remove. The closest of them is reasonably well lit, the farthest mere silhouette. Lit or not, the image trades in their icy and inscrutable presence. Here's how Brian Horrigan, curator of *The 1968 Exhibit*, described the cover:

> Seven young black men—anonymous, black-jacketed, smoking, staring at the camera—are assembled in an ice warehouse. George Lois and photographer Carl Fischer pressed these men (actors? models? guys pulled in off the street?) into a single role, one with a long history in American popular culture—the Black Man who Terrifies White People. Cool. Insolent. Arrogant. Tightly wound. "Powderkegs," each of them. Still, the photograph manages to control them: they are inside; trapped, in a way, in a space that could pass for a prison; like animals or carcasses in a meat locker; isolated from each other, not part of a larger group. Not part of a community at all: no women, no children. Just black maleness, an immense threat to white American males, overwhelmingly the readership of *Esquire*, "The Magazine for Men," as it says just above the head of the black guy on the far right.[65]

Horrigan, in his professional capacity as curator, recognizes black threat in the aesthetics of Lois's image, and ties it to the threat of black masculinity. As a viewer I cannot myself see these men as animal or carcass-like, nor do I see insolence or arrogance in their expressions, which seem to me reservedly skeptical. Yet this is exactly the point, that the aesthetics of black threat—the fact of their looming—invites a quick trick in which the unknown black men ("actors? models?") become a known affective quantity (insolent object) through the aesthetic fact of their looming.

It is with this image in mind that I see David Hammons's *Cold Shoulders* (fig. 2.8) enacting its aesthetic intervention. As a work of minimalism, *Cold Shoulders* might be placed in conversation with Robert Morris's *Untitled (Four Mirrored Cubes)* (1965). Yet I think it makes as much sense to think about the ways *Cold Shoulders*, as a work of minimalism, is in dialogue with Lois's image. In *Cold Shoulders*, massive blocks of ice suggest human forms. In substituting looming blocks of ice for the looming black body, Hammons is able to signify on the aesthetic traditions of black threat—for even if he isn't responding to this exact image, the assumptions that underlie Lois's image hold beyond its borders. Coats of fur and wool—rather than the haptically cooler

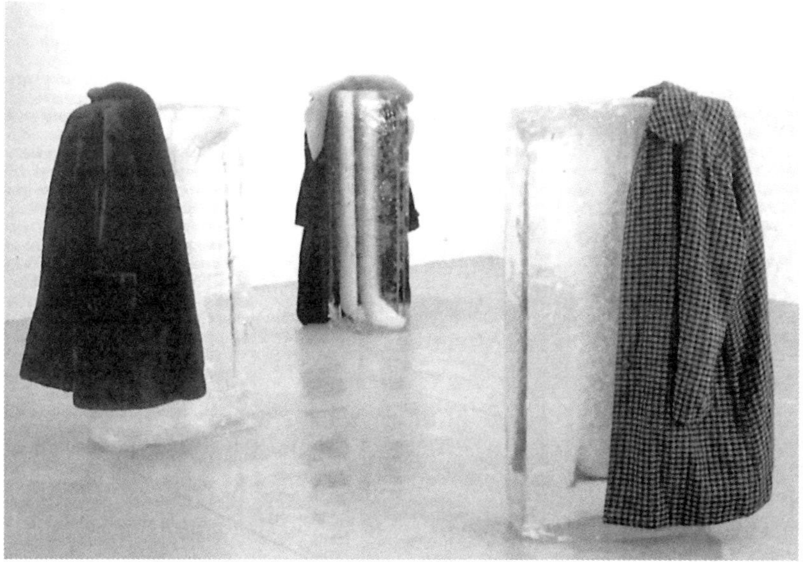

Figure 2.8. David Hammons, *Cold Shoulders*, 1990. Installation view, Jack Tilton Gallery, New York.

leather—are draped on the ice blocks, softening and warming the presence of these "bodies" at the same time that his substitution of ice renders them harder and colder. But importantly, the substitution of ice for bodies allows for a degree of fugitivity for the black subject that the sculptural hoodie of 1992 might not (or might no longer). Threat melts into nothing.

Hammons threads his needle quite exactly—he doesn't defuse threat, as Puryear does, nor does he embrace it as Piper does. Instead, he proffers a performance of conspicuous abstention. "Blackness appearing tonight!" he seems to promise, yet *blackness* fails to show—for some. Some relic of the raptured black body always remains behind, but he leaves it to his viewers to determine whether, or how, to invest that relic with meaning.

ROBERT MORRIS

Unlike the other artists I have discussed in this chapter, Robert Morris is white. He shows no explicit preoccupation with blackness in the course of his extensive progressive activism. Morris is, however, acknowledged as a leading practitioner of minimalism, and his works can be seen as instances of a phenomenon in which blackness disappears from view yet infuses other scopic and affective vehicles. To consider this possibility, I will take up two of Morris's works that evidence hints of blackness: *Site* (1964) and *Untitled (Box for Standing)* (1961). There is no evidence that Morris intended to inflect these works with a cross-racial chromatic. Still, both flirt with aesthetics of black threat by surrogating the black body.

Theorized by Joseph Roach, surrogation is a cultural process by which people who experience a hole in their social fabric—most often caused by death or departure—attempt to find a satisfactory substitute. "Because collective memory works selectively, imaginatively, and often perversely," he says, "surrogation rarely if ever succeeds." Success, however, matters less than the attempt. "I believe," he continues, "that the process of trying out various candidates in different situations—the doomed search for originals by continuously auditioning stand-ins—is the most important of the many meanings that users intend when they say the word *performance*."[66] Although Roach focuses on losses caused by death or departure, the peculiar institution's afterlives have, for many white Americans, rendered the black American an unknown (or unknowable) entity—an unspectral absence deserving effigial proxy. And there is reason to believe that Morris's works offer such effigies by tapping the cultural tropes of blackness—especially, if not exclusively, through the aesthetics of looming.

Morris's sculptural works "radicalized the heretofore passive relationship between art object and spectator," in the words of art critic Maurice Berger.[67] This was Morris's intention all along: he was well aware that human-sized objects insist upon person-like relations. "This is undoubtedly why subliminal, generalized kinesthetic responses are strong in confronting [the new sculpture]," he wrote. "Such responses are often denied or repressed since they seem so patently inappropriate in the face of non-anthropomorphic forms, yet they are there."[68] As Fried makes clear in "Art and Objecthood," he experienced this relation with an impassive object as confrontational. Morris predicted this, too, explaining that the large size of much minimalist sculpture was "one of the necessary conditions of avoiding intimacy."[69] By intimacy he means, in particular, the instinct to get very close to or to touch objects smaller than oneself. Morris wants his objects to insist upon the distance of interpersonal relations. He knows that he is aligning qualities of sculpture to a purpose that is aesthetic but also phenomenological.

Moreover, Morris objects to additions that might detract from the *physical* relationship of the object to a viewer. Take, for example, his thoughts on the addition of color. He writes, "The qualities of scale, proportion, shape, mass, are physical. Each of these qualities is made visible by the adjustment of an *obdurate*, literal mass. Color does not have this characteristic. It is additive. Obviously things exist as colored. The objection is raised against the use of color that emphasizes the optical and in so doing *subverts the physical*. The more neutral hues, which *do not call attention to themselves*, allow for the maximum focus on those essential physical decisions that inform sculptural works" (emphasis added).[70] In not calling attention to themselves, neutral hues are a form of quietude that complements the stubborn, inexpressive presence of human-sized objecthood (and here we might hear the faint echo of Jefferson's immovable veil of black). Morris's own favorite neutral was a signature gray, a mix of black and white hues.

Morris knew that he was aligning qualities of sculpture to a purpose that was aesthetic but also phenomenological. "Unitary forms do not reduce relationships. They order them," he wrote.[71] This assertion comes at a turning point in Morris's first "Notes on Sculpture." Just before making it, he discusses various elements of the new sculpture, so that one could read the "relationships" as those between shape, color, size, and so forth. But immediately afterward, he turns to the human-object relation—meaning that a "unitary" form might also order human-object relations. Yet curiously, even while acknowledging that the object has the power to order relations, Morris doesn't say much about the *nature* of this anthropomorphic object thrust into relation with the human spectator by virtue of its size. The object approximates a human relation, and that is enough. Yet mightn't we think of black threat as the presentation of a unitary form that orders relations through performance?

Untitled (Box for Standing) (fig. 2.9) is an example of looming anthropomorphism in Morris's work. Originally a fir wood structure, *Box for Standing* accommodated Morris's body with little room to spare. He himself called it coffin-like, and said it emerged during a period of his artistic practice—the early 1960s—when he wanted a "totalising, enclosing space within which I exist with the object." Morris roots the works of this time in a particular set of personal circumstances, saying that his exploration of the premises of sculpture coincided with

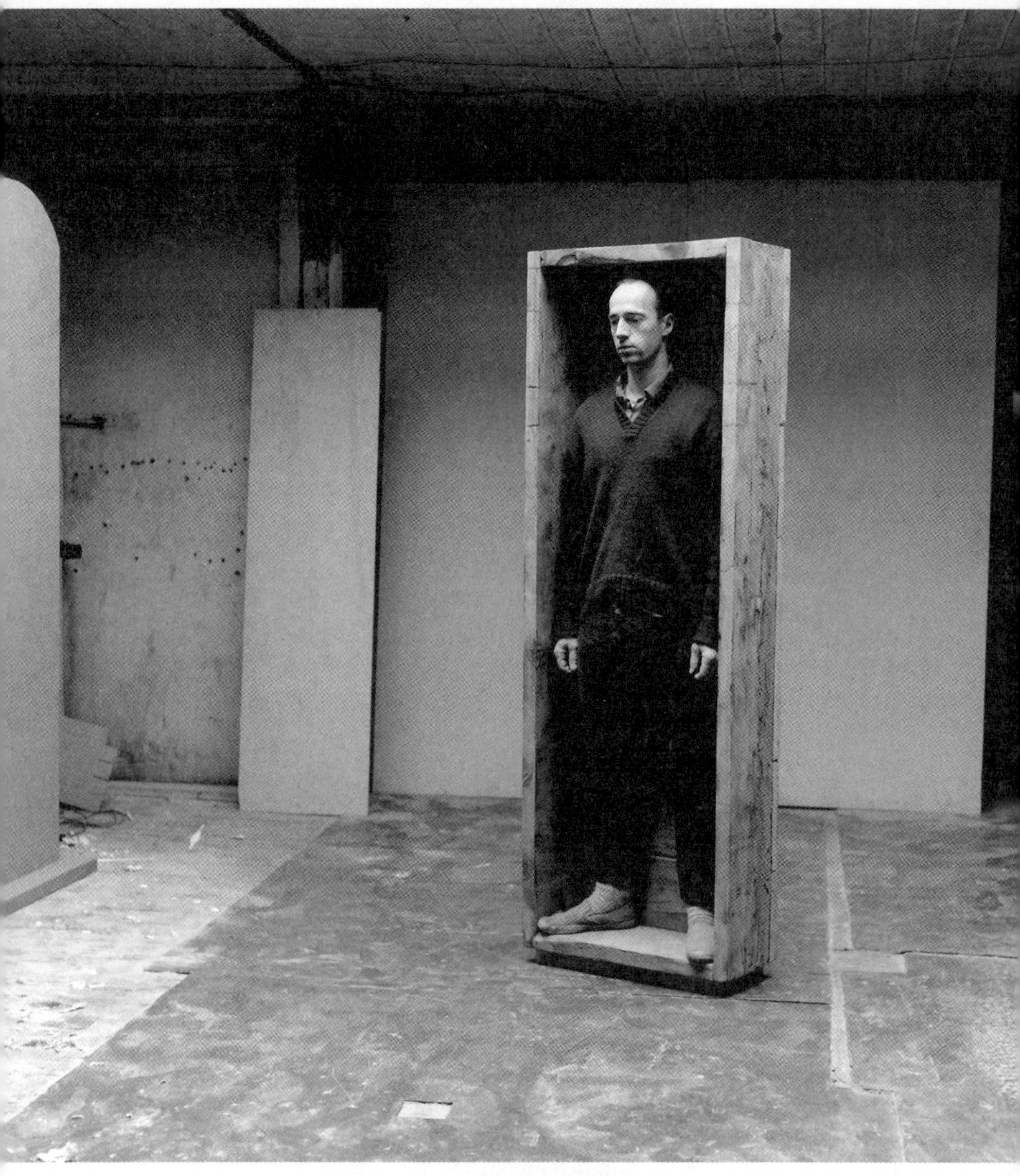

Figure 2.9. Robert Morris in *Untitled (Box for Standing)*, 1961. © 2021 The Estate of Robert Morris/Artists Rights Society (ARS), New York. Courtesy of the Castelli Gallery.

"an increasing negativity toward and incapacity for personal relations. [. . .] Only the inanimate object is alive for me in these years, and making objects becomes my bulwark against the threat of the other, and every other is regarded as threatening, especially those who would try to get close to me."[72] While I often avoid the biographical in discussing an artist's work, Morris's plainspoken admission of his desire for the object to stand in lieu of human relation supports the sense that *Box for Standing* explicitly surrogates the human form in addition to calling the body into relation with it.

Indebted to Fried, many critics of Morris's sculpture focus on what his objects do to the spectator through their imitation of the body's phenomenology. Therefore, a good deal of criticism focuses on the viewer's experience of the sculptural object.[73] Much rarer is an interrogation of *the object's experience of the viewer*. Yet as a hybrid sculpture and performance work, *Box for Standing* suggests an interchangeability between the box and the person standing within in, reinforced by Morris's own expressionless affect when he inhabits the box. They feel of a piece, as though Morris without the box, or the box without Morris, would essentially continue to exhibit the same thing. The human, in other words, is a surrogate for this box as much as the box is a surrogate for the human. And what does the box want of out its exchange with the people who view it?

According to Morris's sculptural ideals, it wants physical presence more than an optical one; it wants to loom. But also—as "Notes on Sculpture" suggests and Morris's personal description of the era seconds—the box wants to force its viewer into relation without abandoning a bulwark of protective objecthood. Morris suggests that this objecthood is adopted in response to a perceived threat. I do not mean to negate or disregard Morris's personal experiences, or to suggest that they were not highly individual. But at least as these feelings have manifested in Morris's objecthood, transfigured into art "as a closed space, a refusal of communication, a secure refuge and defense against the outside world, a dead zone and buffer against others who would intrude"—*that* objecthood resonates with a certain performed and/or performative mode of blackness.[74]

Morris's works—sculptural or live—never perform black threat per se. They tug at the edges of it by performing objecthood, looming, and an unreadability that trades unitary form for intimacy or detail *while simultaneously* (and, for some, uncomfortably) insisting on human relation.[75]

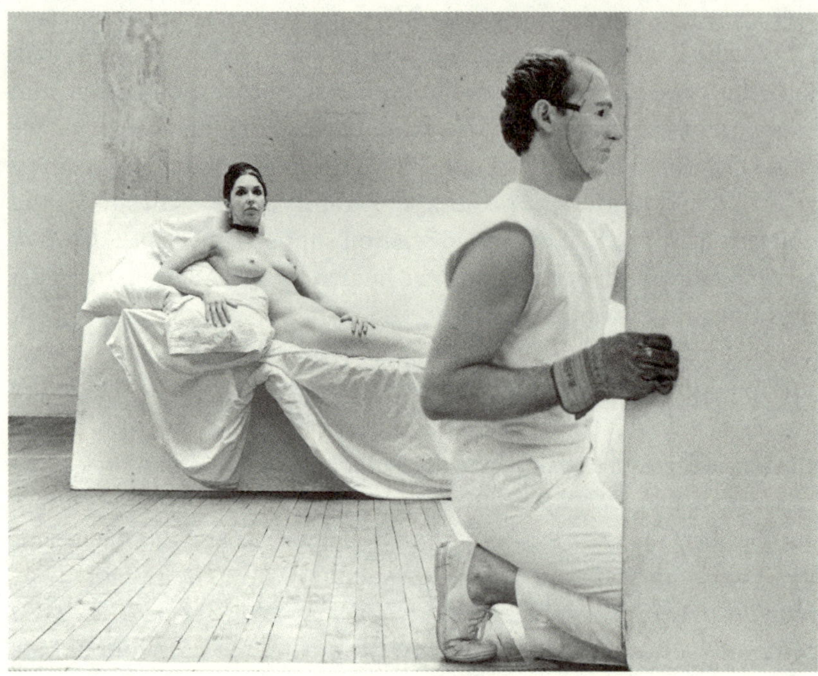

Figure 2.10. Robert Morris with Carolee Schneemann, *Site*, 1964. © 2021 The Estate of Robert Morris/Artists Rights Society (ARS), New York. © 2021 Carolee Schneemann Foundation/Artists Rights Society (ARS), New York. Courtesy Galerie Lelong & Co., Hales Gallery, and P·P·O·W, New York. Courtesy of the Castelli Gallery. Photo by Peter Moore; Peter Moore Photography Archive, Charles Deering McCormick Library of Special Collections, Northwestern University Libraries, © Northwestern University.

As I hope is clear by now, my contention is not that black Americans are the only people who connect to or perform these embodiments, but rather that we have a long and societally reinforced (perhaps even mandated) relationship with them. Morris's reliance on looming does not, therefore, constitute a "true" performance of blackness—if such a thing can be said to exist at all; instead, his reliance illuminates one way that the aesthetic realm can call on the cultural imaginary of blackness in order to do its work. Admittedly, it is something of a trace in *Box for Standing*, but that isn't always the case in Morris's oeuvre. *Site*, a performance piece conceived by Robert Morris and executed together with Carolee Schneemann in 1964, is far clearer in its hail.

Simply put, *Site* (fig. 2.10) riffs on the iconography of Édouard Manet's well-known painting *Olympia* (1863) (fig. 2.11), which portrays a prostitute and her black attendant. At the start of *Site*, as it is

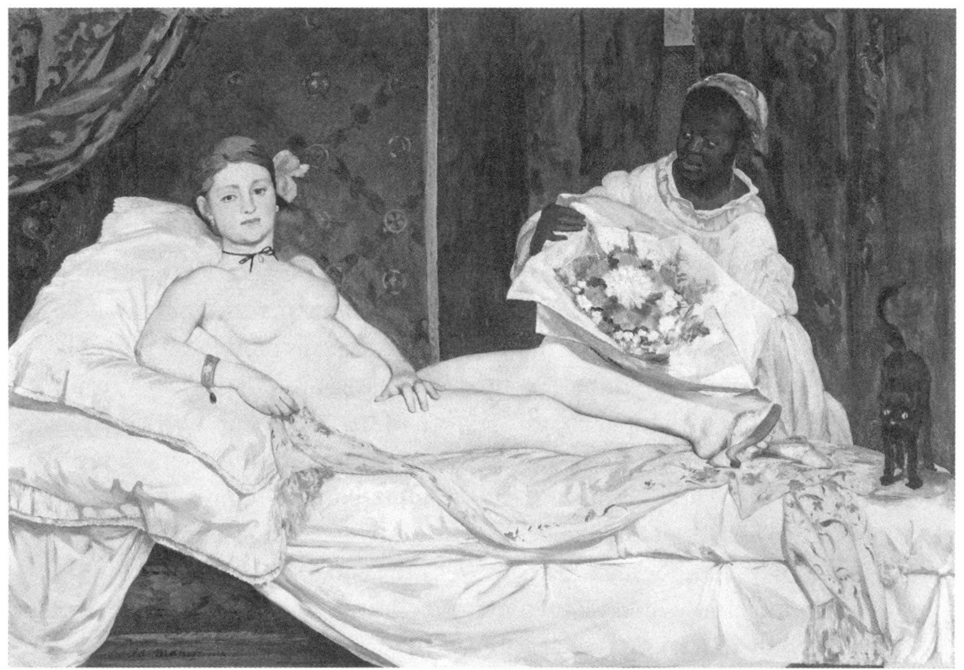

Figure 2.11. Édouard Manet, *Olympia*, 1863. Image courtesy of the Musée d'Orsay.

described by Berger, Morris's audience sees three objects: downstage right, a white box, out of which issue the sounds of jackhammers; upstage center, a large structure of whitewashed plywood; and upstage right, Morris, standing with his back to the audience, dressed in work clothes, boots, and gloves. After several minutes, Morris walks to the plywood structure and begins to disassemble it. As he turns to this work, the audience can see that Morris wears a papier-mâché mask "designed to reproduce, without expression, his facial features."[76] As Morris moves the heavy boards of the upstage structure, he reveals Schneemann reclining in the manner of Olympia, wearing nothing but "a dusting of white powder and a ribbon around her neck."[77] "After Schneemann is fully revealed," Berger says, "Morris walks downstage left, where he moves one of the sheets of plywood into various positions (e.g. carrying it on his back, kneeling next to it). Several minutes later Morris walks back to Schneemann and covers her with the board. He then returns downstage left and turns his back to the audience as the house lights dim."[78] Morris and Schneemann both seem object-like in this performance, although her purpose is stasis while his is motion—he is an object that makes other objects move, impassively.

Site amounts to repetition with a difference: it cites Manet's painting in the iconography of Olympia herself and in picturing two figures, one of whom labors and one of whom reclines (although certainly another form of labor is implied in this reclining). Yet while Manet's work offers two female figures, one white and one black, Morris's piece offers one male figure and one female figure, both white. The fact that it *is* a repetition allows us to parse the symbolic structures that underlie this substitution. For one thing, Morris's piece is consistent with Manet's in making Olympia's companion a worker—support staff, even. In both cases Olympia pays little heed to her attendant, but the attendant's labor nevertheless helps dictate the terms on which Olympia is seen: in Manet's painting, the woman behind Olympia holds flowers; in Morris's performance, his labor reveals and obscures Olympia. Moreover, the boards Morris moves are echoed in the dimensions of the lounge on which Schneemann reclines, implying that she is supported by that labor as well as revealed through it.

For Berger, a comprehensive critic of Morris's works, *Site* stages an analogy between workers and artists in which "the affectations of 'artistic temperament'" are eschewed.[79] Berger reads Morris's masked face as operating against an art historical modernism that elevated the rarefied, avant-garde artist, thereby returning the artist's affiliation to the industrial order that had spurred modernism's idealization of individual expression in the first place. He also reads the mask as reflecting the anonymity of labor. To a large extent I agree with Berger, especially as he emphasizes the anonymity of labor. Building on his insight, however, I want to highlight the fact that anonymous labor has racialized associations in the American context, especially as anonymity intersects with expressionlessness and objecthood. Whether or not Morris's larger oeuvre calls the unnamed worker into being as an unraced (or even deraced) figure, Morris's masked labor in *Site* steps into a structure of meaning already established by Manet. Given this fact, Morris's labor *here* substitutes for a *particular* unnamed laborer who is certainly not unraced. Olympia's attendant is black, and she is inscrutable.

Olympia's attendant is not expressionless, exactly, but neither does her expression give itself over to easy naming. Is this because she wishes to be an unnameable entity (whether "she" refers to the character in the painting or the model who portrayed her)? Or is it because Manet cannot himself *see* her expression? I pose an unanswerable question, but its consequence for Morris's embodiment might be the same: the mask. The expressionless mask that Morris wears is not a race-neutral prop, but rather a substitution for unreadable blackness. Once again, my point here is not that Morris is performing blackness per se, but rather that *cultural* blackness infuses the signifiers that Morris has substituted for blackness's visible (physiognomic) presence.

A final substitution occurs via gender: the flower-wielding woman of Manet's painting becomes a plywood-toting male; the copious pink fabric that obscures her body (in contrast to Olympia's) becomes instead a T-shirt and jeans, work gloves and boots. I read this change to Manet's painting through Hortense Spillers's insights regarding the ungendering of the black female wrought through the workings of slavery—the denial of family integrity, the denial of feminine delicacy and its commensurate calls to protection, and so forth, until, "in the historic outline of dominance, the respective subject-positions of 'female' and 'male' adhere to no symbolic integrity."[80] Morris might easily step into the black female's place because in his cultural imaginary she, as a placeholder, isn't all that "female" to begin with. Morris's mask, stationary pose at the beginning of the piece, and unaffected dance with the wooden boards all suggest that Morris envisioned his own performing body to be an object among objects in this piece and, as an object, perhaps genderless. But in surrogating his body for hers, thereby overwriting the black woman's body with masculinity, Morris flirted with the signal sources of black threat that we recognize so readily in the cross-gendered performance of Piper's Mythic Being.

In suggesting that signifiers of blackness reverberate in Morris's work, I follow the example of Petrine Archer-Straw, who, in the stellar *Negrophilia*, diligently draws out the (white) European avant-garde's fascination with black essence and forms.[81] While certainly not *all* of American culture is at its core about blackness, blackness informs far more than is widely acknowledged. This blinkered view is due partly to Americans' persistently narrow view of what blackness is and how it operates—that is, we fail to recognize blackness in a certain aesthetic because culturally, we have denied that aesthetic as a register *of* blackness. In discussing the work of black abstractionists, art historian Darby English suggests the term "racial discomposure" as a way to discuss, in positive terms, the cultural mixing that he believes to be the true province of black modernism. He writes, "Racial discomposure [. . .] occurs whenever a politico-aesthetic event jeopardizes the chromatic stability underwriting blackness at the level of cultural description. [. . .] At one level, *discomposure* is just a way to refer to the contested and changing nature of historical signifiers of difference [. . .]. But the term may also apply in any number of instances that present blacks' embeddedness in a larger scene of differences [. . .]. *Discomposure* is apt whenever the objective conception of racial blackness encounters an incontestably subjective factor. Discomposure is what happens when blackness *adapts*."[82] English, in this passage, suggests that racial discomposure happens when blackness doesn't present as *obviously* black, when it reveals instead its constructed and contested nature in a wider field of difference. "Discomposure" is what happens when race begins to come apart at its seams through aesthetic means.

I am grateful for English's formulation and its attention to blackness as expansive, contested, and constructed, and in pointing out how Morris's artworks might quietly trade on the cultural signal of black threat, I hope to push against any implicit sense that black people's embeddedness in a larger scene of difference should influence *only* blackness and black cultural makers. Blackness is not the only chromatic subject to destabilization, nor the only one that can benefit from it. As I have previously suggested, racial discomposure can apply as well to whiteness, which, in spite of its tremendous ability to absorb otherness due to its dominance, is not immune to the gravitational effects of other racial bodies. In Morris's work, I spot the possibility of a black influence in white cultural production that is not simply a surface appropriation but rather a deeper pull. Furthermore, if Morris's work can be thought of as performing a mode of black inexpression, other realms of performance—across other bodies and forms—also come into play. For example, how might we think differently about raced inexpression if, say, Yvonne Rainer's minimalist dance could be thought of as working through or alongside the knowledges of deadpan performance?[83] How might Rainer's famous "No Manifesto," and the task-based movement that it described, change if viewed through a darker lens?[84] Though I've elected to raise this possibility without adding a movement analysis adventure to the aesthetic modes already explored, I nevertheless invoke Rainer's minimalist, modernist embodiment as a way of moving into the next chapter, where more feminine embodiments entangle with raced inexpression.

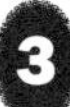

THE OPACITY GRADIENT

> She did not deny them, yet the fact was that they were denied.
> —Jean Toomer, from "Fern," *Cane*

At the outset of this chapter, I want to return briefly to Don Cox, the field marshal of the Black Panther Party featured in Tom Wolfe's article "That Party at Lenny's." As described in the last chapter, the vast majority of Wolfe's description of Cox emphasizes his looming indiscernibility. In a small variation on this theme, Wolfe also asserts that when conversation gets tough at the party (Otto Preminger leads an offensive), a change is apparent in Cox's eyes. "Cox takes the mint and stares at Bernstein with a strange Plexiglas gaze," Wolfe writes.[1] A few pages later: "And Cox stares at him, and the Plexiglas lowers over his eyes once more . . ."[2] Context clues suggest that Wolfe is witnessing (or at least experiencing) a kind of opacity through this change in Cox's gaze, for once the Plexiglas drops Wolfe has no more insight to offer his readers. Still, opacity is not necessarily a material quality of Plexiglas, which is generally transparent. Plexiglas is a synthetic substitute for glass's truer substance—an ersatz window to the soul. Plexiglas also suggests impermeability through its greater resistance to breaking. Cox's gaze mustn't be opaque, exactly—or at least not from a *visual* standpoint. Rather, the thoughts or feelings Cox's gaze could reveal are protected more haptically: Cox secures them behind a sturdy polymer where they remain *inaccessible* to Wolfe, even if they are not invisible.

Of course, Wolfe could be projecting this quality onto Cox. But I think not. To my mind, the metaphor of Cox's eyes bears too much similarity to a passage from Patricia Williams's "On Being the Object of Property." The passage begins with a reference to a black teenage mother of three, whose own mother, together with a doctor, has decided that she should have a tubal ligation:

> She told the story of her impending sterilization, according to my friend, while keeping her eyes on the floor at all times. My friend, who is white, asked why she wouldn't look up, speak with him eye to eye. The young woman answered that she didn't like white people seeing inside her.
>
> My friend's story made me think of my own childhood and adolescence. My parents were always telling me to look up at the world; to look straight at people, particularly white people; not to let them stare me down; to hold my ground; to insist on the right to my presence no matter what. They told me that in this culture you have to look people in the eye because that's how you tell them you're their equal. My friend's story also reminded me how very difficult I found that looking back to be. What was hardest was not just that white people saw me, as my friend's client put it, but that they looked through me, as if I were transparent.
>
> By itself, seeing into me would be to see my substance, my anger, my vulnerability and my raging despair—and that alone is hard enough to show. But to uncover it and have it devalued by ignore-ance [*sic*], to hold it up bravely in the organ of my eyes and to have it greeted by an impassive stare that passes right through all that which is me, an impassive stare that moves on and attaches itself to my left earlobe or to the dust caught in the rusty vertical geysers of my wiry hair or to the breadth of my freckled brown nose—this is deeply humiliating. It rewounds, relives the early childhood anguish of uncensored seeing, the fullness of vision that is the permanent turning-away point for most blacks.
>
> The cold game of equality staring makes me feel like a thin sheet of glass: white people see all the worlds beyond me but not me. They come trotting at me with force and speed; they do not see me. I could force my presence, the real me contained in those eyes, upon them, but I would be smashed in the process. If I deflect, if I move out of the way, they will never know I existed.[3]

It seems significant that Cox's eyes are likened to a transparent sheet when he is engaged in his own game of "equality staring." Instances of containment or withholding that embody such material transparency, I argue, critically nuance the opacity of the deadpan. My naming of transparency is critically indebted to, though different from, transparency as described in the work of Édouard Glissant. In the of *Poetics of Relation*, "transparency" (*transparence*) is held in counter-distinction to "opacity," which Glissant describes as "opportune obscurity."[4] Glissant uses the term "transparency" to name occasions of self-evidence or literalism (and not necessarily literalism in the sense that Michael Fried would use it, though neither am I certain it is so different). In the examples of this chapter, performances muster "opportune obscurity" by being seen *through* rather than or in addition to being seen, placing opacity and transparency on a gradient of obscurity, *both* standing in counter-distinction to literalism.

If this materialist sense of variable scopic saturation seems to refigure the longstanding African American interpretive paradigm of fugitivity, that sense is partially correct. Fugitivity is critically important within African American cultural and visual theory for obvious reasons, and my thinking builds on works that analyze black strategies of visual fugitivity that include anti-portraiture and the material trace.[5] Material transparency is therefore not synonymous with fugitivity, but rather is one strategy within the larger, graduated set of strategies that might be called fugitive. Unlike forms of fugitivity that tropologize the disappearance of escape, transparency does not absent the black body from sight. Rather, it references, performs, or surrogates, in whole or in part, the black body in ways that complicate its scopic availability. Uri McMillan has written that "sensing the surface, rather than searching for the interior life, paradoxically, inches us closer to the mysteries of the black artist"; in this chapter I attend to surface aesthetics through the sense of visual saturation or density.

FEMININITY AND SCOPIC SATURATION

Compared with the looming of the last chapter, the performances of this chapter are framed as a more (though again not exclusively) feminine mode of deadpanning. Though I believe gender is a continuum, I here reproduce its constructed and, therefore, variable poles because the cultural ideals of masculinity and femininity, mutable as they are, play a role in determining how embodiments signify within cultural structures. This cuts both ways, rewarding those whose bodies and performativities meet cultural expectations and punishing those whose fail to. Nevertheless, I would here also emphasize that, given that any black body may be interpellated at either extreme of hypervisibility and invisibility's well-documented simultaneity, black bodies of all genders can perform (or be seen to perform) looming or transparency.[6]

Consider, for example, Naomi Campbell's guest appearance on the British comedy series *Absolutely Fabulous*. At the episode's opening, the show's two protagonists, Patsy Stone and Edina Monsoon, share an awards banquet table with the supermodel. Campbell neither smiles nor frowns, but fans herself looking nowhere in particular. Her affect seems quiet but not uncomfortable, like an introvert having their own thoughts in company. When Edina asks Campbell, "Do you want a drink, are you all right?" Campbell answers, "I'm fine, thanks." She looks at Edina, she answers quietly, she adds a "thanks," but still Edina loudly mutters, "She's very difficult, very difficult," in response. When a competing head of PR, Claudia Bing, tries to convince Campbell to be the face of a liposuction-a-thon to provide human blubber for whale moisturizer, Campbell listens politely; upon walking away Bing, too, insists that Campbell is "very difficult." Later, Bing says that Campbell, who is reading a magazine as her hair is done, is "behaving very, very badly."[7] The joke is that, despite Campbell's reputation for violent outbursts, she is nothing but measured and polite in the episode, even in the face of white women who are entitled, demanding, vapid, and vain. Still, Campbell is the one who is accused of being difficult because she does not respond effusively or subserviently to those around her.

Though Campbell is beautiful and feminine, her muted affect is perceived as intransigence—a mode closer to the black threat of the last chapter. Given the longstanding association of (universal/white) femininity with emotion, the deadpan's withholding runs counter to (universal/white) femininity's expressive expectations. Said differently, if a "neutral" face for a man is inexpressive, a "neutral" face for a woman may require the slight smile of pleasantness—hence "resting bitch face" as the commonly embraced descriptor of failure to strike the affectively appropriate face-at-ease.[8] This can be even more acute for the black woman, called on to be effusive (or, at a minimum, to actively signal her benignity) on account of both her gender and her blackness. Yet Spillers's insights regarding the historical ungendering of the black female body also come into play here; the relative ease with which the black female body has, historically, been uncoupled from the feminine in the American imaginary contributes to the stereotype of the angry black woman.

Furthermore, if the black woman can be perceived as threatening—and I will simply invoke the name Renisha McBride as an example of this phenomenon's costs—it is equally true that black men can be invisible. Ralph Ellison's *Invisible Man* is, of course, an extended portrait of being seen through rather than seen. "I am invisible, understand, simply because people refuse to see me," the novel's opening explains. "Like the bodiless heads you see sometimes in circus sideshows, it is as though I have been surrounded by mirrors of hard, distorting glass. When they approach me they see only my surroundings, themselves, or figments of their imagination—indeed, everything and anything except me."[9] His is hardly the only example. For much of the twentieth century, to say nothing of earlier years, black men in service positions occupied social scripts of invisibility or forgettability rather than threat—think of Pullman porters, for example. Erving Goffman's *Presentation of Self in Everyday Life* goes so far as to describe the servant or the slave as a "non-person" who "in certain ways [. . .] is defined by both performers and audience as someone who isn't there." Borrowing from Mrs. Trollope, Goffman includes, in his illustrations of the non-person, an instance of a young woman who performed great feats of modesty before a fellow white man and yet could lace her stays before a black man "with the most perfect composure."[10] And yet, to linger with the example of Pullman porters for a moment, their concern with "manhood rights"—which included the right to self-defense and their exercise of the vote, as well as the more mundane right to be assertive or strident without fear of reprisal—shows how strongly invisibility correlates with the (black) feminine.[11]

Ultimately, I take Spillers's insight that slavery transformed the black woman into "the principal point of passage between the human and the non-human world" to mean that black femininity is fertile territory for deadpanned aesthetics.[12] McMillan's *Embodied*

Avatars avidly seconds this insight, illustrating how black womanhood can signal with, or through, or as, objecthood.[13] McMillan's work also reminds readers that those whose subjectivities instantiate objecthood *may or may not* embrace that embodiment. Following his example, in this chapter I attempt to parse shades of aesthetic opacity without attempting to discern the enjoyment or disdain of those whose performances illustrate these positions. Thinking with an opacity gradient, I will attempt to distinguish five strategies of opacity, each of which relies upon a different degree of saturation or density of presence. Generally moving from most transparent to most opaque, they are: transparency, sheerness, obscurity, awayness, and opacousness. Though the black body can be subject to violent scrutiny upon a whim, the examples below serve to illustrate how, through aesthetics, it may also court, and be granted, a degree of scopic fugitivity.[14]

TRANSPARENCY

As the closest to invisibility, transparency is the hardest opacity to illustrate. Literal translucency is of course impossible for the human body. While there are artworks that incorporate or approximate aspects of literal transparency—for example, Radcliffe Bailey's *Pullman* (2010), comprising a blue glitter-coated heart enclosed in a clear glass cloche—I am thinking instead of a more metaphorical instantiation: presence that makes it possible to see the invisibility of the black subject without simply creating hypervisibility instead.[15] Transparency, in other words, functions like a scratch or a glare in a pane of glass, highlighting what is most often simply seen through. As an example of this most difficult opacity, I propose the figure of Byrdwoman as performed by Sheryl Sutton.

Sutton is herself a figure of some transparency, having largely disappeared from the annals of avant-garde theater and dance.[16] To offer the briefest glimpse of her work beyond what is discussed here: Sutton choreographed work that appeared in the Kitchen's 1976–1977 season, which also included work by Simone Forti. She danced in the Museum of Modern Art's Sculpture Garden with Andy de Groat (1978), and she collaborated with Bill T. Jones in two performances in 1978 and 1979. Also in 1979, she presented movement work in Paris's

Autumn Festival alongside Deborah Hay and Merce Cunningham. In 1980 she performed in the Holland Festival's Beyond Dance, which also included butoh luminary Min Tanaka. That same year she again performed at the Kitchen in Richard Gallo's *A Killer Is Loose but Nobody's Talking*. Peter Hujar photographed her in 1975, and Laurence Sudre in 1983. She performed with the Squat Theatre, a Hungarian company that relocated first to Paris and then New York, where they made their home in the Chelsea Hotel. In 1982 she appeared in director Gábor Altorjay's black-and-white, German-language film *Tscherwonez*. And she inspired János Pilinszky's strange 1977 work *Beszélgetések Sheryl Suttonnal* (*Conversations with Sheryl Sutton: The Novel of a Dialogue*, translated into English in 1992). In spite of all this, Sutton is an inexplicably under-known figure, best recognized in the context of her longstanding collaboration with Robert Wilson, which included roles in *Deafman Glance* (1970), *Einstein on the Beach* (1976), and *A Letter to Queen Victoria* (1974). Even in this context, as with so many muses, critics have too easily elided Sutton's contributions to Wilson's vision.

In Wilson's plays, Sutton often reprised the Byrdwoman, an enigmatic figure who first appeared to Wilson in "an inner vision" in 1968. A representative of birth, death, and timelessness, Byrdwoman "was neither sad nor happy and somehow encompassed the incomprehensibility of life itself."[17] By 1969, when Wilson staged *The Life and Times of Sigmund Freud* at the Brooklyn Academy of Music, his vision had coalesced into a woman in a black Victorian dress, a single black glove, and a stuffed black raven. The role consisted of sitting perfectly still throughout the first act of the play, which lasted over an hour. "Absolute stillness," Sutton said of playing Byrdwoman. "No expression. The facial muscles are so relaxed that the eyes nearly close, which gives the face a very strange mask. It's almost like you're looking but not seeing."[18]

The next year, 1970, Sutton played Byrdwoman in *Deafman Glance* (fig. 3.1), which Arthur Holmberg called "the signature piece of [Wilson's] first period." In the original production, Byrdwoman, again dressed in a high-necked black Victorian gown, nourishes and then murders two black children in a ritual of excruciating slowness. Another black boy watches and screams in terror. Byrdwoman comes to the screaming child and covers his mouth; he goes quiet and enters

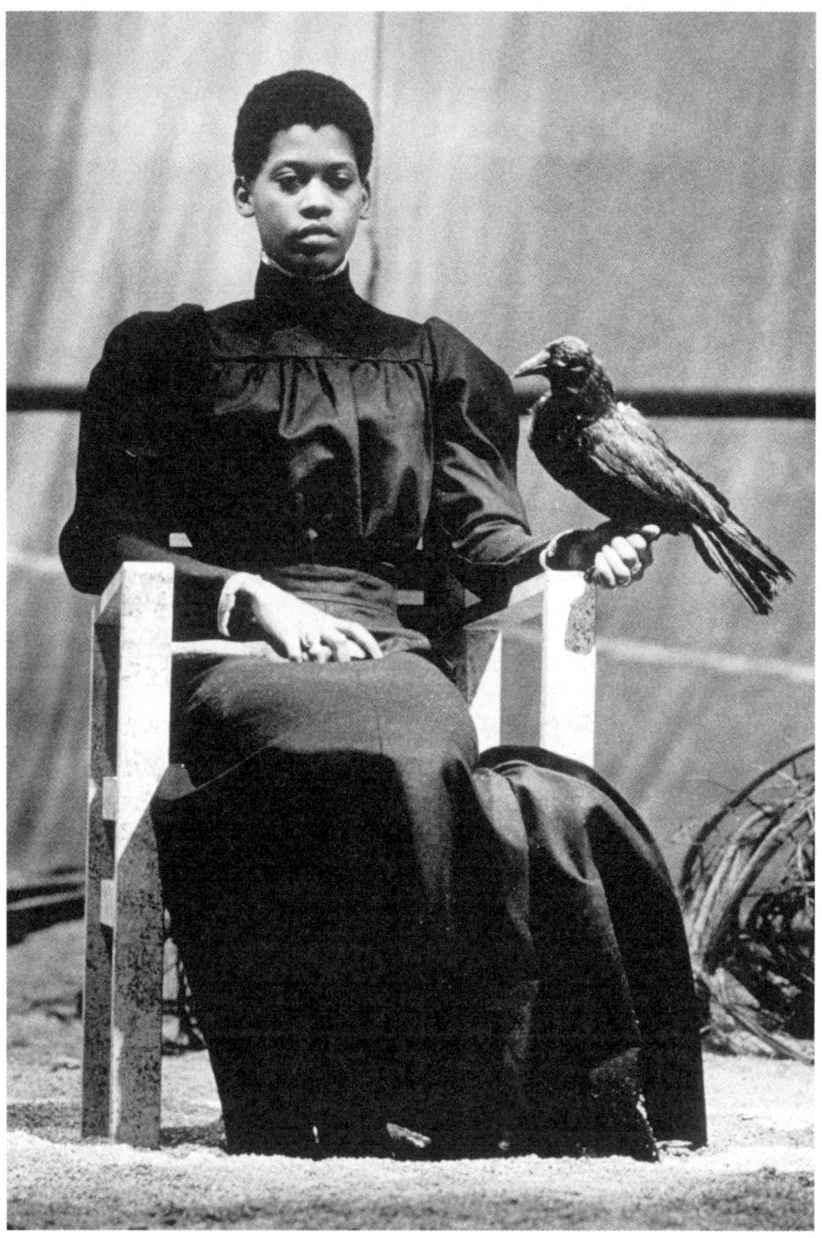

Figure 3.1. *Deafman Glance*, 1971. Photo by Ivan Farkas.

an elaborate dream world that features a martini-drinking frog in a smoking jacket and an ox who swallows the sun.[19] The original work was inspired in part by the drawings of a deaf boy adopted by Wilson, and the play tipped, in its proportions, toward the fantastical dream world.[20] Though the murders of the stage production were mere prologue, the video version of *Deafman Glance* created in 1981 eliminates the screaming boy and the wondrous world he enters, centering instead on Byrdwoman and her Medean murders. Perhaps this is because if *Deafman*'s imagistic method resides in the visual thought of the deaf,[21] its contents, for Wilson, better resided in the Byrdwoman.

I will admit that my experience of the film is one of queasy dread, but neither Wilson nor Sutton sees the figure as violent, likening her instead to a priest or an angel, both vehicles of (a) God's will.[22] As Robert Brustein points out, the video's final image shows "the woman looking out of the kitchen window in front of a naked incandescent lightbulb as we focus on the back of her head."[23] Though the Byrdwoman of this *Deafman* is less transparent than some of her other instantiations—it is impossible *not* to feel her presence—this final view of the back of her head underscores the way that she, like the window or lightbulb (or an angel), both is and is not scopically available.

Before delving further into Sutton's performative iterations, I want to note that it seems important to Wilson that Byrdwoman is black. According to Laurence Shyer, Sutton did not originate the role in *The Life and Times of Sigmund Freud*, the production that first consolidated Wilson's personal archetype. He writes, "The part was not then played by Sutton—she didn't meet Wilson until the following year—but by a young black woman he had cornered in a New York antique store. Upon assuming the role, Sutton made it her own."[24] Shyer also explains that when Wilson has himself stepped into the Byrdwoman character, his body doesn't necessarily evacuate her blackness. "Wilson himself has performed the ritual numerous times throughout the world," Shyer informs us, "usually dressed in a coat and tie but on one recent occasion in a long dress and blackface" (fig. 3.2).[25] Furthermore, as Hilton Als has discussed, other explicit signifiers of blackness have surrounded the Byrdwoman. In *Sigmund Freud*'s production,

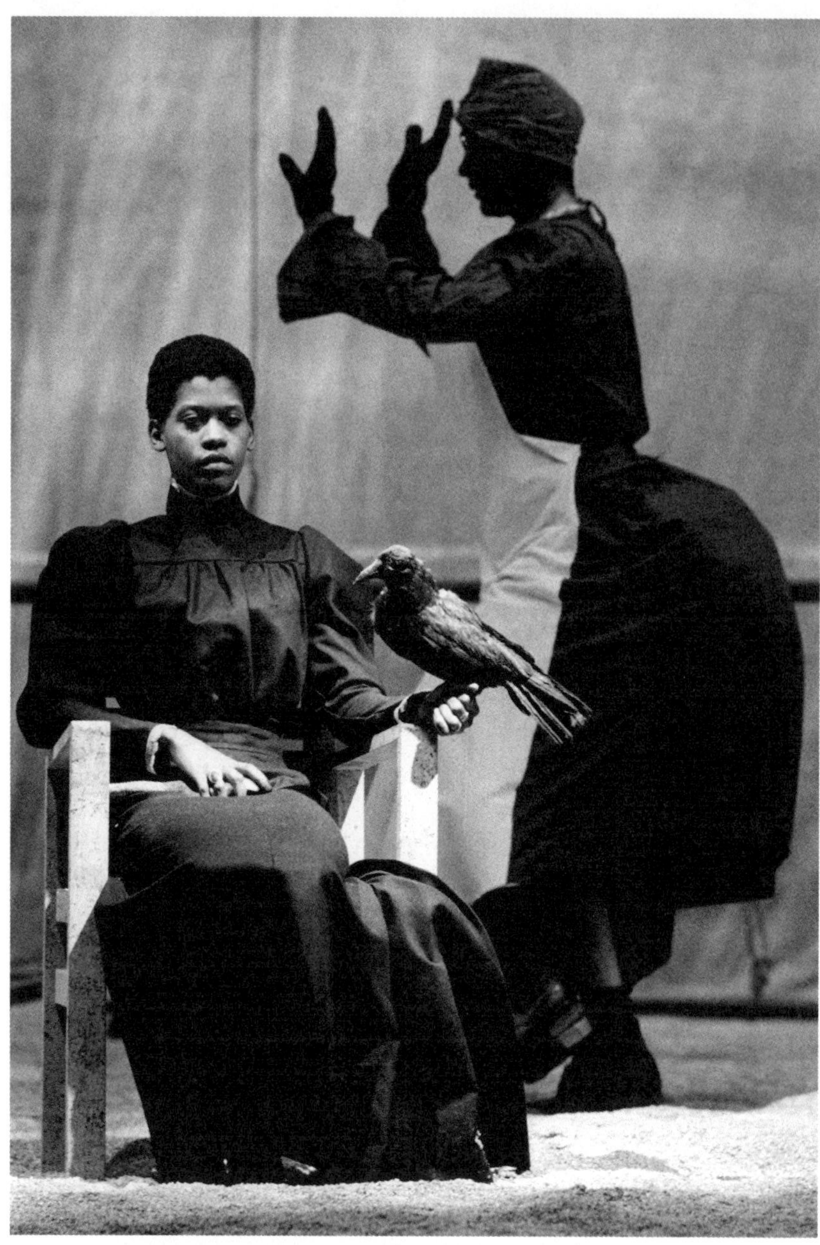

Figure 3.2. *Deafman Glance*, 1971. Photo by Ivan Farkas.

The play included a troubling scene: several performers in Mammy costumes and blackface cavorting to "The Blue Danube." Like Freud, Wilson wanted people to question the notion of motherhood. But the image was also tinged with the acknowledgment that Wilson himself had grown up in a racist environment. (His one close childhood friend was a black boy who worked as a domestic for his family. "My father was not a Klansman, but segregation was part of his education and environment," Wilson told Otto-Bernstein.) The kind of visual and political integration that Wilson was proposing is still rare in the largely white avant-garde. But, at the time, there was no critical inquiry into this aspect of his work, because there was no ongoing conversation on the subject: few of his contemporaries were putting that kind of painful baggage out there. (The Wooster Group's tricky and distanced use of blackface came more than a decade later.)[26]

Als is clearly a Wilson fan, and delicately raises the stickiness of this imagery without condemning Wilson for it—a move that seems fair given Wilson's progressive politics and casting decisions. As Als rightly notes, whatever the espoused politics of individual practitioners, the avant-garde is often not a sphere of integration. Moreover, contemporary blackface performances are often more complex and multilayered (which is not to say untroubling) than is easily or commonly acknowledged due to their deeply offensive history. Therefore, I want to sit a little longer with the blackness of Byrdwoman, and with Sutton's embodiment of her as devised in partnership with Wilson—a partnership that has lasted his entire career.

Indeed, a quarter decade before Sutton's most recent appearance in Wilson's *Zinnias: The Life of Clementine Hunter* (2013)—which is about an African American painter, and in which Sutton once again reprised the role of Byrdwoman—Shyer noted the unusually long collaboration between Wilson and Sutton and suggested that Sutton *uniquely* had the skill to bridge the stylistic transmutations within Wilson's overriding vision. Shyer writes:

Though few have been able to master the skill, Sutton offers a simple explanation for her own uncanny ability to hold an audience with so little. "What it is really is the ability to hold yourself back and give up so much space. Most people can't do that. It's like you turn your flame down low. That's very necessary to Bob [Wilson]'s performing technique and it's also very attractive to the audience. Then they come to you." While Sutton believes any person could develop this quality and would be equally interesting on stage, she admits this might be her special gift.[27]

Taking nothing away from Sutton's exceptional accomplishments as a performer, I want to consider the extent to which she excelled in the execution of Wilson's roles not *only* because of her outstanding technical achievements but *also* because of her racialized and gendered embodiment. Another way to say this is that being black might have formed part of Sutton's artistic training, for it seems to me that Sutton's virtuosity in enacting Byrdwoman echoes ways of being black and female in the world—turning your flame down low, holding your self back, and giving up space. "What people have to find," Sutton says, "is a way to be people somehow in a very aesthetically defined space while performing very minimalistic kinds of actions."[28] If we concede that blackness itself is an aesthetically defined space—and given that race is a visual regime, I don't know how we could deny that it is—this seems to me as striking a definition of day-to-day black womanhood (or, at least, one way of inhabiting it) as I have ever read.[29]

At the suggestion of Sutton herself, I would like to propose that the aesthetic she performs so adeptly is transparency. Sutton described Byrdwoman's presence in *Sigmund Freud* by first noting the importance of people ceasing to notice her presence on the stage: "I was a really kind of silent person in those days and I could occupy myself very easily. I used to go for days without speaking so an hour was nothing to me. People used to tell me that after a while they'd forget about the fact that I wasn't moving and the whole idea of whether I was a statue or a person." Having established that an important part of the role is that someone might forget she is there, she next turns from being forgotten to being seen through, rather than seen: "Her peaceful presence is also related in some way to the setting—in fact you can see the ocean through her. You can look at her the same way you would look at the sea. You can watch for a long time and just have your thoughts."[30] We sense Byrdwoman's surface only insofar as it, like glass or water, reveals something else. Sutton's gestus of invisibility is supported by at least three specific and interrelated techniques: stillness, gliding, and inexpression. Because Harvey Young has already written a thorough account of black stillness, I will instead touch upon gliding and inexpression, again relying upon Sutton's self-description and the descriptions of critics who observed her performances.[31]

Sutton described the working process around the development of Wilson's 1969's *King of Spain* by saying, "It was like a laboratory. [. . .] And each of us had a forte, something we did especially well, and he would incorporate it into the play. My shtick was floating."[32] This sense of floating or gliding is recurrent from her first collaboration with Wilson to her last; the *New York Times* reviewer Zachary Woolfe described Sutton in 2013's *Zinnias* as "gliding darkly on the edges of scenes." Gliding depends upon a sense of continuous motion, floating or not touching the floor, or needing no support. Both descriptors convey movement without friction, an effect achieved in part through extreme or exacting slowness. Sometimes that slowness travels; at other times it is channeled into a discrete action such as pouring water or peeling an onion, as in *KA MOUNTAIN* (1972). Here is Shyer, again: "Both of these scenes [slowly pouring water, slowly peeling an onion] attest not only to Sutton's concentration and control but to her curious ability to be strongly present and absent at the same time. The body is absolutely still except for the action being performed (and an occasional tear running down her cheek from the onion), which is accomplished with the smallest expenditure of energy. As in the Zen arts she becomes the action she is performing; it is as though the water were flowing of its own power and the onion using her to peel itself."[33]

Shyer's description of Sutton as "strongly present and absent at the same time" resonates with the simultaneous invisibility and hypervisibility theorized in black feminist scholarship. It is also consonant with examples from black cultural history, such as Chester Himes's short story "Headwaiter."[34] In that story, Dick, the headwaiter of an upscale hotel restaurant, floats through a dining room, managing everything and attaching to nothing, expending tremendous affective labor (some of it kind and some of it not), every small detail of service modulated just so, in control of everything except his inner life. Dick's example reveals that gliding as a mode of transparency is not limited to women; at the same time, Dick's role also highlights the physical grace and expressive deference required of those in service, both feminized qualities. Sutton's ability to remain expressionless enhances the impression of gliding: Robert Brustein describes Sutton as moving in *Deafman* with "the deliberateness of an anaesthetized zombie," linking her expression and her movement quality.[35] While zombies aren't paradigms

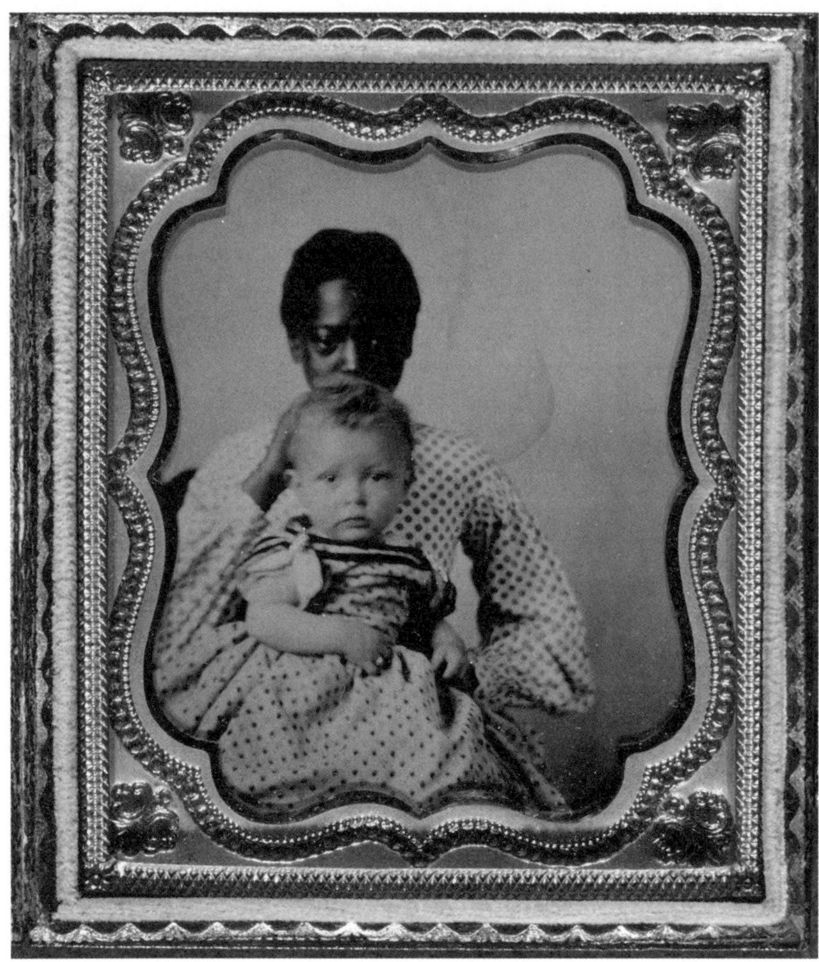

Figure 3.3. African American Woman Holding a White Child, Arkansas, circa 1855. Ruby ambrotype, sixth-plate, hand-colored, 9.0 × 8.1 cm (case) (3.5 × 3.2 in.). Library of Congress Prints and Photographs Division, Washington, DC.

of grace, one wonders at the redundancy of Brustein anaesthetizing the already undead. Is it perhaps a softening and smoothing of their physical manner?

Brustein also asserts that "the total lack of affect in these transactions curiously underlines the mysterious link between nurture and aggression, love and hate, in the lives of some families."[36] A constant thread of the theatrical criticism surrounding Wilson's work is the haunting figure of his mother, whom he describes thus: "My mother was a beautiful, intelligent, cold, and distant woman. . . . She sat beautifully in chairs . . . there was no personal communication. We could sit in a room together for hours and not talk."[37] On one level, the beautiful, aloof, chair-bound Byrdwoman of *Sigmund Freud* seems to reference this fierce and lovely mother. Yet on another, against this cold and elegant woman—someone to be looked at and not touched—Sutton's nineteenth-century costuming surrogates the black nanny who is invisible *but* for touch (fig. 3.3). Consider figure 3.1 alongside figure 3.3—eliding, for a moment, the hauntingly exaggerated mammy of figure 3.2. One could replace Sutton's stuffed raven with a white infant and the folds of time would collapse around Wilson's archetypal angel.[38] Like the invisible maid, the invisible porter, the invisible nanny, the black best friend, the magical negro who chauffeurs any proximate whiteness into new self-actualization, Sutton performs a labor that absents itself in consideration of the objects which spring to life in her stead: the peeled onion, the poured water, the invisible ocean, the gleaming knife, the black raven, the white child.

SHEERNESS

Sheerness is still relatively light in weight or translucency; one can think of scrims, veils, mesh, and so forth. The sheer object can be shaped, draped, worn, or projected onto. Given such versatility, it is not surprising that sheerness is another aesthetic that spans across racial bodies, but also holds distinct significance when linked to blackness. In fact, although I had long been acquainted with Martin Puryear's airy but rigid mesh sculptures, I first recognized sheerness as a black aesthetic looking not at the work of a black artist, but rather at the textile sculptures of Paraguayan artist Claudia Casarino.[39] Ironically, it was the feeling of deep familiarity with Casarino's aesthetics—a sense of kinship—that made me realize I had internalized sheerness as a mode of black femininity.

The first work of Casarino's I encountered, *Puente Kyha* (*Hanging Bridge*) (fig. 3.4), consists of four enormous double-ended dresses, hung from the ceiling and crossed over one another such that smooth, unbroken expanses of dark, translucent cloth connect loose bodices at either end. The work is awe inspiring and placid, but unlike many monumental sculptures its haptics are soft and billowy. The installation speaks to a sense of connection over distance through the long, graceful lines of the dresses' folds. Though there are no bodies present,

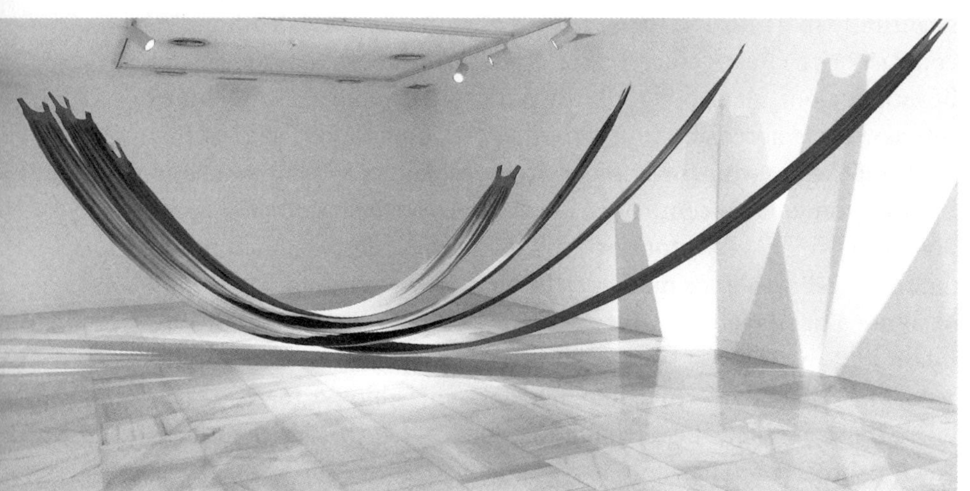

Figure 3.4. Claudia Casarino, *Puente Kyha* (*Hanging Bridge*), 2013. Dresses made of ao po'i (traditional Paraguayan fine cotton fabric). Variable dimensions. Courtesy of the artist.

the sense is not exactly one of absence or invisibility, as the feminine embodiment they reference is all-pervading. Yet if they evoke a sense of femininity, they also resonate with certain modes of black femininity: structured yet pliant, supporting and suspended, present yet unaggressive. *Apyte Ao* (*Corona de tela* [*Cloth Crown*]), figure 3.5, is similar in that oversized dresses (though here oversized only in length) hang in a circle. Of a natural white rather than black cotton, the dresses face into the circle toward one another as if in unbroken community—the impression of facing into one another is subtly achieved through necklines and the lengths of the dresses layering with one another in their continuous circle. Something of the ritual pervades their even spacing, and something of the familial or communal in their braided, unidirectional lengths. I am reminded of *Daughters of the Dust*, Julie Dash's lyrical, associative film about a Gullah family's decision to leave or remain on the island of their forebears, narrated by an as-yet-unborn girl child.[40] The family splits physically, but the grandmother attempts to bind them by sewing packets that contain generations of women's hair. Sheerness runs through the film, which abounds in its nets and curtains and white linen and cotton lace dresses, Spanish moss and parasols and paper pages lifted in the wind.

Casarino names her own intellectual concerns as the political issues of "gender, migration, otherness and identity," later restated as violence, departures, history, and bodies.[41] These issues—a number of which intersect with concerns of the economic underclasses of America—manifest for Casarino in the cotton dresses, which reference the specificity of Paraguayan textile arts. The materiality of cotton also connects to a broader network of cotton-driven economies, as well as extractive colonialism writ large. In the words of Gabriela Salgado, curator at the Atlantic Center of Modern Art (CAAM) in Gran Canaria (Spain), who showed Carasino's works in the exhibit *Illuminating the Absence*, "Cultivated since ancient times by the Guaraní people, cotton

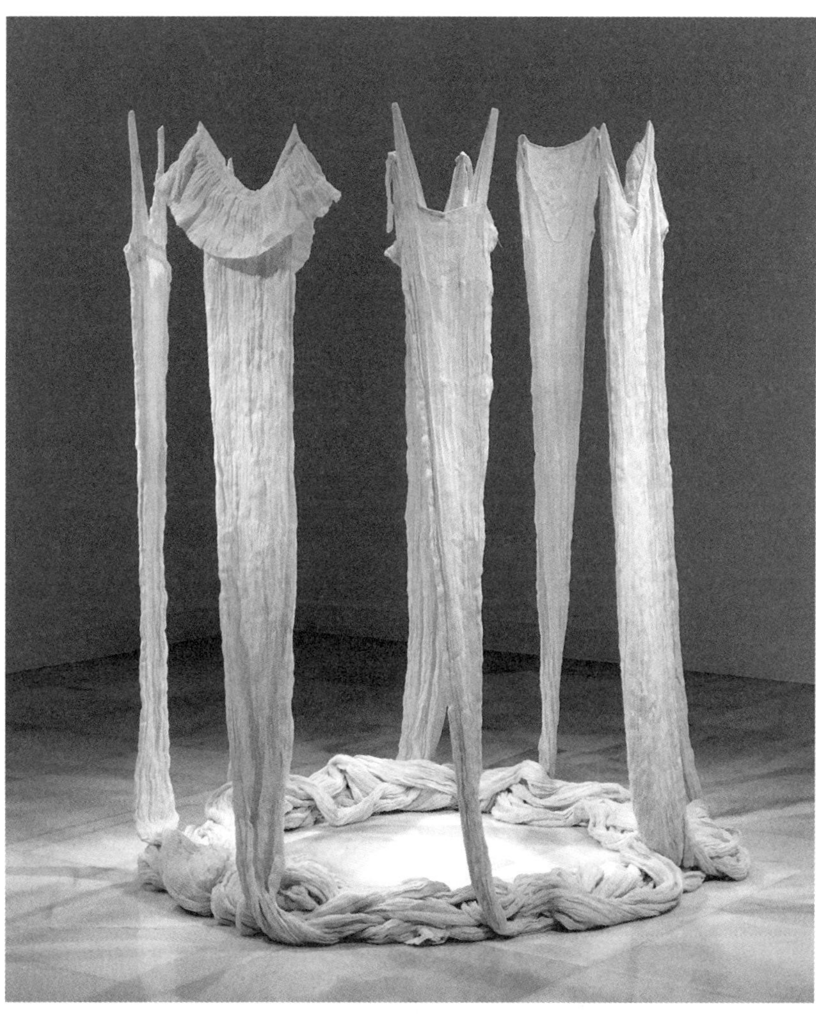

Figure 3.5. Claudia Casarino, *Apyte Ao* (*Corona de tela*), 2011. Raw cotton canvas, variable dimensions. Courtesy of the artist.

was the material that stimulated European penetration in Paraguay. This indissociable link between raw material and colonialism seems fundamental to me, since it introduces global historical narratives that position the practices of artists from Africa, Asia, Oceania and the Caribbean in dialogue with one another, as those for whom the profusion of one or several raw materials caused a rift: the establishment of a before and after the arrival of the colonial empires."[42] According to CAAM's website, Achille Mbembe's *Critique of Black Reason* provided the theoretical underpinnings of the show. "In this essay," the website reads, "the author defines resistance to the influence of 'necropolitics' as the struggle of human bodies to make themselves visible when faced with the absence and silence imposed by power, 'because power today works by producing absence: invisibility, silence, oblivion,' says Mbembe."[43]

But if I am not the only one to find in Casarino's work an aesthetic familiar from blackness, neither would I need to rely on her work to argue this point. Take, for example, the work of Canadian artist Alanna Lynch. Lynch creates performance and installation artworks that consider themes of identity, disgust, contagion, and care through a variety of media, including insects, body fluids and hair, bacterial growth, and smells. Often smell is a primary vehicle. As summarized on one gallery page, "Lynch is drawn to smells for their ability to resist containment and cross boundaries, using them to engage in theoretical discussions about power, identity and the movement of bodies. Though it is well known that smells can evoke strong emotions associated with personal memories, the artist demonstrates that their potency is also evidence of their ability to dominate space and influence human thoughts and behaviour."[44] Her exhibition names—*Vulnerable and Resistant* (2018), *Emotional Labor* (2018), *Gut Feelings* (2017), *Concealed and Contained* (ongoing since 2009)—evidence both the feminist ethics and the play with visibility and withholding with which this book is concerned.[45]

Most relevant here is Lynch's work with bacterial cellulose, also known as bioplastic or SCOBY (symbiotic culture of bacteria and yeast). While several bacterial strains can produce cellulose, Lynch uses one created as a byproduct of kombucha fermentation (fig. 3.6). According to Lynch's own published description of her performance, she reaches into a glass vat full of liquid (kombucha) and the skin-like substance of the cellulose. Her action causes the liquid to spill over, making pools and releasing intense smells. Though her conceptual

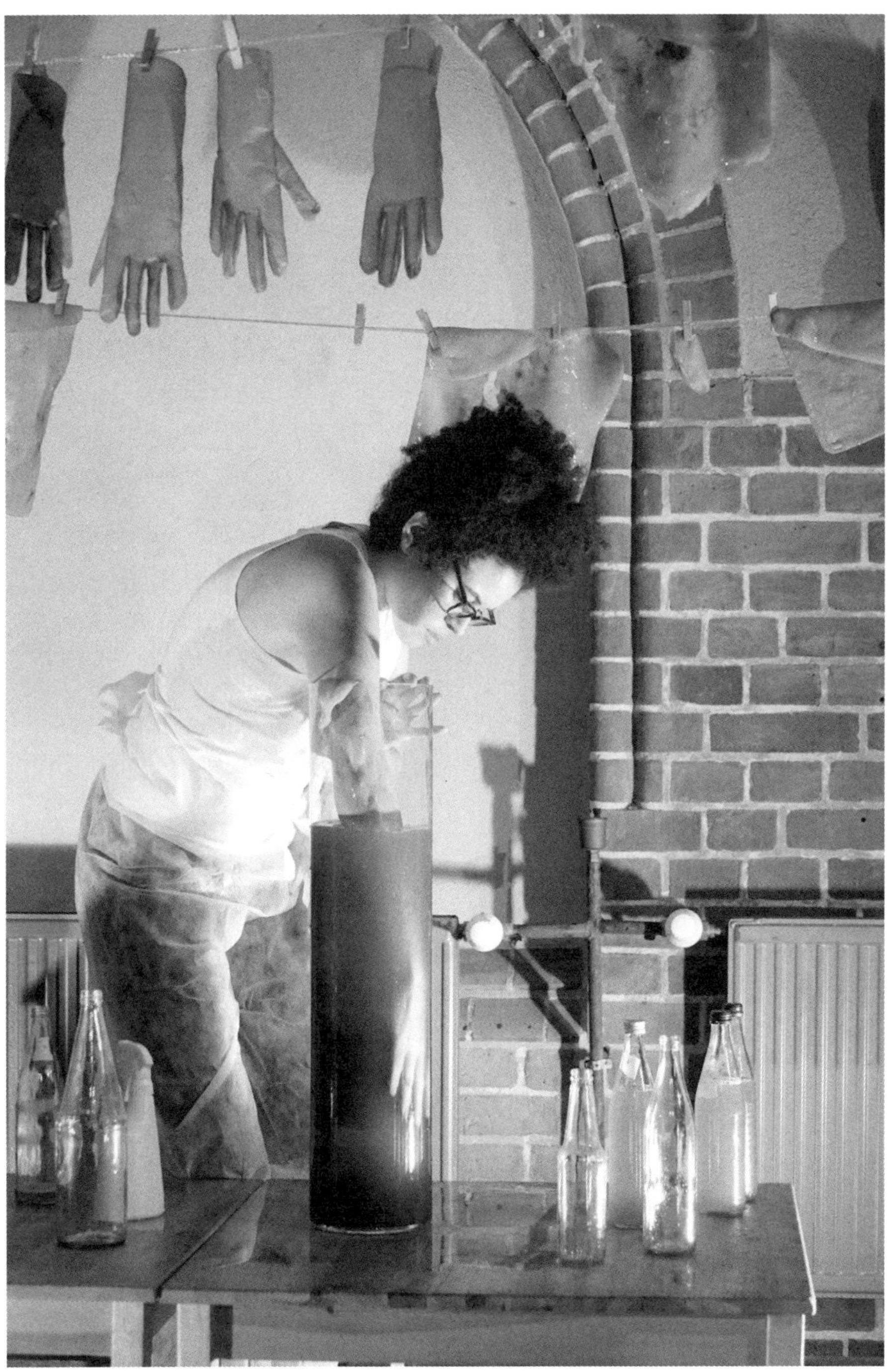

Figure 3.6. Alanna Lynch, *Gut Feelings*. Performance at Goldrausch 2016, St. Johannes-Evangelist, Berlin, Germany. Photo by Matthias Reichelt.

writing focuses on the smells—how they permeate, what they code, who they render loved or reviled—her actions concentrate on the skins. She pulls them from the container, full of the liquid they have been swimming in. The "slabs of matter," as she describes them, are "slimy, stinky, both thick and thin with trailing brown stringy yeasts."[46] She unfolds and stretches the skins, then hangs them to dry. They continue to drip, to stink and pool.

Like the smells they evoke, the skins are affectable and reminiscent of the body, an association only strengthened through their warm, brown tone. They are translucent—sheer—permeable to light. They look fragile, an impression seconded by their variable thicknesses. Lynch demonstrates their malleability, unfolding them in order to hang them up. She also fashions gloves from these sheets (fig. 3.7). A partial description from Vancouver's Access Gallery is as follows:

> The work features sculptural objects such as gloves made from dehydrated kombucha SCOBYs—a bacterial cellulose "fabric." The gloves, which are typically meant to protect a human wearer from a contaminating agent or material, are themselves composed of the contaminating material—in this way, they come to symbolize a cross-species, "contamination as collaboration" ethos of feminist fermentation. The co-mingling of contamination and protection reflects the blurred lines of mind and body, gut and bacteria, self and other, human and non-human, of the microbiome and its intermeshing of borders and bounds. Lynch is energized by the idea, now echoed in science discourse, that "symbiosis is not mutually beneficial" (notably: in biology, the term "symbiosis" has recently been redefined to reflect the often disproportionate dynamics in symbiotic relationships).[47]

Though the Access Gallery description refers to the substance forming the gloves as fabric, in truth—as Lynch's description highlights—a closer analog might be leather. Indeed, bacterial cellulose has spawned interest in the fashion industry, where, so far, it seems largely to approximate leather—fundamentally, skin—though now it is leather with translucency. Indeed, the fleshy qualities of bacterial cellulose are remarkable: it can be fashioned into bioactive cartilage implants for ear and nose reconstruction; it has been prototyped to replace blood vessels; and it is used for dressing wounds and burns.[48] In short, Alanna Lynch's work plays with an eerie approximation of fleshiness.

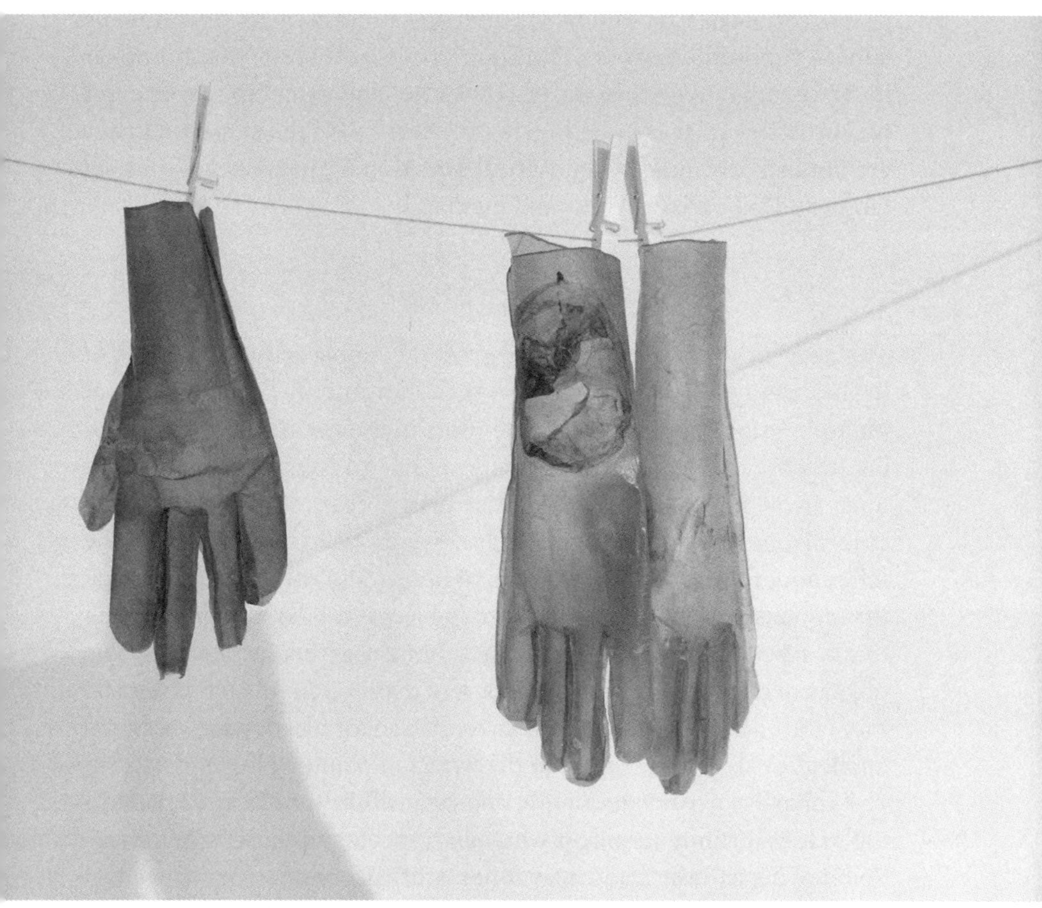

Figure 3.7. Alanna Lynch, *Gut Feelings*, 2019. Detail of installation at Access Gallery. Photo by Rachel Topham.

This sheer skin fascinates me as an aesthetic gesture for its ability to stand mimetically for the raced body. This skin seems at once representative of the raced subject, and an instantiation (which is to say, to externalization) of her labor. Bacterial cellulose is wet, loose, and smelly—at once alarmingly durable and disgustingly fragile. The vulnerabilities of feminine embodiment are displayed as the laundry line of sheets and hands, which evoke the histories of laundress labor and piecework, of hanging flesh, or both. In Lynch's work, the abject and tender intermingle. To interact with the bacterial cellulose skin is to acknowledge associations with smell and disease *and* to dramatize care and use—without requiring that the black body itself should appear.

Instead of the black body, we are left with sheerness. Sheerness is able to communicate both continuity (in that there is something coherent enough to be thought of as a whole) and vulnerability. The mutual presence of these qualities—and, moreover, the sense that they are importantly linked—is a critical assertion of translucency, linking fabric and skin across works and media.

OBSCURITY

The next location on the opacity gradient is obscurity. At the risk of belaboring the etymological, the verb "to obscure," while likely of multiple origins, has at least some roots in the Latin *obscūrāre*, meaning "to obscure, darken, to overshadow, dim, to conceal, hide, to make unclear or unintelligible, to render insignificant."[49] To obscure an object is generally not to completely cover it; when clouds obscure the full moon, for example, some halo of brightness will let us know that the moon is present. But an obscured object is rendered more difficult to see, its edges not only less distinct, but altogether less certain. The objects of obscurity invest in this lack of distinction. In fact, obscurity may court a sense of contagion, interrelation, or bleed, whether literal or allegorical. One sees both in the works of painter Titus Kaphar.

Kaphar's artworks frequently engage visibility and erasure, providing material ruminations on who can be seen and under what terms. Some of his paintings add a layer of historical commentary as well, altering surface or materiality to shift who or what is revealed. For example, *Behind the Myth of Benevolence* (2014) consists of two layered canvases. The topmost indexes the iconic Rembrandt Peale portrait of Thomas Jefferson. As the portrait is described by the White House Historical Association, "The face has the glow of health, a warm complexion. The sitter here looks directly at us and does so with candor, as our equal. The splendid eyes and mouth convey reason and tolerance."[50] In Kaphar's work, this canvas is unfastened from its frame except for its upper right-hand corner; now draped and pleated, the canvas nevertheless reveals the recognizable warm brown background, black suit and white ruff, white hairline, high pink cheekbone, and eye of Peale's painting. But we also see another canvas behind this one, which pictures a young black woman.

The woman in Kaphar's painting is partially obscured by the Jefferson canvas, but one can see enough of her shoulder, arm, and thigh, to know that she is nude or scantily clad. She wears a headwrap with a band of gold, which highlights serving vessels to her right, and a lighter spot of Jefferson's canvas background on her left. The fold of the canvas closest to her mimics the shade of her skin, emphasizing their connection and her role as background. The young woman's expression is hard to name. It is perhaps a little sad, perhaps a little defensive, perhaps somewhat indicting, certainly somewhat closed. Referencing Sally Hemings without picturing her directly (Hemings was light skinned; this woman is not), Kaphar's layered canvases pull back the curtain on the figure of Jefferson, as described by the White House Historical Association (and in countless other histories), revealing the slave labor that supported his ventures and the sexual precarity and exploitation that was so fully part of the chattel slave system.[51]

Whereas *Behind the Myth of Benevolence* exposes the traditionally hidden, others of Kaphar's works highlight registers of opacity that I would like to call obscurity. Like sheerness, obscurity offers partial revelation. But while sheerness highlights materiality, often as a substitute for the otherwise surveilled black body, Kaphar's obscurities present the black body in a manner that makes full surveillance impossible. Two very different works provide examples of this technique.

Mother with Child (fig. 3.8) is one of a number of paintings in which Kaphar renders black subjects partially visible. The painting features a woman in a blue, full-skirted, floor-length nineteenth-century dress, holding a child of perhaps six to eight months. The baby wears a short-sleeved, full-length white gown that, due to its fullness and the suggestion of a matching headpiece, seems more reminiscent of a christening or other special occasion than sleepwear. The child is dark-skinned and the mother, somewhat lighter, bears the suggestion of blackness (or, at a minimum, is darkened through her relation to the child). The nose above her full lips matches the baby's. In the voluminous fabric on their persons and in the suggestion of a parlor room behind them—and, more subtly or insidiously, in the lightness of the woman and the suggestion in the baby's skin tone that the father is darker yet—one senses the upward class striving of free blacks. One can see just enough of the mother's face to recognize the inexpression common in portrait photography, but not much more. Both the mother and child exist in a visual limbo: they are covered by a white wash of paint *and* re-outlined in black. The white paint that obscures them is differentially applied and in motion; while a more uniform wash of erasure renders their

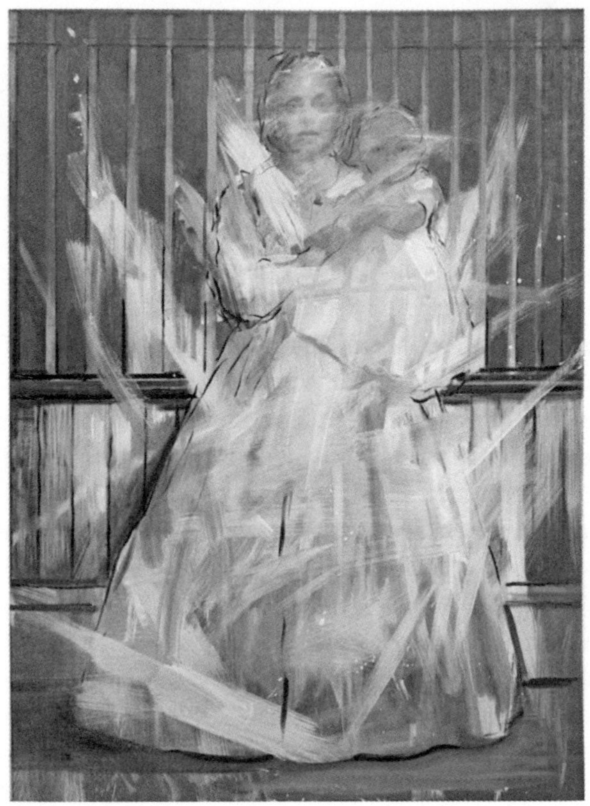

Figure 3.8. Titus Kaphar, *Mother with Child*, 2014. Oil on canvas, 60 × 48 in. © Titus Kaphar. Courtesy of the artist.

features faint, more concentrated strokes of white suggest wings, or an absent hand on a shoulder. If they are becoming shade, it is not, it seems, an inert dissolution.

Kaphar has produced several paintings in this vein, and some of these works have titles that invite the viewer to consider how some subjects risk fading into historical obscurity. I choose *Mother with Child* over others in part because of the consonance between this image and the floating black femininity of Sutton's Byrdwoman, but also to point to the fact that *Mother with Child* doesn't narrativize its rhetorical work in the same manner as *A Fight for Remembrance*, which features a black Civil War Soldier, or *Another Fight for Remembrance*, which shows black protesters in "Hands Up, Don't Shoot" poses. *Mother with Child* instead evokes a lineage of Christian iconography, supported by the mother's blue dress—blue is the traditional iconographic color of Mary's robes. Therefore, the obscurity referenced by *Mother with Child* occurs on two different levels. First, it highlights the inherent obscurity of black women and children, who rarely enter historical narratives in the first place (let alone fight to remain there). Second, Kaphar's delicate art historical references suggest, without picturing, the mother and child's inevitable iconographic companion piece: the *Pietà*. In evoking without showing the child's fated martyrdom, Kaphar's piece resonates with Claudia Rankine's short essay for the *New York Times*, "The Condition of Black Life is Mourning."[52] In that essay, Rankine renders the constant worry and preemptive mourning that is mothering black children, but she also offers a sustained consideration of the merits and degradation of pictured violence. With this context in mind, the white paint of forgetfulness that touches, too, the room in which the mother and child stand, begins to call forth the bars of a cell in its tracing of the boards in the room's upper portion.

If *Mother with Child* enacts obscurity by highlighting the historical erasure of its figures and literally obscuring their visibility under a layer of white, Kaphar's *Jerome Project* enacts obscurity of a different sort. As described in materials produced by the Jack Shainman Gallery,

> While researching his father's prison records, Kaphar came across a startling number of men who shared his father's full name. Intrigued by the pattern, Kaphar began a series of small portraits of these men based on their mug shots. He then dipped each painting into tar up to at least their mouths, obscuring parts of their faces and affording them the privacy they had lost when their mug shots became part of the public record. In Asphalt and Chalk, Kaphar continues The Jerome Project by drawing composite portraits of multiple Jeromes with chalk on asphalt paper. As he layers the contours and features of each face, one becomes disoriented as each individual begins to bleed into the next. Viewed as groups, both explorations of this series represent a community, specifically of African-American men who are statistically overrepresented in our nation's prison population and the criminal justice system.[53]

The Shainman Gallery emphasizes the theme of privacy in Kaphar's *Jerome Project*, describing first a project in which mugshots were rendered and then obscured through tar. While the faces of mugshots in themselves perform deadpan, Kaphar exacerbates their obscurity in *Asphalt and Chalk*.

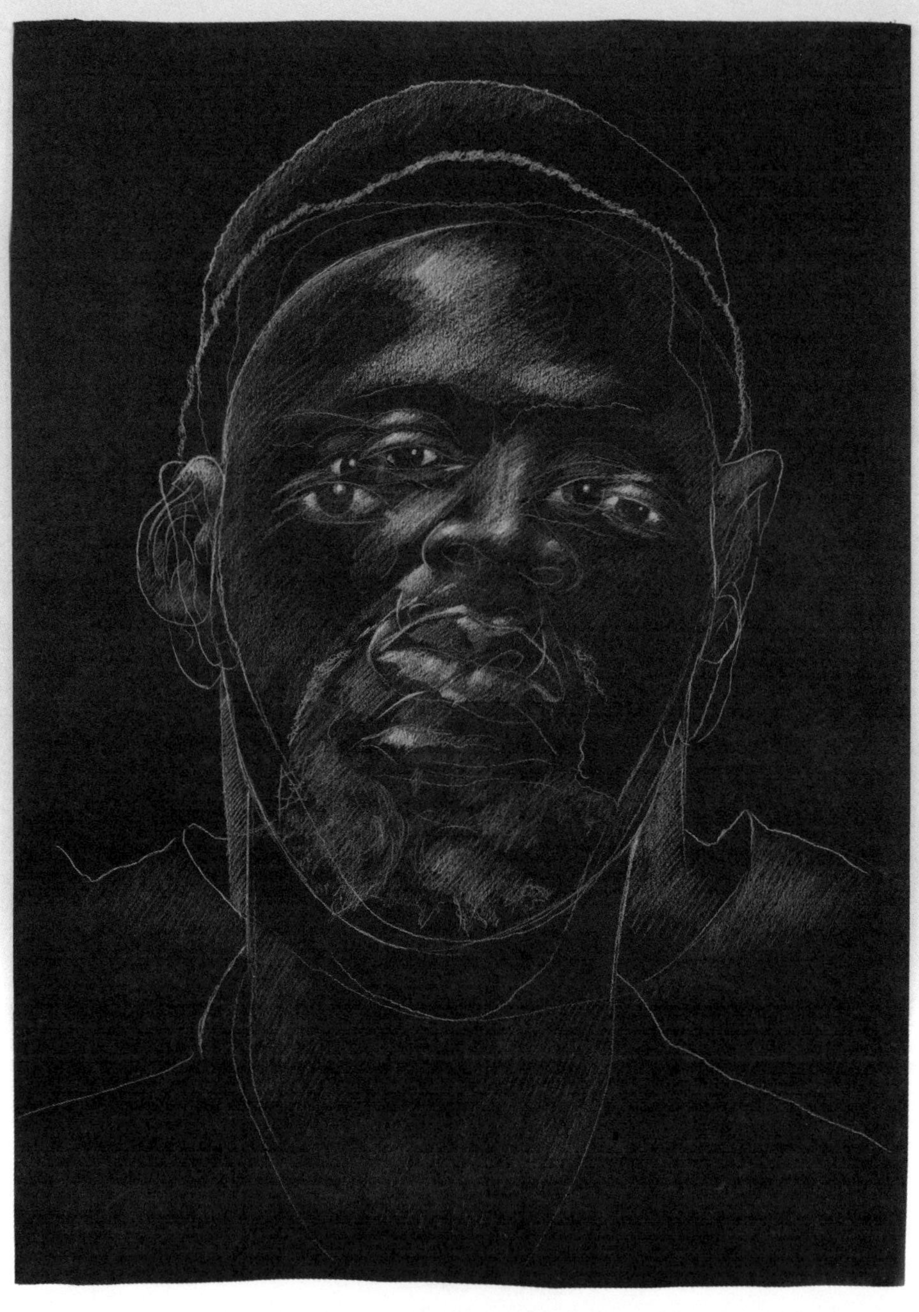

Figure 3.9. Titus Kaphar, *The Jerome Project* (*Asphalt and Chalk*) *III*, 2014. Graphite on asphalt paper, 49 × 35½ in. (drawing), 54 3/8 × 40 7/8 × 2 1/8 in. (framed). Courtesy of the artist. © Titus Kaphar.

Asphalt and Chalk III, for example, layers white-on-black drawings of at least two (and possibly three) male faces (fig. 3.9). Stacked on top of one another as if drawn on the cellulose acetate sheets of overhead transparencies, it is clear that the men perform relative inexpression. One head seems cocked at an angle that might perform an aloof defensiveness. Even this affect is hard to name with any certainty, however, due to the blurring of features. There are at least two chins and sets of shoulders, but one eye appears tripled, and the top of the head is a confusion of crowns and hairlines. A composite face refuses to cohere, even though the stacking places the iterative faces close enough to try—that is, there is an area of lips, and area of noses, and area of left eye and another of right eye. But if a composite face is impossible to locate, neither can one pull out individual faces from their stacked transparency. The men are at once are amalgamated individuals and a deindividuated community. Obscurity renders the black figure as liminal, present but impossible to fully discern.[54]

AWAYNESS

I borrow the term "awayness" from Erving Goffman's *Behavior in Public Places*, a text I find gloriously odd both in its idiosyncratic mounting of evidence and its disarmingly avuncular tone ("Some data have been drawn from a study of a mental hospital [hereafter called Central Hospital], some from a study of a Shetland Island community [hereafter called Shetland Isle], some from manuals of etiquette, and some from a file where I keep quotations that have struck me as interesting. Obviously, many of these data are of doubtful worth").[55] Goffman's approach is not without reason—he sets about to discern the often-implicit codes and practices of social interaction, which may be most obvious when explicitly outlined, accidentally broken, or context dependent.

The awayness Goffman describes in this context is essentially a psychological defense. He writes,

> Perhaps the most important kind of away is that through which the individual relives some past experience or rehearses some future ones, this taking the form of what is variously called reverie, brown study, woolgathering, daydreaming, or autistic thinking. At such times the individual may demonstrate his absence from the current situation by a

preoccupied, faraway look in his eyes, or by a sleeplike stillness of his limbs, or by that special class of side involvements that can be sustained in an utterly "unconscious" abstracted manner—humming, doodling, drumming the fingers on a table, hair twisting, nose picking, scratching. [. . .] In any case, reverie constitutes an eloquent sign of departure from all public concrete matters within the situation.[56]

"Awayness" here refers to a state in which the body is present but the mind is elsewhere, in whole or in part (unconscious, abstracted actions like doodling and hair twirling seem to me methods of being partially rather than wholly absented from proceedings). I would like to propose deadpanned awayness as an inverse instance of visibility and withholding, one in which the mind is present but the body is absented in whole or part. In this withholding of the body, awayness is closest to fugitivity as described in the work of Huey Copeland and others.[57]

My illustration for this aesthetic is the early work of Lorna Simpson, especially those works that pair text and image to convey and modulate presence and absence. I also choose Simpson for the affective tenor of her works, for in reading Goffman's description, I am predictably intrigued by the phrase "brown study." *The Oxford English Dictionary* teaches me that this phrase means "gloomy meditations"—though the glum association seems to be fading—and originated at a time (circa 1555) when brown was associated with gloom.[58] Therefore, while "daydreaming," "woolgathering," or "reverie" might be more or less appropriate in any given context, only "brown study" and "autistic thinking" carry connotations of psychological disorder. Thinking with brown study as racialized (and perhaps also pathologized) melancholy—akin to José Esteban Muñoz's "Feeling Brown" or Anne Anlin Cheng's racial melancholy—makes Simpson's works a logical choice.[59]

Especially in her earlier works, Simpson's images render the black body in segmentation, substitution, and fungibility, making awayness available to the physical body rather than the psyche—though at times she also maintains the sense of psychological abstention or gloomy pathology implied by the phrase "brown study." In *You're Fine* (fig. 3.10), a black woman lies horizontally in a white shift, before a white background, with her back to the viewer. Her body is sectioned over four square photographic panels, with only the soles of her feet

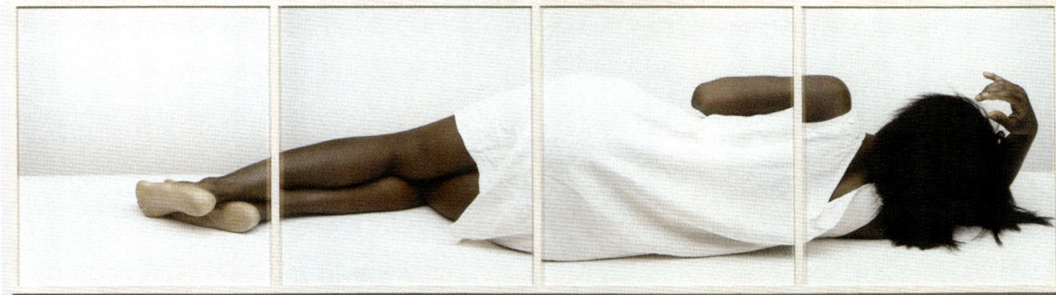

Figure 3.10. Lorna Simpson, *You're Fine*, 1988. Four Polaroid prints, fifteen engraved plastic plaques, twenty-one ceramic pieces (nineteen letters, two apostrophes), 40 × 103 in. overall. © Lorna Simpson. Courtesy of the artist and Hauser & Wirth.

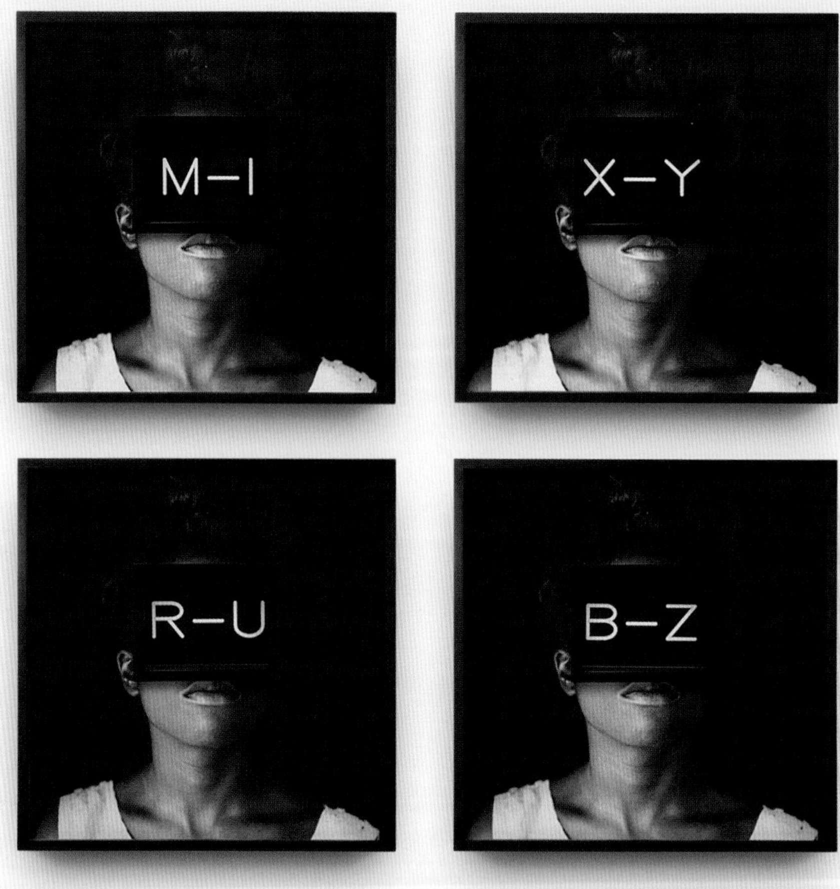

Figure 3.11. Lorna Simpson, *Proof Reading*, 1989. Four Polaroid prints, four engraved plastic plaques, 40 × 40 in. overall. © Lorna Simpson. Courtesy of the artist and Hauser & Wirth.

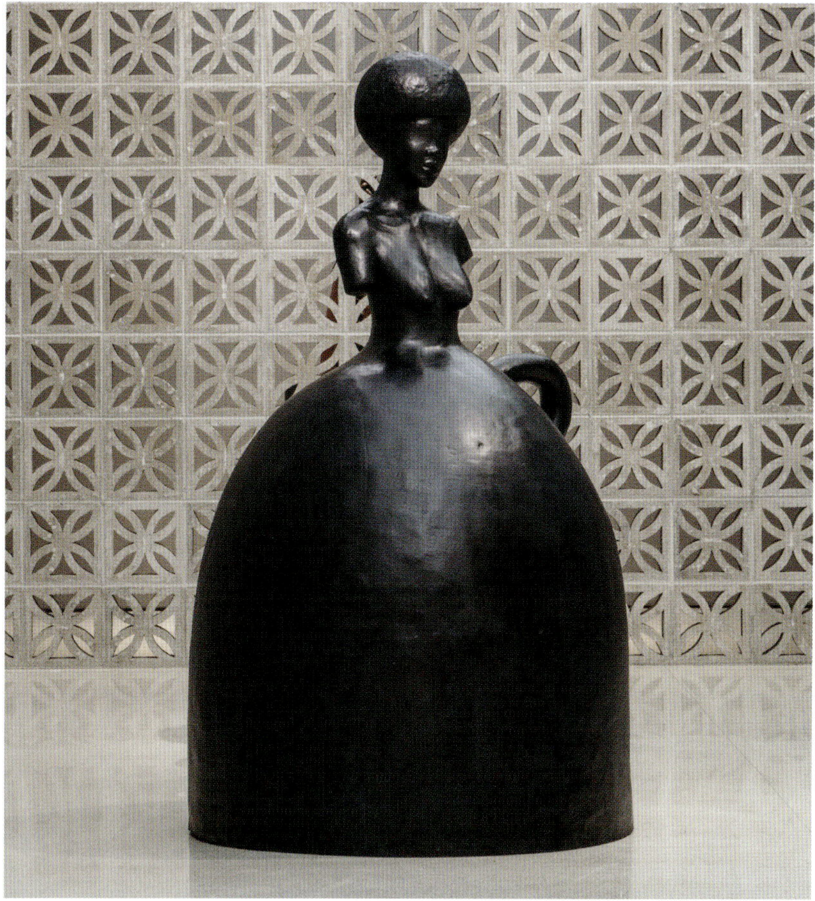

Figure 3.12. Simone Leigh, *Jug*, 2019. Bronze, from an edition of three and one artist proof, 83¼ × 51½ × 51½ in. © Simone Leigh. Courtesy of the artist.

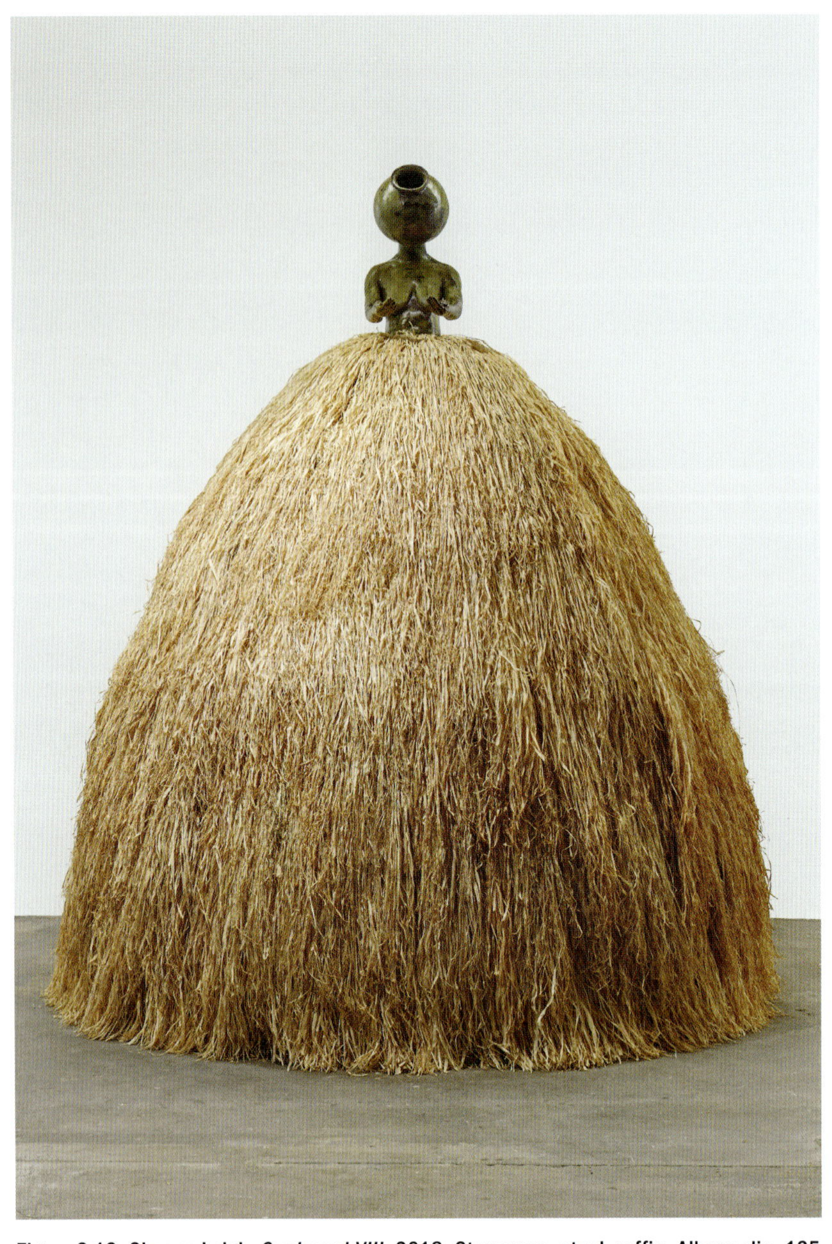

Figure 3.13. Simone Leigh, *Cupboard VIII*, 2018. Stoneware, steel, raffia, Albany slip. 125 × 120 × 120 in. © Simone Leigh. Courtesy of the artist.

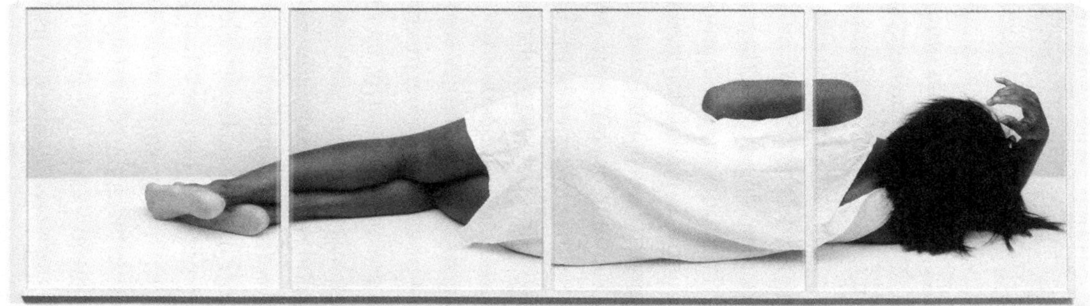

Figure 3.10. Lorna Simpson, *You're Fine*, 1988. Four Polaroid prints, fifteen engraved plastic plaques, twenty-one ceramic pieces (nineteen letters, two apostrophes), 40 × 103 in. overall. © Lorna Simpson. Courtesy of the artist and Hauser & Wirth.

in the leftmost, and only her shoulders and head, over which one hand is draped, in the rightmost. To the left of this image is a vertical stack of thirteen plaques headed "Physical Exam," which list the body parts and procedures that constitute such an exam (abdomen, urine, lung capacity, and so forth). To the right of the woman, another two plaques read "Secretarial Position." Above her are the words "You're Fine"; below her, the words "You're Hired." Because we read from left to right, the job can seem the outcome of the medical examination, implying incommensurate amounts of bodily examination, with "You're Fine, You're Hired" reading as the single outcome of one long process. Alternately, the words might be read as the outcome of two events by linking them diagonally in either direction. But is the outcome of the medical exam "You're Fine," or "You're Hired"? Is the outcome of the job interview "You're Hired," or "You're Fine"?

Suspended between the assessing eyes of the medical complex and the employer of secretarial labor, the woman performs both presence and awayness. Her body is available for examination, but also it is not—we could not identify her again, and we have no access to her emotional experience of our prying eyes. Nevertheless, and especially for black viewers whose experience of the medical industrial complex (and, in truth, of job interviews) might be especially bad, the list(s) carry a tinge of melancholy or pathology. Given this association, I would again emphasize my continuity with those thinkers, especially prevalent in queer-of-color critique, interested in the embrace of survival strategies that are not necessarily "good."[60] While one can readily read the woman's awayness as an anonymity foisted upon her undesired—and there is good reason to read the woman in that way—it is important to leave open the possibility that in the face of surveillance structures she cannot change, she herself elects to leave. To leave something of herself in her place, to be sure—but nevertheless to leave.

In *Proof Reading* (fig. 3.11), Simpson pictures awayness achieved through the fungibility of the black female subject. In this work, Simpson also presents four Polaroid panels, but this time the panels, which are stacked in a 2 × 2 square, show identical portraits of the head and shoulders of a young black woman. She stands in a white shift before a black background, but once again, she is away; here each iteration of her face is covered by a black panel containing a seemingly random pairings or ranges of letters (M–I, X–Y, R–U, B–Z). All we see of her head is her hair, one ear, her lips, and her chin; no facial expression

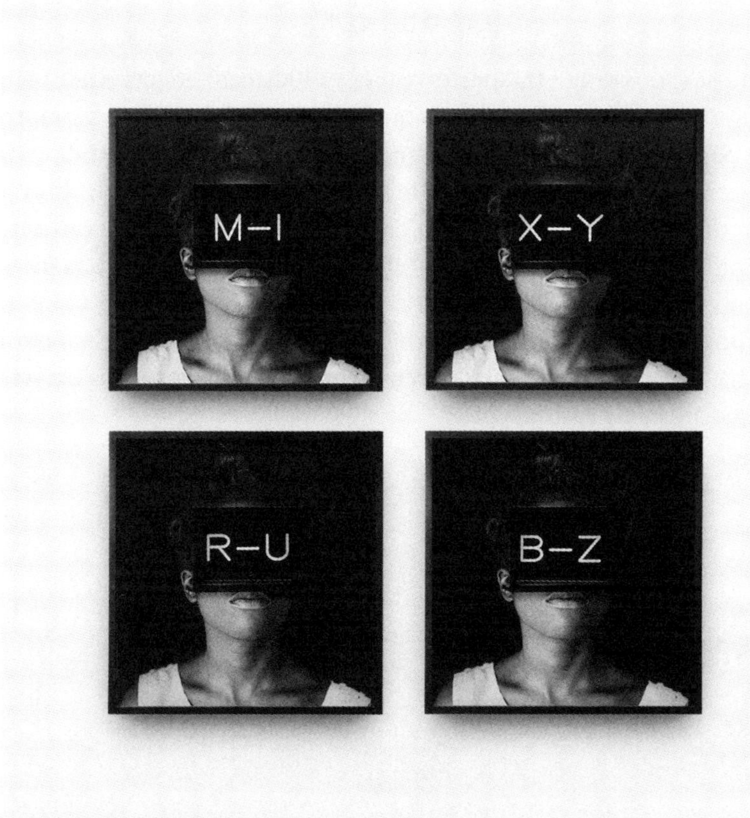

Figure 3.11. Lorna Simpson, *Proof Reading*, 1989. Four Polaroid prints, four engraved plastic plaques, 40 × 40 in. overall. © Lorna Simpson. Courtesy of the artist and Hauser & Wirth.

is discernible. Eyes might be open or closed, beautiful or misshapen. Each woman becomes nothing but the range of letters that stand in her place, identical but not quite. While the title references reading, words and their meanings are, for many observers, subsumed into the dashes of the letter pairings, where they remain indiscernible. The cryptographer, however, finds a coded message ("Am I sexy? Are you busy?")—an ironic invitation, given that the obscuring placards scupper the viewer's ability to judge the sexiness or reciprocal attention of the presumed invitation-issuer. Said differently, there is no reliable way to read for the proof suggested in the work's title. In the end, Simpson's *Proof Reading* (like *You're Fine*) reveals a mind that is present and a body that is away. And, like *You're Fine*, parsing here the comingling of anonymity, indiscernibility, and desire is no easy task.

OPACOUSNESS

The most saturated of the performances I'll discuss enacts what I am calling opacousness—an unspectacular opacity that allows one to seem part of the background or landscape, especially as a product of skin and/or shape. This blending in may or may not have been chosen, but in the ability to marshal it to ends, the opacous subject exhibits the unified duality of gestalt switch. Though they are too beautiful for truly unspectacular mundanity, my principle example lies in two monumental sculptures by Simone Leigh, *Jug* (fig. 3.12) and *Cupboard VIII* (fig. 3.13), both of which reference the female form and/as objects of domestic labor and succor.

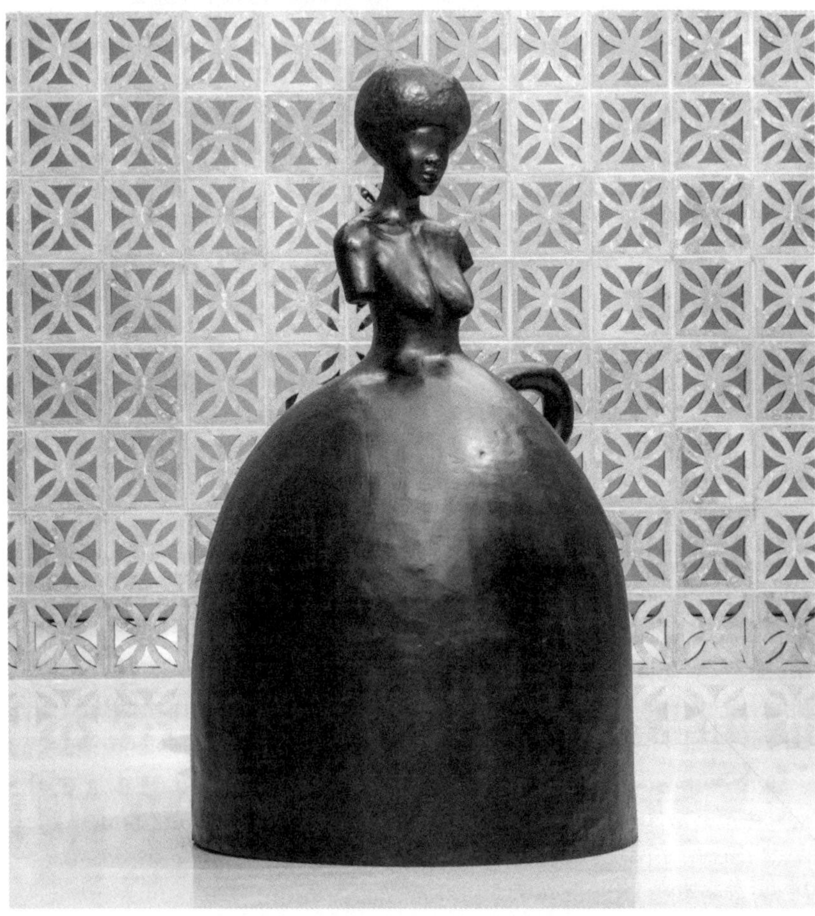

Figure 3.12. Simone Leigh, *Jug*, 2019. Bronze, from an edition of three and one artist proof, 83¼ × 51½ × 51½ in. © Simone Leigh. Courtesy of the artist.

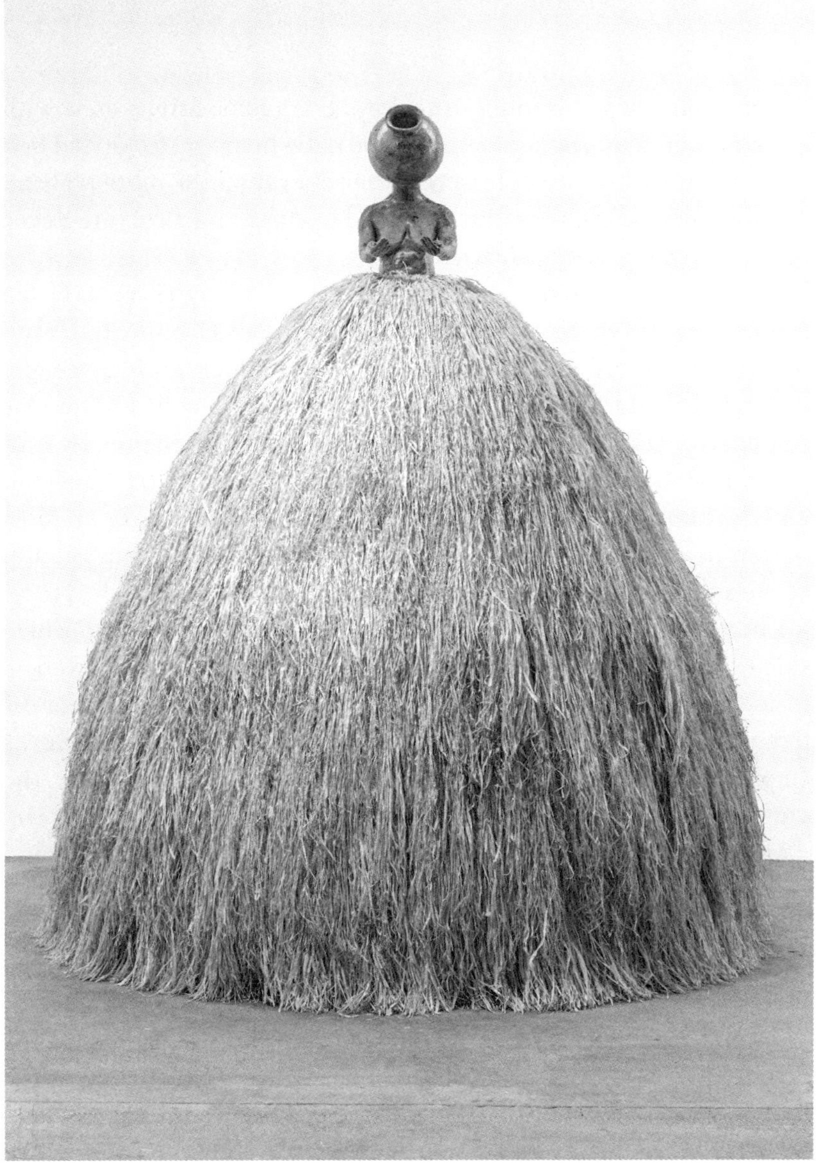

Figure 3.13. Simone Leigh, *Cupboard VIII*, 2018. Stoneware, steel, raffia, Albany slip. 125 × 120 × 120 in. © Simone Leigh. Courtesy of the artist.

Standing at just over eighty-three inches tall, the bronze statue *Jug* has a lower half that takes the smoothly rounded shape of a stoneware beehive whiskey jug, complete with finger handle. Rather than an opening, however, the mouth of the jug transforms into the waist of a woman, whose head and nude, armless torso complete the container. This also gives the jug the association of an enormous skirt. The stately upper half of the sculpture is more archetypal than realistic; besides the unavoidable associations of sculptural feminine armlessness with the Venus de Milo (not quite mimicked), the figure's Afro-styled hair is rendered with a hint of texture rather than anything more realistic, and the figure's face is eyeless. Its facial features and structure nevertheless convey a sense of black heritage.

The base of *Cupboard VIII* is also bell-shaped, though here, as Helen Molesworth points out, the associations are more architectural, ranging from the more general Musgum huts of Cameroon to a specific decorated shed restaurant in Natchez, Mississippi, called Mammy's Cupboard.[61] The sense of the architectural is supported, too, by *Cupboard VIII*'s size and textures: the sculpture is more than ten feet tall and the figure's skirt, made of tiered layers of raffia, makes up most of that height. Again a bare-breasted female figure crowns the top of the sculpture; however, in this case, the head becomes the vessel. Slightly more rotund than *Jug*, the vessel once again evinces a beehive shape that can be seen, for example, in the works of the enslaved artisan David Drake (also known as Dave the Potter). One further difference lies in the arms, now present and extended. In the Mammy's Cupboard building, the mammy figure holds a serving tray. Here, the empty arms, which are rendered in the warm brown of Albany slip glaze, extend toward the viewer in an enigmatic gesture that could be reaching for love or mercy but for the overall sense of contained placidity. Helen Molesworth sees in Leigh's oeuvre an actualization of the ideal "holding space"; in this case that holding seems to me literal.[62]

I hope my reader already recognizes that this, the densest of the opacity gradient's performances, abuts the least threatening of the looming opacities detailed in the previous chapter. To my mind Leigh's sculptures are deeply consonant with Martin Puryear's and, while I won't here reengage Puryear's corpus of work, he has produced a number of sculptural forms, in wire or wood lattice, that are far *less* opaque than Leigh's looming sculptures. Nevertheless, I included Puryear in my discussion of black threat in order to emphasize blackness's right and ability to call others into relation through formal assertion. If these assertions invoke the aesthetic of looming, then looming can be beautiful—which is to say that black male subjectivity can be beautiful. Leigh's monumental works also loom, though I suspect that for many (though certainly not all) viewers, an identifiably female form lessens the sense of threat.

Molesworth calls Leigh's figures "silent," a curious appellation, given that most sculptures are silent, and the mouth (whether of woman or jug) is never the feature lacking. Still, I understand what she means; just as in Kevin Quashie's work, quietude comes to stand for the presence of interiority.

> The figures don't have eyes per se; instead the forms register the eyes as a depression, each eye about the size of the thumb that made it. The texture of these gentle depressions, the smoothness caused by a thumb rubbing their surfaces over and over again, makes them a ravishing combination of the iconic and the indexical. Their lack of eyes might seem to invite viewers to regard them in a classically colonializing matter: You can look and they cannot look back. But this is not the sensation I have when looking at them. I feel as if it is I who cannot "see" them. They do not, importantly, "refuse" my gaze (because that dynamic would still place me at the center of the event). Rather, their lack of eyes counterintuitively means that they are "unseeable," and hence unknowable, to me. They remain self-possessed, looking inward, contemplating and thinking things that I cannot fathom.[63]

For Molesworth, these gynomorphic figures are impenetrable containers, but not out of refusal. She *almost* locates a failure to see in herself ("It is I who cannot 'see' them"), but ultimately she describes a relation that approaches the opacity of Glissant, "the penetrable opacity of a world in which one exists, or agrees to exist, with and among others," one in which, "to feel in solidarity [. . .] it is not necessary for me to grasp."[64]

My own relation to Leigh's works is somewhat different from Molesworth's. I don't feel I cannot see them, or that their lack of eyes structures our relation. When I look upon these sculptures, I feel love and admiration and calm. I feel a sense of recognition: I do see my experience of black womanhood in these works, or, more truly, I *feel* myself in them. This is not, of course, to claim that I understand the full history and plight of the black female domestic laborer, to the extent that this labor history is evoked. Nor is my experience of black female subjectivity itself monumental. But these statues are not, to my mind, only or even primarily about domestic labor, nor about a singular sense of subjectivity. What I recognize is my own containment and containerliness, the sometimes relief of being unseen, the interiority that is always one's first and last recourse, the sizable nobility of these moments extrapolated over time and space as a way of being in the world, the simultaneous solidity and fragility of that work—the work of presence—and, indeed, that work as the source of refreshment made available to a family or a community or a single one in need. The sense of being simultaneously one's use value, and more. The sense of being overlooked rather than looked through, and, perhaps, of not minding that very much.

Lest my sense of recognition imply that opacousness is a distinctly female grammar, I restate my conviction is that gender is no more (or less) a fixed a category than race; I presume that an aesthetic of opacousness is available to anyone. Nevertheless, opacousness may be a *feminine* register even if it is not a *female* one—at least in our current American context, with its historically gendered modes of racial subjection. Said differently, opacousness might bear a special relationship to what Jasmine Elizabeth Johnson calls the "vocabularies of black misrecognition" as they apply to black female embodiment.[65] In the face of these misrecognitions, Johnson theorizes a body of gestures she names "hush acts."

"'Hush,'" she tells us, "dials down noise to make room for a feeling that clamor might distract from. Thus, hush is not complete silence but rather an invitation to receive a different register of vibration or feeling."[66] Aside from this fundamental description, two other qualities of hush are critically important. First, as Johnson describes (building on the work of Hortense Spillers), hush does not deny the embodied hieroglyphics of one's enfleshment. Second, while hush acts claim the space of a subject's interior, "that turning inward is about a practice of self-naming that includes herself yet also spills over the singular autobiographical subject."[67] Hush acts, in other words, constitute opacousness as a more encompassing space of relation than the insistently autonomous opacities of minimalism.[68] Finally, then, even the densest end of the opacity gradient may contain a scale of its own—a porousness within some performances refused inside of others.

4

EXCESS AND ABSENCE (OR, THE NEGRO BELIEVES ____)

Practical exercises demonstrate through color deception (illusion) the relativity and instability of color. And experience teaches us that in visual perception there is a discrepancy between physical fact and psychic effect.

—Josef Albers, *Interaction of Color*

When I tell fellow academics I work on forms of black expressionlessness, a remarkably common response goes something like, "Ah, yes! 'We Wear the Mask'"—a reference to Paul Laurence Dunbar's 1896 poem. This response, common as it is, has always surprised me. After all, the entire first line of Dunbar's poem reads, "We wear the mask that grins and lies." That is, *expression* is written into the poem from the first, even if it is a superficial, artificial one. More perplexingly, while the speaker's mask is full of a false expression, the speaker him- or herself is not expressionless either. The poem reads, in its entirety:

> We wear the mask that grins and lies,
> It hides our cheeks and shades our eyes,—
> This debt we pay to human guile;
> With torn and bleeding hearts we smile,
> And mouth with myriad subtleties.
>
> Why should the world be over-wise,
> In counting all our tears and sighs?
> Nay, let them only see us, while
> We wear the mask.

We smile, but, O great Christ, our cries
To thee from tortured souls arise.
We sing, but oh the clay is vile
Beneath our feet, and long the mile;
But let the world dream otherwise,
  We wear the mask![1]

Torn and bleeding hearts, cries to Christ from tortured souls—the deadpan this is not. So why does this poem so often come up?

If this is a relatively simple matter of people misremembering the contents of the poem in full, I'm intrigued by the texture of that forgetting. On the whole, the people who have suggested "We Wear the Mask" know African American literature quite well, and I'm inclined to think that my interlocutors are not so much mistaken as they are on to something. Their collective association suggests that an easy slippage may occur between surface excess and deadpanned affects. Perhaps Dunbar's injunction to *let* the world "only see us, while / We wear the mask," is, in fact, a redundant command—that once someone's attention is drawn to the mask, the subject who wears it will more than likely be forgotten.

In this chapter I explore this most abstracted iteration of deadpan's simultaneous visibility and withholding in works of contemporary drama that pair visual excess with gestures of evacuation, confusion, or flatness, for, in the words of scholar Ryan Anthony Hatch, "the meaning of race is always formed via the logic of fantasy, [which] not only makes use of theatrical forms to consolidate its effects, but must in itself be understood as a kind of structurally primary theatricality."[2] Said succinctly, in this chapter I show that (the fantasy of) blackness is not only represented in theatrical forms, but is itself a theatrical form. What race *is* depends on the aesthetics of race, and what those aesthetics make politically available and imaginable, as much as it depends upon any other constitutive category. In particular, this chapter examines two plays that amplify racial stereotype in order to render race, as a category, hypervisible to the point of being confounding. Before visiting the theater, however, I want to linger a little longer in the visual history of racial excess and stereotype.

THE AESTHETICS OF BLACK EXCESS

The 1883 Exposition des Arts Incohérents in Paris grew from an initial fundraiser for victims of a gas explosion. The exposition featured "drawings made by people who can not draw," though when the show opened in Jules Lévy's small apartment at 4 Rue Antoine Dubois two months later, it included works by artists as well as non-artists.[3] Édouard Manet, Camille Pissarro, Pierre-Auguste Renoir, and Richard Wagner are said to have been among the two thousand who filled Levy's apartment over four hours.[4] The *Catalogue de l'Exposition des arts incohérents* lists, as entry 15 of 159, *Combat de nègres pendant la nuit*, a work by poet Paul Bilhaud.[5] Phillip Dennis Cate calls this the first documented monochromatic painting.[6] Though the term "deadpan" would not appear for a number of years, the title—*Negroes Fighting at Night*—is itself a bleak example of what we might now call deadpan humor, in so far as it seems to state an absurdity with seriousness. Its absurdisms are racist, but also show a keen appreciation for the play of absence and excess. This occurs most literally, in this purported first showing of an entirely black field, in the act of displaying a field of uniform blackness as though it is pictorial. It also informs the rhetoric of hypothetical figuration, as the void of night's darkness rhetorically embraces the rhetorical excess (or void?) of blackness, and the excessive act of fighting.

A short time later, Bilhaud's painting was followed by Alphonse Allais's *Combat de nègres dans une cave, pendant la nuit* (*Negroes Fighting in a Cellar at Night*; fig. 4.1), reproduced in 1897 in his *Album primo-avrilesque* (*April Foolish Album*). In this series, Allais's monochromes—each a printed block of color in a drawn frame—are each captioned as a particular embodiment engaged in a particular action. Other titles are even more bombastic, including *Tomato Harvest by Apoplectic Cardinals on the Shore of the Red Sea (Aurora Borealis Effect)* and *Some Pimps, Still in the Prime of Life, Lying on Their Stomach in the Grass, Drinking Absinthe.*[7] Given these fantastical titles, the consistency between Bilhaud's and Allais's titles is remarkable. Even if situating "black" people in a dark field is conceptually predictable, the act of fighting is more consistent than is required by the *visual* trope of a black field. Rather, what is being signaled is the cultural trope of a black field, with its attendant associations with violence, darkness, and animality. Monochrome as a modernist artistic gesture or genre

Figure 4.1. Alphonse Allais, *Combat de nègres dans une cave, pendant la nuit* (*Negroes Fighting in a Cellar at Night*), reproduced in 1897.

was, then, like so many others, informed from the beginning by the intersection of European imagination with African bodies.[8]

Between these two events, and also in France, the physician-engineer Étienne-Jules Marey devised the geometric chronophotograph as part of his extensive documentation of movement. While the longer trajectory of Marey's experiments is fascinating, the relevant development here is when, in 1883, his attempts to picture motion in time took an abstract turn. Having first captured movement in photorealist frames similar to those of Eadweard Muybridge (who was less concerned with mapping movement into time and more interested in movement's shapes), Marey attempted to strip away all complicating visual information. He designed a black suit with silver stripes attached to the axis points of the limbs, which, when photographed at regular intervals against a black background, created an abstract representation of movement (fig. 4.2). Historian Anson Rabinbach convincingly argues that turn-of-the-century attempts to graphically represent the body's movement in time and space resulted from the larger perceptual crisis that defined aesthetic modernism, and he shows that a number of French artists—including Marcel Duchamp, Paul Valéry, Edgar Degas, and Georges Seurat—were influenced by Marey's images.[9] The Italian Futurists, too, learned the "non-reality of the motionless body" from Marey. If contemporary artists recognized the "invisibility" of the motionless body to the chronophotographic eye, it seems not so great a stretch to think that Marey's images confirmed that the black body against a black field was equally "invisible." If the ironic nature of Les Incohérents has meant that critics view this first monochrome as a joke even while they celebrate it for its avant-garde forwardness, Marey's contemporaneous image-making suggests that the joke might have been more winking than absurd.

Moreover, if the monochromes of Bilhaud and Allais are sometimes disqualified from the lineages of monochromatic art, the same cannot be said for those of Kazimir Malevich, progenitor of Suprematism. Malevich premiered *Black Square* (fig. 4.3), along with other monochromatic works, in Petrograd in December 1915. These are considered the first "serious" monochromes, and *Black Square* occupied a special place of prominence in the showing (it was hung in the traditional location of religious iconography in Russian Orthodox homes). Nevertheless, X-ray technology recently revealed that the phrase "Negroes Battling at Night" is written in Russian in the lower left-hand corner

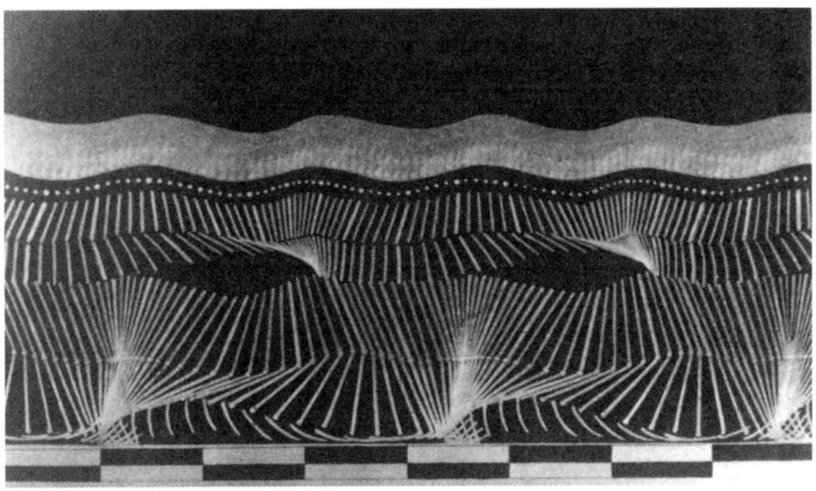

Figure 4.2. Étienne-Jules Marey, *Walking Man*, 1884. Chronophotography. Courtesy of the Músee Marey, Beaune (France).

Figure 4.3. Kazimir Malevich, *Black Square*, 1915. Courtesy of the State Tretyakov Gallery, Moscow (Russia).

of *Black Square* under its black paint, revealing a greater aesthetic continuity than has previously been supposed.[10] Before this revelation, scholars often linked the development of Malevich's monochromatic ideas to his work for the theater. Two years before the Petrograd showing, Malevich had designed sets and costumes for the Russian Futurist opera *Victory over the Sun*, which were in keeping with the stark, symbolist designs of Adolphe Appia and Edward Gordon Craig. Malevich's backdrop for act 2, scene 5, consisted of a large square, divided diagonally, and shaded black in its upper left-hand side. Malevich later called it the first display of Suprematist art.[11] Of course, the fact that the monochrome has roots in the theatrical and the racial might have less to do with the painterly genre of the monochrome *itself* than with the nature of the twentieth century's modernist preoccupations, in which theatricality and racial otherness played no small part. Regardless, the fact that the history of the monochrome is intertwined with blackness and performativity is hard to shake.[12]

Art historian Angeline Morrison addresses these threads in her essay "Autobiography of an (Ex)Coloured Surface," which explores "the simultaneous (and apparently contradictory) qualities of high visibility and near-total *illegibility*" that characterize (Western) monochromatic art.[13] Morrison's central provocation comes from what she sees as two stock responses to the monochrome. In the first, critics "attempt to find the tiniest area of surface differentiation and cling desperately to it"; in the second, critics do not actually engage with the artwork, but engage instead with a theory (such as the "End of Painting") to avoid the fact that there is nothing there. For Morrison, this prompts the question, "Is it precisely this tendency to *not see* or to *explain away* the blankness that we should be trying to read?"[14]

In lieu of these responses, Morrison focuses on the monochrome's resolute illegibility. For her, the monochrome reveals a fundamental slipperiness or trickiness in its ability to escape visual and psychic systems of meaning. The monochrome, she suggests, might be considered to conceal a transgressive secret—much like the narrator of James Weldon Johnson's *Autobiography of an Ex-Colored Man* (1912) or the mixed-race heroine of Douglas Sirk's *Imitation of Life* (1959).[15] These mixed-race subjects defy the logic of the prevailing visual regimes and use that uncomfortable disjuncture to create possibilities for themselves. As Morrison explains, "just as the mixed-race subject is not reducible to a single racial identity, so monochrome is not reducible to either side of the representational binaries [. . .] that have underpinned the stories told by western art history. Apparent visual blankness is both confounding and intriguing, a feature of monochrome's essential *doubleness*."[16] Morrison uses the phrase "critical indeterminacy" to describe the artwork that slips such binary constraints.[17] However, Morrison's arguments rest not so much on *what* the monochrome is (or even isn't), but rather on the affects it inhabits and inspires through its irreducibility. This means that while Morrison's focus is ostensibly *critical* indeterminacy, what comes through as much or more is a kind of *affective* indeterminacy.[18] For Morrison, monochrome's meanings are intimately connected with its resistance to being read—its "eternal deferral of fixed signification."[19]

But if Morrison's point is that one might read an analogous subjectivity at work in the monochrome and the racialized subject, I would posit that the mixed-race subject is not the only racialized subject who confounds fixed signification, nor the only one for whom aesthetic illegibility and affective indeterminacy are linked. As Nicole Fleetwood has argued, "the visible black body is always already troubling to the dominant visual field."[20] Fleetwood's use of the word "trouble" points to the affective as well as aesthetic destabilization that can be effected through black embodiment. Said differently, black subjects beyond Morrison's mixed-race protagonists can and do find ways to "trouble" the scopic regimes that would render the black body as flesh and the black subject as known. Indeed, given that the monochrome as we know it originated with a conceptual blackness in which racial tones became indistinguishable from a black field, there is more than ample confirmation that the darkest hues can be confounding in their excess.

To illustrate this point, consider two monochromes from Glenn Ligon's "Stranger in the Village" series. Ligon produced nearly two hundred works as part of a series that grapples with James Baldwin's 1954 account of living in Switzerland, where he was the only black person most villagers had ever seen. For these works, Ligon used oil

Figure 4.4. Glenn Ligon, *Untitled (Conclusion)*, 2004. Oil stick, acrylic, coal dust and glue on canvas and wood panel, diptych, overall 90 × 144 in. Photo: Studio Scan. © Glenn Ligon. Courtesy of the artist, Hauser & Wirth, New York; Regen Projects, Los Angeles; Thomas Dane Gallery, London; and Chantal Crousel, Paris.

Figure 4.5. Glenn Ligon, *Self-Portrait*, 2002. Coal dust, printing ink, oil, synthetic polymer paint, oil stick, glue, and graphite on canvas, 47.5 × 35.5 in. Photo by Ronald Amstutz. © Glenn Ligon. Courtesy of the artist, Hauser & Wirth, New York; Regen Projects, Los Angeles; Thomas Dane Gallery, London; and Chantal Crousel, Paris.

stick, synthetic polymer, oil, coal dust, glue, and graphite to render sections of Baldwin's text in black relief lettering against a black background. In *Untitled (Conclusion)* (2004) (fig. 4.4), the text of Baldwin's last three paragraphs appears in coal dust, present but barely legible. The uniform blackness of the work swallows the color differentiation that would lend the letters autonomous form and legibility even as light and textural differentiation insist that something is there. The text is available but inaccessible, allowing connection as a visual whole but resistant to acts of decoding. This simultaneous invitation and resistance is all the more acute in Ligon's 1996 work *Self-Portrait* (fig. 4.5). Struggling with this particular painting, Ligon scraped off its text, leaving the painting's surface effaced and abraded. Traces of letter forms persist as glittering vestige or dark, shadowy blur. These remnants impart no textual meaning. Instead they offer the sense that meaning was once present. This black "portrait" displays "self" to us as something held back from the viewer—a now gleaming, now empty, always multiplicitous blackness displayed in its place. Through his introduction of dimension and texture, Ligon also seems to propose that haptics accompany optics in the full conveyance of meaning.

Ligon's work is a beautiful portrait of elusive black subjectivity. Moreover, in their use of coal dust, *Self-Portrait* and *Untitled (Conclusion)* complicate the terms of black monochrome. In modern color theory, black isn't considered a color at all, as blackness is neither a hue of the visible light spectrum nor the white that results from their simultaneous presence.[21] Rather, as early monochrome titles asserted again and again, blackness is the absence of light (luminosity). Since at least 1902, the term ascribed to variations of achromatic white and black is "value."[22] On a value scale or gradient, light represents value and blackness its absence. Yet Ligon's black-on-black work contains a muted luminosity, a shimmer that asserts value in a supposedly valueless expanse. Ligon's work suggests, paradoxically, that excessive blackness can baffle even those identificatory systems informed by and reinforced through stereotype. Stereotype is, after all, its own bewildering schema of expression, valuelessness, and excess, and, just as in the case of "We Wear the Mask"—or, I argue, the plays that follow—stereotype can also tip into incomprehension, illegibility, or resistance.

SOME UNIDENTIFIABLE WEIRDNESS

Young Jean Lee's *The Shipment* is a black identity play written by a Korean American dramatist. Composed through a collaborative process with Lee's all-black cast, *The Shipment* wrestles with black racial stereotypes and the possibility or impossibility of destabilizing them through dramatic structures. The play is composed of two parts. The first is structured like a minstrel variety show, and includes (in order) a dance number, a standup routine, sketches, and a song. The second half of *The Shipment* is, in Lee's own words, "a relatively straight naturalistic comedy." As Ryan Anthony Hatch succinctly describes the dilemma presented by this diptych, "*The Shipment* is a two-act play played in a single, continuous act. Or rather, it is a one-act play divided into two irreconcilable halves, which it refuses either to synthesize or to hold completely apart as distinct theatrical works."[23] These two halves themselves align with the dichotomous trope of visibility/invisibility, with one half invoking the outlandish visibility of minstrelsy, and the other the deraced bodies of bourgeois parlor drama.

During the first half of *The Shipment,* cast members regularly invoke minstrel tropes even while they also constantly subvert them. The show opens with a frenetic dance sequence, in which an actor performs "*bordering-on-goofy choreographed moves that are unidentifiable in genre,*" through which flashes an occasional "*possible minstrel reference—a gesture, a bit of footwork.*"[24] Yet if this is minstrelsy, its appearance is incomplete and further eroded by the dancer's affect: "*Sometimes Dancer 1 is smiling, sometimes not. It's difficult to tell what his relationship is to what he's doing and to the audience.*"[25] When a second dancer joins him, their movements are "*reminiscent of a tap routine, except that neither of them has any coordination and they look as if they are about to fall.*"[26] If this is a performance of "blackness" it's not a great one, invoking neither black authenticity nor black stereotype convincingly. Moreover, as performed by Mikéah Ernest Jennings and Prentice Onayemi, the huge and unsteady gestures of the dance have the ultimate effect of making the dancers seem like life-sized marionettes.[27] This puppeteered quality pervades the first half of the play, wherein, as Lee describes, "the performers [wear] stereotypes like ill-fitting paper-doll outfits held on by two tabs."[28] In this pairing of explicit minstrel reference and deactivated personhood, Lee makes explicit the tension noted at the outset of this chapter: the razor-thin line between the registers of excess and deadpanned affect.

Discussing Ishmael Reed's sometimes cartoonish novel *Flight to Canada,* Glenda Carpio provides additional insight into the work of racial excess. She writes,

> Reed defetishizes the stereotype by aggrandizing its distortions. In his hands, it comes alive, as if newly produced, and overwhelms the reader's senses. He makes it bigger, louder, more grotesque, and more insufferable than it already is in order to arrest our attention and induce us to explore the fears and fantasies that the stereotype, like the fetish, seeks to keep at bay. [. . .] As he parades the host of distortions

produced by the institution of slavery, he creates a comic atmosphere with a cathartic and deconstructive effect, which allows him to conjure the difficult, hidden ideas and emotions that the stereotypes at once suggest and mask. He thus conjures mysteries in a dual sense: while he uses certain narrative techniques to evoke the ancestors or *mystères* of slavery, he aggrandizes the human distortions slavery produced to conjure the thoughts and emotions that the stereotype, as an obscuring phenomenon, renders mysterious.[29]

Although Carpio is here discussing stereotypical depictions of enslavement, her argument can be extrapolated to minstrelsy, an institution that, like slavery, is "over" but for its persistently undead afterlives. And while there is a difference between novels and plays, the live negotiation of racial scripts carries the possibility—though not the guarantee—of alienating audiences from stereotype through just the sort of metatheatrical mashup that *The Shipment* stages.[30]

Next in the variety-show sequence, a standup comedian offers a routine in the mold of leading black comedians, alternating between sexual and scatological jokes on the one hand, and jokes trading in racial stereotypes on the other. Stand Up Comedian (as the character is called) can't quite hew to the line, however, as when a bit about going to the gym derails into a confession ("maybe it's happened to you"): "you standin' by a railroad track, and you hear the train comin', and you get a strong desire to step onto the railroad track, get hit by the train, and die?"[31] While this statement doesn't escape the realm of black signification—if anything, it contains an echo of the black-authored blues standard "Trouble in Mind"—it does considerably undercut the surface stereotypes of the black comedic form. Further, Stand Up Comedian explicitly evokes the specter of minstrelsy only to get lost in it, saying, "If I was to take a shit onstage, use my own shit as blackface paint, fuck a human brain until I came, suck my come back out of the brain, and spit it at the audience. . . . I really don't know where I'm going with this."[32] As a critic, I don't have any special insight into what's going on within this quotation. What is clear to me, however, is that this quotation interrupts assumptions of form within the play. In its aggression (excess) and its trailing off from any punchline (deadpan), it violates the conventions of standup comedy and the larger minstrel tradition from which it derives.

The third variety-show number is a series of sketches following a character named Omar (performed at On the Boards by Jordan Barbour) through a variety of stereotypically black subcultures: basketball, hip-hop, drug dealing, prison, and so forth. These sites are generally loud—full of movement, violence, trash-talking, and so forth. Yet Lee scripts a remarkably flat affect in the characters: "*In the following series of sketches*," the stage directions instruct, "*none of the performers should put on any kind of 'black-sounding' or 'white-sounding' accent. They should deliver their lines and move as flatly as possible*."[33] Even the character Sashay, clearly meant to be flamboyantly gay, sings "Sashay! Sashay is truly outrageous / truly truly truly outrageous" as an awkward song-and-dance performed to the tune of a 1980s cartoon (*Jem*). Sashay's assertion of fabulousness enacts failure, self-consciousness, and flatness rather than black flamboyance.[34]

In performance, this flatness extends beyond inflection of dialogue and into all facets of characters' performativity. Stage directions specify that Omar acts his "rap" by "*covering his mouth with his hand and swaying his hips from side to side while making clumsy 'beatboxing' noises that sound like: 'Puh, puh chuh. Puh, puh, puh chuh*'"; meanwhile, "*Sidekick Michael 'dribbles' by jerking his hand up and down flatly in rhythm with an imaginary basketball*."[35] As becomes clear in performance, the recurrence of Omar's rap rhythms creates an effect that is not only flat but monotonous. His expressive register remains an unchanging beat. As Sidekick Michael, Jennings dribbles his basketball at an angle rather more reminiscent of paddleball—there is, in other words, nothing athletic or natural in his basketball playing; instead this stereotype is again reduced to a monotonous expressivity. Actors practically shout the dialogue of the sketches, further eroding (or, alternately, caricaturing) their emotional register.[36] Characters Desmond and Drug Dealer Mama move "*in a* Grand Theft Auto-*style holding pattern*,"[37] adding yet another layer of inhumanity to their scene of conflict. Again, Lee confronts us with caricature tipping into flatness—excess and deadpan collapsed.

In her book *Ugly Feelings*, Sianne Ngai theorizes a cluster of bemused, amoral, noncathartic, suspended, and/or indistinctly aimed feelings, which she names "Bartlebyan" after the quintessential character of refusal. Performance theorist Karen Shimakawa notes two of the seven ugly feelings identified by Ngai as particularly at work within

Lee's oeuvre.[38] Animatedness refers to "the ambiguous interplay between agitated things and deactivated persons."[39] Stuplimity, on the other hand, is "a concatenation of boredom and astonishment—a bringing together [. . .] of sharp, sudden excitation and prolonged desensitization, exhaustion, or fatigue."[40] Both are on display in *The Shipment*, from the puppeteered nature of the opening dance to the bored-ironic inventions of a game called "Library," (discussed below). Ngai theorizes that Bartlebyan feelings "give rise to a noncathartic aesthetic: art that produces and foregrounds a failure of emotional release."[41] If, for Ngai, noncathartic feelings give rise to noncathartic aesthetics, I would argue that the deadpan's aesthetics complete this circuit, revealing how noncathartic art fosters noncathartic feeling in turn, here marshaled particularly and pointedly around race.

The final part of the variety-show half of *The Shipment* is a song sung by the actors in three-part harmony. The song is "Dark Center of the Universe" by Modest Mouse, the lyrics of which begin "I might disintegrate into the thin air if you'd like / I'm not the dark center of the universe like you thought." While in the context of a black identity play, the "dark center of the universe" has obvious resonance, the song returns repeatedly to the trope of thin air and apparent invisibility. The lyrics revisit this idea several times, offering "If you can't see the thin air then why the hell should you care?" as well as "If you can't see the thin air what the hell is in the way?" (subtly altered, on its repetition, to "what the hell is in your way?").[42] Like the critical responses to monochrome named by Morrison, the lyrics of this song trade on the sense that the singer is interpellated as the universe's dark center, or threatens to disintegrate into the nothing that is thin air.

If Lee's formal experimentation intervenes in the representational structures of race, the use of Modest Mouse is its own assertion. To borrow the simple and insightful phrase of a colleague, Modest Mouse, an indie-rock group based in Portland, Oregon, is "like the whitest band around, but not."[43] The band personifies angsty, late capitalist, American ennui. On albums with titles like *The Lonesome Crowded West* or *This Is a Long Drive for Someone with Nothing to Think About*, the band's lyrics often take the form of slightly incoherent missives rather than the sugary descriptions of love or heartbreak more common to radio play. Further, the band's singer, Isaac Brock, delivers his vocals in a manner that is one part singing, one part talk-yelling. Yet Lee's directions for the song's performance invert "whiteness" as embodied and voiced by Brock. Before the song begins, Lee's stage directions instruct the actors to line the stage and look at the audience "an uncomfortably long time."[44] Next, Lee specifies that the song should be sung with feeling, though with no change of expression or movement on the part of the actors. With harmony and emotion in the voice (excess) and stasis in the body and face (absence), Brock's delivery style is turned on its head. Furthermore, as the actors sing their dissociative lyrics while staring at the audience—which, at most theatrical productions, is mostly white—they call the audience into complicity as they become the "you" sung to.

This song is the transition to the second half of *The Shipment*, a deceptively straightforward parlor play made funny (and, at moments, poignant) by the quirkiness of the characters, who nevertheless interact in realistic ways. And while I largely agree with Hatch's assertion about the overall irreconcilability of these halves of the play, this song acts as something of a bridge and pivot point. Lee's author's note states that her goal in writing the first half of *The Shipment* "was to walk the line between stock forms of black entertainment and some unidentifiable weirdness to the point where the audience wasn't sure what they were watching or how they were supposed to respond."[45] Although she doesn't say so, the second half of Lee's play—in which a strange mélange of characters attend a devolving dinner party—might be described as walking the line between stock forms of white entertainment and some unidentifiable weirdness.

Until the very last moments of the second half's parlor drama, the audience appears to be spared the racially inflected traps that litter the play's first half. There is dramatic tension—the host of the party is having a nervous breakdown—but its roots do not appear to bear any explicit relation to race. While waiting for an ambulance to come for the host, the actors begin playing a parlor game called "Library," in which players invent sentences that might have come from a selected book. When the character called Thomas selects a book called *Black Magic: African American Religion and the Conjuring Tradition*, the invented sentences are to begin with the phrase, "The Negro believes." The completed sentences are submitted anonymously. One says, simply, "The Negro believes." On the other extreme, another reads, "The Negro believes that a Negro's hands and feet are white because the moon done touched 'em in Africa!"[46] After this last selection is read out, the character Omar (now different in disposition and played by a different actor than the Omar of the first section) announces, "I'm sorry. I'm sorry, but I have to say that I'm really uncomfortable with all of this. I just don't think we'd be doing this if there were a black person in the room," to which Desmond—the most literal, inexpressive character—says simply, in the last line of the show, "I guess that would depend on what kind of black person it was."[47]

Are these characters actually white? Perhaps. This is the reading that seems to color Hilton Als's suggestion that "this is so ingenious a twist, such a radical bit of theatrical smoke and mirrors, that, in rethinking everything that has come before—all that 'black' language, all those 'black' situations—we are forced to confront our own preconceived notions of race. And to agree with Lee that we may not live long enough to purge ourselves of them."[48] Indeed we might not, as one reviewer reveals in her one-column review: "The remarkable and versatile cast is African-American, yet Asian-American and African-American relations never come up (though it would have been an interesting topic.)"[49] She believes, even after seeing the show that Lee has created, that "African-American" and "Asian-American" remain stable enough containers to have relations worth categorical exploration, and, more importantly, that this is the expected territory of a play produced by an Asian American and developed with an assistance of an African American cast.

In fact, Lee's text seems to anticipate just such a persistent reinscription of the *fact* of race, if not the inevitability of its meaning. While most reviewers cast the ending as a surprising turn (and Lee reinforces this impression with a sudden blackout), this is in fact the *third* assertion that characters are not black. In the minstrelized sketches of the first half, Drug Dealer Desmond and Bad Cop 2 have both stated that they are not black. And in both instances, Rapper Omar counters that in fact they are. Thus the audience is, I think, *as* invited to adopt Rapper Omar's refrain as they are to take at face value the idea that the characters of this parlor scene have been white all along. The point is that Lee places the decision, and its commensurate implications, in the hands of the audience—leaving them, in Als's words, to "walk a knife's edge of race and meaning."[50]

In the end, says Hatch, Lee's work "mocks the ambition to traverse appearances and plumb the inner depths of the subject for an authentic identity, treating this impulse to a stylistically cavalier contempt, and instead locates the real of its subject in the gaps, failures, and ruptures in signification."[51] Herein lies one link to the monochrome and *its* affects. Morrison suggests that a significant part of the creative power of the monochrome lies in the ways it inspires both "the perpetual desire to decode" and "the impossibility of its satisfaction."[52] This is equally true of plays that stage the deadpanned duality of excess and absence: the creative power of this theatrical vein resides in the ways it inspires the *desire* to decode blackness even as it perpetually frustrates that desire. But, too, Lee stages the monochrome's joke: just as the excess blackness of *Negroes Fighting in a Cellar at Night* results in a picture of nothing, the excess of "The Negro believes" envelops blackness, too.

This is *The Shipment*'s deadpan aesthetic—the play's determination to trade in high visibility and excess while insisting that nothing secures this currency as stable or valuable. This aesthetic is easily spotted in *The Shipment*'s first half, where weirdly mechanical and affectless gestures are grafted onto minstrel forms. But it is equally (if more subtly) at play in *The Shipment*'s second half, where the genre of realist parlor drama invites audiences into the affective expectation that character will be central to the drama—and that race, as a facet of character, will be apparent to the audience and to the character him- or herself. When Lee pulls out the rug, she leaves audiences with a jumble of noncathartic feelings and the sense that, as in the monochrome's deadpan tradition, an absurdity has been stated with seriousness. Unless it hasn't.

AN ALERTNESS OF SOME SORT

In his exceedingly smart article, Hatch asserts that the enjambment of minstrelsy and dramatic realism in *The Shipment* reveals how these dramatic forms are not opposites but rather "two points on an aesthetic Möbius strip. The discourse of [Lee's] plays—the language of characters and the actions that comprise plots—effectively traces a path along the entire surface of this topology, proposing an estranging continuity between discourses usually regarded as being worlds apart."[53] Branden Jacobs-Jenkins traverses the same looping course in his play *Neighbors*. In *Neighbors*, a (black) family of blackface minstrels, the Crows, moves in next to a mixed-race couple and their teenage daughter. In the mind of the father, Richard Patterson—a black man who has newly landed a visiting lectureship in classics, and who hopes for permanent appointment—the new family threatens to destabilize all he has worked for. He fears the Crows will contaminate the "good impression" he has strived to make in a neighborhood full of his academic superiors, explaining to his wife, "People will see them and . . . think we're related! Somehow!"[54] Uncomfortable with her husband's out-of-hand dismissal of the neighbors—especially after hearing him call them "niggers" at first sight—Jean goes out of her way to make nice, becoming quite friendly with the uncle of the family, Zip.[55] In the meantime, Richard and Jean's daughter, Melody, becomes romantically involved with Jim Crow, Mammy Crow's retiring son.

The Crow family is not just a family of minstrel *performers*—though they are also that. They appear in blackface and minstrel garb at all times, whether or not they are performing—or, rather, as if they are *always* performing. Their blackface is naturalized within the world of the play, unmentioned by anyone. Burnt cork seems to represent something essential about the Crows—about, to employ the terms of Lee's provocation, "what kind of black person(s)" they are, rather than simply what kind of performers they are. It is this essential difference to which Richard immediately responds. (More subtly, one black man calling out others as "niggers" might, for certain demographics, reference Chris Rock's infamous "Niggas vs. Black People" bit as effectively as Lee's Stand Up Comedian does.)

Yet the Crow family's racial essentialism is undercut in a variety of ways, perhaps most thoroughly in the pairing of Jim Crow and Melody. Jim Crow has never, until the time of the play, been part of his family's act, serving instead as the troupe's stage manager. Jim Crow wears blackface—a fact he neither mentions nor seems particularly uncomfortable with—even though he doesn't act especially minstrel-like. He is uncomfortable with his family's show, but not the skin he is in (perhaps even born into?). Jim's romance with Melody throws the nature of this blackface into ever more question. Moreover, Melody's name suggests she may in fact belong in the world of the minstrel show, regardless of what her fair skin and integrationist upbringing might otherwise indicate. Indeed, when Jim and Melody make out, his makeup comes off on her:

JIM: You have, um—
MELODY: Another eyelash?
JIM: No, um, it's—
MELODY [*reaching for her face*]: Oh my God, what is it?!

[*She looks at her finger.*]

Oh?

[*She looks at* JIM.]

Oh.
JIM: I'm sorry.
MELODY: Oh, no, no. It's fine. I don't mind . . .[56]

Though Jim is apologetic for his makeup (or essence?) having rubbed off on her, Melody's reaction is first surprise, then acceptance—if not something even more positive.

Melody follows this exchange with a long monologue about her skin changing color around the age of five, and how her mother's "Alabaster Lily" makeup suddenly "appeared" when applied to her face. Seeing the white makeup streak, Melody, says: "I think to myself, there must have been dirt on my face—days and days of dirty had accumulated on my face—so I took the makeup off and I washed my face and I reapplied and it was still streaking. And I washed my face so many times and so hard until I'd basically rubbed my face raw and finally was like whatever and put the makeup on anyway, but when I looked in the mirror, I didn't see my mother anymore. I saw this clown, basically."[57] Melody explains that it never occurred to her that "this had anything to do" with her father, and that the experience of looking like a clown so traumatized her that she resolved afterward "that, rather than wash my face, I was going to let it get so dirty that I was just black—just totally black."[58] Although she eventually forgot all about it, Melody's early trauma instilled a resolution to become totally black—a hue possible for her only through the accrual of artificial layers. Melody's mixed-race identity could align her with the passing subject whom Morrison likens to the monochrome through their shared indeterminacy and secret keeping, yet Melody moves to the other extreme in her desire to become monochromatically black.

If, in Lee's play, the fixity of race is destabilized through the assertion that visually black actors are not playing black characters (unless they are), Jacobs-Jenkins plays a similar trick by destabilizing the nature of skin versus makeup, or essence versus surface. While Jim would seem to be naturalized into a skin of makeup, it can come off. But can it? Even though makeup can come off Jim onto Melody, stage directions never indicate that it lessens or becomes streaky on Jim. Is this an artificial skin, or his true one? Can it be true on one person (Jim) and artificial on another (Melody)? Just what kind of black people are they?

Another similarity between Lee's and Jacobs-Jenkins's work is the conjoining of realist and minstrel forms. Jacobs-Jenkins interspersed minstrel "Interludes" throughout his largely realist play—they are raunchy and surreal portrayals of black stereotype performed by members of the minstrel family (except Jim). They contain watermelon, breast, penis, and anus jokes, and they tropologize black hyperfecundity, stupidity, immorality, and the like. As Jacobs-Jenkins explained this dramaturgical decision to Rebecca Rugg, "Formally, my initial impulse was to smash together these two historical poles of black dramatic representation. [. . .] The idea is that we would be constantly moving back and forth between two very different types of dramaturgy, both having to do with 'race' but with very different relationships to the audience, and maybe at some point they'd synthesize into something else—maybe I'd find the continuous thread. And the shifting back and forth for the audience would create a kind of weird destabilization, and alertness of some sort."[59] This smashing together of historical poles recalls the Möbius strip Hatch senses in Lee's work, in which two apparent poles of black representation are revealed to be continuous. The stated intentions of the two playwrights also seem remarkably similar; "the weird destabilization, and alertness of some sort" that Jacobs-Jenkins aims for in his combination of realism and minstrelsy mirrors the "uncomfortable, paranoid watchfulness in everyone" that Lee hopes will result from her work.[60]

While both playwrights foster alienation effects by merging black representational forms, comparing Lee and Jacobs-Jenkins raises questions about staging and the role of flatness in fostering or amplifying affective difficulty.[61] Contrary to the flat or mechanical tone with which Lee's most stereotypical racial scenes are played,

Jacobs-Jenkins's directions invite a surplus of affect by including adverbs such as "hungrily."[62] Indeed, in one production these Interludes were labeled "cartoons," which a review indicates were delivered "in a confrontational style directly to the audience."[63] Perhaps the interludes were framed as "cartoons" to highlight the impossibility of realistic staging. Still, that framing also references excessiveness and playfulness—and again, Jacobs-Jenkins's stage directions urge such a tone. Jacobs-Jenkins's descriptions of the interludes do not necessarily *preclude* a kind of affectively flat performance. But I would suggest that Jacobs-Jenkins understands exactly the dynamic affective workings of excess described by Carpio earlier in this chapter: "As he parades the host of distortions produced by [minstrelsy], he creates a comic atmosphere with a cathartic and deconstructive effect, which allows him to conjure the difficult, hidden ideas and emotions that the stereotypes at once suggest and mask."

Jacobs-Jenkins seems to acknowledge that he is playing a dangerous game through the tone of the self-aware persona who voices the play's stage directions. These directions are explicitly embodied, as from the beginning of the play, the voice indicates parenthetically, "*(You can't even hear me.)*"[64] This voice issues directions full of propositions and retractions. "*Who knows?*" it says, and "*maybe*" and "*or something.*" Jacobs-Jenkins described this persona, saying, "There is something about the voice (if we want to call it that—the stage directions, or whatever . . .) that is very unsure. It's kind of passive-aggressive, and also kind of coy and self-effacing, with all the 'if you wants' and 'I don't knows'. [. . .] That has to do with the play itself, which is purposely very unsure about something."[65] Here, then, Jacobs-Jenkins purposefully incorporates affective difficulty into the work, though in a way that depends upon directorial choices to translate its tone to an audience.

Jacobs-Jenkins also scripts an explicit moment of affective difficulty for the audience at the end of the play:

> *The atmosphere is soaked in the ash cloud that is Jim Crow Sr. The* CROW FAMILY *sans* ZIP *take their place on "stage," standing in a straight line. Minstrel music plays, but they don't move. Instead, they simply look into every face in the room.* ZIP *and* RICHARD *are still fighting in half-light, and they are the only sound we hear, as the entire family looks the entire*

audience over. The minstrel music finishes, and there is silence before the entire theater, stage and all, is ever so slowly and completely washed in amber light. It is awkward and goes on forever. We watch them. They watch us. Occasionally, they point to people in the audience and whisper to each other, sometimes mockingly, sometimes out of concern. Occasionally, they giggle.[66]

For Jacobs-Jenkins, this is the moment in which the minstrel show and the drama of Richard converge completely. As he explains, "If the whole play was about the effects of images, of the power of the visual, of race as a visual construction, I wanted to see if I could turn both of these weird arcs into one image, and then see how much the image could contain."[67] Again, there is a parallel with the monochrome's various interpretations. One might insist that a theatrical interpretation of race is true or false, everything or nothing, just as one might focus on a monochrome's small surface differentiations or determine that nothing is present at all. Or, one might focus instead on the resolute indeterminacy of racial representation—the revelation that it might all be but one continuous Möbius strip.

This final tableau is, like the similar moment of observation that precedes "Dark Center of the Universe" in *The Shipment*, scripted to present audience members with a moment that is awkward and that goes on forever. More importantly, Jacobs-Jenkins links the fostering of this emotion in the audience with the affects of racial hypervisibility. He says, "For me the ending is simply about the audience experiencing the sensation of being watched. I don't think the Crows really give a crap about having a relationship with the audience at this point. They've been relating to the audience all night. Now they just want to relate to each other and see a show."[68] The audience now gets to experience the feeling of being observed in absence of desired relationship—a feeling that has underwritten volumes of black scholarship ("Look, a Negro!"). As Jim Crow Sr. renders the thin air visible, the Crows assert that they're not the dark center of the play's universe after all. But it is up to the audience to say whether they agree—whether they, and not the Crows, are the observed actors. The Crows may yet be hypervisible as they suspend their meaning-making venture for the audience, turning the tide on the what and where of excess and absence. The evidentiary gaze is awkward—and that might go on forever.

(IN)CONCLUSION

Race is similarly destabilized at the emotional center of *The Shipment*—where stereotypes are hollowed out—and in *Neighbors*, where excesses tip into the weird and uncanny. These works *seem* to participate in a radical refiguring of race. And indeed, for some audience members, they might. But this isn't in the only possible outcome, or even a particularly likely one. Rather, these plays' formal innovations—the ways they exceed genre, how their proliferations and contestations of speech and skin both invoke and undermine authenticities—render their affective register incoherent, inscrutable, or highly individualistic: as subject to blackness's reinscription as its abandonment.

In framing the play of excess and absence as part of a black aesthetic, I hope to illustrate that black cultural producers marshal these linked dynamics to purposeful effect, demonstrating that in contemporary blackness—just as in the blackness of *Combat de nègres pendant la nuit*—there is everything *and* nothing to see. Therefore, a turn to Adrian Piper's *Self-Portrait Exaggerating My Negroid Features* (1981) seems an appropriate move to close this discussion.[69] The pencil drawing, done on a yellowish-brown paper, pictures Piper from the neck up. Her hair, parted in the middle, is long and loose; a hint of a white collar sets off her long neck, with the image's title printed in a neat, small hand; and the neat, rounded arcs of her eyebrows emphasize her eyes, which stare directly forward (presumably at the viewer), and the tired bags beneath them. Through the title, audiences are invited to surveil "exaggerated" signs of blackness to their own ends. Piper's title implies, but never delivers, a complementary *Self-Portrait Exaggerating My White Features*. It is Ligon who finally delivers that ironic, deadpanned work (fig. 4.6). In it, Ligon offers identical, silk-screened photographs of himself with the captions "Self-portrait exaggerating my black features" *and* "Self-portrait exaggerating my white features." As the photographs are identical (and, one might add, indexical), no such exaggeration exists. Yet the audience is invited to look for it anyway—to color Ligon with their own sense of what, and where, his racial "truth" can be found.

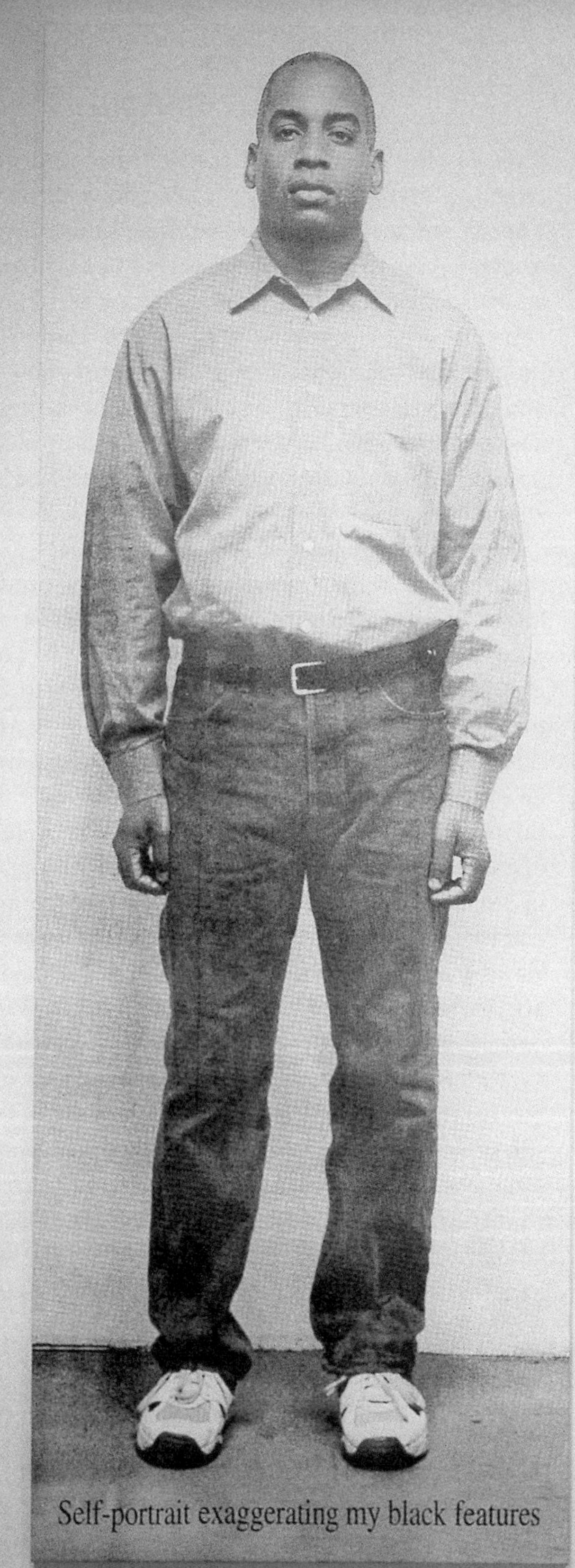
Self-portrait exaggerating my black features

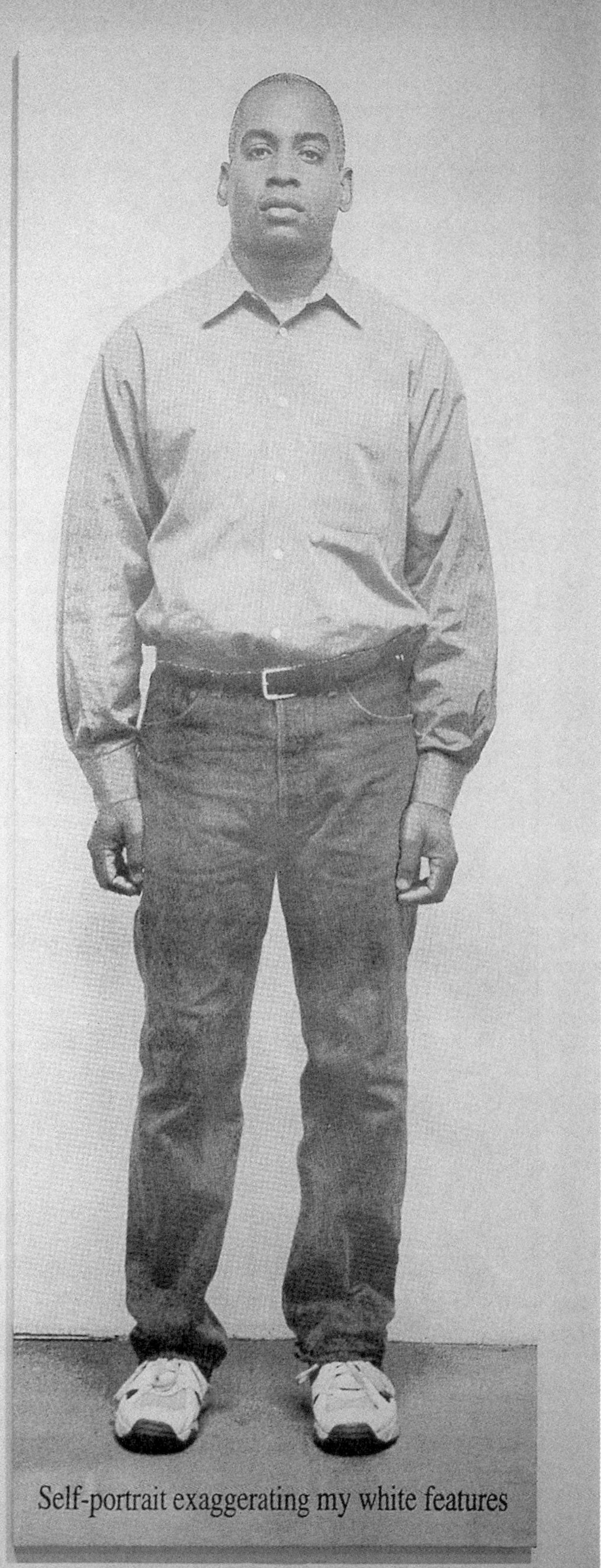

Figure 4.6. Glenn Ligon, *Self-Portrait Exaggerating My Black Features* and *Self-Portrait Exaggerating My White Features*, 1998. Silkscreen on canvas, two panels, each 120 × 40 in. © Glenn Ligon. Courtesy of the artist, Hauser & Wirth, New York; Regen Projects, Los Angeles; Thomas Dane Gallery, London; and Chantal Crousel, Paris.

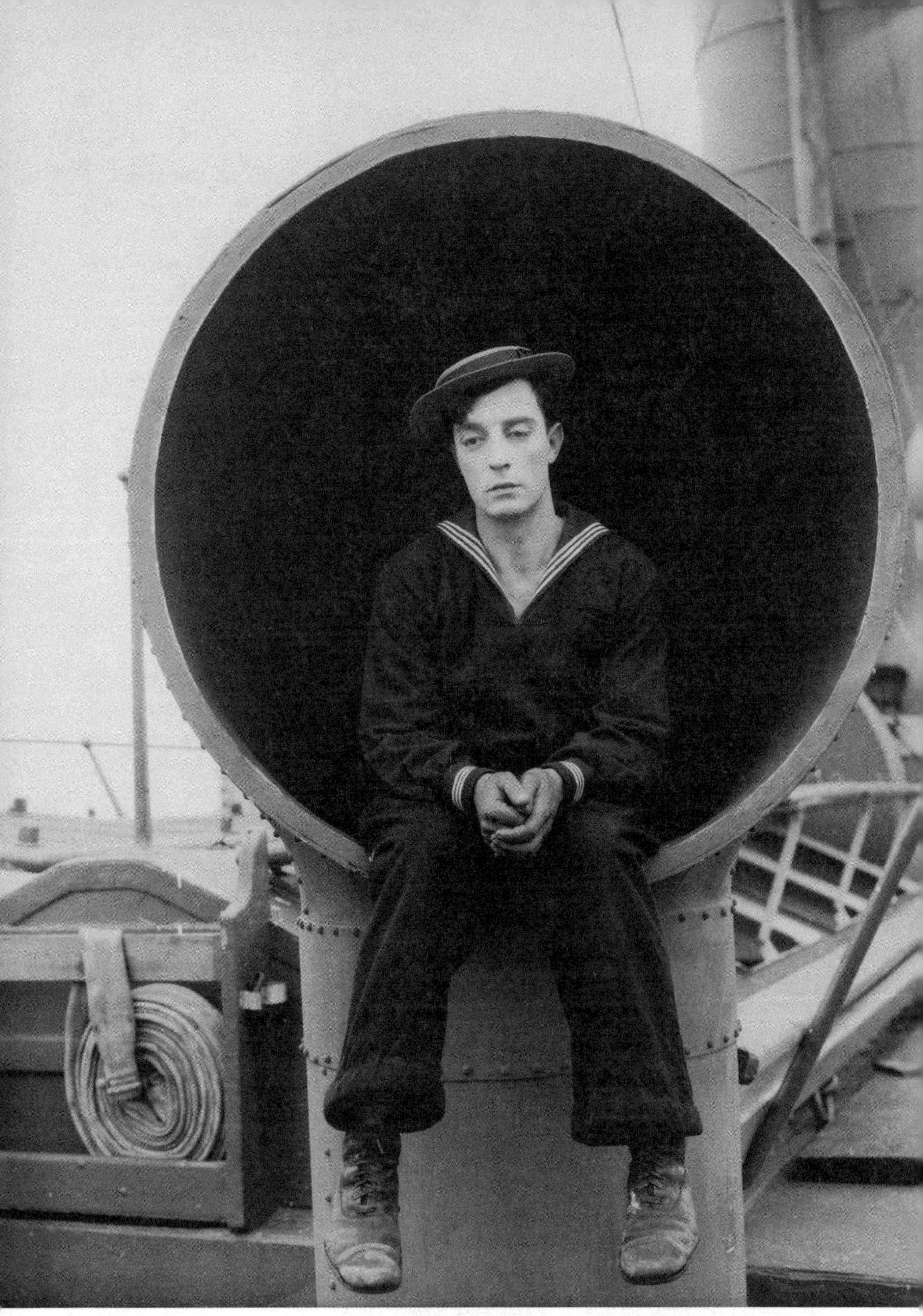

Figure 5.1. "Funnel Vision," promotional still from *The Navigator*, 1924. Courtesy of the John Kobal Foundation.

5

BUSTER KEATON'S BLACK DEADPAN

Over the course of this book, I have followed instances of deadpan into contexts progressively less wedded to black faces and bodies. Nevertheless, up to this point I have largely, though not exclusively, considered examples of expressionlessness and emotional withholding that have originated with black cultural actors. This last chapter is at once a completion of the arc that lessens its dependence on black bodies in order to follow a black aesthetic, and a departure from the through-line that has focused on black cultural production. If, in my second chapter, I identify the ways that minimalist sculpture can be seen to enact an idea of blackness as anthropomorphic looming in order to show that black *and* white artists have taken up this provocation, here I once again attend to the ways that white artists use blackness as it is constructed (and as they, in turn, continue to construct it) within the American cultural imaginary. In this final chapter, I explore the ways that Buster Keaton, the paradigmatic white cultural enactor of deadpan aesthetics, can be seen to borrow from blackness of a sort (fig. 5.1).

Joseph Frank "Buster" Keaton was one of the great comedic film stars of the early twentieth century, and a pioneering filmmaker. He joined the fledgling movie business in 1917 and made a series of two-reelers with Roscoe "Fatty" Arbuckle and Al St. John from 1917 to 1919. His best-known feature-length films were made between 1920 and 1927. Although he enjoyed a resurgence late in life, Keaton's fortunes generally declined after 1928 due to the breakup of his first marriage, increasing alcoholism, an ill-suited contract with MGM, and, perhaps most significant of all, the advent of sound in film. In all his films, Keaton reprised a certain kind of character—one who wore a deadpan expression in the face of any boon or hardship (more often the latter). While the early two-reelers contain a few moments when Keaton cracks a smile, his persona, throughout his career, remained that of one moving through the world with an unflappable stoic bemusement. This characteristic earned Keaton the nickname "The Great Stone Face." While film scholars and critics widely acknowledge that Keaton's deadpan is central to his comedy, the fact that blackness is central to his deadpan earns far less attention. Nevertheless, blackness underwrites this palest of American performances, constituting another instance of blackness suffused in the American experience—"not lying at the bottom of it," in Ralph Ellison's words, "but intertwined, diffused in its very texture."[1]

Before finding his way to film, Keaton was a vaudeville performer. He was born in Kansas in 1895, the eldest child of traveling medicine show performers. He officially joined his family's act at the age of three, but supposedly made his way onto the stage first at the age of nine months when he escaped from the theatrical trunk that served as a playpen and joined his father onstage during a blackface minstrel routine.[2] Related documentation exists—there's a photograph of baby Buster sitting beneath the wide stance of Joe Keaton, who is blacked up and in oversized clothes.[3] Simply put, Keaton grew up in intimate proximity to the blackface stereotypes prevalent throughout the nation and its stages. Keaton occasionally blacked up, but as I will show, he deployed blackness's cultural signage in subtler ways that would have been implicitly or explicitly apparent to contemporaneous audiences, effectively pioneering a kind of non-blackface minstrelsy. This signage has become less clear as the American collective has determinedly forgotten its minstrel legacy. Nevertheless, if, as Henri Bergson has argued, humor requires indifference in the observer, blackness helped to foment this detachment. "Laughter has no greater foe than emotion," Bergson explains. "I do not mean that we could not laugh at a person who inspires us with pity, for instance, or even with affection, but in such a case we must, for the moment, put our affection out of court and impose silence upon our pity. [. . .] The comic demands something like a momentary anesthesia of the heart."

Keaton's comedy allows for pity and affection; it wields blackness as its ether.

I am an admirer of Keaton as a physical actor and an early filmmaker, and this research has in no way lessened my sense of his artistry or his cultural importance. Yet neither am I blind to the fact that he was an actor and filmmaker of cultural importance during an imperfect age. In revealing how cultural signifiers of blackness buttressed Keaton's performance, I am interested in exploring what such use of blackness suggests about American racial imaginaries. Transracial scripts—whether visual, sonic, or affective—are significant because they reveal what is imagined into a racial other and why. Transracial scripts are not *about* the other, but rather are about qualities one group has imaginative use for, yet believes itself to lack and another group to have.[4] This is ultimately what I am after in discussing Keaton's appropriations of blackness: to name the qualities of blackness as it is constructed in the white (hegemonic) cultural imaginary of Americans and subsequently (re-) instated upon black people.

A vivid illustration of such a racial projection can be seen in *College* (1927), one of the relatively rare occurrences in which Keaton donned blackface in his films (fig. 5.2).[5] In the film, Keaton plays Ronald, a poor, unathletic high school valedictorian who attempts to work his way through sports-infested Clayton College, where both the girl he loves and his nemesis for her affections are also enrolled. While most of the plot centers on Ronald's attempts to win over Mary through athletic feats, a subplot features Ronald's attempts at employment. He first lands a job as a soda jerk at a lunch counter, but is fired for abandoning his post when Mary enters the student hangout. Later in the movie, a sign advertising for a colored waiter appears in a restaurant window; Keaton next appears in blackface and waiter's whites, his thumb absentmindedly dipped in the bowl of soup he is serving to a wealthy collegiate peer. When the student demands something Ronald can't stick his thumb into, he returns with an unopened coconut, then heads back to the kitchen without facial expression, staring at the patron over his shoulder a bit too long—a more insolent posture than (white) Ronald has heretofore managed. The personification of black defiance, as performed by otherwise demurring Ronald, depends upon wit, staring, and a lack of expression.

When Mary enters this restaurant accompanied by Ronald's competitor, Ronald fears being recognized under his blackface.

Suddenly—and in notable contradistinction to the black waiters, played by uncredited black actors, who continue to sail through the kitchen doors with upright posture and trays held aloft—Ronald ups the ante on his "colored" performance, shuffling back to the kitchen with his head forward and his arms swinging loose behind him. When the chef sends Keaton back out with coffee, he drops a napkin; in retrieving it he is hit with the opening door and tumbles over in a somersault. He saves the coffee, which has remained upright through the roll, but the blacking from one side of his face has transferred to his whites and he is exposed—first to the dining room and then to the kitchen. The diners look on incredulously, turning their heads and leaning out of their seats. In the kitchen, with its close proximity, the black staff freeze (fig. 5.3). Then, after the chef touches Ronald's face to confirm that he is indeed wearing blacking, she grabs a cleaver and the (already) knife-bearing staff follows suit. Given their far more dignified embodiment of blackness up to this point, the staff's violent response seems less primitive overreaction than justified incensement at finding an impostor in their midst.

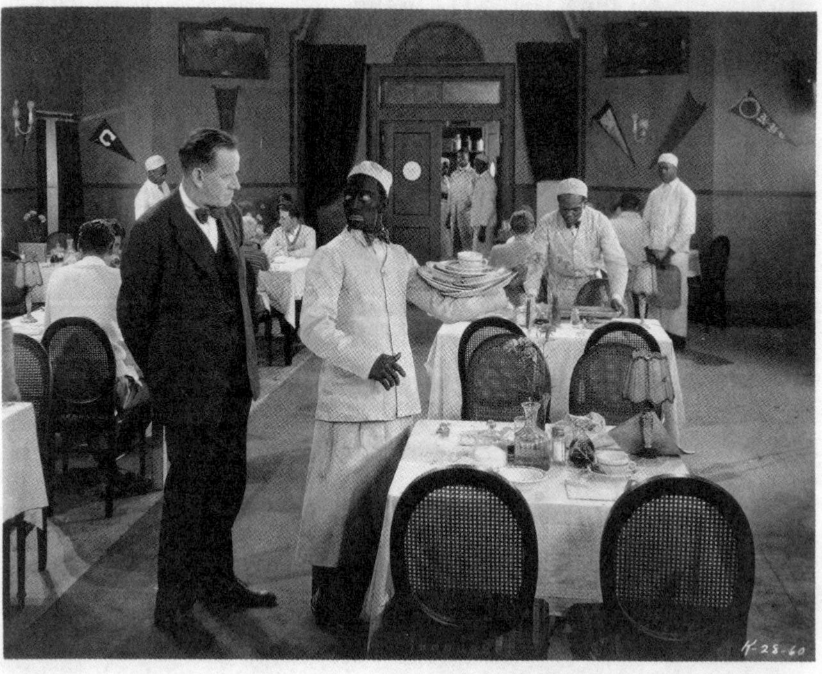

Figure 5.2. Buster Keaton in *College*, 1927. Courtesy of the Film Studies Center, MoMA.

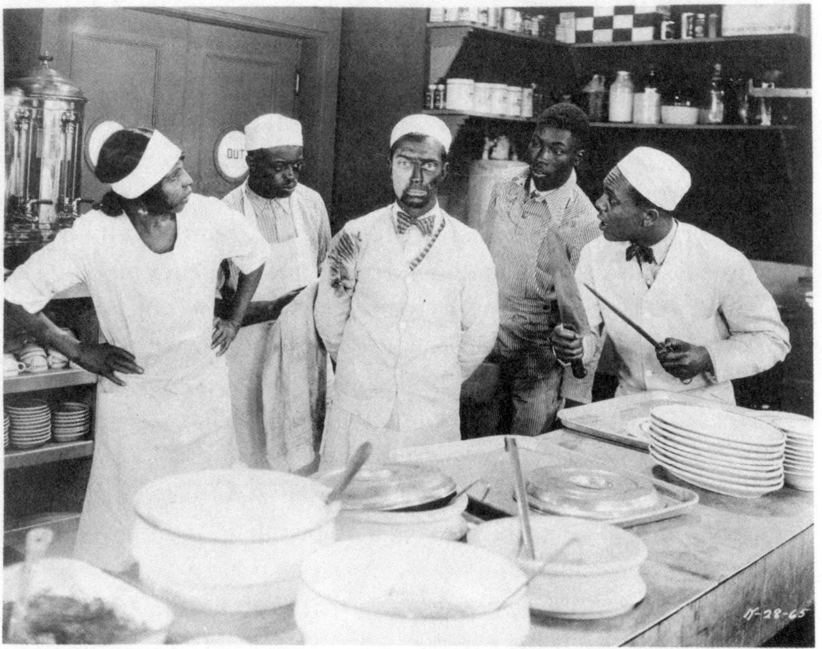

Figure 5.3. Buster Keaton in *College*, 1927. Courtesy of the Film Studies Center, MoMA.

Keaton's blackface performance in this film, while not devoid of stereotype, is more nuanced than many of the era—in part because Keaton in this segment is never intended to represent a black person; rather, he is playing a white man pretending to be black. That is, blackness is used as a vehicle for a *particular* white character to attempt his view of the abstraction that is blackness. Nevertheless, that abstraction carries its own imagined particularities, including a dumb wit, a primitive gait, and a deadpanned stare. In this light, Keaton's performance of being mastered shows itself to be a different sort of minstrelsy, one that did not require blacking to portray an object's insensate, insentient indestructibility—a minstrel abstraction, to riff on Susan Manning's terms.[6]

AN OBJECT AMONG OBJECTS

Biographers and film critics alike highlight the importance of lively objects in Keaton's oeuvre. This liveliness is due, at least in part, to the fact that "object force" is intrinsic to slapstick comedy.[7] "Slapstick," André Bazin notes, "is first and foremost, or at least is also, the dramatic expression of the tyranny of things."[8] Keaton is a master of slapstick, therefore the objects around him are unusually forceful. However, beyond the extent to which Bazin's observation about slapstick is generally true, one can assume that the tyranny of things is likely to look different when it presses the symbolic structures of blackness into its service. Slapstick of this sort might look like Keaton's comedy does: like the tyranny of objects *over another object*. Countless film critics have noted that Keaton's films upend traditional "animacy hierarchies," not only rendering objects as lively but also himself as object-like.[9] In the words of French film critic Robert Benayoun, "Buster merges with his obstacles and becomes an obstacle himself, an 'immovable object' [. . .]. Faced with the perverse uncertainly of a shifting, unreliable reality, Keaton merges with things—he becomes football, canoe, bicycle, wooden Indian, target, package."[10] "Essentially, Buster's character is a thing," he states, "a straw tossed in the windstorm or ground to a powder in society's mill."[11]

Biographers and film critics also note that Keaton's cinematic world seems especially lively because he so often interacts with mechanical objects. Furthermore, this sense of mechanization seeps beyond the literal contraptions of Keaton's world, becoming a ubiquitous state. As critic Gilberto Perez explains, "The arrangements of the inanimate world exert everywhere in Keaton a governing influence on the dramatic development. All his films may be said to enact a dramaturgy of mechanics: [. . .] and the mechanics not only of machines but of other physical formations, sports, a herd of cattle compounded with city traffic in *Go West*, natural phenomena such as a cyclone, a waterfall in *Our Hospitality*, an avalanche in *Seven Chances*."[12] For Perez, the natural consequence of all this lively thingness is the ultimate situation of the human as one machine among many. For example, as film scholar George Wead notes of *The General* (1926), "the mortar [Keaton] contrives as a weapon threatens to kill him, but then helps him—and through the logical consequences of the mechanics involved. In this sense, Keaton and machines always complement one another—the one suggesting a machine, the other becoming more human."[13]

Explanations for this have varied. For Wead, the trope of mechanization is a product of the filmic medium. Wead delves into early film experiments, from the Lumières to Thomas Edison to Mack Sennett, in order to trace filmed humor—or, more exactly, the humor of embodied movement—as a matter of speed and sequence.[14] "The gag is stylized time and causality," he writes. "It is man's immediate environment turned into a mechanism, and *men occupying a mechanized environment tend to be funny*. There is no such thing as an instantaneous gag, though there may be instantaneous facial humor. [. . .] The man in a gag is not just *being* funny. He is engaged sequentially with the space around him" (emphasis in original).[15] The gag, in other words, is reminiscent of an assembly line in its engagement of time and space. Keaton is the object traversing the conveyor belt, acted upon by the levers and gears that surround him. Keaton's biographer Rudi Blesh, on the other hand, attributes this particularity to Keaton's natural proclivity for engineering and a fatalism forged through early traumas involving machines. Keaton's belief in "animate constructions," Blesh believes, informs his films' "strange dual concept of machines that are alive and human beings that are machines."[16]

In their focus on the mechanical elements of Keaton's humor, Wead and Perez channel Bergson's assertion that the comic results from "something mechanical encrusted on the living." In his own words (rendered in italics in the original, so important is this point to his overall consideration of laughter): "The attitudes, gestures and movements of the human body are laughable in exact proportion as that body reminds us of a mere machine."[17] Several interrelated qualities of the mechanical are the true seat of the humorous for Bergson. The mechanical removes or circumvents will ("They laugh because his sitting down is involuntary"); lacks cognizance ("a comic character is generally comic in proportion to his ignorance of himself"); and substitutes automation for these lacks ("a certain fundamental absentmindedness, as though the soul had allowed itself to be fascinated and hypnotised by the materiality of a simple action"). Regardless of its source, the mechanical encrustation is one way that Keaton's minstrel abstraction works.

Importantly, even as Bergson argued that a mechanical quality rendered people laughable, he also argued for the simultaneous primacy of the human in begetting laughter: "Several [philosophers] have defined man as 'an animal which laughs,'" he noted. "They might equally well have defined him as an animal which is laughed at; for if any other animal, or some lifeless object, produces the same effect, it is always because of *some resemblance to man*, of the stamp he gives it or the use he puts it to."[18] As with the ways that a mutual subject/object status haunts the black figure into minimalism, Bergson's analysis suggests that minstrelsy (or any comedic form that casts the black figure at the butt of its joke) was not only a political development but also an *inevitable aesthetic consequence* of the chattel condition.

In chapter 2 I discussed the connection between the black body and aesthetic objecthood in order to examine the concatenation of black inanimacy and threat. Here I want to briefly explore some other ways in which general inanimacy rebounds upon the black body. As a way to ground this discussion, consider Ben Shahn's 1935 photograph *A Medicine Show, Huntingdon, Tennessee* (fig. 5.4). In this image, a black-bodied blackface performer sits in profile with his face turned toward the camera. His lips are enlarged with white paint and he wears a small black cap. The framing of the image surrounds him with the torsos of white men: we cannot see their faces, but each offers a sliver of skin—a wrist, a bit of neck—that confirms their race for the viewer. In the foreground, three smaller figures stand. At the far left, a young white boy faces the camera. His face is blurred, but we can see he wears a slight scowl. He has a birthmark or perhaps the traces of a bloodied nose. A blond boy next to him is turned away from the camera. And finally, of comparable size, a black doll or marionette sits facing the camera. Through compositional lines and spots of white, the photograph draws one's eyes in a counterclockwise spiral—the performer's lips to the straw cap of the doll, through peripheral cardboard boxes to a white hand, along a watch chain to men's white shirts, and finally down to the white boys of the lower left-hand corner. Within the central space of the photograph, there's a tight visual relationship between the black man and the black doll, as they are connected through the lapel of the man's coat. Both look to the camera, both are without a discernible or agential expression, both are unseen by any except the camera.

Shahn's photograph shows that the relationship between black people and objects resonated well beyond slavery's suggestion of their fundamental interchangeability, or, at least, changeling ability. This would seem to be confirmed by the fact that the Library of Congress holdings of Shahn's photographs from Huntingdon, Tennessee, include a tight crop of only the man and doll. As a sympathetic Farm Security Administration photographer, Shahn likely intended this equation as critique. But the fact that he expected it to resonate indicates the strength of the

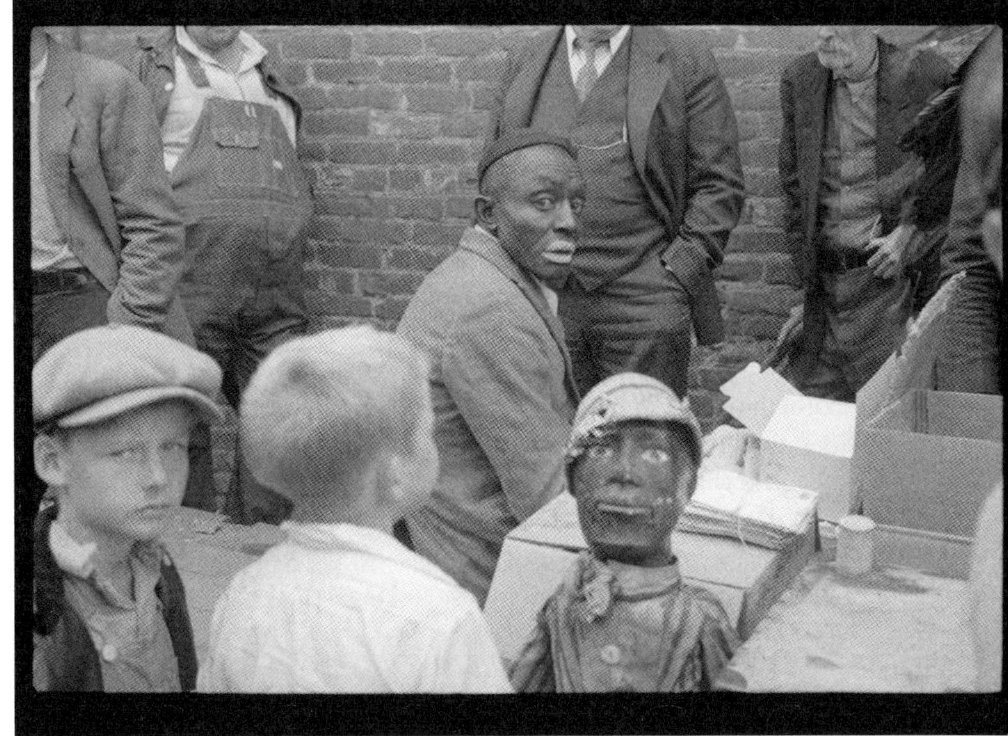

Figure 5.4. Ben Shahn, *A Medicine Show, Huntingdon, Tennessee*, 1935. Gelatin silver print, 6½ × 9¾ in. Harvard Art Museums/Fogg Museum, Transfer from the Carpenter Center for the Visual Arts, © President and Fellows of Harvard College, 2.2002.3000. Gift of Bernarda Bryson Shahn.

association: there is parity between the black man and the black marionette surrounded by a field of agents.

The subject of racialization and an in/animacy resembling man is huge. This discussion could range from the eighteenth century's Mechanical Turk to the 1921 drama *Rossum's Universal Robots*, by Karel Čapek, which introduced "robot" (derived from the Czech word for "slave") into the English language.[19] Even limiting this discussion strictly to the American context produces more than ample evidence of cross-contamination. From the enslaved performer Joice Heth to the 1868 work *Steam Man of the Prairies*, from mechanical "Jolly Nigger" banks to the robotic movements of black dance, black mechanization haunts the American imaginary.[20]

IF I ONLY HAD A BRAIN

At the height of Keaton's career, the signal example of minstrel mechanization was likely to have been Frank L. Baum's Nick Chopper, better known as the Tin Woodman, a character who first appeared in Baum's novel *The Wonderful Wizard of Oz* in 1900. Originally a human, Chopper lost his body to an enchanted axe after he fell in love with a girl who cooked and cleaned for an old woman. The old woman did not wish her servant to marry and so paid a witch to enchant Chopper's axe so that it would slip when he wielded it. The axe severed his body parts one by one, and Chopper had each replaced by a helpful tinsmith, though he was left without a heart when the axe finally cleaved his entire body in two.[21]

Baum's character is suspiciously reminiscent of another character, created twelve years before the publication of *The Wonderful Wizard of Oz*. In May of 1888, Charles W. Chesnutt published the short story "Po' Sandy" in the *Atlantic Monthly*, and the story reappeared in a collection by Chesnutt, *The Conjure Woman*, the following year.[22] In the story, a slave named Sandy is turned into a tree by his conjure-woman wife, Tenie, to prevent their separation, only to be cut down while she is away. Sandy is not the only black character in Chesnutt's story to suffer accidents of lumberjacking. Earlier in Sandy's life as a tree, a slave sent to make turpentine boxes unluckily lands upon Sandy:

> Nudder time, Mars Marrabo sent a nigger out in de woods fer ter chop tuppentime boxes. De man chop a box in dish yer tree, en hack' de bark up two er th'ee feet, fer ter let de tuppentime run. De nex' time Sandy wuz turnt back he had a big skyar on his lef' leg, des lack it be'n skunt; en it tuk Tenie nigh 'bout all night fer ter fix a mixtry ter kyo it up. Atter dat, Tenie sot a hawnet fer ter watch de tree; en w'en de nigger come back ag'in fer ter cut ernudder box on de yuther side'n de tree, de hawnet stung 'im so hard dat de ax slip en cut his foot nigh 'bout off.[23]

The slave's near-loss of his foot to an ax in the course of his labor, and due to magic, bears a striking resemblance to Nick Chopper's lot and suggests that Chopper may have borne a racial tinge from his conception. Conjecturally, I might add that the state in which Nick Chopper is found—having rusted in place—evokes the repertoires of stillness suffusing constructions of blackness, as Harvey Young has written.[24]

Or that Baum's decision to change "Nick" to "Niccolo" for the stage production, so that "Niccolo" could rhyme with "piccolo," might be a subtle allusion to the drum-and-fife bands that constituted black military participation from colonial militias through the Civil War.[25] Far more obvious, however, is Nick's uncanny indestructability, such that his body can be split in two and he can still survive.

Whether or not Baum had blackface in mind when he created the Tin Woodman and his companion character the Scarecrow, the two were certainly minstrelized when they moved to the American stage, where they were performed by blackface duo David Montgomery and Fred A. Stone (fig. 5.5), and it was the show, rather than the book, that was "the best-known and best-beloved iteration of Oz" in the early twentieth century.[26] Minstrel traditions figured prominently in the stage show, both through coon songs and through the performed embodiments of the Scarecrow and Tin Woodman.[27] So well did the blackface team inhabit Baum's roles that Baum dedicated his 1904 *The Marvelous Land of Oz* to them, and, as Robin Bernstein points out in her fabulous book *Racial Innocence*, the dedication page illustrates Montgomery and Stone in character.[28]

Bernstein convincingly argues that *The Wizard of Oz* was not simply a text that was adapted for the stage, but rather "a set of multidirectional calls and responses, repetitions with differences, all of which suffused popular culture." The Scarecrow's minstrelized tossability was one of these recursive phenomena, making floppiness a racially inflected quality during this era. Bernstein argues that the 1915 creation Raggedy Ann is among the Scarecrow's progeny, and that illustrator Johnny Gruelle "consciously saturated" the doll with racial meaning.[29] Gruelle "imprinted" his creation's face with that of the Scarecrow as illustrated in Baum's book, "especially its flat surface, triangular nose, perfectly round eyes, and semicircular smile [. . .], and he imbued his cotton creation with the physical floppiness of Stone's body in performance."[30] Raggedy Ann was from her inception both a doll and a book, and uniting both—the quality at the heart of the brand—was "raggedyness."[31] Like the Scarecrow, Raggedy Ann is thrown about during her many "bumpy adventures" without any lasting harm, and the doll invites rough play and bumpy reenactments through its flexible and mendable body. The books scripted, and the doll accommodated, "raggedy plot lines involving harmless violence, sentient property, and loving devotion to Mistress."[32] These three

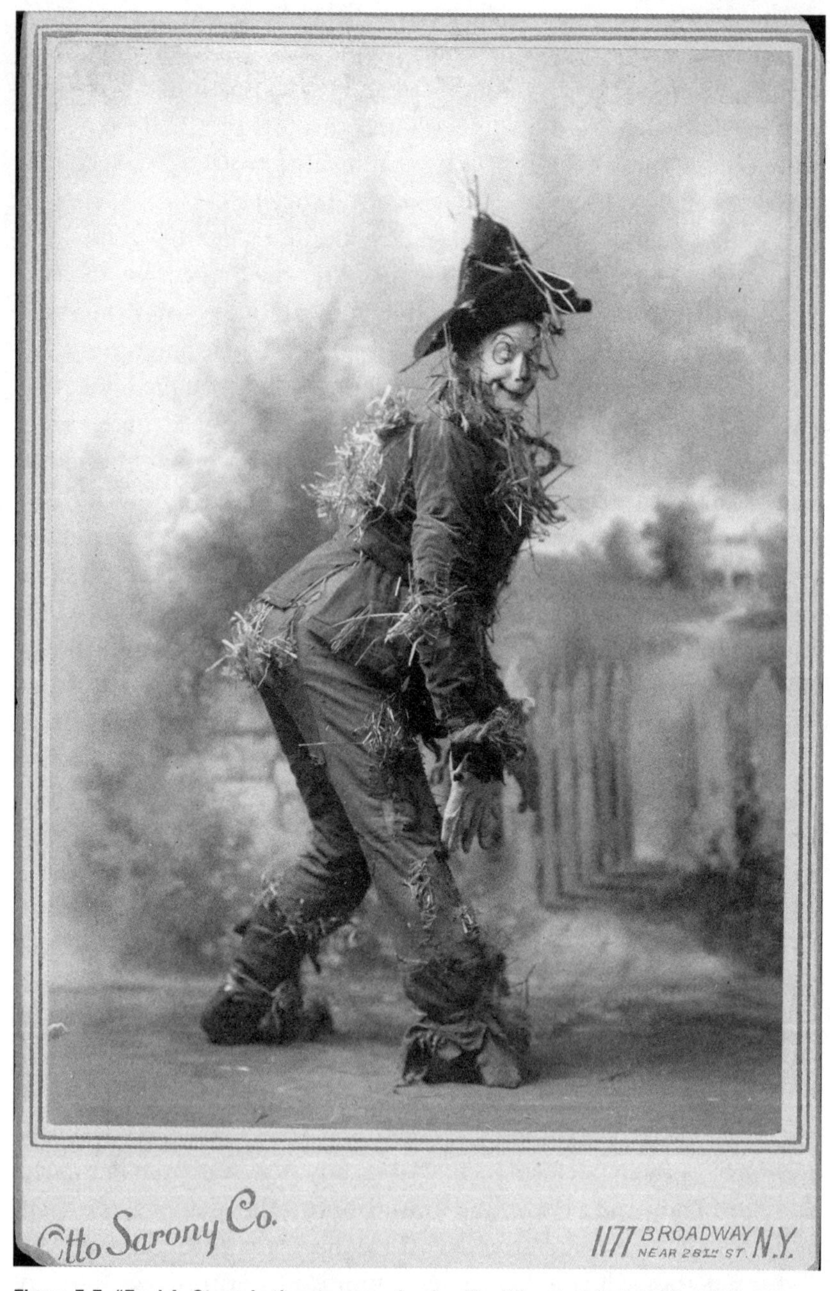

Figure 5.5. “Fred A. Stone in the stage production The Wizard of Oz,” 1903–1905. Otto Sarony Co. Billy Rose Theatre Division, The New York Public Library. New York Public Library Digital Collections.

narrative tropes summarize, as well, much of Buster Keaton's oeuvre, in which a hapless man with unchanging expression is harmlessly battered in his devoted (and generally successful) attempts to win the girl. I would like to argue that Keaton performed "raggedyness" through his uncomplaining receipt of abuse, and that his paired employment of expressionlessness and floppiness evoked blackness in the popular imagination. Keaton isn't exactly floppy, but he is thrown about, performing a tossability that goes well beyond simple slapstick pratfalls. Like the Scarecrow and Raggedy Ann, he seems light, loyal, and freakishly indestructible. He can be dragged (fig. 5.6), pulled (fig. 5.7), and patched again—his tensile endurance and reparability part and parcel of his desirability. Keaton's comedy also relies on imperviousness and insensibility. One still from his archive shows him sitting on a can marked "POWDER," staring pensively into the middle distance. His head rests on one hand, the other dangles at his side, the cigarette in his fingers a hairsbreadth from the powderkeg's fuse. In another still, from *The General* (fig. 5.8), a movie in which the protagonist is denied enlistment in the Confederate Army and yet saves the day for them, Keaton has stuck his head into a cannon, with collection of head-sized cannon balls just below, implying equivalence and fungibility between the two. Such imperviousness to ballistics is in keeping with the durability that is a staple of racist Americana, such as that seen in E. W. Kemble's *A Coon Alphabet* (fig. 5.9).[33]

It is clear that Keaton's audience understood his bumpy adventures to communicate the same three tropes of raggedyness: harmless violence, sentient property, and loving devotion. Writing for *Esquire*, Paul Gallico described his lasting adoration for Keaton, first formed in his childhood: "This was my deadpan boy, hero of a hundred movies, frustration's mime, pursued, put upon, persecuted by humans as well as by objects suddenly possessed of a malevolent life and will of their own."[34] Gallico links the maliciousness of objects, Keaton's inexpressiveness in the face of their persecution, and his own tender possessiveness. Like the black dolls that, as Bernstein shows, scripted abusive play, surely Buster Keaton dolls like that illustrated in figure 5.10 would be used to (re-)enact the violent material world of Keaton's films. It is not surprising that Keaton was among the metal dolls produced by Swiss company SABA/Bucherer that had articulated metal joints that allowed them to be shaped in, and to hold, any number of lifelike *or* humanly impossible positions.

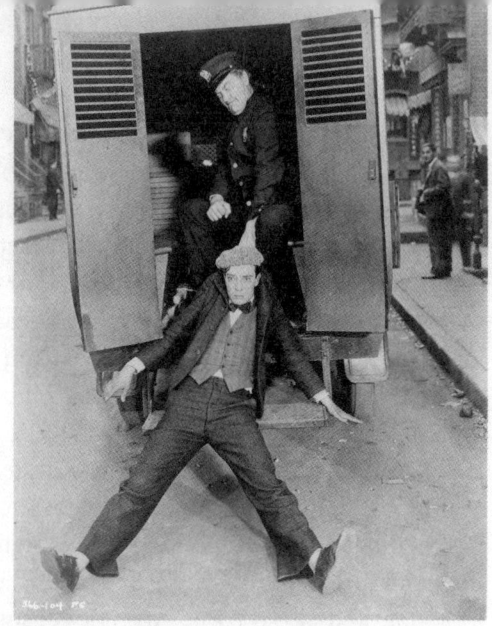

Figure 5.6. Buster Keaton in *The Cameraman*, 1928. Courtesy of the Film Studies Center, MoMA.

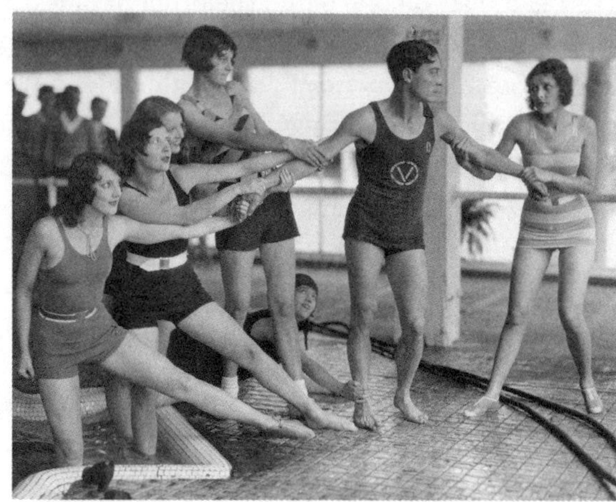

Figure 5.7. Buster Keaton in *The Cameraman*, 1928. From the Metro-Goldwyn-Mayer production and biography photographs and core collection photographs of the Margaret Herrick Library, Academy of Motion Picture Arts and Sciences.

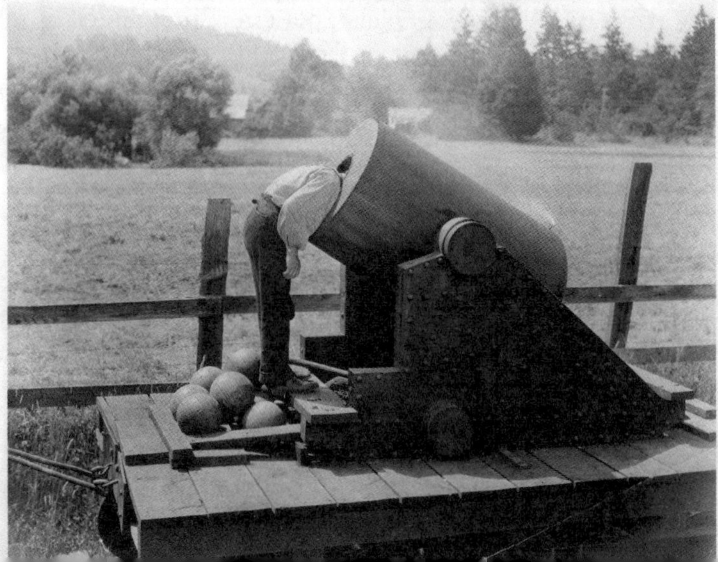

Figure 5.8. Still from *The General*, 1926. Courtesy of the Film Studies Center, MoMA.

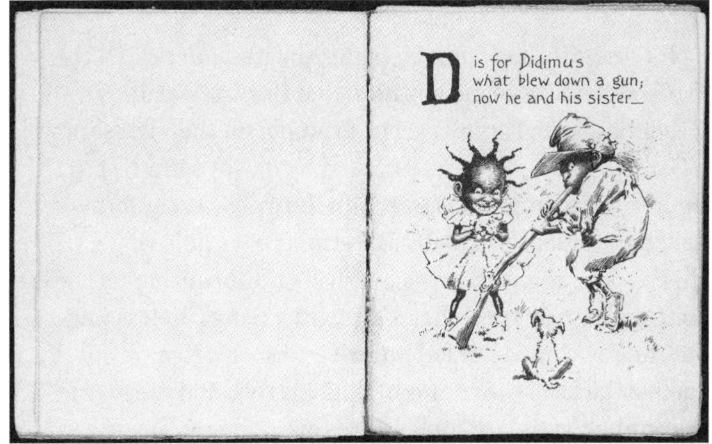

Figure 5.9. E. W. Kemble, *A Coon Alphabet*, 1898. James Weldon Johnson Memorial Collection in the Yale Collection of American Literature, Beinecke Rare Book and Manuscript Library.

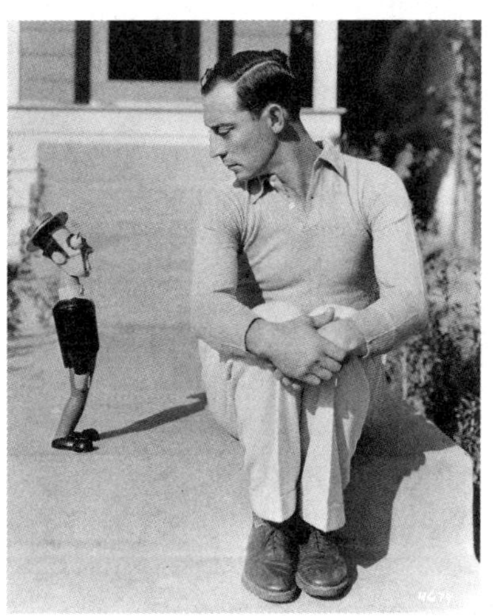

Figure 5.10. Buster Keaton with Keaton Doll, 1928. © Hulton-Deutsch Collection/CORBIS/Corbis via Getty Images.

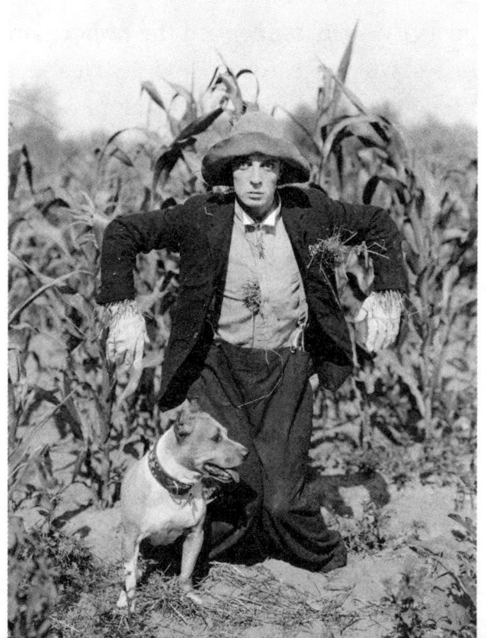

Figure 5.11. Buster Keaton in a promotional still for *The Scarecrow*, 1920. Courtesy of the John Springer Collection, Corbis Historical Collection, Getty Images.

Beyond the plot lines of "cuddling interposed with violence,"[35] the particular symbolic structures of racialization that Bernstein names can also be seen in Keaton's visual archives. For example, in the 1920 short comedy titled *The Scarecrow*, Keaton, pursued by his love interest's father and having lost his own clothes, not only borrows a scarecrow's garb, but also takes a moment to inhabit the scarecrow's pole (fig. 5.11). Hanging with his back to the camera as his rival and the girl meet, he animates just long enough to sneak her a kiss, then hangs lifeless once more. When she runs away and her father arrives instead, Keaton again comes alive to deliver kicks in the rumps of both his rival and the love interest's father. He immediately reassumes lifelessness after each whaling.

Links to Raggedy Ann and her racial coding are even more profound in the short film *Neighbors* (1920).[36] The two-reeler's minimal plot revolves around a boy and girl, the children of feuding families who live on opposite sides of a tall fence. The film ends, of course, with their marriage—and in the middle an elaborate series of gags makes up their courtship and attempt to make it to the altar. As in any Keaton film, these gags highlight durability and floppiness. Additionally, *Neighbors* relies on blackface gags even more than *College*. Early in the film, Keaton falls headfirst through a barrel and lodges upside down with his head buried completely in mud. His father tries to get him out a number of ways before finally succeeding—at one point even threatening to try a pickaxe (a tool that would require rather more durability than even Keaton could muster). Keaton reemerges covered in mud, as if corked. Keaton's character then attempts to whack his girl's father over the fence, but a policeman is wearing the hat that Keaton believed to be on the head of his nemesis. Keaton peers over the fence, and the policeman sees a "black" man. A chase ensues, which Keaton escapes by cleaning his face. The policeman fails to recognize him and picks up an innocent (racially) black man walking down the street. In the eyes of the law, they are interchangeable enough. The innocent manages to escape when the policeman is momentarily distracted. In the meantime, Buster has had a can of black paint dropped on him and so, once again, the policeman takes him in hand. In one final gag in this line before Keaton escapes for good, Keaton wipes off only half his face. As he turns around, the startled policeman watches his quarry turn from black to white.

Keaton lands in the mud in the first place because the father of his love interest finds him on their third floor (he has climbed in through a window). Keaton tries to ride a clothesline back to his house in escape, but his speed sends him around the bend and back through her second-floor window. Her father promptly tips Keaton upside down, hangs him on the clothesline by his slap shoes, and sends him back across the yard. Keaton comes to rest in the place of a rug his father had been beating, and gets the expected whack as a result. Keaton hanging from his feet explicitly overlaps with images of Raggedy Ann, in that Ann is hung by her feet or her (empty) head after a washing in Gruelle's illustrations (fig. 5.12). A promotional still from *Nothing but Pleasure* (1940), in which Keaton hangs from a clothesline by his shoulders, shows the trope was a long-lasting one (fig. 5.13). Yet another still from Keaton's archive shows Keaton posing lifelessly with a life-sized Raggedy Ann–style doll (fig. 5.14). We can read Raggedy Ann as oversized, or we can read Keaton as shrunken, but this latter reading is further suggested by other images from his archive in which Keaton appears with oversized objects that similarly dwarf him. Keaton and the doll appear as fellow figures on a shelf. He sits in her lap, as if desiring matronly attentions—though none are forthcoming at present. (One might note, too, the resemblance of Keaton to a doll on the shelf in figure 5.1).

Here I find my way back to the deadpan, for this pairing highlights one difference between Raggedy dolls and Keaton, which is the smile sewn permanently onto Raggedy Ann's face. No matter how much abuse rag dolls take—and the Frankenstein stitching around the doll's neck indicates that she has taken some—she smiles through it, able to enjoy damage as much as cuddles. Yet, as one more anecdote from Bernstein will confirm, this does not write Keaton's expressionlessness out of perceived blackness; it writes it further into it. In an unpublished story that likely dates between 1920 and 1926, Gruelle created a character named Raggedy Auntie—a black, homemade doll stuffed, like her indestructible counterparts, with clean white cotton.[37] In this story, upon the appearance of Raggedy Auntie in the nursery, one of the other dolls announces he dislikes her on account of her blackness. Though the other dolls attempt a welcome, Raggedy Auntie just sits and smiles, unmoving to all their invitations. Only when convinced that the dolls are genuine in their welcome does the doll come alive. Gruelle writes, "'Raggedy Auntie wipe[s] her white button eyes with her rag hand, 'I jess guess we all will be frens!' she [says], 'But I jes thought if you all didn't like me I would jess pretend I wasn't alive!'"[38] The black character pretends an inanimacy beyond that of the other

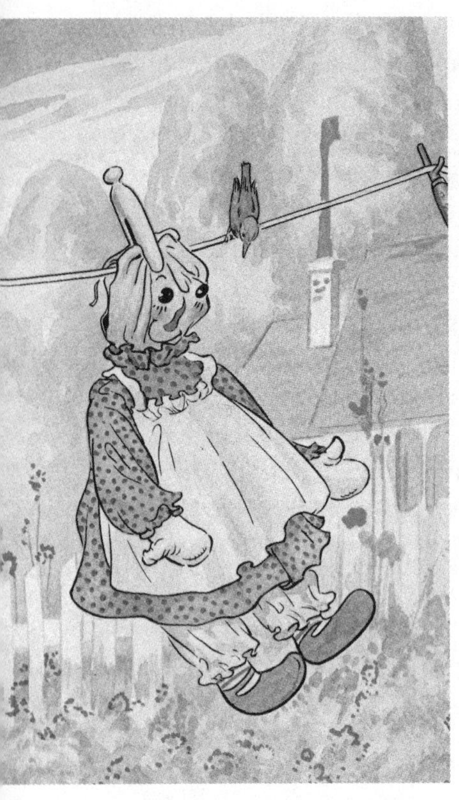

Figure 5.12. Raggedy Ann hung up to dry. Johnny Gruelle, *Raggedy Ann Stories*, (Joliet, IL: P. F. Volland, 1918), 47. Image courtesy of Robin Bernstein.

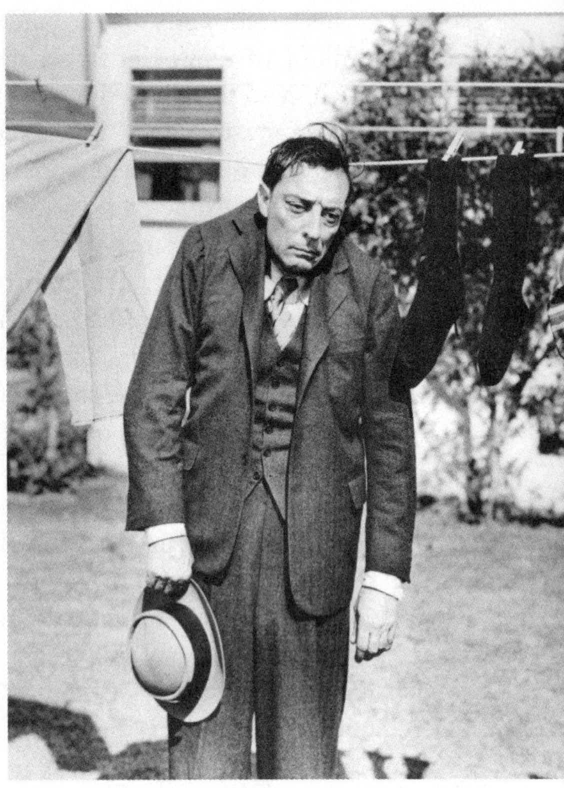

Figure 5.13. Buster Keaton hung up to dry, 1940. Courtesy of the Film Study Center at MoMA.

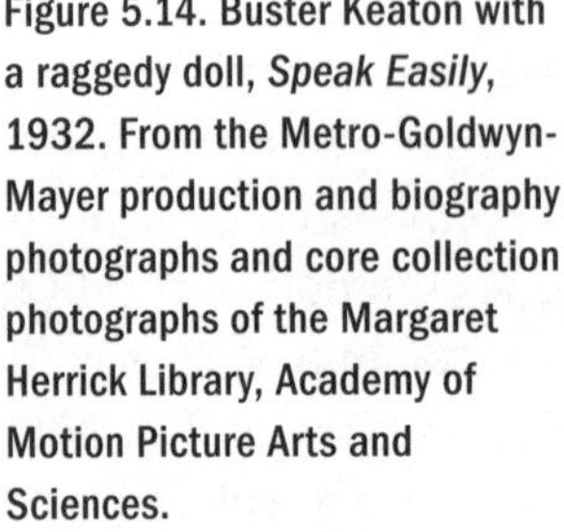

Figure 5.14. Buster Keaton with a raggedy doll, *Speak Easily*, 1932. From the Metro-Goldwyn-Mayer production and biography photographs and core collection photographs of the Margaret Herrick Library, Academy of Motion Picture Arts and Sciences.

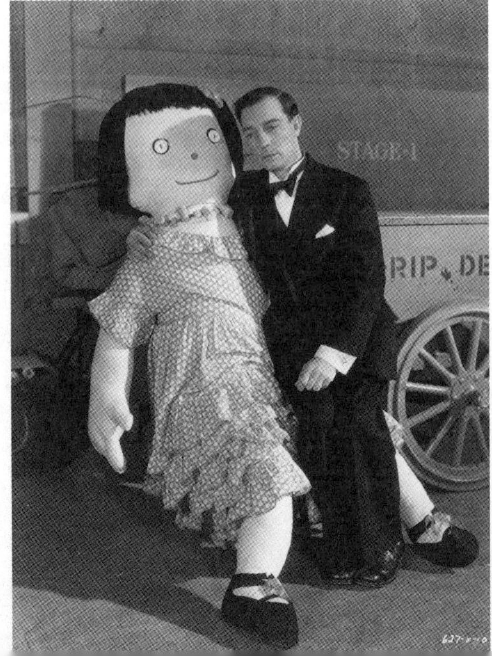

dolls, who are only inanimate around people, as her defensive social stratagem. The manuscript indicates that Raggedy Auntie sits still and smiling in the course of pretending *not to be alive*. In the case of dolls, whose smiles are sewn and painted on, a state of unliveliness is characterized by smiling. Humans, on the other hand, animate upon smiling. *Un*liveliness is instead wedded to expressionlessness—as reflected in the term "deadpan," which, as stated in the introduction, etymologically means "dead face."

For my purposes, the important thing to note is the pairing of indestructability and imperturbability. Black people in America have been disproportionately subject to the whims of the social and material worlds: the whoopdee breaks down, the levees break. It would be a stretch to declare this *uniquely* the province of blackness, even if it is *especially* so, for anyone in poverty or at a structural disadvantage is inevitably subject to the whims of breakage and collapse, or the absurd and dire consequences of material absence or excess. This is why Charlie Chaplin's recurrent character was "The Tramp," after all. But if the material world is agential, how one *reacts* in the face of that willfulness has a lot to do with the extent to which one's self-assertion might or might not matter. Many books from the first half of the twentieth century—Nella Larsen's *Quicksand* (1928), William Attaway's *Blood on the Forge* (1941), Chester Himes's *If He Hollers Let Him Go* (1945), Ann Petry's *The Street* (1946), Ralph Ellison's *Invisible Man* (1947)—feature black subjects attempting to determine how active to be in the face of larger societal machinations.[39] More than one of these works ends with central characters essentially surrendering their sense of agency—*Quicksand* is perhaps the best example of such abandonment. Others—such as Richard Wright's *Native Son* (1940)—all but suggest that black subjects' attempts to assert their agency can result in nothing but disaster.[40] Although it is unclear what kind of mercy the white world might have shown Bigger Thomas had he availed himself of it at that novel's outset, it *is* clear that every subsequent move Bigger makes—every willful step taken in the face of white racism and informed by racism's former privations—drives him into more desperate straits as he is hounded toward his terrible and inevitable end. For the black subject, one strain of black letters suggests, it might be useless to try—for to try is only to ask the world to prove you to be the object that you are. (Recall, too, the rhetorics of the Ben Shahn image

Medicine Show, Huntingdon, Tennessee—the visual equivalence it proposes between the man and the marionette.)

In short, one way to render blackness is to perform resignation rather than self-assertion. Keaton's deadpanned expression was a critical part of the resignation with which his character met his fate. As Perez describes, "At one point in *Our Hospitality* Buster is on a cliff, tied by a long rope to a man above him who loses his footing and plummets into the river below. The look on Buster's face, as he registers the inescapable gravitational consequence that he is himself imminently to be pulled down into that river, memorably summarizes his sense of his dealings with the physical universe. The universe, that look acknowledges, dictates its own terms: nothing to be done, at this point, against the pull of gravity."[41] "Nothing to be done" in the face of a looming catastrophe isn't all that funny unless the consequences aren't all that serious. Unless nobody is going to get hurt. Unless that body on the line is only a thing after all.

KEATON'S COMEDY OF IMPERVIOUSNESS

If, for Perez, Keaton's deadpan enacts a kind of stoicism (nothing to be done), not every critic frames Keaton's deadpan in these terms. For many others, Keaton's placid response is more (or at least also) a function of innocence or stupidity ("absentmindedness" in Bergson). On the side of innocence, there's Joanna Rapf: "It is commonplace to describe Keaton as a man who seems to have descended from another planet, a man who is somehow installed in the wrong universe and has to cope with a world he does not fully understand. Yet he refuses to be surprised, incarnating a sense of calm equilibrium at which we can only marvel. [. . .] Behind Keaton's remarkable deep eyes, staring out at a baffling, belligerent world, is an innocent wisdom that seems untouched by the fall of man."[42] For Rapf, in other words, Keaton is not stoic, because stoicism would imply that he understands his fundamental helplessness and is determined to accept it. Rather, he is not in a position to understand what might be coming next. All is baffling to this innocent, who is left with little choice but to bumble through with a lucky reliance on his indestructibility.

On the side of stupidity—although it is meant in as complimentary a manner as possible—there's Benayoun: "What gives Buster his inwardness," he says, "is the fact that he embraces reality with a natural sense of marvel and a serene conviction that everything can be explained with a minimum of thinking, leading to an immediate physical conclusion."[43] In Benayoun's formation, thinking is not so much abandoned as it is displaced into the body. J. P. Lebel seems to agree, asserting, "Keaton's body is the *expression* of his personality" (emphasis in original).[44] Personality—its emotions, its judgments and deductions—is located not in Keaton's brain but in his body. Moreover, the bodily insentience of Keaton's characters has repercussions for their cognition. Simply put, Keaton's characters aren't only indestructible; they are slow to feel their abuse.

This quality of his characters was developed in Keaton's earlier stage life in the "five-second ouch," which Keaton described for Blesh:

> "The old man would kick me," Buster once recalled, "a hell of a wallop with a number twelve slapshoe right on my fanny. Remember, we wore no pads. I rode the punches or got hurt. Now a strange thing developed. If I yelled ouch—no laughs. If I deadpanned it and didn't yell—no laughs. 'What goes?' I asked. 'Isn't a kick funny?' 'Not by itself it ain't,' said Joe. So he gives me a little lesson: I wait five seconds—count up to ten slow—grab the seat of my pants, holler bloody murder, and the audience is rolling in the aisles. I don't know what the thunder they figured. Maybe that it took five seconds for a kick to travel from my fanny to my brain. Actually, I guess, it was The Slow Thinker. Audiences love The Slow Thinker."[45]

For the signature Keaton character, forged through the stage, it takes a whole five seconds for a pain to travel to the brain that registers it. Or perhaps there's a fundamental disconnect between the body and the brain, and the brain must register what *should* hurt, for in its fundamental state of inanimacy, the body *wasn't* hurt. In either case, the brain wasn't *quick* (and "quick," we might recall, once meant *alive.*) Given the long association of blackness with a lack of intelligence—or, at best, an embodied rather than an intellectual set of intelligence—the simpleness or stupidity of Keaton's characters rebounds upon blackness, just as their insensitivity does.[46]

Keaton's early days, which occurred at the height of Jim Crow, must have been rife with such associations—and if anything it is remarkable the extent to which Keaton's black-bodied peripheral characters largely avoid such stereotypes (although as peripheral characters, they also don't contain much depth).[47] According to Keaton himself, the two

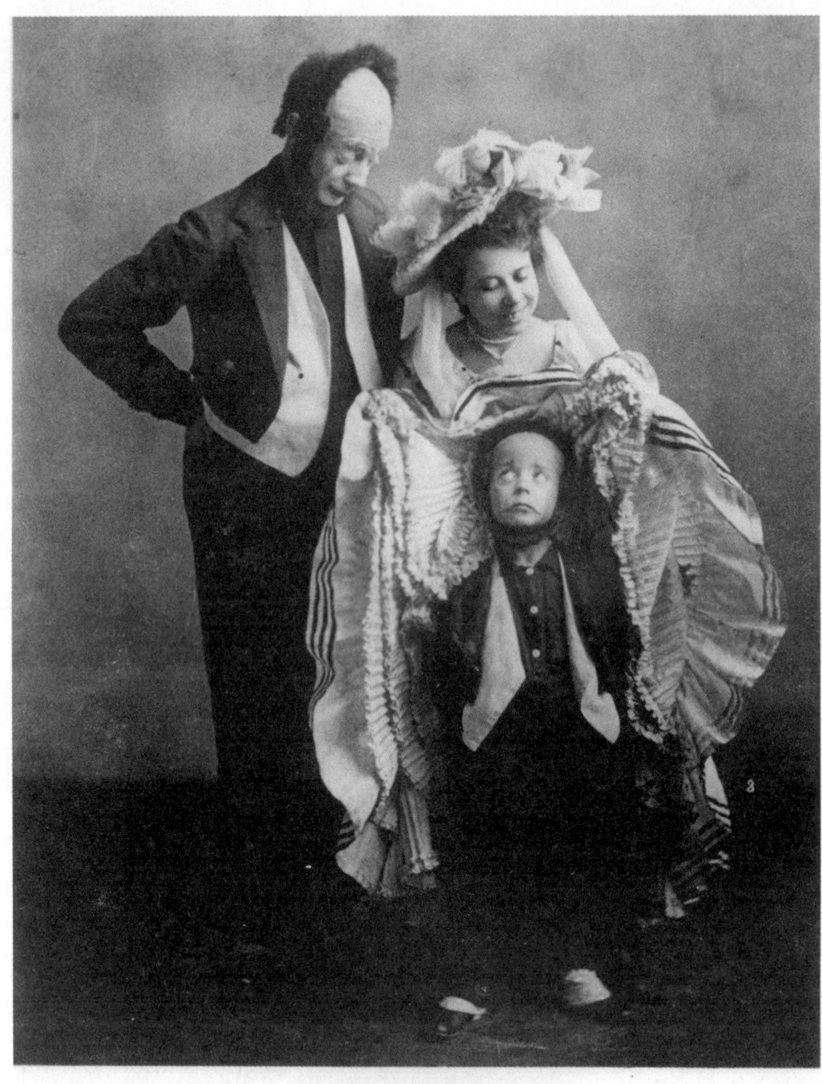

Figure 5.15. The Three Keatons, circa 1900. Courtesy of the Film Study Center at MoMA.

signature and intertwined features of his act—his uncanny indestructibility and his deadpanned affect—were forged in the vaudeville act of his childhood (fig. 5.15). Keaton describes the act in his autobiography: "Even in my early days our turn established a reputation for being the roughest in vaudeville. This was the result of a series of interesting experiments Pop made with me. He began these by carrying me out on the stage and dropping me on the floor. Next he started wiping up the floor with me. When I gave no sign of minding this he began throwing me through the scenery, out into the wings, and dropping me down on the bass drum in the orchestra pit."[48] As Keaton grew, the act remained largely a slapstick routine, featuring an acrobatic dishing and taking of punishments. That wasn't all there was to the act—his mother, Myra Keaton, played instruments, and sometimes Buster sang—but slapstick abuse of father upon son was certainly at its core. And, from the beginning, Keaton's signature mode was expressionlessness.

According to Keaton, the deadpan quality of his acting was born alongside the abuse of his childhood vaudeville act. The stories of its origins vary slightly, but follow the same general theme. In interviews with Blesh, Keaton supposed that his deadpan may have originated with the concentration it took to time his falls, but his father soon deliberately cultivated the expressive mode. Joe Keaton realized that audiences laughed more when the child was frozen-faced, and urged Buster to play to the crowd. In Blesh's biography, Keaton says: "If something tickled me and I started to grin, the old man would hiss, 'Face! Face!' That meant freeze the puss. The longer I held it, why, if we got a laugh the blank pan or the puzzled puss would double it. He kept after me, never let up, and in a few years it was automatic. Then when I'd step onstage or in front of a camera, I *couldn't* smile. Still can't."[49] Keaton's autobiography tells a similar story, and one that emphasizes floppiness alongside. He writes:

> Before I was much bigger than a gumdrop I was being featured in our act, The Three Keatons, as "The Human Mop."
>
> One of the first things I noticed was that whenever I smiled or let the audience suspect how much I was enjoying myself they didn't seem to laugh as much as usual. I guess people just never do expect any human mop, dishrag, beanbag, or football to be pleased by what is being done to him. At any rate it was on purpose that I started looking miserable, humiliated, hounded, and haunted, bedeviled, bewildered, and at my wit's end.[50]

Hollywood memoirs are a literary genre of extravagant embellishment, but it seems as though the most exaggerated element of this account is young Keaton's imperviousness to pain. Joe Keaton was by all accounts exceedingly rough with his son, and, although scholars have since pointed to and tried to correct the inaccuracies that occur in both Keaton's autobiography and Blesh's early biography, to the extent that Joe Keaton is misrepresented, it is insofar as Buster shielded him from criticism. I draw from this biographical information several interpretive facts: (1) Buster sustained a good deal of physical punishment in the course of the family act; (2) a performed expressionlessness accompanied the show of abuse; and (3) American audiences relished this expressionless receipt of abuse. And, notably *only* American audiences, for the Keatons tried taking their act to England in 1909 with disastrous results. The perceived "brutality" of the act was an issue.

According to Joe's report in *Variety* and Buster's subsequent retelling, the stage of London's Palace Theater was uneven and full of splinters; as a result, Joe couldn't "mop" with Buster.[51] Their usual repertoire was reduced to Joe throwing Buster around. Blesh summarizes the result: "Nine-tenths of the time, the lad was in the air; the other tenth, he was on his neck. From each fresh assault he bounded up unhurt. Visually it was funny but appalling."[52] "We did get a few titters from the gallery," Buster said of the performances in his autobiography, "but the stalls, the boxes, and the balcony greeted us with absolute silence. [. . .] Even when Pop, in desperation, said after a bit of hurly-burly, 'It loses a bit in the translation, doesn't it?' he was greeted by the same blood-chilling silence."[53]

Fellow acts and Palace manager Sir Alfred Butt advised the Keatons to tone down the violence.[54] After this the Keatons changed their act to what Blesh describes as "more pantomime and travesty, less slapstick, no assault and battery." Instead of being thrown around the stage by the suitcase handle sewn into his clothes, Buster impersonated Bert Williams, the blackbody blackface performer, who was beloved by British audiences. Again according to Blesh, Buster ended his act singing the Williams favorite "Somebody Lied," with special lyrics that Williams had written two years before for Buster's personal use.[55] British audiences' love for Williams is certainly one reason the Three Keatons added his persona to their act. But Williams was not the only popular American performer who could have been ghosted into the Keaton's act.[56] Why Williams in particular?

INTERCHANGEABLE PARTS

I suggest that Williams slid into Buster's place in the Three Keatons' show in just the way that Raggedy Auntie's performance of blackness moved from inanimacy to minstrel dialect upon coming alive for the other dolls. Both of these substitutions reveal that American repertoires of (imagined) blackness comprise interchangeable elements, such that Williams's performance of blackness—perhaps especially in tandem with his black*face*—could be substituted for Keaton's indestructibility. Williams's most famous song, readers might recall, was "Nobody" (1905), a trope that Williams extended to encompass much of his performative persona. In Louis Chude-Sokei's words, "[Williams's] signature was 'Nobody.' His persona was Mr. Nobody. His performance was erasure, not invisibility."[57] The terms Chude-Sokei uses here are fitting: "erasure" and "not invisibility." To my mind, this choice of terms hearkens back to the African American railroad porters and the simultaneous omnipresence and nonbeing they performed. It also loops in the ubiquitous and elided blackness of rag dolls' scriptive use—the way their blackness is subsumed into the cotton innards that is the source of their imperviousness.

Moreover, this instance from Keaton's childhood isn't the only occasion in which blackness and physical durability stand as interchangeable in Keaton's work. In 1921, Keaton was at work on a film titled *The Electric House*, the plot of which unfolds when a botany major is accidentally awarded an electrical engineering degree and consequently rewires a house from top to bottom. During the filming of an escalator scene, Keaton's slapshoe got caught in the machine's stair treads; before his crew could turn the escalator off, Keaton's ankle was shattered.[58] Forbidden to do stunts for at least five months, Keaton's next film, *The Playhouse*, relied on camera work to create its gags. It also relied on blackness.

The Playhouse is a fanciful two-reel film. It opens in the lobby of a small opera house in which a poster announces "Minstrel Show Tonight." Keaton arrives, buys a ticket, and enters the theater. In the theater, a group of musicians is playing—and all of the instrumentalists are Keaton. There are shots of audience members—a rich old couple, a more modest younger couple, a mother and a son—all of which are played by Keaton. And onstage, nine minstrel performers sit in line—end men Sambo and Bones with woolly wigs and whitened lips—and all of them are Keaton. In the audience, the man from the younger couple eyes the program, in which "Buster Keaton Presents BUSTER KEATON'S MINSTRELS." Keaton is listed as every performer, top to bottom. Eventually Keaton is roused as a stagehand who is dreaming this one-man show. The second half of the picture proceeds with the variety act, and includes a number of performers alongside Keaton.

Due to his ankle injury, Keaton was unable to exhibit his extraordinary indestructibility in this short film, just as he was (albeit for different reasons) in his short-lived British stage career. And, as on the British stage, his solution was the substitution of minstrel performance. In asserting this as "his" solution, it is not my intention to make this substitution purely a matter of Keaton's artistic vision. Rather, as an astute comedian and filmmaker, Keaton constructed a gag based on cultural legibility. That is, this gag would not have worked for audiences unless "blackness" is a viable substitution for "indestructibility" in the cultural imagination of the audience. It is worth noting that the duration of the blackface scene is actually quite short, and one might reasonably argue that this lessens its impact. Visually, this is true. Yet from the opening movie poster to the production list that conscripts everyone into a minstrel cast list, the narrative trope that is substituted wholesale for durability is that of blackface minstrelsy.[59]

If my argument is convincing to this point, I would propose yet other image of blackness's symbolic interchangeability, though it is, on first glance, a little harder to recognize. A publicity photograph for the 1932 film *The Passionate Plumber* shows Keaton sitting in a low armchair, playing a ukulele and gazing at a life-sized female statuary bust (fig. 5.16). The bust rests in his lap, but leans away from him and onto the arm of the chair. Keaton, in profile, wears his typical non-expression, but other elements of the picture—his proximity to the woman's face, the ukulele's suggestion of a serenade, the manner in which Keaton's feet telegraph the posture of a nervous child—suggest infatuation. As with the rag doll, this statuary head pays Keaton no mind. Turned to face the camera, her own expressionless face does not acknowledge Keaton at all. If anything, the elongated hand on which her face rests suggests grace, but perhaps also boredom.

Rapf captions this picture: "A darling of the surrealists, Keaton in a publicity photograph for *The Passionate Plumber* (1932)."[60] Indeed, Keaton was not only beloved by surrealists but has drawn comparison to surrealism from critics such as Benayoun. Rapf's caption is brief and unqualified, as if surrealism's appearance in this photograph is amply obvious. Keaton's connection to surrealism isn't obvious to every eye, however. Reviewing Benayoun's *The Look of Buster Keaton* for the Buster Keaton Society, David B. Pearson and Patricia Eliot Tobias write, "This pretentious photo-oriented book [. . .] is pretty to look at, but proposes a convoluted philosophical treatise. Benayoun compares Keaton to the

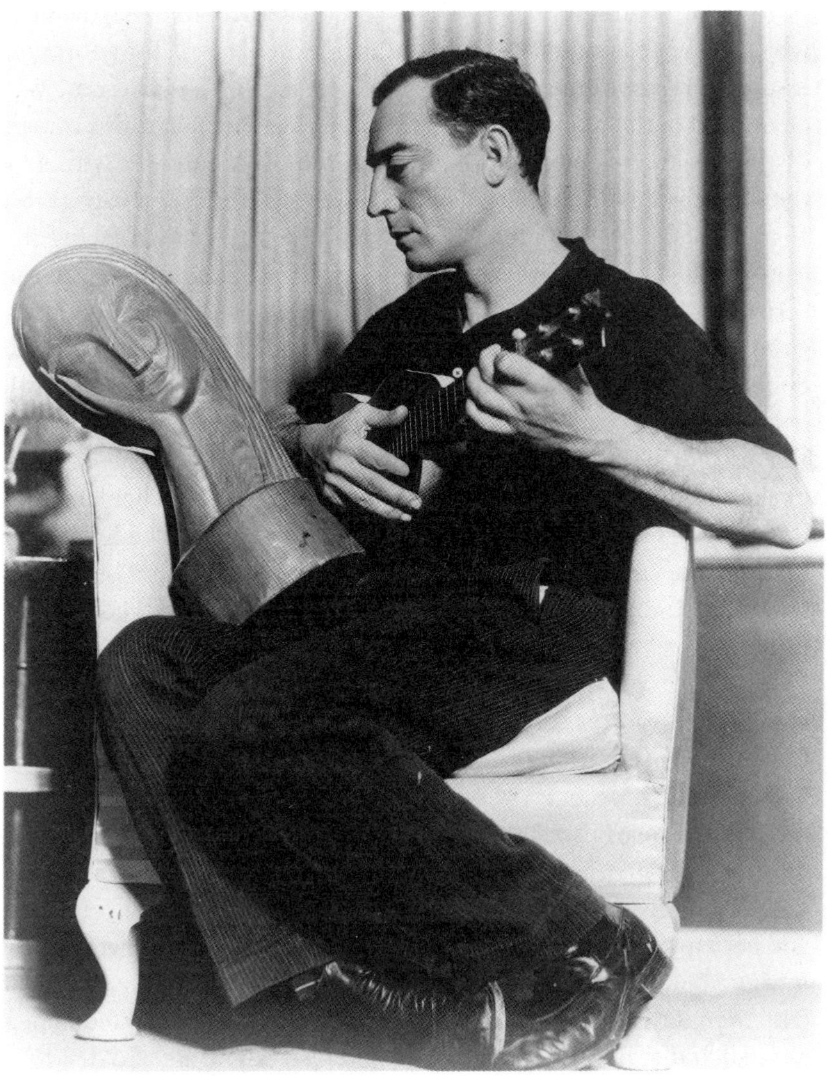

Figure 5.16. Buster Keaton in a promotional still for *The Passionate Plumber*, 1932. Courtesy of the Film Studies Center, MoMA.

great surrealists, existentialists and dada-ists. Buster would have laughed. Very expensive, if you're lucky enough to find a copy. Out of print, but a favorite with many."[61] Just because Buster would have laughed doesn't mean there's nothing to the connection. And while there are many linkages one might draw between surrealism and Keaton—to name the most persistently invoked art movement—surrealism, too, confirms the racial tinge of Keaton's performative archive.

To begin with Rapf's image and caption choice: one may wonder why *this* image is submitted as the illustration of surrealist adoration. A superficial answer lies in the suggestion that Keaton is in some way enamored of the wooden figure in his lap. But the image also carries distinct echoes—compositionally and in its contents—to works by the surrealist photographer Man Ray, especially the 1926 image series *Noire et Blanche*. Though Keaton is in profile rather than facing the camera, this image hearkens to Man Ray's most famous image of the series (fig. 5.17). In addition to the doubling of the faces (two similarly sized, one upright and one on its side, or nearly), there is, too, a subtle doubling of the hands. In Man Ray's image, Kiki de Montparnasse's hand holds an African mask upright, her fingers visible to the camera. The distinct digits of her hand find echo in Keaton's on the neck of his ukulele. Keaton's sculptural counterpart holds the side of her face, and the shape of her hand mirrors the shape of the rounded shadow under Kiki's prone visage. In fact, the pose of Keaton's sculptural beloved is strikingly similar to Constantin Brâncuși's 1918 bronze *A Muse*. I have not been able to confirm the identity of the sculptor—someone of little renown may well have produced this work as a set piece—but the abstraction of features is reminiscent of those modernist sculptors who took formal inspiration from African masks (Pablo Gargallo, Amedeo Modigliani). Moreover, though the color variation between their faces is not nearly so stark here as in Man Ray's work, *The Passionate Plumber*'s photograph features a variation in tone between Keaton and that of his statuary companion—a subtle hint of racial variation and perhaps, given his pose of infatuation, hints of miscegenation. The intrigue of this racial variation is only compounded for those familiar with Man Ray's series, which included this same image printed in negative such that the African mask appeared starkly white and de Montparnasse as black. The relative placements of Keaton (upright) and the modernist—that is to say, slightly Africanized—sculpture (prone) thereby mirror the placements of whiteness and blackness in the negative image of *Noire et Blanche*, subtly suggesting the interchangeability of whiteness and blackness.

Unlike the Scarecrow and Raggedy Ann, Man Ray's surrealist photographs were probably not well known to most members of the audiences who consumed this promotional image. It seems far more likely they *were* known to the transatlantic studio forces on the *production* end of this photograph. Regardless, as with Raggedy Ann, audiences

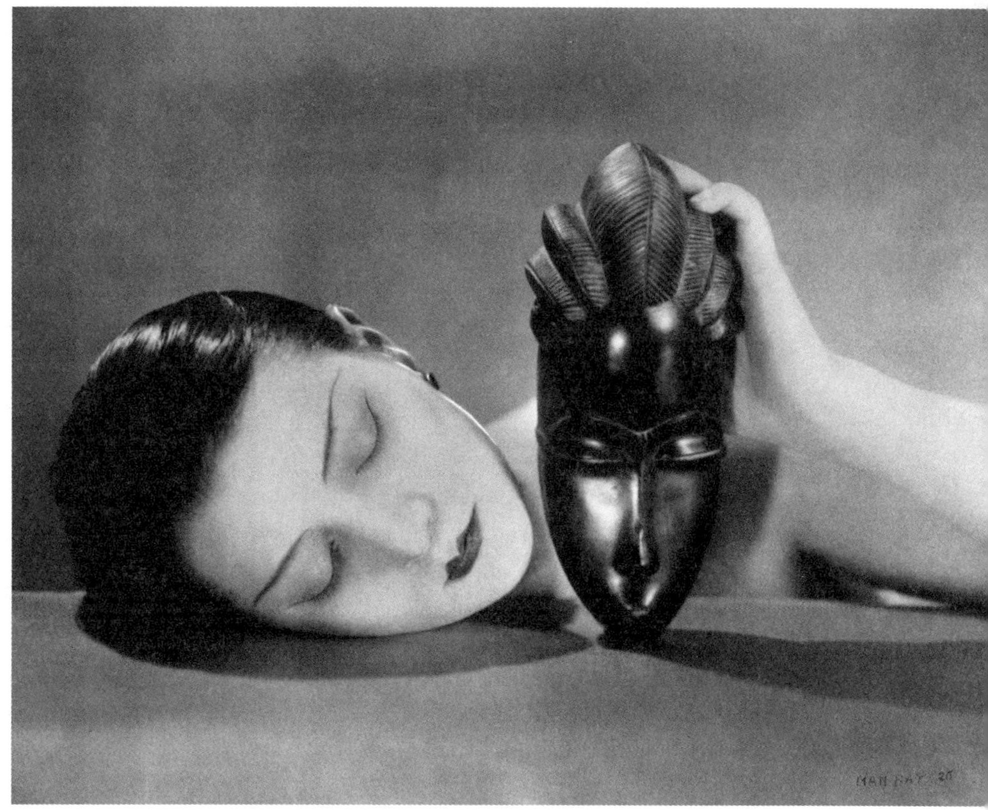

Figure 5.17. Man Ray, *Noire et Blanche*, 1926. © Man Ray 2015, Trust/Artists Rights Society (ARS), NY/ADAGP, Paris, 2021.

did not need to understand what they were seeing *as* an evocation of blackness in order to understand it as timely, compelling or affective because it *was* an evocation of blackness.

Benayoun's manuscript is particularly a case in point. Though the volume contains several essays, they exist largely to highlight the lavish illustrations. The evidentiary weight of Benayoun's assertions lies in his curation of film stills, movie posters, and artworks, and he claims Keaton's relation to various movements in art and philosophy based on these images. (This, I think, is the reason reviews find the volume convoluted even while it is beloved: its primary assertions do not lie in its text.) Keaton—either on film, or as he's been abstracted in illustrated movie posters—is juxtaposed with a wealth of artworks, including paintings by René Magritte, Alexei von Jawlenski, Giorgio de Chirico, and André Derain.

As I touched upon in chapter 4, modernists of the early twentieth century were indebted to encounters with racial and ethnic others. De Chirico, for example, kept regular company with Paul Guillaume, collector of African art and presenter of "the first public exhibition of negro art in Paris"; Derain claimed African art as a transformative inspiration.[62] Race earns no mention in the text through which Benayoun directs our gaze, yet also among his juxtapositional illustrations are explicit markers of racial otherness: pictured alongside Keaton we find a moai tangata sculpture of Polynesia, a Hawaiian feather mask, and Picasso's *Les demoiselles d'Avignon*—the most famous example of an African-inspired Western art in the modernist canon, born from Picasso's fateful 1907 visit to the Trocadéro.

Picasso's painting of prostitutes is often cited as the beginning of cubism—a proto-cubist work, evidenced by the fracturing of the figures in the painting, and the abstraction of a cube in the breasts of the woman of the upper right. the woman of the upper right. The faces of the prostitutes themselves exhibit the abstracted forms of African masks, which are, in this case, also inexpressive. Picasso later described his encounter with the other in the museum, saying "men had made those masks and other objects . . . as a kind of mediation between themselves and the unknown hostile forces that surround them . . . At that moment I realized what painting was all about . . . a way of seizing the power by giving form to our terrors as well as our desires."[63] In Benayoun's book, Keaton becomes just such a figure, a stolid intermediary of the hostile word, an object among objects, bolstered by ubiquitous and invisible blackness.

THE RIDDLE AROUND KEATON

If all this blackness seems a little too removed from Keaton's Hollywood life as we know it, I offer a reminder that Keaton's life included black *people* as well as black stereotypes. It's clear that the vaudeville circles in which he ran included some black actors; over the years Keaton relayed anecdotes about Bill "Bojangles" Robinson and Bert Williams.[64] Even more significantly, if one reads around the glaring silences and subtle suggestions of biographical sources, one can discern the likelihood that Keaton spent more than a decade of his adult life—including his most productive years—with a black man as a constant companion.

Various accounts say Keaton met Willie Riddle (also known as Willy Caruthers or Willie Carruthers) on the train home from World War I in

April of 1919, or on the train to New York for his wedding in May of 1921.[65] All agree that Riddle worked as a dining car chef on the Santa Fe line, "one of the gourmet cooks who made traveling on the Santa Fe *Super Chief* as luxurious an experience as sailing on a deluxe ocean liner."[66] Keaton took to Riddle's cooking, liked the man personally, and offered him a job as his own cook.[67] By all accounts, Riddle not only excelled as a personal chef but became Keaton's "manservant"—not so much out of an affectation of wealth on Keaton's part as out of Keaton's fundamental dependence (although wealth certainly facilitated this arrangement).[68] Put simply, Keaton was not a man who was good at looking after himself. It seems that for more than a decade—including the years in which Keaton's children were born and well into the aftermath of his first marriage—Riddle played an outsized caretaking role. Blesh describes Riddle's function as "cook, valet, wet nurse, errand boy, and secretary."[69] Marion Meade goes into more detail: "Willie Riddle became Keaton's cook and bartender, and he also took care of his wardrobe, shopped, telephoned, ran errands, wrote letters, made appointments, warded off pests, and attended to the hundred and one matters that helped keep Keaton functioning. In Keaton's dressing room Riddle operated an open bar throughout Prohibition. Friends could go into the kitchenette at any hour and count on getting a drink or a meal. For a dozen years he would be the glue of Keaton's daily life."[70]

No biographer mentions Riddle's race. Still, large and small references suggest a reasonable inference. To begin, the immeasurable list of tasks that fell to a professional chef insinuates that Riddle was exceptionally devoted, had limited options, or both. Still, that's hardly an ironclad indicator. Descriptions of Riddle are, at times, far more suggestive. Take this passage from Tom Dardis's biography:

> Willy Caruthers, Buster's servant since the end of the twenties, stayed on with 'little Bussy,' as he called him, until it became impossible for Buster to pay his weekly salary. In the mid-thirties Willy was converted to the religious movement led by Father Divine in Harlem. He changed his name to Ely Prosper; his wife changed hers to Lotus Flower. Willy made a new life and vowed to change his evil, thieving ways, for over the years he had been stealing from Buster. He attempted to make restitution for everything; figuring that he had stolen 287 chickens over the years, he returned exactly this number. After leaving Buster, Willy took a job with the Southern Pacific Railroad. When times got harder

> for Buster, Willy and his wife came once a week to clean his house from top to bottom. Like Buster, Willy always drove a Cadillac, even in the worst of times; one maddening year Buster could not afford a new one, but Willy managed to get himself one.[71]

Dardis does not indicate from whence this information comes. Regardless of its origins, this brief description seems to encode blackness at every turn—from mention of the black Harlem preacher Father Divine to the minstrel routine of chicken theft and childlike attempt at exact restitution; from devoted housecleaning to new Cadillac driving; railroad job to self-anointed prosper.[72] Of course it is possible that not all of this is true—and ultimately I'm less interested in its truth than its suggestion that blackness accompanied and served Keaton night and day.

While Dardis's passage is the most explicit suggestion that Riddle was black, it is hardly the only one. Strange wordings seem to follow Riddle's name. For example, in her description of Keaton's "war of independence" with the MGM studio, Meade writes, "Top stars at MGM were assigned elaborate accommodations. Instead, Keaton rented a house across the street from the main entrance of the studio and gathered his people there. Instead of lunching at the studio commissary, where the meals were both tasty and cheap, he had the devoted Willie Riddle make his food. Instead of behaving like an employee, he conducted himself as if he were *separate but equal* to Mayer and Thalberg" (emphasis added).[73] Why separate but equal? What does Keaton's self-assertion have to do with the Plessy v. Ferguson case that made that particular phrase famous? So far as I can tell, nothing whatsoever (especially since Keaton *preferred* his separate accommodation)—except, maybe, that this separate accommodation included Riddle.

Perhaps the most telling aspect of Riddle's legacy in Keaton's biography is how little of it there actually is, especially considering another point upon which all accounts are consistent: that Riddle was a critical member of the tiny cadre that surrounded Keaton after his first divorce. Keaton coped largely by taking off in his "land yacht," "a monstrous vehicle that had originally been ordered [. . .] by the then-president of the Pullman Company, who had placed it up for sale shortly after obtaining it. [. . . Keaton's] manservant, Willy Caruthers, was the nominal chauffeur for the land yacht, in addition to his duties as bartender and cook."[74] During his divorce, Keaton, together with friend Lew Cody, took off in the land yacht as admiral and captain, complete with uniforms taken from MGM's wardrobe department. "Carruthers," Blesh says, "was crew." With Riddle as driver, Keaton would escape in the land yacht, "fishing, duck hunting, visiting San Francisco, or just cruising. [. . .] Just as suddenly Buster would be home—he had bought a small house, where he lived alone except for Carruthers—sitting by himself, fighting to calm down and to kick the alcohol."[75]

I have been unable to find any certain image of Riddle; however, two images of Keaton with his land yacht include an unnamed black figure that, at least so far as biographies indicate, seems likely to be him. In the first of these (fig. 5.18), the unnamed black man stands at the land yacht's rear exit, his hands clasped behind his back and legs set in what a dancer would call a close fourth position. He hangs at the photograph's margin, only there, it seems, to bolster Keaton's absurd, deadpanned grandiosity in his admiral's outfit. Though Keaton has one arm tucked into his jacket in Napoleonic style, the chauffer's form carries a slight echo of Keaton's

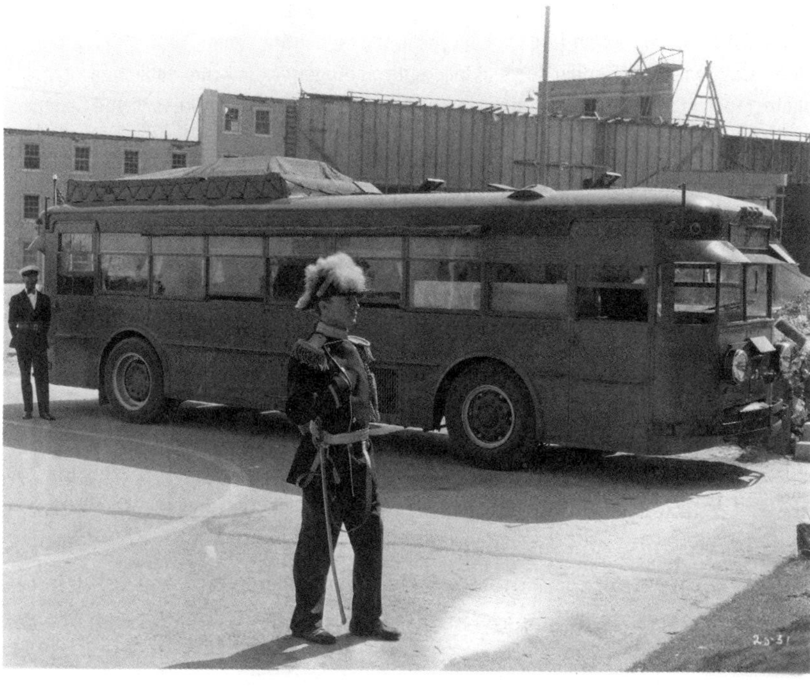

Figure 5.18. Buster Keaton with his land yacht and unidentified man, circa 1931. From the Metro-Goldwyn-Mayer production and biography photographs and core collection photographs of the Margaret Herrick Library, Academy of Motion Picture Arts and Sciences.

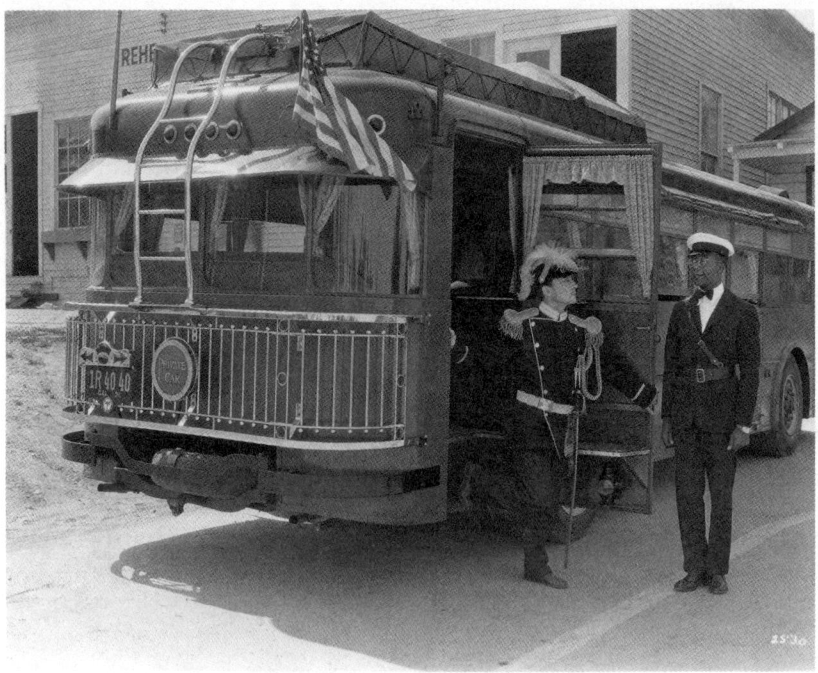

Figure 5.19. Buster Keaton with his land yacht and unidentified man, circa 1931. From the Metro-Goldwyn-Mayer production and biography photographs and core collection photographs of the Margaret Herrick Library, Academy of Motion Picture Arts and Sciences.

in the set of their legs and in the visual pop of their belts—the attendant's belt is fastened over his jacket, perhaps added as a last-minute prop. Indeed, the man himself seems added as a prop, one meant to buttress the land yacht as a set piece and Keaton as an actor before it.

A second image (fig. 5.19) shows Keaton emerging from the land yacht, his nose in the air. Here the man who might be Riddle is brought in on the joke. He is close enough that we can take in some of his details: his fine watch, his hemmed trouser cuffs, his wire-rimmed glasses, his shoes (which are, one notes, more highly shined than Keaton's own). His lips are upturned in a slight smile, though the more one zooms in on this photograph, the more staid this smile appears. With his heels smartly together and his bowtie fastened tightly to his collar, he looks far more bookish than descriptions of a chicken-thieving bartender would lead one to believe. Furthermore, given that he looks no older than Keaton, Dardis's assertion that Riddle called Keaton "little Bussy" seems all the more unlikely. Either this is not Riddle, Riddle is much older than he looks, or "little Bussy"—whether originated by Riddle or invented by someone else—is inflected with a minstrel dialect. This address also subtly emphasizes Riddle's railroad service, both before and after his time as Keaton's chef, and through the land yacht's narrated origins with the Pullman Company. As Beth Tompkins Bates has explained in her work on Pullman porters, older, southern black men were considered particularly adept at performing the simultaneous omnipresence and invisibility that was a hallmark of the Pullman porter.[76] Porters relied on their invisibility to increase the comfort (or, more exactly, the "psychological luxury") of their passengers. "Although pretending not to understand or be privy to conversations," Bates writes, "porters took mental notes of likes and dislikes, interests, and habits of clients as a way of anticipating the patrons' needs."[77]

Given the likely proximity of a black companion for at least a decade of his life, Keaton's inexpressive performance of not-knowingness and contingent existence highlights how the deadpan is a cousin of other black expressive traditions such as dissemblance and signifyin' discussed in the introduction.[78] To be clear, I'm not elevating this minor character of Keaton's biography in order to suggest that Keaton was embodying or acting *as* Willie Riddle. I suggest, however, that Keaton may have had quite an intimate view of deadpan gesture as a mode of being in the world.[79] At the least, I feel confident suggesting that the gesture of black deadpan informs the contours of the biographical *character* of Carruthers, who in turn haunts the margins of Keaton's life story. Here is a man who lived around—if not with—Keaton for some dozen years, who was part of three-man treks into the mountains for duck hunting or fishing in the face of Keaton's alcoholic divorce, and who possibly returned weekly to clean his house for some years after. Yet Riddle appears by name in no pictures (if indeed he is pictured at all), with an inconsistently spelled name, largely as a side-note tinged with racialized overtones. "Like the Negro," Blesh writes in attempting to describe Keaton's downfall in the face of sound pictures, "the thinking clown was an Invisible Man."[80]

Like the Negro indeed.

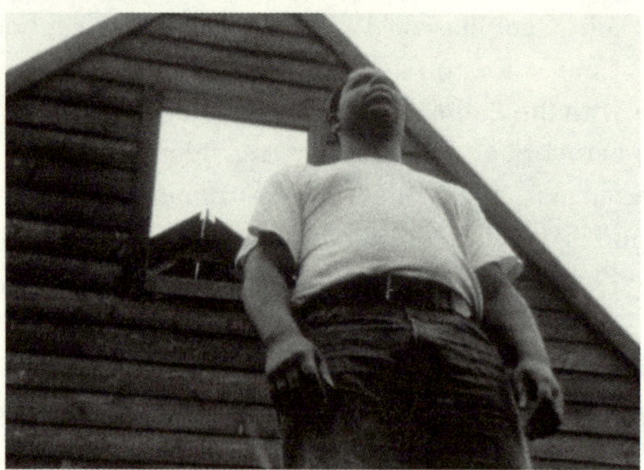

Figure C.1. Steve McQueen, still from *Deadpan*, 1997. 16mm black-and-white film, transferred to video, silent, 4:35. © Steve McQueen. Courtesy of the artist, Marian Goodman Gallery and Thomas Dane Gallery, London.

CODA

Steve McQueen Takes It Back

In 1996, Steve McQueen produced a film called *Deadpan,* now housed at the Film Study Center of the Museum of Modern Art, which riffs on a scene from Keaton's 1928 *Steamboat Bill, Jr. Steamboat Bill* contains one of Keaton's most famous scenes: the façade of a house falls onto Keaton, who is saved because he stands in exactly the location of a window. McQueen's 4:35 film reprises that moment over and over, from a variety of camera angles (fig. c.1). Besides the differences in camera angles there are some other differences. Keaton's house was located in a town, for example, while McQueen stands in an open field. Keaton's house was clearly a house; McQueen's appears rather more like an unpainted barn. There are also some similarities. Of course, the action of the house façade falling is the same. So, too, is the unflinching, deadpanned response of McQueen.

But while Keaton's stunt happened once in a fast-moving sequence of events representing a cyclone blowing through town, no atmospheric event prompts the fall of the barn wall over McQueen. In *Steamboat Bill, Jr.*, Keaton stands facing the camera as the house façade drops. In *Deadpan,* the first time the wall falls, the shot we see is of McQueen's back and the grassy field that he faces. And rather than happening once, the façade's fall happens (or, at least, is sequentially pictured) over and over again. The second shot is of his unlaced boots; the camera stays tightly focused on them as the façade drops, sending up a small shower of dirt. At other points in the film, we see just McQueen's hands and legs experience the fall, or watch from overhead, or watch in profile, or watch from below. Moreover, not all of the camera angles feature McQueen at all. In one shot we watch the window drop away from the camera's pictured area, leaving a view of the ceiling joists instead.

As mentioned above, McQueen remains deadpanned throughout the film, but this is especially highlighted in a couple of moments. One occurs during the one moment of seeming "effect" in the film, beyond the use of camera angle and shot length. At this point, rather near the end of the film, it seems the shot has been rewound. There is a close-up of McQueen's face as the shadows of the barn pass over it—then the shadows appear to move *up* across his face before once again passing down. McQueen remains placid throughout, save a slight shift in his brow. The other occurs at the end of the film, where, after a blackout, McQueen's face returns to the screen just before the film ends. *Blackout.*

Obviously, this short film borrows from Keaton in its content and in its title. But it also *takes back* from Keaton, *re*-situating deadpan in black cultural production through McQueen's black body. Even more than in Keaton's singular façade drop, for example, McQueen's tight camera angles and the exclusion or partial exclusion of the human render inanimate objects willfully lively. The picture of the barn window letting go of its wall to expose the joists behind it demonstrates this sense of liveliness. It also lets the black male escape our scopic gaze for a moment, though we know he's there (for where else could he be?). At another point, a shower of dirt jumps up at the façade's landing, but McQueen's rooted boots do not. The dirt, then, is similarly lively. Given all this movement, McQueen's stillness is all the more striking. The sense of scale pivots around this stillness: the barn and the man loom over the ground, the wall looms over the man, the man looms over the hole, the trees loom over it all.

Similarly, McQueen's use of timing has an uncanny effect. While the façade drop of *Steamboat Bill, Jr.* was a surprising twist for its viewers, the same cannot be said for the viewer of *Deadpan*. We know the façade is going to drop. Moreover, we know it is going to drop over and over again. What we *don't* know is its timing. Some of McQueen's shots are uncomfortably long—we are looking at not much of anything, waiting and waiting. At other times, more than one iteration of the drop happens in quick succession—we've hardly appreciated the last one's effects before we're on to the next one. At least for me, this increases both the anxiety and the sense of uselessness—*nothing to be done*—that surrounds McQueen's figure.

And yet, though McQueen appears as an object among objects, less lively than a barn side or a spray of dirt and no livelier than the boots he wears, he is not still in order to better take abuse. While a great deal of anxiety surrounds the façade's weighty drop, the protagonist of the film is never forced to perform his durability, even if he does perform his endurance, as he never comes to any physical harm. This is not to suggest that he is free. So long as the barn side will drop, he must be in the space of the window. And so he waits, object-like, for the material world to do what it will. The world is not benevolent, but the fact that McQueen's protagonist isn't a rag doll offers a significant revision of Keaton's character—and suggests, ever so subtly, that he never was that. Above all, and most intangibly, I have the sense, when I watch *Deadpan*, that I am, for once, the intended audience. That in this case, McQueen's inexpression is speaking to me, with me, about the shared condition of embodied racialization and of the kinds of psychic durability and physical stilling that it can call for. Of course I can't say whether or not that was McQueen's intention. But, as with the girl in the Gee's Bend window, in the end, intention isn't the thing that matters.

Ultimately, in this book I have argued that deadpan is a black gesture because of the kinds of associations that trail blackness, and because of the ways that black people can and do work with and through these associations. Deadpan is capable of hiding, deflecting, or amplifying expressive content without being loud or expressive in itself. This quiet has given it short shrift in performance analysis. Therefore, this book tracks an omnipresent yet undernoted gestural repertoire across a range of media and genre, for it is only through assembling this repertoire that the full range of deadpan's malleability and rhetorical efficacy becomes clear. Deadpan can signal the ways that blackness calls for, and calls forth, performances of inanimacy and insensibility. Yet deadpan can also beget affects that bind community, or that gift a sense of belonging, or, perhaps at the most utopic, allow others to experience, if just for a moment, a box or a hole for standing. Most often, deadpan's doings live somewhere in between—an ambivalent and eloquent *some type of way*.

# ACKNOWLEDGMENTS

Countless people have helped bring this project to fruition. In attempting to enumerate them I am likely to have forgotten someone, and if so I offer my deepest apologies. It is only a measure of the sheer numbers of friends and colleagues to whom I owe a debt of gratitude. I hope that if you do not see your name, you at least see your community listed among the benevolent forces below.

To begin at the beginning: Bruce Bennett, Catherine Burroughs, and Cynthia Garrett inexplicably believed in the world's messiest undergraduate. Sherry Simpson was a beloved friend and mentor and she remains the teacher I strive to be. I miss her more than she would believe, and I can, in fact, imagine her scoffing at that idea in her humble and hilarious way from the shag-carpeted benches of the Blue Fox.

Aaron Sachs, Crystal Feimster, and Jonathan Holloway emboldened me to dream of Yale. Jennifer Brice's encouragement was invaluable in a moment of great transition. I raise a glass to Sue Edinger, a model of women's mentorship, for encouraging me to go when it would have been easier not to. Professors Elizabeth Alexander, Jafari Allen, Hazel Carby, Jonathan Holloway, Matthew Frye Jacobson, Erica James, Kathryn Lofton, Paige McGinley, Joseph Roach, Marc Robinson, and Robert Stepto made Yale an intellectual home. Jacqueline Goldsby served on my orals committee with good cheer and great advice. George Chauncey, Toni Dorfman, Jonathan Holloway, and

Kathryn Lofton guided my pedagogical development. Elise Morrison, Kimberly Jannarone, and La Marr Jurelle Bruce offered camaraderie and mentorship. So did Douglas Jones, Shane Vogel, and Soyica Colbert. Albert Laguna and Greta LaFleur were the Fairy Godpeople of job market materials preparation—may they be forever blessed. Jodie Stewart-Moore, Lisa Monroe, Jennifer Fleischer, Susan Shand, and Jean Cherniavsky made everything work. Michelle Nearon was also a great support.

Thanks to my cohort members in American Studies and African American Studies: Wendell Adjetey, Anusha Alles, Susie An, Danielle Bainbridge, Jorge Cuéllar, Melissa Castillo-Garsow, Anya Montiel, Sebastian Perez, Usha Rungoo, Aaron Sweeney; and the members of my RITM Dissertation Working Group. Additional thanks to Nicholas Forster, Madeline Whittle, and Chris Kramaric for keeping us young. Matt Keaney, we'll always have French for Reading. Heather Vermeulen, Fadila Habchi, and Danya Pilgrim, thank you for holding it down, intellectually and interpersonally, in quiet and key ways. Above all, I thank Claire Schwartz and Lauren Meyer for their love and trust, Michelle Morgan for her example, and Alex Ripp for her constant companionship.

Robert Stepto and Mary Lui midwifed this project from a sprawling idea into a coherent prospectus. Joseph Roach, Kathryn Lofton and Daphne Brooks served on my dissertation committee, and Erica James had a profound effect before leaving for warmer shores. Each of them has made this work immeasurably better, though two deserve an extra word. Joseph Roach inherited me from a departing faculty member and has been a paragon of generosity ever since. His faith in this project has never wavered—but as far as I can tell, his faith never wavers in any of his former students. Furthermore, the Performance Studies Working Group of IPSY (Interdisciplinary Performance Studies at Yale), which Joe convened, provided me with a cherished community of scholars at Yale, and brokered my connections to the broader performance studies world. Kathryn Lofton, too, convened a group of scholars in her magical way. Alex Kaloyanides, Emily Johnson, Kati Curts, Michelle Morgan, Molly Greene, Shari Rabin, Sarah Koenig, Lucia Hulsether, Cody Musselman, Catherine Mas, and Lewis West modeled what an intellectually and personally supportive academic community can be, and I thank them all. As a teacher, KL validated my wackiest scholarly impulses and invalidated my crippling doubts. As a dear friend, she held up my entire house in a time of sudden need. No words can amply express my gratitude.

Chapters in development benefited from additional conversations with Colleen Kim Daniher, Kyle C. Frisina, Christopher Grobe, Vivian Huang, Bettina Judd, Christina Leon, Christine Mok, Amber Jamilla Musser, and Sarah Stefana Smith. Unbeknownst to him, a question from Vincent Brown had a profound effect on chapter 1. Many of my colleagues in the English Department of the University of Chicago read this manuscript in whole or in part and offered their thinking to strengthen my own. In particular, I thank Ellen McKay, Frances Ferguson, C. Riley Snorton, Adrienne Brown, and Sianne Ngai for detailed chapter discussion, and I bless up to Lauren Berlant, who is so very missed. Timothy Harrison, Benjamin A. Saltzman, James Chandler, Bill Brown, Timothy Campbell, Deborah Nelson, Christopher Taylor, and Noémie Ndiaye also offered keen and thoughtful feedback. Deborah Nelson and David Levin have offered their levity, strategic thinking, and constant encouragement. In their different ways, Allyson Nadia Field and Kenneth Warren have gone above and beyond in being helpful and welcoming. Ellen McKay's humor, insight and everyday vocabulary are astounding. Adrienne Brown, Edgar Garcia, and Christopher Taylor hang tough, and I thank them for playing the role of older academic siblings in offices, homes, and cash-only establishments. Sianne Ngai and C. Riley Snorton have become friends as well as mentors, and I thank them for their willingness to field a call about anything. Zachary Samalin, Sonali Thakkar, and Rachel Galvin always bring the good fight with articulate grace. Thanks to Honey Crawford and Julia Rhoads for their camaraderie and support.

I am tremendously thankful for my community at the University of Chicago. In the pre-pandemic days, SJ Zhang and Kaneesha Parsard invested many a morning in the study rooms of the Rubenstein, and their support and camaraderie was invaluable. A number of other postdoctoral fellows lent their support and company in writing and in life; my thanks to Carmen Merport Quiñonez, Marcia Tan, Loren Saulsberry, Aresha Martinez-Cardoso, Natacha Nsabimana, Kathryn Takabvirwa, Tulio Bermúdez, Sharese King, and Sophia Azeb. Tracye Matthews and Tierra Kilpatrick helped secure spaces for us to work communally. Many discussions with Michael Dango, over ambivalence and drinks, form the backdrop of this book. Since the beginning of the pandemic I have benefited from the wisdom, kindness, and fortitude of Leslie

Rogers, Victoria Saramago, Sophie Salvo, and Kathryn Takabvirwa, and I thank Melissa Gilliam and Regina Dixon-Reeves for bringing us together. Deisy Del Real, Holly Guise, and Roya Ebtehaj, thank you for sharing your lives with me for the last four years. I thank all of my students, but especially the graduate students of Get the Ax and MTRG. Shirl Yang, Marissa Fenley, Eva Pensis, Arianna Gass, Bellamy Mitchell, Michael Stablein Jr., Clara Nizard, Fabien Maltais-Bayda, Lily Scherlis, and Jenny Harris, it is a pleasure learning with and beside you. And, as ever, department administrators make the world go 'round. My thanks to Lex Nalley Drlica, Racquel Asante, Angeline Dimambro, Katie Kahal, Laura Merchant, Anna Dobrowolski, Vicki Walden, Jessi Haley, Starsha Gill, and Annette Lepique for answering my countless inanities and for securing vegan food.

Brian Herrera, Stephanie Leigh Batiste, and especially Robin Bernstein provided early support and encouragement. I thank Uri McMillan, Sandra Ruiz, and Shane Vogel for including me in the Minoritarian Aesthetics Series. Eric Zinner, Furqan Sayeed, and Ainee Jeong have been responsive at every turn. My editors Amy Sherman and James Harbeck found countless little errors, redundancies, and tics, and improved the manuscript tremendously. My gratitude to Josh Rutner for indexing this work. Two anonymous readers were extremely insightful and generous, and I thank them both. Ella Nagle, research assistant extraordinaire, invested hours in securing image files and permissions for this manuscript. This book could not have made it across the finish line without her calm organization, diligent persistence, and unflappable good humor.

Research was facilitated by funding from the Beinecke Rare Book & Manuscript Library's Gallup Fellowship in American Literature and the Dean's Emerging Scholar Award at Yale. At the University of Chicago, research was funded through the Humanities Division and the College. Additional gratitude goes to the Mellon Foundation and the University of Chicago's Center for the Study of Race, Politics, and Culture (CSRPC), whose generosity secured the many images this book contains. Marilyn Willis helped to administer these funds. For their generous administrative help, I thank Simon Crocker, Chairman of The John Kobal Foundation; Ashley Swinnerton and the Film Study Center at MoMA; Kristine Krueger, NFIS Coordinator at the Margaret Herrick Library of the Academy of Motion Picture Arts and Sciences; Erin Harris at the Richard Avedon Foundation; and Lexi Campbell at the Matthew Marks Gallery. I also offer my gratitude to Martin Puryear for sharing his time and his thoughts.

Finally, this project could never have come to be without the help and support of a number of friends in New Haven, Chicago, and around the world. I am sorry to offer the fewest words to and about you, but you are too many and my heart is too full. My thanks to Friends Center for Children; Cold Spring School; Connie Razza; Adam Solomon and Brenda Carter; Jim Baron; Jen Grace Baron; Paul North and Carolina Baffi; Julie Krishnaswami; Matt and Sarah Keaney; Tori and Ronnie Rysz; Benjamin Saltzman and Ashleigh Langs-Saltzman; Tim Harrison and Christina Smit; Cristi Alvarado and Joe Stadolnik; Rachel DeWoskin and Zayd Dohrn; Rachel Cohen; everyone in 5411–15, but especially Hoyt Long and Mea Konopasek; Joshua Dumas; Liz Bradfield and Lisa Sette; Kelly Carlisle; Sarah Malena and Don Wallace; Phil Wittman; Sabrica Barnett; Ben Tevelin; Tim Marvin; and Susan Deacon and Mark Ferrari. Thanks, as well, to my family: the aunts (Marilyn, Linda, Nancy, Vivian, and Janet); Andy Post; Barb Post and Keith Batman; Caleb Batman and Dylan Hohmann; Emma Batman and Zac and Oliver Mosely; Johanna Batman and John and Nanami Person; my sister Anna; and my parents Ken Post and Mickie Cuevas-Post.

Last but not least, thanks to Arlo, Phineas, and Mark. You make all things possible, and all work worthwhile. Thank you for your patience, wit, love, and grounding influence. This book is for you.

NOTES

INTRODUCTION

1 These rows represent enraged, ashamed, cautious, smug, and depressed; and overwhelmed, hopeful, lonely, lovestruck, jealous.

2 An idiosyncratic observation: if, to my child-of-the-'70s mind, the cultural artifact most conjured through the seriality of Borgman's illustration is the album sleeve of REO Speedwagon's *Nine Lives* (in which nine otherwise identical cat faces are individuated through their choice of sunglasses and coordinating cat-nose color), the photographic head of Quan brings to mind the poster for Grandmaster Flash and the Furious 5 at the Twin City Roller Rink, Sept. 10, 1981: https://digital.library.cornell.edu/catalog/ss:1334248. The signification of photographic realism in the grid, in other words, may activate a broader set of aesthetic legacies for black audiences familiar with hip hop lineages.

3 *Urban Dictionary*, s.v. "some type of way," accessed February 2, 2018, www.urbandictionary.com.

4 *Oxford English Dictionary Online*, s.v. "dead-pan" (Oxford University Press, December 2014), www.oed.com.

5 "Deliberate" is the first word of the definition that appears in the *New Oxford American Dictionary*, s.v. "deadpan" (Oxford University Press, 2010), online version.

6 *Oxford English Dictionary Online*, s.v. "dead-pan" (Oxford University Press, December 2014), www.oed.com.

7 Sid Sutherland, "Firpo Lucky if He Lasts Five Rounds with Dempsey," *Los Angeles Times*, August 6, 1923, ProQuest Historical Newspapers: Los Angeles Times (1881–1989).

8 Tom Fletcher, *The Tom Fletcher Story: 100 Years of the Negro in Show Business!* (New York: Burdge & Company, 1954), 114–15.

9 By asserting that corporeality can communicate in and of itself, I do not mean to suggest that what a body communicates is necessarily chosen. Indeed, a fundamental assumption of performance studies is that there is no such thing as a neutral body. Our gender, our race, our shape each carry assertions through the structures and assumptions that precede us. Judith Butler, *Gender Trouble: Feminism and the Subversion of Identity* (New York: Routledge, 1990).

10 Tina Post, "Williams, Walker, and Shine: Blackbody Blackface, or the Importance of Being Surface," *TDR/The Drama Review* 59, no. 4 (2015): 83–100; V. I. Pudovkin, "Film Technique," in *Film: An Anthology*, ed. Daniel Talbot (Berkeley: University of California Press, 1959), 189–200.

11 Édouard Glissant, *Poetics of Relation*, trans. Betsy Wing (Ann Arbor: University of Michigan Press, 1997).

12 An airshaft is defined in the *Oxford English Dictionary* as a straight, vertical passage that admits air into a mine or tunnel, or a ventilating a shaft for a building or room. *Oxford English Dictionary Online*, s.v. "airshaft" (Oxford University Press, December 2016), www.oed.com.

13 Richard O. Boyer, "The Hot Bach (1944)," in *The Duke Ellington Reader*, ed. Mark Tucker (New York: Oxford University Press, 1993), 214–45.

14 Though it is hard to make out, the woman is featured in a cellophane ad. In a decorative blouse or dress, with a watch prominently displayed above manicured hands, she holds an elaborately braided bread suggestive of elegance and refinement. "Your baker offers you a tempting variety!" the ad says, and, "Really fresh thanks to 'Cellophane.'"

15 Uri McMillan, *Embodied Avatars: The Art of Black Female Performance* (New York: New York University Press, 2015), 7.

16 I say more about awayness in chapter 3.

17 For more on the important topic of black interiority, see Kevin E. Quashie, *The Sovereignty of Quiet: Beyond Resistance in Black Culture* (New Brunswick, NJ: Rutgers University Press, 2012); Darby English, *1971: A Year in the Life of Color* (Chicago: University of Chicago Press, 2016).

18 Nor is black interiority necessarily less prone to racial overwriting. In the specific ecology of this image, granting the girl an imaginative, contemplative, or spiritual inner life risks not divorcing her from the crude materiality of the cabin but instead figuring black interiority as a matter of essential human origins, reinforced by the girl's youth.

19 Sylvia Wynter, "Rethinking 'Aesthetics': Notes Towards a Deciphering Practice," in *Ex-Iles: Essays on Caribbean Cinema*, ed. Mbye B. Cham (Trenton, NJ: Africa World Press, 1992).

20 José Esteban Muñoz, *Disidentifications: Queers of Color and the Performance of Politics* (Minneapolis: University of Minnesota Press, 1999).

21 I do not invoke stoicism in relation to the deadpan, because as I understand it, stoicism presupposes a person's emotional state and implies their ethical commitments. As much as possible, I wish to avoid ascribing emotions or ethics to the performing black subject without a supporting account, attempting instead to read the performative scene. Said differently, even if the aesthetic e/affect of a scene were to be such that stoicism seems called for, I would prefer to ascribe the stoic affect to the observed assemblage rather than the subject at its center. My colleague Tim Campbell also helpfully suggests that deadpan's relationship to sympathy has interesting implications for Adam Smith's spectator, in whom sympathy is increased through stoic reserve. While I've elected to avoid this exploration in this text, I am grateful to Tim for introducing this point for further consideration.

22 For example, see Hortense Spillers's foundational distinction between the discursive body and the maimable flesh, where discourse's abstract body leaves blackness's flesh behind. Hortense J. Spillers, "Mama's Baby, Papa's Maybe: An American Grammar Book," in *Black, White, and in Color: Essays on American Literature and Culture* (Chicago: University of Chicago Press, 2003), 203–29.

23 Noa Steimatsky, *The Face on Film* (New York: Oxford University Press, 2017), 21.

24 Steimatsky, 3.

25 The phrase "archaic power" appears in the book's summary paragraph on the back cover.

26 Calvin L. Warren, *Ontological Terror: Blackness, Nihilism, and Emancipation* (Durham, NC: Duke University Press, 2018); Miguel Gutierrez, "Does Abstraction Belong to White People?" *BOMB*, November 7, 2018, https://bombmagazine.org. I recognize that I am moving quickly between between abstraction and metaphysics, and that they are not identical terms. While I cannot here provide a theorization of the dislocations of twentieth-century secularism, S. Elise Archias and Juliet Bellow's introduction to their special issue of *Arts* helps explicate the slippage that allows me to move between these terms. S. Elise Archias and Juliet Bellow, "'Dance and Abstraction' Special Issue Introduction," *Arts* 9, no. 4 (December 2020): 120.

27 Phillip Brian Harper, *Abstractionist Aesthetics: Artistic Form and Social Critique in African American Culture* (Durham, NC: Duke University Press, 2015), 1–67. For Harper, the difficulty of untethering black representational abstraction from historical oppression prompts a turn to the sonic and literary as spheres of abstractionist aesthetics. While I concede the promise of these other realms, I refuse to abandon the attempt to redeem black visuality, for, as I say elsewhere in these pages, blackness will not (and should not) cease to be seen.

28 Harper, 63.

29 Allan Sekula, "The Body and the Archive," *October* 39 (Winter 1986): 3–64; Sander L. Gilman, "Black Bodies, White Bodies: Toward an Iconography of Female Sexuality in Late Nineteenth-Century Art, Medicine, and Literature," in *"Race," Writing, and Difference*, ed. Henry Louis Gates, Jr. (Chicago: University of Chicago Press, 1986), 223–61; Ann Fabian, *The Skull Collectors: Race, Science, and America's Unburied Dead* (Chicago: University of Chicago Press, 2010); Mel Chen, *Animacies: Biopolitics, Racial Mattering, and Queer Affect* (Durham, NC: Duke University Press, 2012); Alexander Todorov, Christopher Olivola, Ron Dotsch, and Peter Mende-Siedlecki, "Social Attributions from Faces: Determinants, Consequences, Accuracy, and Functional Significance," *Annual Review of Psychology* 66 (August 25, 2014): 519–45.

30 Carrie Noland, *Agency and Embodiment: Performing Gestures/Producing Culture* (Cambridge, MA: Harvard University Press, 2009).

31 A reader who doubts the conscriptive or culturally determined nature of facial (in)expression might scan any of black Twitter's periodic parenting-focused hashtags for the phrase "fix your face."

32 Lauren Berlant, "Showing Up to Withhold: Pope.L's Deadpan Aesthetic," in *Showing Up to Withhold* (Chicago: The Renaissance Society at the University of Chicago, in association with the University of Chicago Press, 2014).

33 Kim F. Hall, *Things of Darkness: Economies of Race and Gender in Early Modern England* (Ithaca, NY: Cornell University Press, 1995), 7.

34 Kobena Mercer, "Art History and the Dialogics of Diaspora," *Small Axe* 38 (July 2012): 223.

35 Sunny Xiang locates Asian inscrutability in the tones of the cold war's intelligence apparatus, arguing that the cold war's "most confounding intelligence concern [. . .] was neither containing Oriental enemies nor promoting Asian friends but distinguishing one from the other." While she doesn't use the term *inscrutable*, Karen Shimakawa rightly describes Young Jean Lee's *Songs of the Dragons Flying to Heaven* as "a play that vexes all attempts to situate it neatly in terms of politics or aesthetics [or] affect." Christine Mok notes how artist Nikki S. Lee elucidates "the complexity and complicity of racial surveillance" by frustrating visual legibility for Asian and American audiences alike. Vivian Huang reads performance works by Yoko Ono and Laurel Nakadate as experiments in disidentificatory hospitality, arguing that, through silence and parasitism, the artists perform an inscrutability that accommodates intimacy even as it gestures to the expectation that the Asian/American female is always host and never guest. Sonny Xiang, *Tonal Intelligence: The Aesthetics of Asian Inscrutability during the Long Cold War* (New York: Columbia University Press, 2020), 36; Karen Shimakawa, "Young Jean Lee's Ugly Feelings about Race and Gender: Stuplime Animation in *Songs of the Dragons Flying to Heaven*," *Women & Performance* 17, no. 1 (March 2007): 89–102; Christine Mok, "On The Face of It: Nikki S Lee's Layers" (presented at the Performance Studies Working Group, Yale University, November 3, 2015); Vivian L. Huang, "Inscrutably, Actually: Hospitality, Parasitism, and the Silent Work of Yoko Ono and Laurel Nakadate," *Women & Performance: A Journal of Feminist Theory* 28, no. 3 (2018): 187–203.

36 Eric Hayot, *The Hypothetical Mandarin: Sympathy, Modernity, and Chinese Pain* (New York: Oxford University Press, 2009), 168–70.

37 Hayot, 129.

38 Summer Kim Lee, "Staying In: Mitski, Ocean Vuong, and Asian American Asociality," *Social Text* 37, no. 1 (2019): 31.

39 Lee briefly mentions inscrutability in her discussion about accommodation, but she largely does so through Vivian Huang's work on hospitality. See Huang, "Inscrutably, Actually."

40 Summer Kim Lee, "Staying In," 39–40.

41 Summer Kim Lee, "Staying In," 31.

42 Here I mean "performance" in the same sense as Erving Goffman's in *The Presentation of Self in Everyday Life* (New York: Anchor Books, 1959). He writes, "I assume that when an individual appears before others he will have many motives for trying to control the impression they receive of the situation [. . .] I shall be concerned only with the participant's dramaturgical problems of presenting the activity before others. The issues dealt with by stagecraft and stage management are sometimes trivial but they are quite general; they seem to occur everywhere in social life" (15).

43 In Hall's words, "cultural hegemony is never about pure victory or pure domination (that's not what the term means); it is never a zero-sum cultural game; it is always about shifting the balance of power in the relations of culture; it is always about changing the dispositions and the configurations of cultural power." Stuart Hall, "What Is This Black in Black Popular Culture?," in *Critical*

Dialogues in Cultural Studies, ed. David Morley and Kuan-Hsing Chen (London: Routledge, 1996).

44 Ju Yon Kim, *The Racial Mundane: Asian American Performance and the Embodied Everyday* (New York: New York University Press, 2015), 10.

45 Saidiya Hartman, *Scenes of Subjection: Terror, Slavery, and Self-Making in Nineteenth-Century America* (New York: Oxford University Press, 1997); Nicole R. Fleetwood, *Troubling Vision: Performance, Visuality, and Blackness* (Chicago: University of Chicago Press, 2011).

46 One well-known example from within black culture (and by no means the most egregious one) can be found in Zora Neale Hurston, "Characteristics of Negro Expression," in *Zora Neale Hurston: Folklore, Memoirs and Other Writings*, ed. Cheryl A. Wall (New York: The Library of America, 1995), 830–47.

47 In this and other images, I have elected to consider the pictured subjects as co-creators of their images. I readily concede that this is a particularly messy business: although many of the pictured subjects were aware of the camera's presence, others may not have been. Moreover, at times the photographer may have desired expressionlessness in the black subject, and pictures may have been composed accordingly. The pictured subjects had little control over the circulation of their images and received inadequate, if any, remuneration from the uses that followed (through inclusion in *Life* magazine, for example—a publication whose resounding success resided largely in its savvy and powerful use of the social image). Still, I do not believe these concerns should render the photographed subjects powerless in the moment of their pictured performance of selfhood. I hope it is possible to acknowledge the differential powers at play within a sociopolitical matrix without rendering every black subject a hapless token in someone else's game.

48 Goffman, *Presentation of Self in Everyday Life*; Michel de Certeau, *The Practice of Everyday Life* (Berkeley: University of California Press, 1984).

49 Richard Iton, *In Search of the Black Fantastic: Politics and Popular Culture in the Post-Civil Rights Era* (New York: Oxford University Press, 2008), 8.

50 Iton, 16.

51 Robin D. G. Kelley, "'We Are Not What We Seem': Rethinking Black Working-Class Opposition in the Jim Crow South," *Journal of American History* 80, no. 1 (June 1993): 75–112; Iton, *In Search of the Black Fantastic*, 102.

52 Jeffrey Ferguson, "Race and the Rhetoric of Resistance," *Raritan* 28, no. 1 (Summer 2008): 4–32.

53 Muñoz, *Disidentifications*; Anne Anlin Cheng, *The Melancholy of Race: Psychoanalysis, Assimilation, and Hidden Grief* (New York: Oxford University Press, 2000); Karen Shimakawa, *National Abjection: The Asian American Body Onstage* (Durham, NC: Duke University Press, 2002); E. Patrick Johnson, *Appropriating Blackness: Performance and the Politics of Authenticity* (Durham, NC: Duke University Press, 2003).

54 Susan Manning, *Modern Dance, Negro Dance: Race in Motion* (Minneapolis: University of Minnesota Press, 2004), 10–11.

55 English, *1971: A Year in the Life of Color*, 45.

56 English, 71.

57 Scholars who convincingly argue for opacity as a mode of blackness include Daphne Brooks, *Bodies in Dissent: Spectacular Performances of Race and Freedom, 1850–1910* (Durham, NC: Duke University Press, 2006); Shane Vogel, *The Scene of Harlem Cabaret: Race, Sexuality, Performance* (Chicago: University of Chicago Press, 2009); Huey Copeland, *Bound to Appear: Art, Slavery and the Site of Blackness in Multicultural America* (Chicago: University of Chicago Press, 2013).

58 Vogel, *Scene of Harlem Cabaret*; Harvey Young, *Embodying Black Experience: Stillness, Critical Memory, and the Black Body* (Ann Arbor: University of Michigan Press, 2010); Brooks, *Bodies in Dissent*; Copeland, *Bound to Appear*.

59 See Henry Louis Gates, Jr., "The Blackness of Blackness: A Critique of the Sign and the Signifying Monkey," in *Black Literature and Literary Theory*, ed. Henry Louis Gates, Jr. (New York: Methuen, 1984), 289–93.

60 Darlene Clark Hine, "Rape and the Inner Lives of Black Women in the Middle West," in "Common Grounds and Crossroads: Race, Ethnicity, and Class in Women's Lives," special issue, *Signs* 14, no. 4 (Summer 1989): 915.

61 Brooks, *Bodies in Dissent*, 8.

1. SUBJECTIVITY AND SELF-SPECIMENIZATION

1 Louis was at times pictured smiling with his family or with fellow celebrities. Conversely, a (rare) series of photos depicts Louis *glowering* in his boxing gear. These images can be found at the Hank Kaplan Boxing Archive at the Brooklyn College library. I am thankful to librarian Jahongir Usmanov for his assistance. To contextualize Louis's archive from another angle, *most* fighters in stance photographs are relatively expressionless as a convention of the genre; Louis's stance photos are therefore unexceptional in this regard. Furthermore, from yet another rhetorical position, no face is ever *truly* expressionless, and Louis's forehead bore a deep and affecting furrow from a young age—an easy place to read expression or ground affective information, whether real or projected.

2 Dan Burley, "3 In Mid-West Win as Golden Glovers," *New York Amsterdam News*, March 17, 1934, ProQuest Historical Newspapers: New York Amsterdam News (1922–1993).

3 Bill Gibson, "Hear Me Talkin' to Ya," *Baltimore Afro-American*, April 13, 1935, ProQuest Historical Newspapers: Baltimore Afro-American (1893–1988).

4 Joe Louis and Art Rust and Edna Rust, *Joe Louis: My Life* (New York: Harcourt Brace Jovanovich, 1978); Chris Mead, *Champion—Joe Louis: Black Hero in White America* (New York: Charles Scribner's Sons, 1985); David Margolick, *Beyond Glory: Joe Louis vs. Max Schmeling, and a World on the Brink* (New York: Vintage Books, 2005); Lewis Erenberg, *The Greatest Fight of Our Generation: Louis vs. Schmeling* (New York: Oxford University Press, 2006); Joe Louis Barrow Jr. and Barbara Munder, *Joe Louis: 50 Years an American Hero* (New York: McGraw-Hill, 1998); Randy Roberts, *Joe Louis: Hard Times Man* (New Haven, CT: Yale University Press, 2010).

5 Louis and Rust and Rust, *Joe Louis*, 39. "They did not set down in writing any particular rules and say, 'Now this is what you have to do.' No, just in day by day talking I knew what they wanted."

6 Jeffrey T. Sammons, *Beyond the Ring: The Role of Boxing in American Society* (Urbana: University of Illinois Press, 1988), 98. The same seven-point list consistently recurs in connection to Louis, including (unattributed) appearances in such works as David Remnick's *King of the World: Muhammad Ali and the Rise of an American Hero* (New York: Vintage Books, 1998), 225–6; Mead, *Champion—Joe Louis*, 52; Barrow and Munder, *Joe Louis*, 43.

7 The conclusions of this chapter are also indebted to Tina Campt's discussion of seriality in the black portrait archive. Campt writes of such images: "They are staged. They are predictable. They are posed. They show smartly dressed individuals—black folks putting their best foot forward. But they are also stiff and oddly 'affected' [. . .] Apparently all surface and no depth, they emphasize artifice rather than interiority and seem to lack any form of creativity or spontaneity. Instead of giving us insight into context, individuality, or 'soul' they tantalize us instead at the level of external presentation and display." For Campt, the interest of these photographs lies precisely in their predictability and those qualities that qualify as *studium* within Barthes's critical lexicon. In counterdistinction to *punctum*, the wounding "element which rises from the scene, shoots out of it like an arrow, and pierces," *studium* is "a kind of general, enthusiastic commitment [. . .] without special acuity." Studium images are engaging as politics or as history; one's connection to them is not individual but cultural. Campt asks what might happen if we were to take Barthes's category more seriously, and "reconceptualize and indeed revalue the seriality of studio portraiture, and of the image-making practices of black diasporic communities in particular, *as a significant and revealing form of expressive cultural practice*" (emphasis added). Campt's intervention lies in her willingness to grant the photographic subject not the punctum of their portrait—that element that is striking only to their beloved or to a stranger whose beloved is in some way accidentally recalled—but rather the studium that is projected to all other viewers, and across the folds of time, granting portrait sitters their *un*remarkableness. Tina M. Campt, *Image Matters: Archive, Photography, and the African Diaspora in Europe* (Durham, NC: Duke University Press, 2012), 137–8; Roland Barthes, *Camera Lucida: Reflections on Photography*, trans. Richard Howard (New York: Hill and Wang, 1981), 26.

8 Jack McKinney, "He's Mad And Getting Madder," *Sports Illustrated*, September 24, 1962; James Baldwin, "The Fight: Patterson vs. Liston," in *The Unlevel Playing Field: A Documentary History of the African American Experience in Sport*, ed. David K Wiggins and Patrick B. Miller (Chicago: University of Chicago Press, 2005), 296–303; LeRoi Jones (Amiri Baraka), "The Dempsey-Liston Fight," in *Home: Social Essays* (New York: Akashic Books, 1996), 179–84; Norman Mailer, *The Fight* (Boston: Little, Brown and Company, 1975); Leon Gast, *When We Were Kings* (Gramercy Pictures, 1996).

9 Appropriate and inevitable are not equivalent, but the feeling of the subjects in question on this particular issue are beyond the scope of my investigation (if they are knowable at all).

10 W. E. B. Du Bois, *The Souls of Black Folk* (New Haven, CT: Yale University Press), 5.

11 Young, *Embodying Black Experience*, 35.

12 Alan Trachtenberg, *Reading American Photographs* (New York: Hill and Wang, 1989), 59.

13 Trachtenberg, 54.

14 Trachtenberg, 54.

15 Trachtenberg, 56.

16 Brian Wallis finds Trachtenberg's comparison to Roman busts ironic because Wallis views the daguerreotypes not as portraits but as types. Wallis effectively argues that the purpose for which the images were produced continues to overwrite the figures pictured: "The subject as already positioned, known, owned, represented, spoken for, or constructed as silent; in short, it is ignored. [. . .] Fundamentally nonreciprocal, [the type] masks its subjective distortions in the guise of logic and organization. Its formations are deformations." The type is exceedingly *un*like the nineteenth-century portrait, Wallis suggests, because of portraiture's relationship to individuality—and here individuality is tantamount to personhood:

> The portrait, on the other hand, is of value principally because of the viewer's relationship to the sitter, the ability to recognize the subject when he or she is absent. In this sense, the portrait is like a caricature that accents the telling features of an individual. Generally, the nineteenth-century photographic portrait was designed to affirm or underscore the white middle-class individual's right to personhood [. . .]. Further, the portrait signaled an individual's place in society, which explains why so many daguerreotypes feature sitters posed with the tools of their trade or other attributes.

Wallis does not agree that Agassiz's daguerreotypes constitute portraits, because their commissioner and maker were not interested in the pictured individuals *as* individuals. Yet Wallis seems to align with Trachtenberg in his belief that individuality is created in part through the performance of a social role (what Trachtenberg names a "social persona")—and that "specimen" is not a recognized one. Brian Wallis, "Black Bodies, White Science: Louis Agassiz's Slave Daguerreotypes," *American Art* 9, no. 2 (Summer 1995): 54–5.

17 Young, *Embodying Black Experience*, 48.

18 Young, 43.

19 Young defines the futured as "our ever-evolving present viewed from a past perspective." Young, 49–50.

20 Young, 44.

21 For Young, the "futured" is also at work in the materiality of the daguerreotype. Because a daguerreotype is made of a polished silver-surfaced plate, it is highly reflective. It is difficult to view a daguerreotype without seeing one's own image superimposed. Young pays attention to the affect of this reflective surface, which inserts the viewer into the picture. He suggests that, in looking at reproductions of Agassiz's daguerreotypes, we should imagine our own reflections superimposed onto the surface of the image. In this way we might understand ourselves "as the seer who sees the captives as photographed and as the seen who is photographed (or, more accurately, reflected) alongside the captives. In this way, not only does the distance between the captive in the frame and the

viewer outside the frame disappear, but so does the temporal separation between the 1850 studio session and our third millennial spectatorship. The result is that we enter their present and they join us in our present." Young, 49.

22 Barthes, *Camera Lucida*, 26–7.

23 Barthes, 95.

24 Michael Sacasas, "Dead and Going to Die," *New Inquiry*, October 21, 2013, https://thenewinquiry.com.

25 Trachtenberg, *Reading American Photographs*, 26.

26 Sacasas, "Dead and Going to Die."

27 Erving Goffman named this performance "front." Goffman, *Presentation of Self in Everyday Life*. Goffman doesn't theorize the historical moment that front was born or became critical to interaction. Yet the early debates about the nature of the daguerreotype's capture or corruption of personage, as well as the rampant advice about strategies to render the photographic truth more flattering, suggests that photography played a role in heightening presentational self-consciousness. See Trachtenberg, *Reading American Photographs*, 23–5. Furthermore, although Trachtenberg himself seems not to make the connection to "front" in Goffman's sense of the word, Trachtenberg suggests a contemporaneous architectural analogue when he writes that "the most dramatic development [of the portrait studio] was the metamorphosis of the original 'front' into a 'reception room.' [. . . Not a museum of natural history] but a theater of desire, the gallery had become a new kind of city place devoted to performance: the making of oneself over into a social image."

28 Lauren Berlant, "Thinking about Feeling Historical," *Emotion, Space and Society* 1 (2008): 4. In situating the lived experience of enslaved persons within Berlant's framework of ordinariness, I mean that while the experience of slavery was also traumatic or exceptional, for individuals subject to slavery's abjections, the state of being enslaved was the ongoing, indeterminate experience from which deliverance would have been the event or break. This is not to normalize it in a moral sense, or to inscribe it as a "natural" condition. Rather, it is to point out the voraciousness of the ordinary, such that an instance of being objectified might have come to be "normal" even if it never became "natural"—hence the crisis within the ordinary.

29 Trachtenberg, *Reading American Photographs*, 54.

30 Trachtenberg, 56.

31 Denise Ferreira da Silva, *Toward a Global Idea of Race* (Minneapolis: University of Minnesota Press, 2007).

32 Paul Gilroy, *The Black Atlantic: Modernity and Double-Consciousness* (Cambridge, MA: Harvard University Press, 1995), 8.

33 Kathleen Collins, "Portraits of Slave Children," *History of Photography* 9, no. 3 (1985): 187–210; Gilman, "Black Bodies, White Bodies"; Wallis, "Black Bodies, White Science"; Suzanne Schneider, "Louis Agassiz and the American School of Ethnoeroticism: Polygenesis, Pornography, and Other 'Perfidious Influences,'" in *Pictures and Progress: Early Photography and the Making of African American Identity*, ed. Maurice O. Wallace and Shawn Michelle Smith (Durham, NC: Duke University Press, 2012), 211–43.

34 *Oxford English Dictionary Online*, s.v. "specimen (*n.*)" (Oxford University Press). www.oed.com.
35 *Oxford English Dictionary Online*, s.v. "specimen (*n.*)."
36 Sekula, "The Body and the Archive."
37 Janice Neri, *The Insect and the Image: Visualizing Nature in Early Modern Europe, 1500–1700* (Minneapolis: University of Minnesota Press, 2011), xiii.
38 Neri, 84, xiii.
39 Neri, 7.
40 Neri, xi, 3–4.
41 Neri, 85.
42 Neri, 77.
43 Neri, xiii.
44 Gilroy, *Black Atlantic*, 72–3.
45 My gratitude to my librarian friend Rob Kowalczyk, who first provided me with details of this case. There was canonical debate as to the anatomical location of the soul, with the majority opinion cathecting to the brain or the ventricles of the heart, and the postmortem examination provided assurance that these were two.
46 A. Peña Chavarría and P.G. Shipley, "The Siamese Twins of Española (The First Known Post-Mortem Examination in the New World)," *Annals of Medical History* 6 (1924): 299.
47 Peña Chavarría and Shipley, 298.
48 Chen, *Animacies*.
49 Peña Chavarría and Shipley, "Siamese Twins of Española," 299.
50 Peña Chavarría and Shipley, 300.
51 Peña Chavarría and Shipley, 300.
52 Seltzer, *Official World*, 6–7. Seltzer does not spend much time periodizing modernity for his readers, leaving such work to a quick reference to authors—Max Weber, Carl Schmitt, Michel Foucault, Niklas Luhmann—who note a shift in humanity's self-organization from the eighteenth century on. Nevertheless, it is clear that our self-observation does not indicate a postmodernity, however much it may have come into its own in the digital age.
53 Seltzer, 22.
54 Seltzer, 6–7.
55 Clement Greenberg, *Art and Culture: Critical Essays*. (Boston: Beacon Press, 1961), 6; and Clement Greenberg, "Modernist Painting," in *Twentieth Century Theories of Art*, ed. James M. Thompson (Ottawa: Carleton University Press, 1999), 94.
56 Seltzer, *Official World*, 3, 6.
57 Seltzer, 7.
58 Seltzer, 19.
59 Seltzer, 9; Richard Schechner, *Performance Studies: An Introduction*, 2nd ed. (New York: Routledge, 2006).
60 Seltzer, 154.
61 Seltzer, 20.
62 Joseph Roach, *The Player's Passion: Studies in the Science of Acting* (Ann Arbor: University of Michigan Press, 1993), 15–16.

63 Mark Seltzer, *Bodies and Machines* (New York: Routledge, 1992), 156–7.
64 Seltzer, *Bodies and Machines*, 159.
65 Seltzer, *Official World*, 157.
66 Seltzer, *Official World*, 39.
67 Bertolt Brecht, *Brecht on Theatre: The Development of an Aesthetic*, ed. John Willett. (New York: Hill and Wang, 1992).
68 Seltzer, *Official World*, 15.
69 Seltzer, *Official World*, 166.
70 Joyce Carol Oates, *On Boxing* (New York: Harper Perennial, 2006), 4.
71 Hazel V. Carby, *Cultures in Babylon* (New York: Verso, 1999), 22–39.
72 See Simone Browne, *Dark Matters: On the Surveillance of Blackness* (Durham, NC: Duke University Press, 2015).
73 Nell Irvin Painter, *Sojourner Truth: A Life, A Symbol* (New York: W. W. Norton, 1996), 139.
74 Shawn Michelle Smith, *Photography on the Color Line: W. E. B. Du Bois, Race, and Visual Culture* (Durham, NC: Duke University Press, 2004), 2.
75 Smith, 46.
76 Wallis, "Black Bodies, White Science."
77 Smith, *Photography on the Color Line*, 54–5.
78 Smith, 57.
79 Smith, 65.
80 Smith, 67.
81 Smith, 44.
82 Smith, 108.
83 Smith, 107.
84 Smith, 57.
85 Du Bois, *The Souls of Black Folk*.
86 Richard Wright, *12 Million Black Voices* (New York: Basic Books, 2008).
87 Zora Neale Hurston, "How It Feels to Be Colored Me," in *Folklore, Memoirs, & Other Writings*, ed. Cheryl A. Wall (New York: The Library of America, 1995), 826–9; for further discussion of the primitive in cabaret culture, see Vogel, *Scene of Harlem Cabaret*.
88 Anne Anlin Cheng, *Second Skin: Josephine Baker and the Modern Surface* (New York: Oxford University Press, 2011), 28.
89 For an important discussion of Civil Rights era photography, see Leigh Raiford, *Imprisoned in a Luminous Glare: Photography and the African American Freedom Struggle* (Chapel Hill, NC: University of North Carolina Press, 2011), 27.
90 Associate Director, Richard Avedon Foundation, "Avedon images of William Casby for Deadpan," email, 2021.
91 Richard Avedon and James Baldwin, *Nothing Personal* (New York: Atheneum, 1964).
92 Hilton Als, "Richard Avedon and James Baldwin's Joint Examination of American Identity," *New Yorker*, November 6, 2017. As the associate director of the Avedon Foundation explained over email, the image was included in a press kit promoting the new edition of *Nothing Personal*, which is to say that the editors of *The New Yorker* did not independently decide to elevate this particular image

as an exemplar of Avedon's aesthetic "solely on its own merits." Nevertheless, *The New Yorker* team led the online Photo Booth article with the Casby family portrait, giving it pride of place. Furthermore, *The New Yorker*'s print announcement of the book release, which appeared in the November 13 issue, was accompanied by only this one image. In short, I assert, even if *The New Yorker*'s team didn't choose the photo solely on its own merits, they certainly recognized that it had merits.

93 Jean Toomer, *Cane*, 2nd ed. (New York: Norton Critical Editions, 2011).

94 Barthes, *Camera Lucida*, 34.

95 Barthes, 28.

96 Avedon's own caption was "William Casby, born in slavery, Algiers, Louisiana, March 24, 1963," hence the caption of figure 1.7.

97 On the contrary, one can summon the qualitative descriptors that might accompany a white face that did not have to stand symbolically as everything or nothing. The person bearing an inexpressive face might evoke any number of descriptors: lonely, wise, vacant, contained, meditative, concerned, placid, etc. None of those are invoked here.

98 Trachtenberg, *Reading American Photographs*, 56.

99 Berlant, "Thinking about Feeling Historical," 5–6.

100 Berlant, 6.

101 Berlant, 7.

2. MINIMALISM AND THE AESTHETICS OF BLACK THREAT

1 Tom Wolfe, "Radical Chic: That Party at Lenny's," *New York Magazine*, June 8, 1970, 27.

2 While not of concern for this chapter, it is probably worth stating that this reader's impression of the "superego Negro" is indelibly colored by a cadre of audience/participation characters from black literature, especially those of Toomer's "Black Box" and Ellison's "King of the Bingo Game." See Toomer, *Cane*; Ralph Ellison, *Flying Home and Other Stories* (New York: Vintage International, 1996).

3 Wolfe, "Radical Chic," 33.

4 Curiously, the *OED* definition of "loom" is consistent in the definitional qualities of large size and indistinct or indefinite form, but not a commensurate sense of threat. *New Oxford American Dictionary*, s.v. "loom"; *Oxford English Dictionary Online*, s.v. "loom, v.[2]."

5 Brian Massumi, "The Future Birth of the Affective Fact: The Political Ontology of Threat," in *The Affect Theory Reader*, ed. Melissa Gregg and Gregory J Seigworth (Durham, NC: Duke University Press, 2010), 61–2.

6 Massumi, 54.

7 Massumi, 53.

8 State of Missouri v. Darren Wilson, "Grand Jury Volume V," 225–28, Ferguson Grand Jury Documents, www.documentcloud.org/documents/1371057-grand-jury-volume-5 (see *Washington Post*, September 16, 2014).

9 Glenda Elizabeth Gilmore, *Gender and Jim Crow: Women and the Politics of White Supremacy in North Carolina, 1896–1920* (Chapel Hill: University of North Caro-

lina Press, 1996); Crystal N. Feimster, *Southern Horrors: Women and the Politics of Rape and Lynching* (Cambridge, MA: Harvard University Press, 2009).

10 My gratitude to C. Riley Snorton for posing this question.

11 Jennifer Doyle, *Hold It Against Me: Difficulty and Emotion in Contemporary Art* (Durham, NC: Duke University Press, 2013).

12 Mailer, *The Fight*. See for example 50–1, where Mailer describes Foreman's musical choice, in conjunction with his fighting, through a string of comparisons to witches, gods, trees splitting like bones, caves boiling vapors, and so forth.

13 James Baldwin, *Collected Essays* (New York: The Library of America, 1998).

14 Political choice and media portrayal play a role in creating the impression of threat, but here I acknowledge a cyclical and self-perpetuating relationship between the creators and the consumers of politics and media culture.

15 Jennifer Field, "Chronology," in *Martin Puryear*, ed. John Elderfield (New York: The Museum of Modern Art, 2007).

16 Maurice Berger, *Labyrinths: Robert Morris, Minimalism and the 1960s* (New York: Harper & Row, 1989).

17 John P. Bowles, *Adrian Piper: Race, Gender, and Embodiment* (Durham, NC: Duke University Press, 2011).

18 Maurice Berger, *Minimal Politics: Performativity and Minimalism in Recent American Art* (Baltimore: Fine Arts Gallery, University of Maryland, 1997).

19 Susan E. Cahan, *Mounting Frustration: The Art Museum in the Age of Black Power* (Durham, NC: Duke University Press, 2016); English, *1971*.

20 Thelma Golden, ed., *Black Male: Representations of Masculinity in Contemporary American Art* (New York: Whitney Museum of Art, 1994).

21 Michael Fried, "Art and Objecthood," in *Art and Objecthood: Essays and Reviews* (Chicago: University of Chicago Press, 1998), 152.

22 Fried, 154, 155.

23 Fried, 155–6.

24 Fried, 148.

25 Daniel Patrick Moynihan, *The Negro Family: The Case for National Action* (Washington, DC: US Government Printing Office, 1965).

26 Kyla Schuller, *The Biopolitics of Feeling: Race, Sex, and Science in the Nineteenth Century* (Durham, NC: Duke University Press, 2008).

27 Fried, "Art and Objecthood," 166.

28 Hartman, *Scenes of Subjection*, 40.

29 Hartman, 6.

30 Hartman, 69.

31 It is interesting to consider whether, when blackness is detected in the mute object—even subliminally—it must be re-rendered as theatrical to order to be legible. Readers interested in this point, or in the underlying values and sensibilities of Fried's groundbreaking essay, should consult Christa Noel Robbins, "The Sensibility of Michael Fried," *Criticism* 60, no. 4 (Fall 2018): 429–54.

32 Thomas Jefferson, *Notes on the State of Virginia* (Boston: Lilly and Wait, 1832), 144–5.

33 Jefferson, 145.

34 Hurston, "Characteristics of Negro Expression."

35 Although deadpan does not necessarily invite intimacy or trust, neither does it quite discourage it. To reiterate once more a point of the introduction, the deadpan is remarkably (even eerily) malleable.

36 Perry Morgan, "The Case for the White Southerner," *Esquire*, January 1962, 43.

37 APRA Archivist, "Re: Image permissions for forthcoming book," email, August 24, 2021. I emailed my explanation of the book and its orientations to the unnamed APRA Archivist on April 27, 2021. The quoted reply was addressed to my research assistant Ella Nagle, who had written in the interim to follow up.

38 McMillan, *Embodied Avatars*; Valerie Cassel Oliver, ed., *Radical Presence: Black Performance in Contemporary Art* (Houston: Contemporary Arts Museum Houston, 2013).

39 All five images of *I Am the Locus* are available for viewing or downloading in PDF form on the website of The University of Chicago's Smart Museum: https://smartcollection.uchicago.edu/people/725/adrian-piper/objects. Images from her Untitled Performance at Max's Kansas City can be found at http://foundation.generali.at/en/collection/artist/piper-adrian/artwork/untitled-performance-at-maxs-kansas-city-nyc.html.

40 Bowles, *Adrian Piper*, 6.

41 This image can be seen in Bowles, 250.

42 My reading of Piper's uses of the Afro wig respectfully disagrees with Judith Wilson's assertion that the wig reveals "the inessential nature of racial identity" insofar as Piper's diminutive embodiment could not sufficiently muster menace without it. While is true from *outside* of the artwork, nothing *within* the performance suggests to its audience (unless Piper herself is the intended witness) that the wig's meaning is other than "Third World, working class, overtly hostile male." This is a significant detail because my argument is that the Mythic Being's consciousness exists in tension with the implicit threat of the minimalist male body. Judith Wilson, "Beauty Rites: Toward an Anatomy of Culture in African American Women's Art," *International Review of African American Art* 11, no. 3 (January 1994): 17.

43 McMillan, *Embodied Avatars*, 101.

44 Wolfe, "Radical Chic," 45.

45 Wolfe, 28.

46 Wolfe, 28.

47 Wolfe, 28.

48 Wolfe, 31.

49 Wolfe, 44–5.

50 McMillan, *Embodied Avatars*, 97.

51 Bowles, *Adrian Piper*, 134.

52 Bowles, 135.

53 When the scholars I cite venture into biography, they generally highlight the acquisitional roots of Puryear's craftsmanship: he spent time in Africa in the Peace Corps; he observed furniture making in Scandinavia. These are important details, to be sure; however, when it comes to the materiality of his artwork, perhaps they are not more important than Puryear's identity as an African American. (Nor, of course, do they run contrary to it.)

54 Margo A. Crutchfield, *Martin Puryear* (Richmond: Virginia Museum of Fine Arts, 2001), 3.

55 John Elderfield, "Martin Puryear: Ideas of Otherness," in *Martin Puryear*, ed. John Elderfield (New York: Museum of Modern Art, 2007), 13.

56 Elderfield, "Martin Puryear," 27.

57 Neal Benezra, "'The Thing Shines, Not the Maker': The Sculpture of Martin Puryear," in *Martin Puryear*, ed. Neal Benezra (Chicago: Thames and Hudson/ The Art Institute of Chicago, 1991), 25.

58 Crutchfield, *Martin Puryear*, 36.

59 Elderfield, "Martin Puryear" 24.

60 Elderfield, 24.

61 Elderfield, 35.

62 Elderfield, 24.

63 Robert Storr, "Martin Puryear: The Hand's Proportion," in *Martin Puryear*, ed. Neal Benezra (Chicago: Thames and Hudson/ The Art Institute of Chicago, 1991), 127.

64 James Baldwin, "How Can We Get the Black People to Cool It?" *Esquire*, July 1968.

65 Brian Horrigan, "Esquire–July 1968," *The 1968 Exhibit*, July 7, 2009, accessed August 12, 2016, www.the1968exhibit.org. According to its website, the 1968 Exhibit was organized by the Minnesota History Center in association with the Atlanta History Center, the Chicago History Museum, and the Oakland Museum of California, and was funded by the National Endowment for the Humanities, the Institute of Museum and Library Services, and the Legacy Amendment through the vote of Minnesotans on November 4, 2008.

66 Roach, *Cities of the Dead*, 2–3.

67 Berger, *Labyrinths*, 50.

68 Berger, *Labyrinths*, 50.

69 Robert Morris, "Notes on Sculpture," in *Minimal Art: A Critical Anthology*, ed. Gregory Battcock (New York: E. P. Dutton & Co., 1968), 222–35.

70 Morris, 225.

71 Morris, 228.

72 Simon Grant and Robert Morris, "Simon Grant Interviews Robert Morris," *Tate Etc.*, no. 14 (Autumn 2008), www.tate.org.uk.

73 See, for example, Daniel Sack, *After Live: Possibility, Potentiality, and the Future of Performance* (Ann Arbor: University of Michigan Press, 2015). Sack is interested in the latent or unrealized in performance, and his chapter "Beholding Potentiality" examines registers of withholding or deferral in minimalist sculpture and performance, in conjunction with Fried's critical assertions, in order to consider withholding's effects on viewers.

74 Grant and Morris, "Simon Grant Interviews Robert Morris." This description also alerts one to the possible racial tinge in Morris's monumental sculptural works, including *Passageway*—with its own heartbeat—and the hermetic enclosures of the *Labyrinth* works. Furthermore, once this much is admitted, more and more of minimalism begins to feel as though it performs a whiteness discomposed through enacted of blackness. In turn, David Hammons' stubborn

engagement with Richard Serra's *T.W.U.* sculpture appears in a different light; *Pissed Off* and *Shoe Tree* feel more like acts of complicated reclamation than of a more straightforward indictment. For more on these performances, see Abbe Schriber, "'Those Who Know Don't Tell': David Hammons c. 1981," *Women & Performance: A Journal of Feminist Theory* 29, no. 1 (2019): 41–61.

75 Morris inveighs against detail and intimacy in relation to the new sculpture, specifically as they are instantiated through diminutive size (which, to his mind, begets intimacy) and visual distraction (which stems from detail).

76 Berger, *Labyrinths*, 81.

77 Berger, *Labyrinths*, 81. Schneemann was an important artist in her own right, although none of the sources I have consulted suggest she had a prominent role in the development of this piece. For more on Schneemann as an artist, see Elise Archias, *The Concrete Body: Yvonne Rainer, Carolee Schneemann, Vito Acconci* (New Haven, CT: Yale University Press, 2016).

78 Berger, *Labyrinths*, 81–2.

79 Berger, *Labyrinths*, 86.

80 Spillers, "Mama's Baby, Papa's Maybe."

81 Petrine Archer-Straw, *Negrophilia: Avant-Garde Paris and Black Culture in the 1920s* (New York: Thames & Hudson, 2000).

82 English, *1971*, 45.

83 Virginia Spivey, "Sites of Subjectivity: Robert Morris, Minimalism, and Dance," *Dance Research Journal* 35/36, no. 2/1 (Winter 2003–Summer 2004): 113–30.

84 For more on Rainer and her minimalist, tasked-based dance of the early 1960s, see Carrie Lambert-Beatty, *Being Watched: Yvonne Rainer and the 1960s* (Cambridge, MA: MIT Press, 2011); and Archias, *The Concrete Body*.

3. THE OPACITY GRADIENT

1 Wolfe, "Radical Chic," 48.

2 Wolfe, 50.

3 Patricia J. Williams, "On Being the Object of Property," in *The Alchemy of Race and Rights* (Cambridge, MA: Harvard University Press, 1991), 222.

4 Glissant, *Poetics of Relation*, 120.

5 Copeland, *Bound to Appear*, 9.

6 For hypervisibility and invisibility's simultaneity see, for example, Spillers, "Mama's Baby, Papa's Maybe"; Fleetwood, *Troubling Vision*.

7 Bob Spiers, "Jealous," *Absolutely Fabulous* (BBC, April 27, 1995).

8 As the introduction discussed, blackness might also be subject to the assumptions of expressiveness, emphasizing the ways that race and gender are mutually imbricated, and the ways that the neutral or universal are implicitly white.

9 Ralph Ellison, *Invisible Man* (New York: Vintage International, 1995), 3.

10 Goffman, *Presentation of Self in Everyday Life*, 151–53.

11 Beth Tompkins Bates, *Pullman Porters and the Rise of Protest Politics in Black America, 1925–1945* (Chapel Hill: University of North Carolina Press, 2001).

12 Hortense J. Spillers, "Interstices: A Small Drama of Words," in *Black, White, and in Color: Essays on American Literature and Culture* (Chicago: University of Chicago Press, 2003), 155.

13 Uri McMillan, "Introduction: Skin, Surface, Sensorium," *Women & Performance: A Journal of Feminist Theory* 28, no. 1 (January 2, 2018): 1–15.

14 Copeland, *Bound to Appear*; Ellison, *Invisible Man*; Nella Larsen, *The Complete Fiction of Nella Larsen: Passing, Quicksand, and the Stories* (New York: Anchor Books, 2001).

15 Perhaps neither here nor there, but I have long believed that Francis Picabia's *Américaine*—a stark, isolated illustration of a lightbulb, at once transparent and reflective and quite dark in hue—pictures not just any American woman, but a black one.

16 A reclamation of Sutton's place in the recorded history of avant-garde theatre and dance is an undertaking for the future work of myself or others.

17 Laurence Shyer, *Robert Wilson and His Collaborators* (New York: Theatre Communications Group, 1989), 8.

18 Shyer, 8.

19 Arthur Holmberg, *The Theatre of Robert Wilson*, Directors in Perspective (Cambridge: Cambridge University Press, 1996), 4.

20 Holmberg, 7.

21 Holmberg, 3.

22 Holmberg, 7. Wilson says, "By turns I see her as a mother, a priest, an angel of death. Maybe she's Medea. It's not a violent murder. It's tender. She's a mystery." Sutton: "I never thought of it as evil. No emotion was implied. No anguish. No suffering. It was more subliminal. I thought of it as a ritual, like a mass. Raising and lowering the knife was like raising and lowering a chalice."

23 Robert Sanford Brustein, "MASS MoCa: A Boom in the Boonies," in *Millennial Stages: Essays and Reviews, 2001–2005* (New Haven, CT: Yale University Press, 2006), 203–7.

24 Shyer, *Robert Wilson and His Collaborators*, 8.

25 Shyer, 7. If *King of Spain* and *Freud* both date to 1969, with *King of Spain* occurring in January of that year, it seems factually incorrect that Sutton and Wilson hadn't yet met. Still, I've no reason to doubt this account of another actress in the role.

26 Hilton Als, "Slow Man," *New Yorker*, September 17, 2012.

27 Shyer, *Robert Wilson and His Collaborators*, 15. Because Shyer interviewed Sutton to draft his brief chapter on her, his work contains invaluable statements about her process, Wilson's process, and where she locates success.

28 Shyer, 10.

29 While fragility is not part of Byrdwoman's persona, it can be part of the transparency's aesthetic. Consider the deep connection between Laura Wingfield and her glass figurines in Tennessee Williams's *Glass Menagerie*. Though Laura's transparency is linked to her femininity and disability (and family relations), some productions, such as Tazewell Thompson's in 1989, have very successfully cast the family as black. In asserting Laura's ability to be a black subject, Thompson and others in effect assert the black female's ability to be a subject of glass—fragile, translucent, and smooth; born of transmogrified sand; shaped into uniqueness; cuttingly sharp when broken.

30 Shyer, *Robert Wilson and His Collaborators*, 8–9.

31 Young, *Embodying Black Experience.*
32 Holmberg, *Theatre of Robert Wilson*, 4.
33 Shyer, *Robert Wilson and His Collaborators*, 11.
34 Chester Himes, "Headwaiter," in *The Collected Stories of Chester Himes* (New York: Thunder's Mouth Press, 2000), 1–15.
35 Brustein, "MASS MoCa," 205.
36 Brustein, 205.
37 Als, "Slow Man."
38 To my mind, white child in the lap of the black nanny also raises the specter of cross-racial maternity and the specter of procreative rape. This recalls a passage from Darlene Clark Hine: "Only with secrecy, *thus achieving a self-imposed invisibility*, could ordinary Black women accrue the psychic space and harness the resources needed to hold their own in the often one-sided and mismatched resistance struggle" (emphasis mine). Hine, "Rape and the Inner Lives of Black Women in the Middle West," 915.
39 Sheerness can also be seen in the works of Japanese American Ruth Asawa, Dominican Raquel Paiewonsky, and African American Senga Nengudi.
40 Julie Dash, *Daughters of the Dust* (Kino International, 1991).
41 Erwan Filidori, "Claudia Casarino—On Being Under Pressure," *Metal*, accessed December 16, 2019, https://metalmagazine.eu.
42 Artishock, "Claudia Casarino: Iluminando la ausencia," *Artishock*, February 27, 2018, https://artishockrevista.com. "Cultivado desde tiempos remotos por el pueblo guaraní, el algodón fue el material que estimuló la penetración europea en el Paraguay. Dicho vínculo indisociable entre materia prima y colonialidad me parece fundamental, ya que introduce narrativas históricas globales que colocan su práctica en diálogo con la de artistas de África, Asia, Oceanía y el Caribe para quienes la profusión de una o varias materias primas significó el desenlace de un sisma: el establecimiento de un antes y un después de la llegada de los imperios coloniales."
43 Gabriela Salgado, "Claudia Casarino: Illuminating Absence," *CAAM*, January 25, 2018, www.caam.net.
44 Whose Museum, "Whose Museum x KRETS; Chapter 2: Alanna Lynch & Maria Wæhrens," March 29, 2019, https://whosemuseum.org.
45 Alanna Lynch, *Alanna Lynch*, accessed December 17, 2019, http://alannalynch.com.
46 Alanna Lynch, "Gut Feelings: A Perfomance," in *Musings* (food feminism fermentation, 2019), 31–5.
47 Lauren Fournier, "Fermenting Feminism: Andrea Creamer, Eleonora Edreva & Leo Williams, Alanna Lynch, Sarah Nasby, Walter Scott, and Christine Tien Wang," *Access Gallery*, September 13, 2019, https://accessgallery.ca.
48 Zh. T. Niyazbekova, G. Zh. Nagmetova, and A.A. Kurmanbayev, "An Overview of Bacterial Cellulose Applications," *Eurasian Journal of Applied Biotechnology*, 2018, no. 2, https://biotechlink.org, doi: 10.11134/btp.2.2018.3.
49 *Oxford English Dictionary Online*, s.v. "obscure (*v.*)."
50 Rembrandt Peale, *Thomas Jefferson*, 1800, oil on canvas. White House Collection/White House Historical Association, www.whitehousehistory.org.

51 “Titus Kaphar—Jack Shainman Gallery,” accessed October 25, 2019, www.jackshainman.com. Kaphar is no longer represented by Jack Shainman, so the page is no longer available on that site (although, like many other now-vanished web pages, including some I have cited, it can still be viewed using the Wayback Machine at https:// archive.org). See also kapharstudio.com.

52 Claudia Rankine, “The Condition of Black Life Is One of Mourning,” *New York Times*, June 22, 2015.

53 “Titus Kaphar—Jack Shainman Gallery.”

54 Kaphar’s *Asphalt and Chalk* composites also intervene in the history of criminal composite photographs, such as those devised by eugenicist Francis Galton. See Sekula, “The Body and the Archive.”

55 Erving Goffman, *Behavior in Public Places: Notes on the Social Organization of Gatherings* (New York: The Free Press, 1963), 4. As Goffman notes in a footnote on page 70, he himself borrowed the term from Gregory Bateson and Margaret Mead, who used the term in their own context of racialized observation. Under the heading AWAYNESS, the text reads: “An obverse of the Balinese love of crowded scenes is their habit of withdrawal into vacancy—letting themselves suddenly slip into a state of mind where they are, for the moment, no longer subject to the impact of inter-personal relations. This withdrawal occurs in a large variety of contexts, but is perhaps especially common in parent-child and teacher-pupil relationships, and following some rather definite activity of work or play. The face of a mother or child, or both, will become vacant immediately after unusually active play; or the face of an artist will be similarly unresponsive after he has just finished a carving.” Bateson and Mead, *Balinese Character: A Photographic Analysis* (New York: New York Academy of Sciences, 1942), 68–9.

56 Goffman, *Behavior in Public Places*, 70.

57 Copeland, *Bound to Appear*.

58 *Oxford English Dictionary Online*, s.v. “brown study (*n.*).”

59 See José Esteban Muñoz, *The Sense of Brown*, ed. Joshua Chambers-Letson and Tavia Nyong’o (Durham, NC: Duke University Press, 2020); and Anne Anlin Cheng, *Melancholy of Race*.

60 Lauren Berlant, *Cruel Optimism* (Durham, NC: Duke University Press, 2011); Doyle, *Hold It Against Me*; Amber Jamilla Musser, *Sensational Flesh: Race, Power, and Masochism* (New York: New York University Press, 2014); McMillan, *Embodied Avatars*; Leticia Alvarado, *Abject Performances* (Durham, NC: Duke University Press, 2018); Joshua Chambers-Letson, *After the Party: A Manifesto for Queer of Color Life* (New York: New York University Press, 2018).

61 Helen Molesworth, “Art Is Medicine,” *Artforum* 56, no. 7 (March 2018): 171.

62 Molesworth, 172.

63 Molesworth, 170–1.

64 Glissant, *Poetics of Relation*, 114, 193.

65 Jasmine Elizabeth Johnson, “‘Sheer Pleasure’: Eloise Greenfield, Solange Knowles, and Black Hush,” in *Saturation: Race, Art, and the Circulation of Value*, ed. C. Riley Snorton and Hentyle Yapp (Cambridge, MA: MIT Press, 2020), 187. Although Johnson’s title includes the word “sheer,” the article does not reference sheerness in the definitional sense I use—at least not explicitly. Neverthe-

less, I feel it is not merely coincidence that the word appears in the title of an article whose themes are so consonant with the aesthetic modes I am thinking through.

66 Johnson, 188.

67 Johnson, 189.

68 Indeed, I want to argue that this helps to explain the spaces in which, and objects with which, Solange has performed the aesthetic registers of her muted albums. Placing the "hush acts" of herself and her largely female cadre of performers in embodied conversation with the autonomy of Donald Judd's 15 untitled works of concrete, for example, mobilizes (racially) complementary but (affectively) divergent forms of minimalism.

4. EXCESS AND ABSENCE (OR, THE NEGRO BELIEVES _____)

1 Paul Laurence Dunbar, *Lyrics of Lowly Life (1896)* (New York: Arno Press, 1969).

2 Ryan Anthony Hatch, "First as Minstrelsy, Then as Farce: On the Spectacle of Race in the Theatre of Young Jean Lee," *CR: The New Centennial Review* 13, no. 3 (2013): 92.

3 The editors of *Monochromes* divide the genre into four types, two of which will be considered in this chapter: "the Parisian 'jokes' of the nineteenth century [. . .]; and those created within the fold of Abstraction in the twentieth century." The other two types are works whose color register is singular because of the medium of their creation (such as pencil works), and the Zen monochromes of Asian tradition. Valeria Varas and Raul Rispa, eds., *Monochromes: From Malevich to the Present* (Berkeley: University of California Press, 2006), 15.

4 Phillip Denis Cate, "The Spirit of Montmartre," in *The Spirit of Montmartre: Cabarets, Humor and the Avant-Garde, 1875–1905*, ed. Phillip Denis Cate and Mary Shaw (New Brunswick, NJ: Jane Voorhees Zimmerli Art Musum, Rutgers, 1996), 1.

5 Cate, 31.

6 Rose identifies one earlier monochrome, produced by Jean-Louis Petit in 1843. According to Rose, this painting, *Vue de la Hougue (effet de nuit)*, was intended as a prank, parodying contemporary painters' practice of minimizing light-dark contrasts. See Barbara Rose, "The Meanings of Monochrome," in Varas and Rispa, *Monochromes*, 23.

7 Original titles: *Récolte de la tomate par des cardinaux apoplectiques au bord de la mer rouge (effet d'aurore boréale)* and *Des souteneurs, encore dans la force de l'âge et le ventre dans l'herbe, boivent de l'absinthe*. Some variation exists in translations of these titles. I have followed those used in John C. Welchman, *Invisible Colors: A Visual History of Titles* (New Haven, CT: Yale University Press, 1997), 107–8.

8 Though Barbara Rose draws a line between the avant-garde and pure modernism, thereby disqualifying Les Incohérents from modernist abstraction's monochromatic lineages, I cannot follow this logic. Petrine Archer-Straw, for example, illuminates the extent to which the French avant-garde and modernism are

linked, in no small part by illuminating the extent to which race underwrites both. Archer-Straw, *Negrophilia.*

9 Anson Rabinbach, *The Human Motor: Energy, Fatigue, and the Origins of Modernity* (Berkeley: University of California Press, 1990). See especially chapter 4.

10 Ivan Nechepurenko, "Examination Reveals a Mysterious Message on Malevich's 'Black Square' Painting," *New York Times*, November 18, 2015.

11 Rose, "Meanings of Monochrome," 27.

12 For some, the persistent prominence of the color black in monochrome is notable, for, as Les Incohérents made explicit through their cellars and nights, black connotes the absence of light and sight. As Angeline Morrison notes, "The *Black Square* can [. . .] be read as the ultimate painterly paradox: a visual image that tells of the impossibility of seeing, embodied in an object whose very reason for existing is to be seen." Morrison, "Autobiography of An (Ex)Coloured Surface: Monochrome and Liminality," in *Discrepant Abstraction*, ed. Kobena Mercer (Cambridge, MA: MIT Press, 2006), 140.

13 Morrison, 137.

14 Morrison, 136.

15 Morrison, 138–39. Rose also mentions race in her consideration of monochrome. Yet Rose uses the affective indeterminacy of the monochrome to negate the racialized subject. For Rose, "the reticent, austere monochrome remains a statement of unapologetic elitism, challenging interpretation at every level. Its ethos is at odds with political correctness and represents resistance to all ideologies. The sex, nationality, race, and age of the monochrome artist are irrelevant and usually undiscernable." Rose, "Meanings of Monochrome," 82. Although Rose moves quickly from the affect of the art*work* (reticent, austere, unapologetically elitist, challenging, resistant) to the identity of the art*ist* (undiscernable), her determination not to see race—or at least the possibility of it—is exactly what Morrison reads as evidence of monochrome's position as the "unspeakable" mixed-race relation of modern art. Moreover, the "elitism" of the monochrome links the form with traditional narratives of passing and its theme of ruthless social climbing.

16 Morrison, "Autobiography of An (Ex)Coloured Surface," 139. Morrison specifies these binaries as full/empty, meaning/non-meaning, information/no-information, or figure/ground. Morisson's "or" suggests that this is not meant to be a comprehensive list.

17 Morrison, 144.

18 Morrison, 144. Morrison's essay is full of affective descriptors. Take, for example, her interpretive lens on the work of (mixed-race) Australian artist Gordon Bennett, whose painting *Suprematist Painting No. 1 (Nigger Lover)* (1993) is reproduced in her essay. Morrison quotes four sentences from an article about Bennett, authored by Bob Lingard and Fazal Rizvi. Within those few sentences the words *ambivalence, oppositional, discomfort, uncomfortable,* and *unsure how to react* all appear.

19 Morrison, 149. Rose also finds something affectively compelling and slippery in the monochromatic from, and lists "resistance, withdrawal, rejection, and a radical break from history" among monochromes' uniting characteristics. She

writes, “The monochrome work of art remains mysterious, an enigmatic presence that resists interpretation. Its appearance suggests simplicity and unity, which masks a potential for multivalence and paradox.” Rose, “Meanings of Monochrome,” 53, 21.

20 Fleetwood, *Troubling Vision*, 6.

21 David Hornung, *Color: A Workshop for Artists and Designers*, 3rd ed. (London: Laurence King Publishing, 2021).

22 *Oxford English Dictionary Online*, s.v. “value, n.”

23 Hatch, “First as Minstrelsy, Then as Farce,” 105–6.

24 Young Jean Lee, *The Shipment and LEAR* (New York: Theatre Communications Group, 2010), 7.

25 Young Jean Lee, *The Shipment and LEAR*, 7.

26 Young Jean Lee, *The Shipment and LEAR*, 7.

27 Young Jean Lee, *The Shipment*, October 3, 2009, Young Jean Lee’s Theatre Company. On the Boards, Seattle, Washington, October 3, 2009; video, On the Boards TV, www.ontheboards.tv.

28 Young Jean Lee, *The Shipment and LEAR*, 5.

29 For more on the confounding excesses of stereotype, see also Jennifer C. Nash, *The Black Body in Ecstasy: Reading Race, Reading Pornography* (Durham, NC: Duke University Press, 2014); Glenda R. Carpio, *Laughing Fit to Kill: Black Humor in the Fictions of Slavery* (New York: Oxford University Press, 2008), 124.

30 For more on this topic, see Tina Post, “‘Is That What We Wanted?’: Staging Slavery’s Affective Scripts,” *Modern Drama* 62, no. 4 (Winter 2019): 539–64.

31 Young Jean Lee, *The Shipment and LEAR*, 12.

32 Young Jean Lee, *The Shipment and LEAR*, 13.

33 Young Jean Lee, *The Shipment and LEAR*, 16.

34 Young Jean Lee, *The Shipment and LEAR*, 26.

35 Young Jean Lee, *The Shipment and LEAR*, 17.

36 Young Jean Lee, *The Shipment*.

37 Young Jean Lee, *The Shipment and LEAR*, 22.

38 Shimakawa, “Young Jean Lee’s Ugly Feelings about Race and Gender,” 93.

39 Sianne Ngai, *Ugly Feelings* (Cambridge, MA: Harvard University Press, 2005), 91.

40 Ngai, 271.

41 Ngai, 9.

42 Young Jean Lee, *The Shipment and LEAR*, 30.

43 I am grateful to Michelle Morgan for her insight on this point and its implications.

44 Young Jean Lee, *The Shipment and LEAR*, 29.

45 Young Jean Lee, *The Shipment and LEAR*, 5.

46 Young Jean Lee, *The Shipment and LEAR*, 53.

47 Young Jean Lee, *The Shipment and LEAR*, 53.

48 Hilton Als, “The Theatre: By the Skin of Our Teeth,” *New Yorker*, January 26, 2009.

49 Gwen Orel, “Theatre Reviews: NY (The Shipment),” *Backstage–National Edition*, January 15, 2009, 16.

50 Als, “The Theatre: By the Skin of Our Teeth.”

51 Hatch, “First as Minstrelsy, Then as Farce,” 97.

52 Morrison, "Autobiography of An (Ex)Coloured Surface," 152.

53 Hatch, "First as Minstrelsy, Then as Farce," 94.

54 Branden Jacobs-Jenkins, *Neighbors*, in *Reimagining "A Raisin in the Sun": Four New Plays*, ed. Rebecca Ann Rugg and Harvey Young (Evanston, IL: Northwestern University Press, 2012), 338.

55 Jacobs-Jenkins, 313.

56 Jacobs-Jenkins, 364–5.

57 Jacobs-Jenkins, 365.

58 Jacobs-Jenkins, 355. The audience is invited to connect this externally applied, total blackness with a different kind of clowning, of course.

59 Jacobs-Jenkins, 408–9.

60 Young Jean Lee, *The Shipment and LEAR.*

61 For more on alienation effects, see Brecht, *Brecht on Theatre*; Brooks, *Bodies in Dissent.*

62 Jacobs-Jenkins, *Neighbors*, 358.

63 Marilyn Stasio, "Legit Reviews: Off Broadway: Neighbors," *Variety*, March 15, 2010.

64 Stasio, 311.

65 Rebecca Ann Rugg, "Interview with Branden Jacobs-Jenkins," in Rugg and Young, *Reimagining "A Raisin in the Sun"*, 408.

66 Jacobs-Jenkins, *Neighbors*, 402.

67 Rugg, "Interview with Branden Jacobs-Jenkins," 410. For the time being, I am choosing to ignore the second ending of the play, which brings the actors of Melody and Jim into the audience space as themselves. Jacobs-Jenkins suggests that it did not "work" in its staging at the Public because of the theatre's architecture, and it is not mentioned in any theatre reviews of the play.

68 Rugg, 410.

69 The image can be seen easily at www.nytimes.com/2018/04/19/arts/design/adrian-piper-review-moma.html.

5. BUSTER KEATON'S BLACK DEADPAN

1 Ralph Ellison, "The Art of Fiction: An Interview," in *The Collected Essays of Ralph Ellison*, ed. John F. Callahan (New York: The Modern Library, 2003), 214.

2 Rudi Blesh, *Keaton* (New York: Macmillan, 1966), 5.

3 This image can be seen in Blesh, 6. Unfortunately I have yet to locate it digitized or in an archive.

4 James Baldwin was particularly salient on this point. Recall his speech at the end of 1963 documentary *Take This Hammer* ("You're the nigger, baby, it isn't me"). Richard O. Moore, "Take This Hammer" (KQED San Francisco: National Education Television, 1963), San Francisco Bay Area Television Archive, https://diva.sfsu.edu.

5 He costumed, as well, in Asian and Indigenous American attire. There is plenty to be said about the ways in which inexpression is also marshaled in and through those racial identities, though I will not take up that work here.

6 As discussed in the introduction, Susan Manning uses the terms "metaphorical minstrelsy" and "mythic abstraction" to name the ways that race was, or was

not, acknowledged in its contributions to modern dance. Manning, *Modern Dance, Negro Dance.*

7 For more on object force see Jiří Veltruský, "Man and Object in the Theater," in *A Prague School Reader on Esthetics, Literary Structure, and Style*, trans. Paul L Garvin (Washington, DC: Georgetown University Press, 1964); Andrew Sofer, *The Stage Life of Props* (Ann Arbor: University of Michigan Press, 2003).

8 André Bazin, *What Is Cinema?* vol. 1 (Berkeley: University of California Press, 1967), 121.

9 My understanding of animacy hierarchies is primarily indebted to Chen, *Animacies.*

10 Robert Benayoun, *The Look of Buster Keaton*, trans. Randall Conrad (New York: St. Martin's Press, 1983), 19.

11 Benayoun, 55.

12 Gilberto Perez, "The Bewildered Equilibrist: An Essay on Buster Keaton's Comedy," *Hudson Review* 34, no. 3 (Fall 1981): 344.

13 George Wead, *Buster Keaton and the Dynamics of Visual Wit* (New York: Arno, 1976), 265–6.

14 Wead, *Buster Keaton and the Dynamics of Visual Wit.* Though Keaton did not generally undercrank his cameras as Sennett did (to produce the effect of speed), Wead offers compelling evidence that Sennett's technological intervention primed a certain aesthetic and affective trope. Wead writes, "It would be a few years before Sergei Eisenstein was to compare his concept of montage to the internal combustion engine, but in 1912 Mack Sennett began to stylize the world as a machine. 'In the world of the commonplace,' he said, 'only the extraordinary, the unbelievable almost, is truly amusing or interesting.' Sennett fascinated America with men at the mercy of mechanization." 177–8.

15 Wead, 165.

16 Blesh, *Keaton*, 42. Keaton lost part of an index finger in childhood to a clothes-wringer and experienced an unusual fright from a ventriloquist's marionette.

17 Henri Bergson, *Laughter: An Essay on the Meaning of the Comic*, trans. Cloudesley Brereton and Fred Rothwell (New York: Macmillan, 1914) Project Gutenberg EBook, August 2003.

18 Bergson.

19 Louis Chude-Sokei, *The Sound of Culture: Diaspora and Black Technopoetics* (Middletown, CT: Wesleyan University Press, 2016).

20 For more on Joice Heath as automaton, see McMillan, *Embodied Avatars*; for more on *The Steam Man of the Prairies*, see Joel Dinerstein, *Swinging the Machine: Modernity, Technology, and African American Culture between the World Wars* (Amherst: University of Massachusetts Press, 2003). For more on the umbrella of race and automatism, see "Animatedness" in Ngai, *Ugly Feelings*, and "Reification, Reanimation, and the American Uncanny" in Bill Brown's *Other Things* (Chicago: The University of Chicago Press, 2015).

21 Frank L. Baum, *The Wonderful Wizard of Oz* (Chicago: G.M. Hill Co., 1900), 58–60.

22 I believe my colleague Danielle Bainbridge first connected these texts in our Politics and Performance graduate seminar.

23 Charles W. Chesnutt, "Po' Sandy," The Charles W. Chesnutt Archive, ed. Stephanie P. Browner, Matt Cohen, and Kenneth M. Price, accessed April 5, 2021, https://chesnuttarchive.org.

24 Young, *Embodying Black Experience.*

25 Baum's lyrics to "Niccolo Piccolo" include the lyrics "Defying fell malaria / He'd execute this aria / With marvelous dexterity, / Each night at half past nine." Malaria was most common in the former slave states of the United States. Building on Eileen Southern's research, ethnomusicologist David Evans's research into fife and drum survivals reiterates the "large number of black fifers and drummers that served in the Union Army during the Civil War, and [. . .] one recorded case of such a group in the confederate army." David Evans, "Black Fife and Drum Music in Mississippi," *Folkstreams*, accessed April 2, 2021, www.folkstreams.net.

26 Robin Bernstein, *Racial Innocence: Performing American Childhood from Slavery to Civil Rights* (New York: New York University Press, 2011), 161.

27 Related to the mechanization of blackness mentioned earlier in this chapter, the Tin Woodman also bears consideration as a mechanical iteration of minstrel inflection. Alas, that is for another project.

28 Bernstein, *Racial Innocence*, 161–2.

29 Bernstein, 163.

30 Bernstein, 149, 163.

31 Bernstein, 151.

32 Bernstein, 189, 153.

33 I can't help but mention that Blesh describes the creative process surrounding early Keaton/Arbuckle two-reelers by saying "the story, like Topsy, just grew." Blesh, *Keaton*, 93. As Bernstein shows, the character Topsy was a frequent victim of uncannily survivable violence; although Blesh ostensibly evokes Topsy as a metaphor of uncertain parentage and a preternatural ability to thrive in a harsh environment, tropological blackness carries other meanings along (here, the ability to withstand violence). Said differently, while "just grew" might be an apt description of Keaton and Arbuckle's process, I think it likely that Topsy occurred to Blesh because of the violence common to both her character and the two-reelers in question.

34 Paul Gallico, "Circus in Paris," *Esquire*, August 1954, 108–13.

35 Bernstein, *Racial Innocence*, 188.

36 For more on the classed, raced, and gendered uses of makeup in Keaton's work, see Susan E. Linville, "Black Face/White Face: Keaton and Comic Doubling," *New Review of Film and Television Studies* 5, no. 3 (December 2007): 269–84.

37 Bernstein, *Racial Innocence*, 175.

38 Bernstein, 177. I here rely on Bernstein's transcription, as I have not been able to travel to the manuscript.

39 Larsen, *Complete Fiction of Nella Larsen*; Ellison, *Invisible Man*; Chester Himes, *If He Hollers Let Him Go* (New York: Da Capo Press, 2002); Ann Petry, *The Street* (Boston: Mariner Books, 1991); William Attaway, *Blood on the Forge* (New York: NYRB Classic, 2005).

40 Richard Wright, *Native Son* (New York: Harper & Row, 1966).

41 Perez, "Bewildered Equilibrist," 347.

42 Joanna E. Rapf and Gary L. Green, *Buster Keaton: A Bio-Bibliography* (Westport, CT: Greenwood Press, 1995), 37–8.

43 Benayoun, *Look of Buster Keaton*, 18.

44 J. P. Lebel, *Buster Keaton*, trans. P. D. Stovin (New York: A. S. Barnes & Co., 1967), 32. In Lebel's treatise the deadpan is most valuable for the ways it emphasizes Keaton's eyes and his movement, both of which Lebel finds inordinately expressive. In the assessment that Keaton's deadpan helps to highlight his movement, Lebel would seem to agree with the assertions of my first chapter.

45 Blesh, *Keaton*, 44.

46 Countless sources take up this history, as well as African American attempts to counter its perceptions. For a particularly multifaceted account that brings up aesthetics and performativity, see Wallace and Smith, *Pictures and Progress*; Gilmore, *Gender and Jim Crow*.

47 For example, a brief scene in *Neighbors* shows the innocent black man who was nearly arrested espying Keaton carted away in his place; he laughs and blows an Italianate kiss in appreciation for his getaway. One could read a "jolly negro" into this scene, but in my own estimation it is joyful without being excessive. The scene shows only the actor's head—that is, his whole body isn't called into the testimony of happy-go-luckiness. He also shows no laziness or slowness of cognition in conjunction with his joy.

48 Buster Keaton, *My Wonderful World of Slapstick* (Garden City, NY: Doubleday, 1960), 12.

49 Blesh, *Keaton*, 38.

50 Buster Keaton, *My Wonderful World of Slapstick*, 13.

51 Buster Keaton, 61; Joe Keaton, "'London': 'Mr. Butt and Co.,'" *Variety*, December 11, 1909, 106, Media History Digital Library.

52 Blesh, *Keaton*, 62.

53 Buster Keaton, *My Wonderful World of Slapstick*, 62.

54 Buster Keaton, *My Wonderful World of Slapstick*, 62.

55 Blesh, *Keaton*, 62.

56 For more on ghosted roles, see Marvin Carlson, *The Haunted Stage: The Theatre as Memory Machine* (Ann Arbor: University of Michigan Press, 2001), 7–9.

57 Louis Chude-Sokei, *The Last "Darky": Bert Williams, Black-on-Black Minstrelsy, and the African Diaspora* (Durham, NC: Duke University Press, 2006), 54.

58 Blesh, *Keaton*, 154.

59 I have here skipped over Keaton's portrayal of a monkey in the latter half of the film, though it, too, can be interpreted as harkening to blackness and an interruption of traditional animacy hierarchies.

60 Rapf and Green, *Buster Keaton*.

61 David B. Pearson and Patricia Eliot Tobias, "Keaton Bookshelf," The DamfiNews: The International Buster Keaton Society, accessed May 3, 2016, www.busterkeaton.com.

62 Archer-Straw, *Negrophilia*, 54–64.

63 Cheng, *Second Skin*, 18.

64 Buster Keaton, *My Wonderful World of Slapstick*, 77–8. See also pages 26 (Robinson), 126 and 311 (Williams).

65 The confusion regarding Riddle's name is due to Keaton's rechristening of him. According to Blesh, "When Willie Riddle first came to Hollywood, his own name had struck him as inadequate. 'Willie this, Willie that,' he had complained. '*Willie!*' Buster searched for an imposing name; he got it out of his own sixth year, a Robert Hilliard vaudeville playlet of 1901, *The Littlest Girl*. Hilliard had been Carruthers. Now Willie stepped into the role." Blesh, *Keaton*, 236.

66 Marion Meade, *Buster Keaton: Cut to the Chase* (New York: HarperCollins, 1995), 118.

67 Meade, 118; Blesh, *Keaton*, 236.

68 Tom Dardis, *Keaton: The Man Who Wouldn't Lie Down* (New York: Charles Scribner's Sons, 1979), 75.

69 Blesh, *Keaton*, 236.

70 Meade, *Buster Keaton*, 118.

71 Dardis, *Keaton*, 236. While Dardis suggests Riddle joined Keaton in the late (rather than the early) '20s, he is outnumbered on this point.

72 For more on pan-toting (that is, re-appropriating employers' food stuffs) as a black practice, see Tera W. Hunter, *To 'Joy My Freedom: Southern Black Women's Lives and Labors after the Civil War* (Cambridge, MA: Harvard University Press, 1997).

73 Meade, *Buster Keaton*, 185.

74 Dardis, *Keaton*, 186.

75 Blesh, *Keaton*, 330.

76 Bates, *Pullman Porters and the Rise of Protest Politics*, 18.

77 Bates, 22.

78 Authors also accuse Keaton of dissemblance. In discussing Keaton's autobiography, Joanna Rapf writes, "In almost three hundred pages, Keaton reveals very little about his personal life, despite appearances to the contrary. [. . . For] even here Keaton wears the great stone face which on the surface appears to say nothing but in reality conveys a philosophy of life." Rapf and Green, *Buster Keaton*, 82–3.

79 If I do not completely discount the possibility that Willie "Carruthers" Riddle was white, I nevertheless argue that he has been written into Keaton's narrative in a way that resounds with blackness. Regardless of the race of the actual man, his narrative function has become an authenticating one. I will take up that authenticating blackness as though it is literal—though I would argue that in either case, in its narrative function, it is "real."

80 Blesh, *Keaton*, 310.

BIBLIOGRAPHY

Albers, Josef. *Interaction of Color*. New Haven, CT: Yale University Press, 2013.

Als, Hilton. "Richard Avedon and James Baldwin's Joint Examination of American Identity." *New Yorker*, November 6, 2017.

———. "Slow Man." *New Yorker*, September 17, 2012.

———. "The Theatre: By the Skin of Our Teeth." *New Yorker*, January 26, 2009.

Alvarado, Leticia. *Abject Performances*. Durham, NC: Duke University Press, 2018.

Archer-Straw, Petrine. *Negrophilia: Avant-Garde Paris and Black Culture in the 1920s*. New York: Thames & Hudson, 2000.

Archias, Elise. *The Concrete Body: Yvonne Rainer, Carolee Schneemann, Vito Acconci*. New Haven, CT: Yale University Press, 2016.

Archias, S. Elise, and Juliet Bellow. "'Dance and Abstraction' Special Issue Introduction." *Arts* 9, no. 4 (December 2020): 120.

Artishock. "Claudia Casarino: Iluminando la ausencia." *Artishock*, February 27, 2018. https://artishockrevista.com.

Attaway, William. *Blood on the Forge*. New York: NYRB Classic, 2005.

Avedon, Richard, and James Baldwin. *Nothing Personal*. New York: Atheneum, 1964.

Baldwin, James. *Collected Essays*. New York: The Library of America, 1998.

———. "How Can We Get the Black People to Cool It?" *Esquire*, July 1968.

———. "The Fight: Patterson vs. Liston." In *The Unlevel Playing Field: A Documentary History of the African American Experience in Sport*, edited by David K Wiggins and Patrick B. Miller, 296–303. Chicago: University of Chicago Press, 2005.

Barrow, Joe Louis, Jr., and Barbara Munder. *Joe Louis: 50 Years an American Hero*. New York: McGraw-Hill, 1998.

Barthes, Roland. *Camera Lucida: Reflections on Photography*. Translated by Richard Howard. New York: Hill and Wang, 1981.

Bates, Beth Tompkins. *Pullman Porters and the Rise of Protest Politics in Black America, 1925–1945*. Chapel Hill: University of North Carolina Press, 2001.

Bateson, Gregory, and Margaret Mead. *Balinese Character: A Photographic Analysis*. New York: New York Academy of Sciences, 1942.

Baum, Frank L. *The Wonderful Wizard of Oz*. Chicago: G. M. Hill Co., 1900.

Bazin, André. *What Is Cinema?* Vol. 1. Berkeley: University of California Press, 1967.

Benayoun, Robert. *The Look of Buster Keaton*. Translated by Randall Conrad. New York: St. Martin's Press, 1983.

Benezra, Neal. "'The Thing Shines, Not the Maker': The Sculpture of Martin Puryear." In *Martin Puryear*, edited by Neal Benezra, 13–54. Chicago: Thames and Hudson/The Art Institute of Chicago, 1991.

Berger, Maurice. *Labyrinths: Robert Morris, Minimalism and the 1960s*. New York: Harper & Row, 1989.

———. *Minimal Politics: Performativity and Minimalism in Recent American Art*. Issues in Cultural Theory. Baltimore: Fine Arts Gallery, University of Maryland, 1997.

Bergson, Henri. *Laughter: An Essay on the Meaning of the Comic*. Translated by Cloudesley Brereton and Fred Rothwell. New York: Macmillan, 1914. Project Gutenberg EBook, August 2003.

Berlant, Lauren. *Cruel Optimism*. Durham, NC: Duke University Press, 2011.

———. "Showing Up to Withhold: Pope.L's Deadpan Aesthetic." In *Showing Up to Withhold*. Chicago: The Renaissance Society at the University of Chicago, in association with the University of Chicago Press, 2014.

———. "Thinking About Feeling Historical." *Emotion, Space and Society* 1 (2008): 4–9.

Bernstein, Robin. *Racial Innocence: Performing American Childhood from Slavery to Civil Rights*. New York: New York University Press, 2011.

Blesh, Rudi. *Keaton*. New York: Macmillan, 1966.

Brown, Bill. *Other Things*. Chicago: University of Chicago Press, 2015.

Bowles, John P. *Adrian Piper: Race, Gender, and Embodiment*. Durham, NC: Duke University Press, 2011.

Boyer, Richard O. "The Hot Bach (1944)." In *The Duke Ellington Reader*, edited by Mark Tucker, 214–45. New York: Oxford University Press, 1993.

Brecht, Bertolt. *Brecht on Theatre: The Development of an Aesthetic*. Edited and translated by John Willett. New York: Hill and Wang, 1964.

Brooks, Daphne. *Bodies in Dissent: Spectacular Performances of Race and Freedom, 1850–1910*. Durham, NC: Duke University Press, 2006.

Browne, Simone. *Dark Matters: On the Surveillance of Blackness*. Durham, NC: Duke University Press, 2015.

Brustein, Robert Sanford. "MASS MoCa: A Boom in the Boonies." In *Millennial Stages: Essays and Reviews, 2001–2005*, 203–7. New Haven, CT: Yale University Press, 2006.

Burley, Dan. "3 in Mid-West Win as Golden Glovers." *New York Amsterdam News*, March 17, 1934. ProQuest Historical Newspapers: New York Amsterdam News (1922–1993).

Butler, Judith. *Gender Trouble: Feminism and the Subversion of Identity*. New York: Routledge, 1990.
Cahan, Susan E. *Mounting Frustration: The Art Museum in the Age of Black Power*. Durham, NC: Duke University Press, 2016.
Campt, Tina M. *Image Matters: Archive, Photography, and the African Diaspora in Europe*. Durham, NC: Duke University Press, 2012.
Carby, Hazel V. *Cultures in Babylon*. New York: Verso, 1999.
Carlson, Marvin. *The Haunted Stage: The Theatre as Memory Machine*. Ann Arbor: University of Michigan Press, 2001.
Carpio, Glenda R. *Laughing Fit to Kill: Black Humor in the Fictions of Slavery*. New York: Oxford University Press, 2008.
Cate, Phillip Denis. "The Spirit of Montmartre." In *The Spirit of Montmartre: Cabarets, Humor and the Avant-Garde, 1875–1905*, edited by Phillip Denis Cate and Mary Shaw, 1–94. New Brunswick, NJ: Jane Voorhees Zimmerli Art Museum, Rutgers, 1996.
Certeau, Michel de. *The Practice of Everyday Life*. Berkeley: University of California Press, 1984.
Chambers-Letson, Joshua. *After the Party: A Manifesto for Queer of Color Life*. New York: New York University Press, 2018.
Chen, Mel. *Animacies: Biopolitics, Racial Mattering, and Queer Affect*. Durham, NC: Duke University Press, 2012.
Cheng, Anne Anlin. *Second Skin: Josephine Baker and the Modern Surface*. New York: Oxford University Press, 2011.
———. *The Melancholy of Race: Psychoanalysis, Assimilation, and Hidden Grief*. New York: Oxford University Press, 2000.
Chesnutt, Charles W. "Po' Sandy." The Charles W. Chesnutt Archive, ed. Stephanie P. Browner, Matt Cohen, and Kenneth M. Price, accessed April 5, 2021. https://chesnuttarchive.org.
Chude-Sokei, Louis. *The Last "Darky": Bert Williams, Black-on-Black Minstrelsy, and the African Diaspora*. Durham, NC: Duke University Press, 2006.
———. *The Sound of Culture: Diaspora and Black Technopoetics*. Middletown, CT: Wesleyan University Press, 2016.
Collins, Kathleen. "Portraits of Slave Children." *History of Photography* 9, no. 3 (1985): 187–210.
Copeland, Huey. *Bound to Appear: Art, Slavery and the Site of Blackness in Multicultural America*. Chicago: University of Chicago Press, 2013.
Crutchfield, Margo A. *Martin Puryear*. Richmond: Virginia Museum of Fine Arts, 2001.
Dardis, Tom. *Keaton: The Man Who Wouldn't Lie Down*. New York: Charles Scribner's Sons, 1979.
Dash, Julie. *Daughters of the Dust*. Kino International, 1991.
Dinerstein, Joel. *Swinging the Machine: Modernity, Technology, and African American Culture Between the World Wars*. Amherst: University of Massachusetts Press, 2003.
Doyle, Jennifer. *Hold It Against Me: Difficulty and Emotion in Contemporary Art*. Durham, NC: Duke University Press, 2013.

Du Bois, W. E. B. *The Souls of Black Folk*. New Haven, CT: Yale University Press, 2015.
Dunbar, Paul Laurence. *Lyrics of Lowly Life. (1896)*. New York: Arno Press, 1969.
Elderfield, John. "Martin Puryear: Ideas of Otherness." In *Martin Puryear*, edited by John Elderfield, 13–57. New York: Museum of Modern Art, 2007.
Ellison, Ralph. *Flying Home and Other Stories*. New York: Vintage International, 1996.
———. *Invisible Man*. New York: Vintage International, 1995.
———. "The Art of Fiction: An Interview," in *The Collected Essays of Ralph Ellison*, edited by John F. Callahan. New York: The Modern Library, 2003.
English, Darby. *1971: A Year in the Life of Color*. Chicago: University of Chicago Press, 2016.
Erenberg, Lewis. *The Greatest Fight of Our Generation: Louis vs. Schmeling*. New York: Oxford University Press, 2006.
Evan, David. "Black Fife and Drum Music in Mississippi." *Folkstreams*, accessed April 2, 2021. www.folkstreams.net.
Fabian, Ann. *The Skull Collectors: Race, Science, and America's Unburied Dead*. Chicago: University of Chicago Press, 2010.
Feimster, Crystal N. *Southern Horrors: Women and the Politics of Rape and Lynching*. Cambridge, MA: Harvard University Press, 2009.
Ferguson, Jeffrey. "Race and the Rhetoric of Resistance." *Raritan* 28, no. 1 (Summer 2008): 4–32.
Ferreira da Silva, Denise. *Toward a Global Idea of Race*. Minneapolis: University of Minnesota Press, 2007.
Field, Jennifer. "Chronology." In *Martin Puryear*, edited by John Elderfield. New York: The Museum of Modern Art, 2007.
Filidori, Erwan. "Claudia Casarino—On Being Under Pressure." *Metal*, accessed December 16, 2019. https://metalmagazine.eu.
Fleetwood, Nicole R. *Troubling Vision: Performance, Visuality, and Blackness*. Chicago: University of Chicago Press, 2011.
Fletcher, Tom. *The Tom Fletcher Story: 100 Years of the Negro in Show Business!* New York: Burdge & Company, Ltd., 1954.
Fournier, Lauren. "Fermenting Feminism: Andrea Creamer, Eleonora Edreva & Leo Williams, Alanna Lynch, Sarah Nasby, Walter Scott, and Christine Tien Wang." *Access Gallery*, September 13, 2019. https://accessgallery.ca.
Fried, Michael. "Art and Objecthood." In *Art and Objecthood: Essays and Reviews*. Chicago: University of Chicago Press, 1998.
Gallico, Paul. "Circus in Paris." *Esquire*, August 1954, 108–13.
Gast, Leon. *When We Were Kings*. Gramercy Pictures, 1996.
Gates, Jr., Henry Louis. "The Blackness of Blackness: A Critique of the Sign and the Signifying Monkey." In *Black Literature and Literary Theory*, edited by Henry Louis Gates, Jr., 285–321. New York: Methuen, 1984.
Gibson, Bill. "Hear Me Talkin' to Ya." *Baltimore Afro-American*, April 13, 1935. ProQuest Historical Newspapers: Baltimore Afro-American (1893–1988).
Gilman, Sander L. "Black Bodies, White Bodies: Toward an Iconography of Female Sexuality in Late Nineteenth-Century Art, Medicine, and Literature." In *"Race,"*

Writing, and Difference, edited by Henry Louis Gates, Jr., 223–61. Chicago: University of Chicago Press, 1986.

Gilmore, Glenda Elizabeth. *Gender and Jim Crow: Women and the Politics of White Supremacy in North Carolina, 1896–1920*. Chapel Hill: University of North Carolina Press, 1996.

Gilroy, Paul. *The Black Atlantic: Modernity and Double-Consciousness*. Harvard University Press, 1995.

Glissant, Édouard. *Poetics of Relation*. Translated by Betsy Wing. Ann Arbor: University of Michigan Press, 1997.

Goffman, Erving. *Behavior in Public Places: Notes on the Social Organization of Gatherings*. New York: The Free Press, 1963.

———. *The Presentation of Self in Everyday Life*. New York: Anchor Books, 1959.

Golden, Thelma, ed. *Black Male: Representations of Masculinity in Contemporary American Art*. New York: Whitney Museum of Art, 1994.

Grant, Simon, and Robert Morris. "Simon Grant Interviews Robert Morris." *Tate Etc.*, no. 14 (Autumn 2008). www.tate.org.uk.

Greenberg, Clement. *Art and Culture: Critical Essays*. Boston: Beacon Press, 1961.

———. "Modernist Painting." In *Twentieth Century Theories of Art*, edited by James M. Thompson, 94. Ottawa: Carleton University Press, 1999.

Gutierrez, Miguel. "Does Abstraction Belong to White People?" *BOMB*, November 7, 2018. https://bombmagazine.org.

Hall, Kim F. *Things of Darkness: Economies of Race and Gender in Early Modern England*. Ithaca, NY: Cornell University Press, 1995.

Hall, Stuart. "What Is This Black in Black Popular Culture?" In *Critical Dialogues in Cultural Studies*, edited by David Morley and Kuan-Hsing Chen. London: Routledge, 1996.

Harper, Phillip Brian. *Abstractionist Aesthetics: Artistic Form and Social Critique in African American Culture*. Durham, NC: Duke University Press, 2015.

Hartman, Saidiya. *Scenes of Subjection: Terror, Slavery, and Self-Making in Nineteenth-Century America*. New York: Oxford University Press, 1997.

Hatch, Ryan Anthony. "First as Minstrelsy, Then as Farce: On the Spectacle of Race in the Theatre of Young Jean Lee." *CR: The New Centennial Review* 13, no. 3 (2013): 89–114.

Hayot, Eric. *The Hypothetical Mandarin: Sympathy, Modernity, and Chinese Pain*. New York: Oxford University Press, 2009.

Himes, Chester. "Headwaiter." In *The Collected Stories of Chester Himes*, 1–15. New York: Thunder's Mouth Press, 2000.

———. *If He Hollers Let Him Go*. New York: Da Capo Press, 2002.

Hine, Darlene Clark. "Rape and the Inner Lives of Black Women in the Middle West." *Signs* 14, no. 4 (Summer 1989): 912–20.

Holmberg, Arthur. *The Theatre of Robert Wilson*. Directors in Perspective. Cambridge: Cambridge University Press, 1996.

Hornung, David. *Color: A Workshop for Artists and Designers*. 3rd ed. London: Laurence King Publishing, 2021.

Horrigan, Brian. "Esquire–July 1968." *The 1968 Exhibit*, July 7, 2009, accessed August 12, 2016. www.the1968exhibit.org.

Huang, Vivian L. "Inscrutably, Actually: Hospitality, Parasitism, and the Silent Work of Yoko Ono and Laurel Nakadate." *Women & Performance: A Journal of Feminist Theory* 28, no. 3 (2018): 187–203.

Hunter, Tera W. *To 'Joy My Freedom: Southern Black Women's Lives and Labors after the Civil War*. Cambridge, MA: Harvard University Press, 1997.

Hurston, Zora Neale. "Characteristics of Negro Expression." In *Zora Neale Hurston: Folklore, Memoirs and Other Writings*, edited by Cheryl A. Wall, 830–47. New York: The Library of America, 1995.

———. "How It Feels to Be Colored Me." In *Folklore, Memoirs, & Other Writings*, edited by Cheryl A. Wall, 826–9. New York: The Library of America, 1995.

Iton, Richard. *In Search of the Black Fantastic: Politics and Popular Culture in the Post-Civil Rights Era*. New York: Oxford University Press, 2008.

Jacobs-Jenkins, Branden. "Neighbors." In *Reimagining "A Raisin in the Sun": Four New Plays*, edited by Rebecca Ann Rugg and Harvey Young, 306–403. Evanston, IL: Northwestern University Press, 2012.

Jefferson, Thomas. *Notes on the State of Virginia*. Boston: Lilly and Wait, 1832.

Johnson, E. Patrick. *Appropriating Blackness: Performance and the Politics of Authenticity*. Durham, NC: Duke University Press, 2003.

Johnson, Jasmine Elizabeth. "'Sheer Pleasure': Eloise Greenfield, Solange Knowles, and Black Hush." In *Saturation: Race, Art, and the Circulation of Value*, edited by C. Riley Snorton and Hentyle Yapp, 183–196. Cambridge, MA: MIT Press, 2020.

Jones, LeRoi (Amiri Baraka). "The Dempsey-Liston Fight." In *Home: Social Essays*, 179–84. New York: Akashic Books, 1996.

Keaton, Buster. *My Wonderful World of Slapstick*. Garden City, NY: Doubleday & Company, 1960.

Keaton, Joe. "'London': 'Mr. Butt and Co.'" *Variety*, December 11, 1909, 106. Media History Digital Library.

Kelley, Robin D. G. "'We Are Not What We Seem': Rethinking Black Working-Class Opposition in the Jim Crow South." *Journal of American History* 80, no. 1 (June 1993): 75–112.

Kim, Ju Yon. *The Racial Mundane: Asian American Performance and the Embodied Everyday*. New York: New York University Press, 2015.

Lambert-Beatty, Carrie. *Being Watched: Yvonne Rainer and the 1960s*. Cambridge, MA: MIT Press, 2011.

Larsen, Nella. *The Complete Fiction of Nella Larsen: Passing, Quicksand, and the Stories*. New York: Anchor Books, 2001.

Lebel, J. P. *Buster Keaton*. Translated by P. D. Stovin. New York: A. S. Barnes & Co., 1967.

Lee, Summer Kim. "Staying In: Mitski, Ocean Vuong, and Asian American Asociality." *Social Text* 37, no. 1 (2019): 27–50.

Lee, Young Jean. *The Shipment*. October 3, 2009. Young Jean Lee's Theatre Company. On the Boards, Seattle, Washington. Video, On the Boards TV, www.ontheboards.tv.

———. *The Shipment and LEAR*. New York: Theatre Communications Group, 2010.

Linville, Susan E. "Black Face/White Face: Keaton and Comic Doubling." *New Review of Film and Television Studies* 5, no. 3 (December 2007): 269–84.

Louis, Joe, and Art and Edna Rust. *Joe Louis: My Life*. New York: Harcourt Brace Jovanovich, 1978.
Lynch, Alanna. *Alanna Lynch*. Accessed December 17, 2019. http://alannalynch.com.
———. "Gut Feelings: A Performance." In *Musings*, 31–5. food feminism fermentation, 2019. www.foodfeminismfermentation.com.
Mailer, Norman. *The Fight*. Boston: Little, Brown and Company, 1975.
Manning, Susan. *Modern Dance, Negro Dance: Race in Motion*. Minneapolis: University of Minnesota Press, 2004.
Margolick, David. *Beyond Glory: Joe Louis vs. Max Schmeling, and a World on the Brink*. New York: Vintage Books, 2005.
Massumi, Brian. "The Future Birth of the Affective Fact: The Political Ontology of Threat." In *The Affect Theory Reader*, edited by Melissa Gregg and Gregory J. Seigworth, 52–70. Durham, NC: Duke University Press, 2010.
McKinney, Jack. "He's Mad and Getting Madder." *Sports Illustrated*, September 24, 1962, 24–27, 118–121.
McMillan, Uri. *Embodied Avatars: The Art of Black Female Performance*. New York: New York University Press, 2015.
———. "Introduction: Skin, Surface, Sensorium." *Women & Performance: A Journal of Feminist Theory* 28, no. 1 (January, 2018): 1–15.
Mead, Chris. *Champion—Joe Louis: Black Hero in White America*. New York: Charles Scribner's Sons, 1985.
Meade, Marion. *Buster Keaton: Cut to the Chase*. New York: HarperCollins, 1995.
Mercer, Kobena. "Art History and the Dialogics of Diaspora." *Small Axe* 38 (July 2012): 214–27.
Mill, John Stuart. "Bentham." In *Early Essays*, edited by J. W. M. Gibbs, 327–416. London: George Bell and Sons, 1897.
Moynihan, Daniel Patrick. *The Negro Family: The Case for National Action*. Washington, DC: U.S. Government Printing Office, 1965.
Mok, Christine. "On The Face of It: Nikki S Lee's Layers." Presented at the Performance Studies Working Group, Yale University, November 3, 2015.
Molesworth, Helen. "Art Is Medicine." *Artforum* 56, no. 7 (March 2018): 164–73.
Moore, Richard O. "Take This Hammer." KQED San Francisco: National Education Television, 1963. Video, 44:14. San Francisco Bay Area Television Archive. https://diva.sfsu.edu.
Morgan, Perry. "The Case for the White Southerner." *Esquire*, January 1962, 41–45.
Morris, Robert. "Notes on Sculpture." In *Minimal Art: A Critical Anthology*, edited by Gregory Battcock, 222–35. New York: E. P. Dutton & Co., 1968.
Morrison, Angeline. "Autobiography of An (Ex)Coloured Surface: Monochrome and Liminality." In *Discrepant Abstraction*, edited by Kobena Mercer, 134–53. Cambridge, MA: MIT Press, 2006.
Muñoz, José Esteban. *Disidentifications: Queers of Color and the Performance of Politics*. Minneapolis: University of Minnesota Press, 1999.
———. *The Sense of Brown*. Ed. Joshua Chambers-Letson and Tavia Nyong'o. Durham, NC: Duke University Press, 2020.
Musser, Amber Jamilla. *Sensational Flesh: Race, Power, and Masochism*. New York: New York University Press, 2014.

Nash, Jennifer C. *The Black Body in Ecstasy: Reading Race, Reading Pornography*. Durham, NC: Duke University Press, 2014.

Nechepurenko, Ivan. "Examination Reveals a Mysterious Message on Malevich's 'Black Square' Painting." *New York Times*, November 18, 2015.

Neri, Janice. *The Insect and the Image: Visualizing Nature in Early Modern Europe, 1500–1700*. Minneapolis: University of Minnesota Press, 2011.

New Oxford American Dictionary. Oxford University Press, 2010. Online Version.

Ngai, Sianne. *Ugly Feelings*. Cambridge, MA: Harvard University Press, 2005.

Niyazbekova, Zh. T., G. Zh. Nagmetova, and A. A. Kurmanbayev. "An Overview of Bacterial Cellulose Applications." *Eurasian Journal of Applied Biotechnology*, 2018, no. 2. https://biotechlink.org, doi: 10.11134/btp.2.2018.3.

Noland, Carrie. *Agency and Embodiment: Performing Gestures/Producing Culture*. Cambridge, MA: Harvard University Press, 2009.

Oates, Joyce Carol. *On Boxing*. New York: Harper Perennial, 2006.

OED Online. Oxford University Press, December 2016. www.oed.com.

Oliver, Valerie Cassel, ed. *Radical Presence: Black Performance in Contemporary Art*. Houston: Contemporary Arts Museum Houston, 2013.

Orel, Gwen. "Theatre Reviews: NY (The Shipment)." *Backstage–National Edition*, January 15, 2009.

Painter, Nell Irvin. *Sojourner Truth: A Life, A Symbol*. New York: W. W. Norton & Company, 1996.

Peale, Rembrandt. *Thomas Jefferson*. 1800. Oil on canvas. White House Collection/ White House Historical Association. www.whitehousehistory.org.

Pearson, David B., and Patricia Eliot Tobias. "Keaton Bookshelf." The DamfiNews: The International Buster Keaton Society. Accessed May 3, 2016. www.busterkeaton.com.

Peña Chavarría, A., and P. G. Shipley. "The Siamese Twins of Española (The First Known Post-Mortem Examination in the New World)." *Annals of Medical History* 6 (1924): 297–302.

Perez, Gilberto. "The Bewildered Equilibrist: An Essay on Buster Keaton's Comedy." *Hudson Review* 34, no. 3 (Fall 1981): 337–66.

Petry, Ann. *The Street*. Boston: Mariner Books, 1991.

Post, Tina. "'Is That What We Wanted?': Staging Slavery's Affective Scripts." *Modern Drama* 62, no. 4 (Winter 2019): 539–64.

———. "Williams, Walker, and Shine: Blackbody Blackface, or the Importance of Being Surface." *TDR/The Drama Review* 59, no. 4 (2015): 83–100.

Pudovkin, V. I. "Film Technique." In *Film: An Anthology*, edited by Daniel Talbot, 189–200. Berkeley: University of California Press, 1959.

Quashie, Kevin E. *The Sovereignty of Quiet: Beyond Resistance in Black Culture*. New Brunswick, NJ: Rutgers University Press, 2012.

Rabinbach, Anson. *The Human Motor: Energy, Fatigue, and the Origins of Modernity*. Berkeley: University of California Press, 1990.

Raiford, Leigh. *Imprisoned in a Luminous Glare: Photography and the African American Freedom Struggle*. Chapel Hill, NC: University of North Carolina Press, 2011.

Rankine, Claudia. "'The Condition of Black Life Is One of Mourning.'" *New York Times*, June 22, 2015.

Rapf, Joanna E., and Gary L. Green. *Buster Keaton: A Bio-Bibliography*. Westport, CT: Greenwood Press, 1995.

Remnick, David. *King of the World: Muhammad Ali and the Rise of an American Hero*. New York: Vintage Books, 1998.

Roach, Joseph. *Cities of the Dead: Circum-Atlantic Performance*. New York: Columbia University Press, 1996.

———. *The Player's Passion: Studies in the Science of Acting*. Ann Arbor: University of Michigan Press, 1993.

Robbins, Christa Noel. "The Sensibility of Michael Fried." *Criticism* 60, no. 4 (Fall 2018): 429–54.

Roberts, Randy. *Joe Louis: Hard Times Man*. New Haven, CT: Yale University Press, 2010.

Rose, Barbara. "The Meanings of Monochrome." In *Monochromes: From Malevich to the Present*, edited by Valeria Varas and Raul Rispa. Berkeley: University of California Press, 2006.

Rugg, Rebecca Ann. "Interview with Branden Jacobs-Jenkins." In *Reimagining "A Raisin in the Sun": Four New Plays*, edited by Rebecca Ann Rugg and Harvey Young, 404–14. Evanston, IL: Northwestern University Press, 2012.

Sacasas, Michael. "Dead and Going to Die." *New Inquiry*, October 21, 2013. https://thenewinquiry.com.

Sack, Daniel. *After Live: Possibility, Potentiality, and the Future of Performance*. Ann Arbor: University of Michigan Press, 2015.

Salgado, Gabriela. "Claudia Casarino: Illuminating Absence." *CAAM*, January 25, 2018. www.caam.net.

Sammons, Jeffrey T. *Beyond the Ring: The Role of Boxing in American Society*. Urbana: University of Illinois Press, 1988.

Schechner, Richard. *Performance Studies: An Introduction*. 2nd ed. New York: Routledge, 2006.

Schneider, Suzanne. "Louis Agassiz and the American School of Ethnoeroticism: Polygenesis, Pornography, and Other 'Perfidious Influences.'" In *Pictures and Progress: Early Photography and the Making of African American Identity*, edited by Maurice O. Wallace and Shawn Michelle Smith, 211–43. Durham, NC: Duke University Press, 2012.

Schriber, Abbe. "'Those Who Know Don't Tell': David Hammons c. 1981." *Women & Performance: A Journal of Feminist Theory* 29, no. 1 (2019): 41–61.

Schuller, Kyla. *The Biopolitics of Feeling: Race, Sex, and Science in the Nineteenth Century*. Durham, NC: Duke University Press, 2008.

Sekula, Allan. "The Body and the Archive." *October* 39 (Winter 1986): 3–64.

Seltzer, Mark. *Bodies and Machines*. New York: Routledge, 1992.

———. *The Official World*. Durham, NC: Duke University Press, 2016.

Shimakawa, Karen. *National Abjection: The Asian American Body Onstage*. Durham, NC: Duke University Press, 2002.

———. "Young Jean Lee's Ugly Feelings About Race and Gender: Stuplime Animation in *Songs of the Dragons Flying to Heaven*." *Women & Performance* 17, no. 1 (March 2007): 89–102.

Shyer, Laurence. *Robert Wilson and His Collaborators*. New York: Theatre Communications Group, 1989.

Smith, Shawn Michelle. *Photography on the Color Line: W. E. B. Du Bois, Race, and Visual Culture*. Durham, NC: Duke University Press, 2004.

Sofer, Andrew. *The Stage Life of Props*. Ann Arbor: University of Michigan Press, 2003.

Spiers, Bob. "Jealous." *Absolutely Fabulous*. BBC, April 27, 1995.

Spillers, Hortense J. "Interstices: A Small Drama of Words." In *Black, White, and in Color: Essays on American Literature and Culture*, 152–75. Chicago: University of Chicago Press, 2003.

———. "Mama's Baby, Papa's Maybe: An American Grammar Book." In *Black, White, and in Color: Essays on American Literature and Culture*, 203–29. Chicago: University of Chicago Press, 2003.

Spivey, Virginia. "Sites of Subjectivity: Robert Morris, Minimalism, and Dance." *Dance Research Journal* 35/36, no. 2/1 (Winter 2003–Summer 2004): 113–30.

Stasio, Marilyn. "Legit Reviews: Off Broadway: Neighbors." *Variety*, March 15, 2010.

State of Missouri v. Darren Wilson. "Grand Jury Volume V." Ferguson Grand Jury Documents. www.documentcloud.org/documents/1371057-grand-jury-volume-5.

Steimatsky, Noa. *The Face on Film*. New York: Oxford University Press, 2017.

Storr, Robert. "Martin Puryear: The Hand's Proportion." In *Martin Puryear*, edited by Neal Benezra, 127–34. Chicago: Thames and Hudson/The Art Institute of Chicago, 1991.

Sutherland, Sid. "Firpo Lucky if He Lasts Five Rounds with Dempsey." *Los Angeles Times*, August 6, 1923. ProQuest Historical Newspapers: Los Angeles Times (1881–1989).

"Titus Kaphar—Jack Shainman Gallery." Accessed October 25, 2019. www.jackshainman.com.

Todorov, Alexander, Christopher Olivola, Ron Dotsch, and Peter Mende-Siedlecki. "Social Attributions from Faces: Determinants, Consequences, Accuracy, and Functional Significance." *Annual Review of Psychology* 66 (2015): 519–45.

Toomer, Jean. *Cane*. 2nd ed. New York: Norton Critical Editions, 2011.

Trachtenberg, Alan. *Reading American Photographs*. New York: Hill and Wang, 1989.

Urban Dictionary. Accessed February 2, 2018. www.urbandictionary.com.

Varas, Valeria, and Raul Rispa, eds. *Monochromes: From Malevich to the Present*. Berkeley: University of California Press, 2006.

Veltruský, Jiří. "Man and Object in the Theater." In *A Prague School Reader on Esthetics, Literary Structure, and Style*, translated by Paul L Garvin. Washington, DC: Georgetown University Press, 1964.

Vogel, Shane. *The Scene of Harlem Cabaret: Race, Sexuality, Performance*. Chicago: University of Chicago Press, 2009.

Wallace, Maurice O., and Shawn Michelle Smith, eds. *Pictures and Progress: Early Photography and the Making of African American Identity*. Durham, NC: Duke University Press, 2012.

Wallis, Brian. "Black Bodies, White Science: Louis Agassiz's Slave Daguerreotypes." *American Art* 9, no. 2 (Summer 1995): 38–61.

Warren, Calvin L. *Ontological Terror: Blackness, Nihilism, and Emancipation*. Durham, NC: Duke University Press, 2018.

Wead, George. *Buster Keaton and the Dynamics of Visual Wit*. New York: Arno Press, 1976.

Welchman, John C. *Invisible Colors: A Visual History of Titles*. New Haven, CT: Yale University Press, 1997.

Whose Museum. "Whose Museum x KRETS: Chapter 2: Alanna Lynch & Maria Wæhrens." March 29, 2019. https://whosemuseum.org.

Williams, Patricia J. "On Being the Object of Property." In *The Alchemy of Race and Rights*, 216–36. Cambridge, MA: Harvard University Press, 1991.

Wilson, Judith. "Beauty Rites: Toward an Anatomy of Culture in African American Women's Art." *International Review of African American Art* 11, no. 3 (January 1994), 11–18.

Wolfe, Tom. "Radical Chic: That Party at Lenny's." *New York Magazine*, June 8, 1970, 26–56.

Wright, Richard. *12 Million Black Voices*. New York: Basic Books, 2008.

———. *Native Son*. New York: Harper & Row, 1966.

Wynter, Sylvia. "Rethinking 'Aesthetics': Notes Towards a Deciphering Practice." In *Ex-Iles: Essays on Caribbean Cinema*, edited by Mbye B. Cham, 267–279. Trenton, NJ: Africa World Press, 1992.

Xiang, Sonny. *Tonal Intelligence: The Aesthetics of Asian Inscrutability during the Long Cold War*. New York: Columbia University Press, 2020.

Young, Harvey. *Embodying Black Experience: Stillness, Critical Memory, and the Black Body*. Ann Arbor: University of Michigan Press, 2010.

INDEX

ABOUT THE AUTHOR

Tina Post is Assistant Professor of English, Theater, and Performance at the University of Chicago, where she is also affiliated with the Center for the Study of Race, Politics, and Culture.